SISKIYOU COUNTY LIBRARY

3 2871 00254810 1

D0430684

Birding
Northern
California

John Kemper

598.07
10

FALCON®

Guilford, Connecticut
An imprint of The Globe Pequot Press

SISKIYOU COUNTY PUBLIC LIBRARY
715 FOURTH STREET
YREKA, CALIFORNIA 96097

A FALCONGUIDE®

Copyright © 2001 by The Globe Pequot Press
Previously published by Falcon Publishing, Inc.

All rights reserved. No part of this book may be reproduced or transmitted in any form by any means, electronic or mechanical, including photocopying and recording, or by any information storage or retrieval system, except as may be expressly permitted by the 1976 Copyright Act or in writing from the publisher. Requests for permission should be addressed to The Globe Pequot Press, P.O. Box 480, Guilford, CT 06437.

Falcon and FalconGuide are registered trademarks of The Globe Pequot Press.

Front cover photo: Red-shouldered hawk, by Russ Kerr.
Back cover photo: Townsend's Warbler, by Brian E. Small.
All black-and-white photos by the author.

Library of Congress Cataloging-in-Publication Data

Kemper, John.
    Birding Northern California / John Kemper.
       p. cm.
    Includes bibliographical references (p.) and index.
       ISBN 1-56044-832-6 (pbk.)
     1. Birdwatching—California, Northern—Guidebooks. 2.
Birding sites—California, Northern—Guidebooks. 3. California,
Northern—Guidebooks. I. Title.
QL684.C22K45 1999   99-17148
598.07'234794—dc21   CIP

♻ Text pages printed on recycled paper.
Manufactured in the United States of America
First Edition/Third Printing

CAUTION
Outdoor recreational activities are by their very nature potentially hazardous. All participants in such activities must assume the responsibility for their own actions and safety. The information contained in this guidebook cannot replace sound judgment and good decision-making skills, which help reduce risk exposure, nor does the scope of this book allow for disclosure of all the potential hazards and risks involved in such activities.

    Learn as much as possible about the outdoor recreational activities in which you participate, prepare for the unexpected, and be cautious. The reward will be a safer and more enjoyable experience.

Contents

Bodega Bay to Lake Tahoe

San Francisco Bay Area

Foreword

Birding Northern California, which covers the region from the Oregon border to the northern edge of San Luis Obispo and Kern counties, is an outstanding contribution to the understanding and appreciation of the birds of the Golden State. Its insight into the lives and localities of the state's birds provides a valuable resource to birders, both newcomers and veterans of the sport.

This book is the next best thing to actually going on a birding trip with John Kemper. With a scholarly eye for detail and precision, John guides the reader to the best places to see the species that inhabit our state, and to the rich habitats that offer tremendous displays of bird life, reminiscent of an earlier California.

Acknowledged as a fine teacher on the birds of Northern California, John Kemper has had a lasting influence on birding and bird conservation. We in Audubon see these two activities as extremely important to each other. People tend to value only those elements of nature that they understand and enjoy. It is our hope that the more people who sample the wonder of thousands of migrating geese and cranes, the delicate flight of the hummingbird, and the beautiful song of a warbler, the more they will take action to protect these creatures and make certain generations to follow will be able to experience these wonderful aspects of life, too. John Kemper's birding guide to Northern California is an important contribution to a better understanding and a greater appreciation of birds and nature.

Happy Birding!

Daniel Taylor
Executive Director,
National Audubon Society—*California*

Acknowledgments

I could not have carried out the project of writing a birding guide for Northern California without the help of a lot of people. Those I have listed below all have much greater knowledge of what goes on in their local areas than I possibly could have, and they have caught many errors that crept into the manuscript. If this book proves to be a reliable guide in helping birders get around in the northern part of the state, then in a very real sense the credit goes to them. In like manner, if any errors remain, they are completely my responsibility.

The following people reviewed portions of the manuscript, or in other ways contributed to its development: Lee Ashford, Bob Barnes, Deborah Bartens, Frances Bidstrup, Sarah Blanchette, Ann Brice, Beverly Brock, Jeanne Clark, Terry Colborn, John Coon, Kathy Crane, Donald Crosby, Al DeMartini, Bruce Deuel, Art Edwards, Josh Erdman, Mike Feighner, David Feliz, George Finger, Allen Fish, David Fix, Nick Fittinghoff, Steve Flannery, Bob Garrison, Maurice Getty, Gayle Green, John Green, Brenda Grewell, Bill Grummer, Kevin Gusé, Steve Hampton, Rob Hansen, Ed Harper, John Harris, Stanley Harris, Daphne Hatch, Tom and Jo Heindel, Pamela Helmke, Rob Hewitt, Joan Humphrey, Beth Huning, Ralph and Evelyne Ingols, Wendy Janssen, Deborah Jaques, Ginny Kaminski, Bob Keiffer, Robin Kulakow, Kim Kuska, Tom Leskiw, Ron LeValley, Robin Leong, Larry and Pam Lougheed, Jerry Marinovich, Mike Martin, Jennifer Matkin, Bruce Maxwell, Dave Menke, Liz Merry, Peter J. Metropulos, L. D. Murdock, Mini Nagendran, Kit Novick, Carlos Perada, Michael Perrone, Debbie Petersen, Richard Redmond, Mike Reeves, Cliff Richer, Jean Richmond, Don Roberson, Steve Rovell, Ronnie Ryno, Karine Sande, Susan Sanders, Mary Schiedt, Ron Schlorff, Debi Shearwater, Jill Shirley, Dave Shuford, Craig Stowers, Emilie Strauss, David Suddjian, Lee Summers, Jerry Tacklin, Bobby Tatman, Dan Taylor, Steve Thompson, Dorothy Tobkin, Reed Tollefson, Kent Van Vuren, Dave Wagner, Naomi Walker, Bruce Webb, Judy Whitcombe, Jerry R. White, Peter Whyte, Brian Williams, Ken Wilson, Donald Yasuda, David Yee, and Bob Yutzy.

A special thanks goes to the following people, who each read the entire manuscript and provided suggestions beyond value: Ted Beedy, Sid England, and Tim Manolis. I am especially grateful to Sid England for the many discussions we had of purpose, style, coverage, and content.

1. Introduction

Northern California is incredibly diverse, and is considered one of the most wonderful regions in the country. It has a 14,162-foot volcano, Mount Shasta, as its centerpiece, and the lovely Lake Tahoe and the incomparable Yosemite Valley. Its rocky seashore is so beautiful that whenever Hollywood wants a gorgeous coastline for its movies, it goes straight to Mendocino.

Because the customary location for the separation between Northern and Southern California lies along the northern boundary of Kern County, this means that Northern California also includes Sequoia and Kings Canyon national parks, containing the largest trees on earth, and Mount Whitney, the highest point in the lower 48 states.

For birders, the litany of superlatives goes on. As of 1998, the official list of birds that have occurred within California contains 606 species, 559 of which have been found in Northern California. Only two other states have lists in excess of 500 species: Texas (613) and Arizona (515). One of the reasons for California's bird species diversity is its long coastline, with its abundant deepwater (pelagic) birds. Monterey is commonly acknowledged as the finest pelagic birding location in the country, with Bodega Bay close behind. Birders who have taken pelagic trips on the East Coast have noted that it is necessary to go far offshore to find any appreciable concentrations of birds. At Monterey, however, the birds appear almost as soon as the boat leaves the harbor, sometimes tens of thousands of them at one time.

A large number of the birds that have appeared in Northern California are vagrants from Asia, Alaska, Mexico, or the East Coast, and thus are not considered regulars. Even so, 364 regular species occur in the northern half of the state. Of these, 173 are included in the section titled "Specialty Birds," of which 147 are western specialties that birders from other regions are anxious to see when they come to the West. Fifty-six of them are special to the Pacific Coast.

The *Summer Atlas of North American Birds* (1995) has presented the results of breeding bird surveys for 1985 through 1991, including listings of the top three areas of highest summer counts for each species. Northern California was included in the top three for 97 species (Texas had 76, Arizona had 60, and Florida had 46). The 97 species for Northern California are given in the table labeled "Summer." If more than one area in Northern California is listed, the number of areas is shown in parentheses.

The second table, "Winter," gives the results from Audubon Christmas Bird Counts. It lists species for which Northern California locations had the highest winter counts in North America, for at least one of the three Christmas counts from 1994 to 1996. If there was more than one year in which the count was the highest, the number is shown in parentheses.

If a species (154 of them) is listed in either column, it means that Northern California is a good place to look for that species; however, it is worth a reminder that "highest counts" is a relative term. For example, the "high" Christmas count for a rare species like Black Rail ranged from 7 to 10; for Eurasian Wigeon, it was 19, and for Pacific Golden-Plover, 22.

Species for which Northern California has the recorded highest counts

Summer

Pied-billed Grebe
Eared Grebe
Western Grebe
Clark's Grebe (2)
American White Pelican (2)
Double-crested Cormorant (2)
Brandt's Cormorant
Pelagic Cormorant
American Bittern (2)
Black-crowned Night-Heron (2)
Canada Goose
Mallard
Northern Pintail
Cinnamon Teal (2)
Northern Shoveler
Gadwall
Redhead
Lesser Scaup
Common Merganser
Ruddy Duck
Osprey
White-tailed Kite (2)
Northern Harrier
Red-tailed Hawk
Peregrine Falcon
Ring-necked Pheasant
California Quail
Mountain Quail (3)
American Coot
Killdeer (2)
Black-necked Stilt
American Avocet (2)
Willet

Spotted Sandpiper
Common Snipe
Wilson's Phalarope
Heermann's Gull
Ring-billed Gull (2)
California Gull
Western Gull
Caspian Tern (2)
Forster's Tern
Common Murre (2)
Band-tailed Pigeon
Barn Owl
Northern Pygmy-Owl (3)
Spotted Owl
Anna's Hummingbird
Allen's Hummingbird (3)
Acorn Woodpecker (2)
Nuttall's Woodpecker (3)
White-headed Woodpecker
Olive-sided Flycatcher (2)
Pacific-slope Flycatcher (2)
Black Phoebe (3)
Cassin's Vireo (2)
Hutton's Vireo (3)
Warbling Vireo
Steller's Jay (2)
Western Scrub-Jay
Yellow-billed Magpie (3)
American Crow (3)
Cliff Swallow (2)
Mountain Chickadee (2)
Chestnut-backed Chickadee (2)
Oak Titmouse (2)

Bushtit
Red-breasted Nuthatch (2)
White-breasted Nuthatch (3)
Brown Creeper(3)
Marsh Wren
American Dipper
Golden-crowned Kinglet
Western Bluebird
Mountain Bluebird
Townsend's Solitaire
Wrentit
Phainopepla
Orange-crowned Warbler
Yellow Warbler
Black-throated Gray Warbler (3)
Hermit Warbler
Wilson's Warbler
Yellow-breasted Chat
Dark-eyed Junco ("Oregon")
Western Tanager (2)
Black-headed Grosbeak
Lazuli Bunting
Red-winged Blackbird
Tricolored Blackbird (3)
Brewer's Blackbird (2)
Bullock's Oriole (3)
Purple Finch (2)
House Finch (2)
Pine Siskin
Lesser Goldfinch (3)
Lawrence's Goldfinch (2)

Winter

Pacific Loon
Horned Grebe (3)
Clark's Grebe (2)
Northern Fulmar
Sooty Shearwater (3)
Short-tailed Shearwater (2)
Black-vented Shearwater
Brandt's Cormorant (2)
American Bittern (2)
Black-crowned Night-Heron (3)
Tundra Swan (2)
Ross's Goose
Green-winged Teal
Northern Pintail
Cinnamon Teal (2)
Northern Shoveler (3)
Gadwall
Eurasian Wigeon
American Wigeon
Ring-necked Duck
Lesser Scaup
Surf Scoter (2)
Bufflehead
Ruddy Duck
White-tailed Kite (2)
Northern Harrier
Sharp-shinned Hawk
Golden Eagle
Prairie Falcon
Peregrine Falcon (2)
Mountain Quail (3)
Black Rail (3)
Virginia Rail (3)
Sora (3)

Black-bellied Plover (3)
Pacific Golden-Plover
Snowy Plover
Semipalmated Plover
Black-necked Stilt (3)
American Avocet (3)
Willet (3)
Whimbrel
Long-billed Curlew
Marbled Godwit (3)
Western Sandpiper (2)
Least Sandpiper (3)
Red Phalarope
California Gull (2)
Elegant Tern
Common Murre
Marbled Murrelet
Cassin's Auklet (2)
Rhinoceros Auklet (2)
Band-tailed Pigeon (2)
Western Screech-Owl
Northern Pygmy-Owl (3)
Spotted Owl (2)
Northern Saw-whet Owl (3)
White-throated Swift
Lewis's Woodpecker
Acorn Woodpecker (2)
Red-breasted Sapsucker
Williamson's Sapsucker (3)
Nuttall's Woodpecker (3)
White-headed Woodpecker (2)
Northern Flicker
Black Phoebe
Steller's Jay (2)

Western Scrub-Jay
Pinyon Jay
Yellow-billed Magpie (3)
Mountain Chickadee (2)
Oak Titmouse (3)
Pygmy Nuthatch (3)
Brown Creeper
Bewick's Wren
House Wren
Marsh Wren
Ruby-crowned Kinglet (2)
Western Bluebird (3)
Mountain Bluebird
Hermit Thrush (3)
Wrentit (2)
American Pipit
Townsend's Warbler (3)
California Towhee
Rufous-crowned Sparrow
Lark Sparrow (2)
Fox Sparrow (2)
Song Sparrow
Golden-crowned Sparrow (3)
White-crowned Sparrow
Tricolored Blackbird (2)
Western Meadowlark (3)
Brewer's Blackbird (2)
Purple Finch
Cassin's Finch
House Finch (2)
Lesser Goldfinch (3)
American Goldfinch (2)

Now, for a little reality check. Besides everything mentioned, it is necessary to add that California is also the most populous state in the nation. Most of the population is in the southern part of the state, but the San Francisco Bay Region (6.3 million people) is ranked as the fourth largest metropolitan area in the United States, behind New York, Los Angeles, and Chicago. The Sacramento metropolitan area has 1.5 million; Fresno has 700,000, and Stockton has 500,000 people. But the good news is that Northern California is a vast region. Eleven of the counties in Northern California have populations of less than 25,000. Sierra County (where Yuba Pass, described in this book, is located) has only 3,300, and Alpine County (Hope Valley and Carson Pass) has only 1,100.

There are lots of quiet, wonderful places out there, and this book will help you find them. There also are lots of wonderful, natural birding places tucked in close to the major population centers; this book will help you find those, too.

HOW TO USE THIS GUIDE

The definition of Northern California used in this book is the one used by most birders, who generally consider the state to be separated along the northern border of San Luis Obispo and Kern counties, except that Inyo County is considered part of Southern California. This is approximately the same definition as the one used in *California Birds* by Arnold Small (1994), and in *Birds of Northern California* by Guy McCaskie, et al. (1988). However, the area included in this book also includes the Kern River Valley and the White Mountains, partly because these areas seem to me to be logically attached to the rest of Northern California, and partly because they sometimes don't get included in Southern California guides. Offshore waters out to 200 nautical miles (230 statute miles) are included.

Eighty-one birding sites are described here. The sites are divided into six different regions, and a map is provided for each region, showing site locations.

Each site description includes a detailed map; it is not intended as a navigational tool but rather for trip planning. Instead, use a reputable road map or the California road atlases published by DeLorme (see details under **Additional Help**).

If the site is included in the *California Wildlife Viewing Guide,* published by Falcon, the binoculars icon used to identify wildlife viewing areas is shown next to the name of the site. Likewise, if the site has at least one barrier-free trail, the barrier-free icon appears next to the site name. (See "Other Symbols," page 30.)

Following the number and name of each site, the following headings appear:

Habitats lists the various habitats to be found at the site. Characteristics of these are discussed in depth in Chapter 3.

Specialty birds includes some of the western specialties (see definition below) that are likely to be found on the site, those classified as endangered or threatened, and a few others of special interest. Generally, the list includes species only if they occur at the common or uncommon level (see definitions below), but may include those that are rare if the site is one of the better locations to find such species, for example, Rock Sandpiper at Point St. George.

Other key birds includes some interesting nonspecialty species.

Species are grouped into Resident, Summer, Winter, and Migrant. These seasonal categories necessarily are very loose, and give only a general impression of the season in which significant numbers of that particular species are likely to be present. For many species, there will always be some individual birds that don't "obey" the seasonal designations, and will confound any attempt to categorize them.

Because spring and fall are not listed as separate categories, this means that summer may overlap into both spring and fall to some degree. Likewise, winter may overlap spring and fall. In each case, the birds are placed in the seasonal category in which they are most likely to appear. (See later discussion of summer and winter.)

These lists of specialty birds and other key birds should by no means be taken as complete listings of all the species, even the common ones, to be found at a site, but only those that I think might be of special interest. Thus, the paragraphs can be thought of as highlights, and in the detailed site descriptions many additional species will generally be mentioned. The common species that are generally omitted from these two paragraphs are described later in the section titled, "Qualifications on species to be listed."

Defining our terms

Abundant refers to a species that occurs by the hundreds or thousands.

Common species are generally found easily and sometimes in large numbers.

Fairly common means the species occurs regularly in small numbers, but may not be seen on every trip.

Uncommon species, while regular, usually are present in very small numbers, and may be seen on less than half the trips into the appropriate habitat.

Rare means there aren't very many of that particular species around, and it may be seen only a few times per season.

Western specialty – This is a species that occurs primarily in the western part of the country (meaning mostly west of the Mississippi River), is found in Northern California at least at the rare level, and is considered regular. It excludes those that occur on a casual or accidental basis.

Resident – Some authorities do not use the word *resident* for a species unless the bird breeds at that locality. In this book, the term is used if significant numbers of that species are to be found at the given locality throughout the year, regardless of breeding. In some instances, such as those in which most members of the species withdraw from the area during, say, winter, but a few remain behind, the species will not be classified as resident, but as a summer visitor. An example is Lawrence's Goldfinch: Most individuals move south in winter, but a few remain behind. Also, in the case of many mountain species that are classified as resident, there may be a general movement downslope during periods of heavy snows. Mountain Quail is an example.

Summer category – Species included in this category are those that are called summer visitors in this book. They are present in the area during the summer months, but almost all individuals migrate south for the winter. Some authors make a distinction between summer resident (those that are present in summer and breed), and summer visitor (those that are present in summer but do not breed). In this book, summer visitor refers only to the occurrence of a species in that season, and makes no distinction between breeding and nonbreeding status. Note that "summer" differs for different species. For some, such as Allen's Hummingbird, the summer season may begin as early as February or March and be over by June, but for most it begins later, in April or May, and runs to July or August.

Winter category – Species included in this category are those that are usually referred to as winter visitors. Almost all individuals breed to the north of the particular site described (although a handful may occasionally breed at the site), but move into the site to spend the winter. For some species, such as some of the sandpipers, winter may begin as early as July, but for most it extends from about October through February.

Postbreeding visitor – These are species that breed to the south of our area, but move into the area in substantial numbers in mid- to late summer, and may remain throughout the fall.

Best times to bird is self-explanatory. It helps you plan your trip to each site during the right season.

Directions provide written details on how to reach the site or a logical point to begin birding a large or wide-ranging site. The instructions begin from a city, town, or the junction of two well-traveled roads.

The birding also includes some directions to points of interest and good birding within the boundaries of the larger site. This heading also provides tips on how best to observe birds at the site and lists some of the species you're likely to see there.

ADDITIONAL HELP: A section with this heading is provided at the end of each site description, to aid you in planning your trip.

NCA&G grid refers to the DeLorme *Northern California Atlas & Gazetteer* (1995). Under this heading, the page number and grid coordinates of the site's location are listed. Most of the sites in this guide can be found in the NCA&G. A few others are mapped out in the DeLorme *Southern and Central California Atlas & Gazetteer* (1996). These atlases are available in many bookstores, and can be procured from DeLorme Publishing, P.O. Box 298, Yarmouth, Maine 04032; 1-800-452-5931.

The definition of Northern California used for this book is different from the one used in the DeLorme atlases. This book uses the definition commonly employed by birders, and extends as far south as the northern borders of San Luis Obispo and Kern counties.

Elevation tells the approximate elevation or a range of elevations of the site.

Hazards lists things to be found on the site that require your attention and some caution, ranging from poisonous plants to rattlesnakes to heavy traffic. All the hazards can be avoided with a little care and none should discourage you from visiting and exploring a site.

Nearest food, gas, lodging names towns near the site that can provide the amenities you might need. In selecting towns for these listings, I have picked those with a reasonable selection of services, so that you will not be disagreeably surprised if a town turns out to have only one motel that happens to have gone out of business.

Camping lists the names of campgrounds near the birding site. Most of the sites in this book include this heading, but if there is no acceptable campground within a reasonable distance, the listing is omitted. The things I look for in a campground include attractive natural surroundings, public ownership, and paved interior roads (to keep down the dust). In a few cases I have listed campgrounds that might not meet these criteria but are the only practical choice. A typical case of this latter type is the "campground" that is essentially a big paved parking lot, with white stripes painted between the "campsites." Such campgrounds appear to find favor with folks who have boats and boat trailers, and want to stay near a marina.

Many campgrounds require reservations. The numbers to call for the national parks, national forests, state parks, and for some private campgrounds are given in Appendix F.

For more information provides the name of a reliable agency, office, or organization that can help answer questions not covered in the site descriptions. Because certain organizations may appear in several listings, the addresses and telephone numbers are collected in Appendix A.

Qualifications on species to be listed

The species listed in the highlight paragraphs headed "Specialty birds" and "Other key birds" have been chosen in a way that I hope will seem reasonable. Not everyone will agree on the choices, but I have tended to err on the generous side—that is, in the direction of overlisting. I have tried to keep in mind the interests of both out-of-state and in-state birders.

There are some species that are so common and widespread that I think most would agree they should not generally be highlighted as specialties or as key birds. In some cases, they may be listed in the highlight paragraphs anyway, if there is some special reason for doing so.

Common species often omitted from the **Specialty birds** paragraph: California Quail; California and Western Gulls; Anna's Hummingbird; Acorn Woodpecker; Black Phoebe; Western Scrub-Jay; Mountain Chickadee; Bushtit; Spotted and California Towhees; Golden-crowned Sparrow; and Western Meadowlark.

Common species often omitted from the **Other key birds** paragraph: Pied-billed Grebe; Double-crested Cormorant; Great Blue Heron; Great and Snowy Egrets; Turkey Vulture; Canada Goose; Gadwall; American Wigeon; Mallard; Northern Shoveler; Northern Pintail; Ruddy Duck; Northern Harrier; Red-tailed Hawk; American Kestrel; Ring-necked Pheasant; American Coot; Killdeer; Willet; Western and Least Sandpipers; Dunlin; Ring-billed and Herring Gulls; Rock and Mourning Doves; Belted Kingfisher; Downy Woodpecker; Northern Flicker; American Crow; Common Raven; Tree, Barn, and Cliff Swallows; Brown Creeper; Bewick's, House, and Marsh Wrens; Ruby-crowned Kinglet; American Robin; Northern Mockingbird; European Starling; Cedar Waxwing; Yellow-rumped Warbler; Savannah, Song, and White-crowned Sparrows; Dark-eyed Junco; Red-winged and Brewer's Blackbirds; Brown-headed Cowbird; House Finch; and House Sparrow.

IMPORTANT BIRD AREAS

The "Important Bird Area Program" is a worldwide activity to identify areas that are important to birds. It began in Europe in the 1980s under the International Council of Bird Preservation, since renamed Birdlife International. In 1989 Birdlife International published the results of its work in the book Important Bird Areas in Europe. This book listed more than 2,444 Important Bird Areas (IBAs) in 31 countries.

In the United States, a similar program was initiated in the mid-1900s, and was still under way at the time of the publication of this book. In the U.S., the IBA program is administered by the National Audubon Society and the American Bird Conservancy. The goal of the program is to identify sites in each state that are essential for sustaining naturally occurring populations of bird species, and to protect or manage those sites for the long-term conservation of birds, other wildlife, and their habitats. By 1998, the states of Pennsylvania (77 IBAs) and New York (127 IBAs) had completed the initial phases of their programs, although they continue to evaluate new sites on an ongoing basis. Twelve other states, including California, had IBA programs under way in 1998.

An area may be listed as an IBA for one of the following reasons:

1. It provides habitat for endangered, threatened, or vulnerable species.

2. It provides habitat for endemic species, or species with a restricted range.

3. It provides habitat for an assemblage of species restricted to a unique or threatened natural community.

4. It is a site where birds concentrate in significant numbers when breeding, in winter, or during migration.

Sites may be designated as Global, Continental, National, or State, with the most stringent criteria at the Global level and less stringent criteria through the other levels. Designation of a site at the Global level represents the highest level of recognition.

For the purposes of this book, if a site had been recognized as an IBA by the time of publication, it is mentioned in the site description. However, it needs to be emphasized that the program was still under way at the time of publication, and many additional outstanding sites were expected to qualify.

2. Climate and Topography

Five major landforms dominate Northern California: the coast, most of it rocky and scenic; the great Central Valley, extending for 400 miles through the middle of the state; the Coast Ranges, which run close to the sea throughout, and separate the coast from the Central Valley; the Cascade and Sierra Nevada mountain ranges, with 12 peaks exceeding 14,000 feet; and a bit of the Great Basin. The Great Basin portion has two parts: the Modoc Plateau to the north and east of Mount Shasta, and the region east of the Sierra Nevada, containing Mono Lake.

One of the fascinating consequences of California's topography is the effect it has on the climate. Here is an example of what is possible. On a summer day, you can begin in San Francisco surrounded by fog, and with the temperature in the 50s. (Mark Twain is reported to have said that the coldest winter he ever experienced was a summer in San Francisco.) As you travel inland toward Sacramento, the temperature rapidly rises until it may be 100 degrees F or more, in a distance of only 50 miles. Then, as you climb into the Sierra Nevada, the temperature drops, until it becomes a delightful 80 degrees F at Lake Tahoe.

It has been said that California has only two seasons, spring and fall, or, more simply, the wet season and the dry season. Rains typically begin in October, become heavy in December and January, taper off in April, and virtually cease in May. Summer is almost entirely free of rain.

The two-season rule doesn't apply to the mountains or Great Basin. Summer thunderstorms frequently occur in these regions. In winter the Great Basin can get subzero temperatures, and snow in the Cascades and Sierra can be anywhere from 6 to 20 feet deep. Snow and ice are no problem in most of California, but if you go into the mountains in winter, you will need to carry tire chains.

The rolling hills that dominate much of the state are brown (Californians refer to them as "golden") during the summer, reflecting the lack of rainfall. In December the hills start to turn green, and stay that way until April. Then, when the rains stop, the hills turn brown again and stay that way through the summer.

The major landforms plus other important regions, such as the Bay Region and the Delta, are based on those in *The Jepson Manual—Higher Plants of California* (1993), J. C. Hickman, (ed.). Information on weather, and how to prepare for it, is included.

Coast

The climate in the spring and fall along the Northern California coast has to be among the best this world has to offer. The sun is bright, the air is fresh and cool, mosquitoes are rare, and there is an invigorating quality to everything that makes a person just glad to be there. Although spring and fall are generally gorgeous, there is lots of fog in summer and lots of rain in winter.

In the summer you won't need a raincoat, but you will probably need a jacket, maybe two of them. In the winter, the rainfall along most of the coast is usually

Northern California landforms

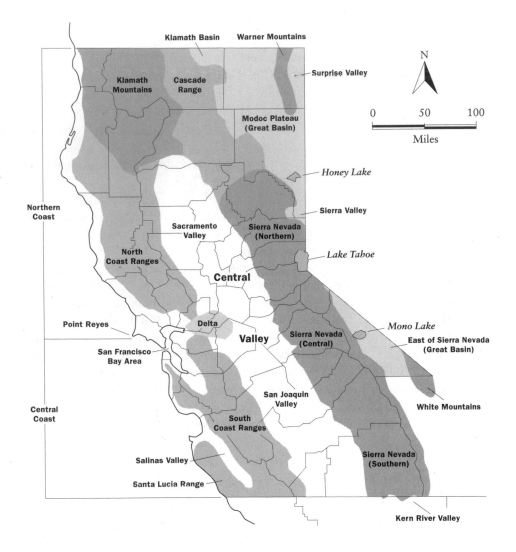

moderate, perhaps 30 or 40 inches, but higher in an El Niño year. In the redwood regions it can be twice that amount. Snow is extremely rare on the coast.

One thing that characterizes the coastal region and sets it off from the region defined as the interior, meaning (mostly) the Central Valley, is the presence of dense conifer forests. Douglas-fir is the most widespread conifer, but there are extensive redwood forests, mostly from Santa Cruz north. The coast also has pine forests in several locations, including Monterey pine (in the Monterey Bay region), Bishop pine, and shore pine.

Because the coastline is so long, there may be substantial differences in the occurrence of bird species along the coast. Hence, a distinction may occasionally be made in this guide between the Northern Coast and the Central Coast, with the approximate division between the two occurring in the region of San Francisco Bay. (The southern coast, which is not included in this book, is the section from Santa Barbara to the Mexican border.)

Central Valley

The Central Valley consists of two valleys—the Sacramento Valley north of the Delta (see page 14 for a description of the Delta), and the San Joaquin Valley south of the Delta. Some people rigorously define the valley to include only those portions that are flat, but others include the foothill regions, at least up to where the pines begin to outnumber the oaks.[1] The birds that inhabit the valley floor will often be markedly different from those in the foothills, but the climate is similar—dry in summer and often hot.

The Central Valley is one of the most productive agricultural areas anywhere. Most of it is flat, and the farm fields extend as far as you can see. These same fields are hosts to many bird species, such as Horned Larks, Western Meadowlarks, and raptors of all kinds. Also, the Central Valley is one of the major winter gathering places on the continent for swans, ducks, and geese. Many of the winter days are sparkling clear, with temperatures in the invigorating 50s and 60s. To stand in the middle of this immense area on such a day, surrounded by thousands of waterfowl filling the sky, and with your vision limited only by the mountains standing on the horizon, has to be one of the grandest wildlife experiences you can have.

However, at times in the winter, especially in December, the valley can fill with dense fog, which creates a hazard for airplanes and automobiles. The temperature hovers in the 40s, and you find yourself wishing it would rain so the fog would go away.

Typical rainfall is only 15 to 20 inches per year. Snow may fall on the valley floor once every 20 years or so. As far as clothing is concerned, the rule is to bundle up in winter, and in the summer an air-conditioned car is pretty welcome. Spring and fall, however, are great. Sometimes there are strong north winds on the valley floor, which generally lessen as you ascend the foothills.

---

1 This is the definition of the Central Valley used by the Central Valley Bird Club, suggested by David Yee.

The foothills usually are above the fog. It can be cold and foggy in Sacramento, whereas only a thousand feet higher in the foothills it will be warm and sunny. The foothill country is characterized by open grassy stretches interspersed with clumps of trees, mostly blue oaks—a kind of country generally referred to as oak savanna. In many places the hills are clothed with chaparral, which consists of shrubs, sometimes thorny, growing together in such density that it is almost impossible to force your way through. People sometimes refer to it as sagebrush, but this is really not quite right. A few species of sage do grow in this region, but the sagebrush people are usually thinking of is a plant of the Great Basin, called basin sagebrush *(Artemisia tridentata)*, generally found at elevations of 4,000 feet or more.

Coast Ranges

The Coast Ranges run almost the entire length of the state, and separate the Central Valley from the ocean. In the north, the Coast Ranges merge with the Klamath Mountains, which in turn merge with the Cascade Range. The Klamath Mountains generally resemble the Cascades and the Sierra in terms of their bird life and forest structure. Farther south, near Clear Lake, the Coast Ranges become lower and drier, with great expanses of oak savanna and widespread distribution of foothill pines (also called gray pines). In many places the ridges are clothed almost exclusively with chaparral and dwarf cypress.

South of the Bay Area, the Coast Ranges essentially split into two parts, divided by the Salinas Valley. The part near the coast, called the Santa Lucia Range, is high, rugged, and plunges directly into the sea, creating the spectacular Big Sur coast. The highest portions have forests and birds that resemble those in the higher portions of the mountains farther north.

The part of the Coast Range lying inland, between the Salinas and Central valleys, is rugged, dry, remote, and wild—often referred to as the unknown California. It has extensive oak woodland, oak savanna, chaparral, and lots of foothill pines. As the mountains slope down to the Central Valley, they generally become great treeless, grassy ridges.

In this book, when there is a difference in the occurrence of bird species in different sections of the Coast Ranges, the terms *North Coast Ranges* and *South Coast Ranges* may be employed, with the San Francisco Bay serving as the approximate dividing point. Note that there is an inconsistency here, because the South Coast Ranges are adjacent to the section of coast that is identified on the map as the Central Coast. However, the names used here correspond to those in general use, as inconsistent as those may be.

Mountains

The word *mountains* as used in this book mostly means the Cascade and Sierra Nevada ranges. However, the term also includes the Klamath Mountains and the northerly portions of the Coast Ranges, because of the similarity in distribution of many bird species to be found in all these ranges. The dividing line between the

Cascades and the Sierra is more or less around Lake Almanor. There is no sharp zone of change, but it may occasionally be necessary here to make a distinction in the occurrence of bird species, between the two mountain ranges.

California's mountains are superb—no other word will do. The summer climate in the middle and higher elevations of the Sierra Nevada and Cascade ranges, is, if anything, even better than that of the coast. The sun is bright, the air is fresh and cool, and the humidity is low. Some summers have little rain, but others have thunderstorms almost every day. I was even surprised by 6 inches of snow once in early September, but times like that are rare.

Summer temperatures in the daytime are typically in the 70s and 80s, depending upon the elevation. Nighttime temperatures frequently are in the 40s, and can go below freezing at higher elevations. In the winter, skiers flock to the mountains, where daytime temperatures are often in the 40s and 50s. But daytime temperatures can also be in the 10s and 20s, and on the eastern slopes nighttime temperatures can go below zero. Some of the heaviest snowfalls ever recorded in the United States occurred in the Sierra.

Generally *mountains* refers to the regions above where the pine forests begin. In the north, this can be as low as 3,000 feet, or even lower, but is around 5,000 feet in the south. In the middle elevations, the trees are mostly ponderosa pine, white fir, incense cedar, Douglas-fir, and black oak. A little higher, around 6,000 or 7,000 feet, the red firs, Jeffrey pines, and quaking aspens begin to take over, and wonderful green jewel-like meadows make their appearance.

Higher yet, lodgepole pines and mountain hemlocks become important, until timberline is reached. At Mount Shasta, timberline occurs at about 8,000 feet, whereas in the southern Sierra, it is around 10,000 feet.

Mosquitoes are not usually a problem at middle elevations, such as at Lake Tahoe or Yosemite Valley, but can be terrible in alpine and subalpine areas in June and July, as the snow melts. At such times, insect repellent is a must, especially the kind containing DEET. (DEET is discussed further in the section on ticks in Chapter 4.)

Great Basin
California's portion of the Great Basin has two parts, the Modoc Plateau and the region east of the Sierra Nevada south of Lake Tahoe. The Modoc Plateau generally includes the region east of the Cascade and Sierra ranges, south of the Oregon border, including Honey Lake and Sierra Valley. The great, wonderful valleys along the Pit River, called Big Valley and Fall River Valley, lie at the edge of the Cascade Range, and share many of the attributes of the Modoc Plateau.

From a strict geological point of view, much of the Modoc Plateau would not be considered Great Basin because it drains either into the Klamath River or the Sacramento River, and thus to the Pacific Ocean, whereas the true Great Basin has no outlet to any ocean. However, the Modoc Plateau has many of the biological features of the Great Basin, and will be treated in this book as a part of it. In a few cases it may be necessary to make a distinction between the region from Alturas to the north and east (called in this book the *northeast*), and other Great Basin areas in California, such as Honey Lake and the area containing Mono Lake (called in this book *east of the Sierra Nevada*).

The Great Basin technically also includes Lake Tahoe because the Truckee River, which empties out of Lake Tahoe, flows east into Nevada. However, this book (and most people) looks upon Lake Tahoe as part of the Sierra Nevada.

The climate of the Great Basin properly belongs to the continental interior and not to the coastal climate typical of most of California. In the summer the higher portions are fresh and invigorating. Summer thunderstorms and lightning are possible. Winter can be challenging, as with any interior location. The snowfall may not be as large as in the neighboring mountains, but subzero temperatures are common.

Personally, I think the Modoc Plateau has some of the grandest scenery in California. The vast green meadows of Big Valley and Fall River Valley, backed by Mount Lassen or Mount Shasta, are magnificent. I even love the great sagebrush flats (yes, this is the real sagebrush) and the vast juniper forests.

San Francisco Bay Area

The Bay Area is transitional between the coast and the interior, and shares features of both. In this book, it is treated mostly as a part of the region defined as "coast," although the foothill regions are actually more representative of the interior region. (See Chapter 8, the Status and Distribution Chart, for a discussion of the interior region.) The mountains on the peninsula just south of San Francisco are usually considered part of the Bay Area, but share many of the features of the coastal regions farther to the north, including extensive redwood groves.

San Francisco Bay is a huge estuary that punches a hole through the Coast Ranges. It acts like a giant air conditioner for the sprawling populations of the region, and provides an answer to why all those people want to live there— it has an outstanding climate.

Redwood City, south of San Francisco, for years has had a sign on display that reads "Climate best, by government test." True, there can be extremes, with temperatures occasionally topping 100 degrees F in summer, and into the 20s in winter, but the climate generally measures up to the brag.

The region's enormous population growth has brought two unwanted consequences: traffic and smog. The smog tends to concentrate in the lower San Francisco Bay, but is actually getting better over time, as more stringent controls are placed upon industry and autos. The traffic? Well, there is only one useful rule: Stay off the main traffic arteries at rush hours, if you can. (Rush hours are from about 6 A.M. to 10 A.M., and from 3 P.M. to 8 P.M.)

Delta

The Delta is where the Sacramento and San Joaquin rivers come together, just west of Stockton. It is usually thought of as a part of the Central Valley, but is transitional between the valley and the San Francisco Bay Area. If you fly over it in an airplane, it can be seen as a vast green area with winding rivers and sloughs. The green areas in most cases are actually below the level of the neighboring rivers, and are protected by levees. In fact, the entire system is protected by levees, which sometimes fail in years of heavy rainfall.

The Delta in winter is highly attractive to birds such as Sandhill Cranes, Tundra Swans, and Snow Geese. Most highways go around the edges of the Delta, but many local roads penetrate the area, though they are likely to deadend against a slough. Woodbridge Road, described in this guide, is just such a road.

The climate is similar to that in the rest of the Central Valley, although it is moderated somewhat by the air conditioner effect of San Francisco Bay.

Tundra Swans in Central Valley in winter.

3. Habitats

The descriptions of the various habitats in this guide generally correspond to those in *Introduction to California Plant Life* (1974), by R. Ornduff, although in a few cases they have been modified on the basis of classifications in *A Guide to Wildlife Habitats of California* (1988), by K. Mayer and W. F. Laudenslayer (eds.). For each habitat, a few typical bird species are listed. No attempt is made to show seasonality, because that information is given in the various site descriptions and bar graphs. Also, some birds show up in several different habitats and may vary in their preferences for various habitats depending upon the season. Nevertheless, the listings give some idea of what to expect.

Pelagic. The term means deepwater areas away from shore, out to 200 nautical miles. Some typical species are Black-footed Albatross; Pink-footed and Sooty Shearwaters; Ashy and Black Storm-Petrels; Parasitic Jaeger; Sabine's Gull; and Cassin's Auklet.

Coastal waters. These are the shallow waters close to shore, generally within a mile or so of land. Typical species found in this habitat are Red-throated Loon; Western Grebe; Black, White-winged, and Surf Scoters; Pigeon Guillemot; and Common Murre.

Sandy beach and mudflats. This applies to wave-swept beaches as well as the wet open flats adjacent to bays, lagoons, and salt marshes. Some typical species are Killdeer; Black-necked Stilt; American Avocet; Greater Yellowlegs; Willet; Marbled Godwit; Sanderling; Western and Least Sandpipers; Dunlin; and Long-billed Dowitcher.

Rocky headlands refers to the headlands at the ocean shore that are generally subject to marine influences such as surf and wind. Some typical species here are Brown Pelican; Brandt's and Pelagic Cormorants; Black Oystercatcher; Black Turnstone; Surfbird; Heermann's and Western Gulls; and Pigeon Guillemot.

Coastal bays and lagoons include open waters and the immediately adjacent plant growth. Some typical species are Pacific and Common Loons; Western Grebe; Canvasback; Lesser Scaup; Surf Scoter; Bufflehead; Red-necked Phalarope; and Forster's Tern.

Coastal prairie. This term applies to the extensive grasslands that occur in some locations immediately adjacent to the coast. Typical plants are various grasses, bracken fern, and Douglas iris. Some typical bird species are Northern Harrier, Red-tailed Hawk, Common Raven, and Savannah Sparrow.

Coastal scrub consists of a mixture of shrubs and grassy meadows. Typical plants on the coast north of Big Sur, where the plant community is referred to as northern coastal scrub, are coyote brush, salal, poison oak, and bush lupine. South of Big Sur this community is called southern coast scrub, and some typical plants are black sage, white sage, and California buckwheat. Typical bird species are Rufous and Allen's Hummingbirds, Wrentit, and Song and White-crowned Sparrows.

Closed-cone pine forest is characterized by Bishop, shore, and Monterey pines, and cypresses. Bishop and shore pine are typical of the coast north of San Francisco, whereas Monterey pine and Monterey cypress are found in the Monterey Bay area. Closed-cone refers to the fact that the cones do not open until several years after maturing, and frequently only after a fire. Typical bird species are Steller's Jay, Pygmy Nuthatch, Brown Creeper, and Pine Siskin.

Redwood forest. This is the coniferous forest close to the coast dominated by redwoods, although other species, such as Douglas-fir, western hemlock, tan oak, and bigleaf maple, may be present. Such forests are extensive in Del Norte, Humboldt, Mendocino, and Sonoma counties, on Mount Tamalpais (but not on Point Reyes), and again in San Mateo and Santa Cruz counties. South of Monterey, redwood forests occur in isolated locations, such as at Big Sur. Some typical bird species are Steller's Jay, Chestnut-backed Chickadee, Winter Wren, Varied Thrush, and Townsend's Warbler.

Douglas-fir forest. Some authorities (Ornduff) lump redwood forest, Douglas-fir forest, and mixed evergreen forest into the single category of north coastal forest. I have chosen to place redwood forest and Douglas-fir forests in separate categories. As used here, the term applies to the coniferous forest close to the coast dominated by Douglas-fir, although it also occurs in other locations in California, such as throughout the Coast Range and in the Cascades and Sierra Nevada. "Mixed evergreen forest" is a special example of this kind of habitat, and includes not only Douglas-fir, but also broadleaf evergreens such as coast live oak, California bay laurel, tan oak, and madrone. Some typical bird species are Pileated Woodpecker; Olive-sided Flycatcher; Warbling Vireo; Steller's Jay; Winter Wren; Golden-crowned Kinglet; Swainson's and Varied Thrushes; and Townsend's Warbler.

Salt marsh. Salt marshes are found in estuaries and bays that are protected from the wave action and strong winds of the coast, such as at Humboldt Bay, Tomales Bay, and San Francisco Bay, with plant species such as cordgrass (*Spartina* spp.) and pickleweed (*Salicornia* spp.). Some typical bird species are Black and Clapper Rails, and Common Yellowthroat.

Freshwater marsh occurs in connection with standing or sluggishly moving shallow fresh water, such as along Central Valley watercourses, next to lakes such as Clear Lake, and in inland areas such as Sierra Valley and the Modoc Plateau. Characteristic plants are cattails and tules. Some typical bird species are American Bittern, Great Blue Heron, Snowy Egret, Black-crowned Night-Heron, Mallard, Cinnamon Teal, Ruddy Duck, Virginia Rail, American Coot, Marsh Wren, and Red-winged and Yellow-headed Blackbirds.

Lake. The word *lake* is used for permanent bodies of fresh water ranging from ponds to very large lakes. Some typical species are Pied-billed and Eared Grebes; American White Pelican; Double-crested Cormorant; Canada Goose; Northern Shoveler; Northern Pintail; Osprey; and Bald Eagle.

Stream. A stream refers to a watercourse with water year-round. Some typical species are Great Blue Heron, Common Merganser, Spotted Sandpiper, Belted Kingfisher, and Black Phoebe.

Riparian woodland applies to the trees and shrubs occurring along stream courses with year-round water. At elevations ranging from sea level to 3,000 feet in the Central Valley and foothills, this habitat can be referred to as valley foothill riparian woodland, often dominated by Fremont cottonwood, valley oak, California sycamore, and willows. Some typical bird species in this habitat are California Quail; Great Horned Owl; Anna's Hummingbird; Nuttall's Woodpecker; Northern Flicker; Western Scrub-Jay; Tree Swallow; Oak Titmouse; Bushtit; Bewick's Wren; Ruby-crowned Kinglet; Spotted and California Towhees; Song Sparrow; Bullock's Oriole; and House Finch. On the coast, riparian habitats at low elevations can be called coastal riparian woodland. Some typical bird species are Pacific-slope Flycatcher; Cassin's and Warbling Vireos; Chestnut-backed Chickadee; Swainson's Thrush; Orange-crowned and Wilson's Warblers; Golden-crowned Sparrow; Purple Finch; and American Goldfinch. At elevations ranging from 3,000 to 8,000 feet, this habitat can be called montane riparian habitat, and some typical tree species are black cottonwood, bigleaf maple, white alder, and various willows. Some of the bird species are Hairy Woodpecker, American Robin, MacGillivray's Warbler, and Chipping Sparrow.

Farm fields. This habitat may range from alfalfa to fruit orchards. Some typical bird species are Great Egret; Northern Harrier; Red-tailed Hawk; American Kestrel; Ring-necked Pheasant; Loggerhead Shrike; Yellow-billed Magpie; American Crow; Horned Lark; Barn and Cliff Swallows; American Pipit; and Brewer's Blackbird.

Valley grassland is intended to refer to grasslands on the floor of the Central Valley, although the habitat also occurs on gentle slopes in the Coast Range. Some typical species are White-tailed Kite, Red-tailed Hawk, American Kestrel, Western Kingbird, Horned Lark, Savannah Sparrow, and Western Meadowlark.

Foothill woodland ranges from elevations of 300 to 3,000 feet, and is generally characterized by oak species, California buckeye, and foothill pine. The distinction between this and the following habitat is the degree of cover. If the woodland has a largely closed cover, it is referred to in this book as foothill woodland. Some typical bird species are Turkey Vulture, Red-tailed Hawk, California Quail, Mourning Dove, Western Screech-Owl, Acorn Woodpecker, Ash-throated Flycatcher, Western Scrub-Jay, Oak Titmouse, Western Bluebird, and Lesser Goldfinch.

Oak savanna. Tree species here are similar to those in the foregoing category, but the trees are more spaced, with much open grassland between. Some typical bird species are Red-tailed Hawk, Acorn Woodpecker, Northern Flicker, Western Scrub-Jay, White-breasted Nuthatch, and Western Bluebird.

Chaparral consists of dense, nearly impenetrable shrub-dominated vegetation. Typical plant species are chamise, ceanothus, California toyon, manzanita, scrub oak, and poison oak. The word *chaparral* is derived from the Spanish word *chaparro*, the name for scrub oak. Chaparral is often extensive in interior foothill locations, and is subject to frequent wildfires because of its dense growth and dry evergreen leaves. Some typical bird species are Blue-gray Gnatcatcher, Wrentit, California Thrasher, and Sage Sparrow.

Yellow pine forest. Some authors refer to this as montane forest. It is the first forest zone above the foothills and is characterized by such species as ponderosa pine, white fir, sugar pine, incense cedar, canyon live oak, and California black oak. Some typical bird species are Western Wood-Pewee, Steller's Jay, White-breasted Nuthatch, Brown Creeper, Dark-eyed Junco, and Black-headed Grosbeak.

Mixed conifer forest. Ponderosa pines are replaced by Jeffrey pines, and white firs become dominant. It is principally found in the Sierra Nevada and southern Cascades. The forest is notably more moist and cool than the yellow pine forest. Some bird species are Blue Grouse; White-headed and Pileated Woodpeckers; Western Wood-Pewee; Olive-sided and Hammond's Flycatchers; Warbling Vireo; Steller's Jay; Red-breasted Nuthatch; Brown Creeper; Golden-crowned Kinglet; Hermit Thrush; American Robin; Yellow-rumped and Hermit Warblers; Western Tanager; and Cassin's Finch.

Lodgepole–red fir forest. In some places the forest may consist almost exclusively of red firs, but in other locations large stands of lodgepole pines occur, along with some western white pines. This is the zone of heaviest snows. Some typical bird species are Blue Grouse; Williamson's Sapsucker; Dusky Flycatcher; Mountain Chickadee; Red-breasted and Pygmy Nuthatches; Golden-crowned Kinglet; Yellow-rumped Warbler; Cassin's Finch; and Pine Siskin.

Pinyon-juniper woodland. This plant community occurs on the Modoc Plateau and on the east side of the Sierra, in regions of aridity. Typical plants are single-leaf pinyon pine, western juniper, and mountain mahogany. In some locations, where there are no pinyon pines, the habitat will simply be referred to as juniper woodland. Some bird species are Gray Flycatcher and Pinyon Jay.

Joshua tree woodland. This applies to a desert plant community dominated by treelike yuccas called Joshua trees. These plants are generally widely spaced, and can be 20 to 30 feet tall. They often occur together with junipers. An example of this habitat occurs at Walker Pass, in Kern River Valley. Some typical bird species are Cactus Wren and Scott's Oriole.

Sagebrush scrub. This is the true sagebrush, which occurs in vast reaches in the Great Basin and Modoc Plateau as well as in various locations in the Sierra Nevada, often mixed with Jeffrey pines and other montane forest species. Some bird species are Sage Grouse, Gray Flycatcher, Sage Thrasher, Green-tailed Towhee, and Brewer's and Sage Sparrows.

Meadow. Usually means a grassy meadow with considerable wetness to it, applying principally to meadows in mountain areas. Some typical bird species are Common Snipe, Mountain Bluebird, and Lincoln's Sparrow.

Cliffs. Usually, montane cliffs are meant, as in rocky gorges, canyons, and mountains. The term includes the piles of rocky debris called talus (TAY-luss) that lie at the base of the cliffs, and is generally not used in this book for cliffs along the ocean shore, which are a natural part of rocky shorelines. Some typical bird species are Prairie Falcon, Black and White-throated Swifts, and Rock and Canyon Wrens.

Subalpine zone. Subalpine country is the region most highly esteemed by backpackers. It is characterized by spectacular views of mountains and meadows, interspersed with lakes and stands of lodgepole pines and mountain hemlocks. Some bird species are Red-tailed Hawk, Dusky Flycatcher, Mountain Chickadee, and Clark's Nutcracker.

Alpine zone. The country above treeline, often containing year-round snow fields is the alpine zone. It can be reached in the Warner Mountains by hiking out of Patterson Meadow, in the central Sierra by hiking from Carson Pass, and from Tioga Pass in Yosemite National Park. Some typical bird species are Rock Wren, Mountain Bluebird, and Gray-crowned Rosy-Finch.

Mountain Chickadees (parent feeding fledgling) in lodgepole pine–red fir forest.

4. Planning Your Trip

The major airport in Northern California is at San Francisco, and it has frequent connections all over the world. Out-of-state visitors who have destinations such as Point Reyes, Monterey, or Yosemite in mind will probably find San Francisco to be convenient. San Jose and Oakland also have major airports.

If you have destinations like Lake Tahoe or the Klamath Basin, the Sacramento airport would be your best bet. Sacramento does not have the coast-to-coast flights that San Francisco does, but has frequent connections to most locations in the United States.

Almost half of Northern California is in public ownership. By far the largest public landholder in the state is the USDA Forest Service, with 21 million acres. The national parks have 2 million acres, the state parks 560,000 acres, state and federal wildlife refuges 490,000 acres, and the Bureau of Land Management 3.4 million acres. This means that an enormous portion of the state is open to public access and free from "No Trespassing" signs.

The sites in this book have been deliberately chosen to be easily reached. Preference has been given to sites that are open every day of the week, do not need special permission to enter, and can be accessed without a group or a guide. Preference has also been given to those sites accessible by good paved roads. In some cases, the areas have unpaved roads, as in national wildlife refuges and state wildlife areas, and these have been noted in the text. In a few cases, as with the road to the Sage Grouse lek north of Honey Lake, the access roads can be treacherous in wet weather. But such roads are rare in this guide, and your attention is called to them if there is a potential problem.

The question of access by canoe sometimes arises. No specifics on canoe access are given in this guide because the great majority of users will not have the appropriate equipment or skills. The mode of travel most frequently assumed in this guide, after you have arrived by automobile, is on your own two feet, although barrier-free trails are mentioned wherever they exist. For those who are equipped for canoe travel, many parts of the Sacramento River south of Red Bluff are ideally suited for canoes, and lead into wild areas that give no hint that intensively managed farmlands lie just beyond the trees.

HAZARDS

Traffic. The greatest risk you will face is driving on the highways, with driving in fog leading the list. The fogs along the seacoast in summer generally are not the kind that produce zero visibility, although it is prudent to slow down in such cases. It is the winter fogs in the Central Valley and sometimes in the San Francisco Bay Area that are the problem. In December and January there are periods of calm weather with no wind or rain, and the fog can close in with remarkable speed after the sun goes down. The best rule is to plan carefully, and don't be out at night.

Generally, even in the worst fogs, the visibility the next morning will improve by 9 A.M. or 10 A.M.

If, in spite of your best planning, you find yourself in dense fog, then the first thing you must do is slow down. However, the very worst thing you could do is to come to a stop in the traffic lane, because that is how chain collisions happen. If you must stop, get off the roadway and onto the shoulder—way off, as far as you can.

Poison oak. Poison oak should come well toward the top of any list of hazards. Poison oak is almost everywhere in California, except in the higher mountains and in the plateau region. People who are familiar with poison ivy in the East may not recognize poison oak. The leaves are shiny and occur in groups of three, just like poison ivy, but true to the name, they have a scalloped appearance resembling oak leaves, and do not have the pointy look of ivy leaves. (See the accompanying photo.)

Poison oak comes in many forms. The most typical is in bushy clumps, but it also sometimes grows alone, like a small tree. It can even take on a vinelike form and climb high into big trees. Most insidious of all, poison oak can lie flat on the ground among short grasses, rendering it almost invisible until it is too late. Learn what it looks like and keep your distance. If you are unsure, a good rule is to stay on the trail and don't stray into the bushes. Be alert to the possibility that a poison oak branch may reach out across the trail from surrounding underbrush and take you unaware full in the face. Also, you should know that it can still do its damage

Learn to recognize the lobed, glossy leaves of poison oak, which grow in groups of three.

22

in winter, when the branches are bare. If you find yourself near suspicious-looking bushes, don't touch anything if you can help it.

Don't burn poison oak wood in a campfire. The smoke can carry the oils, and people who are especially allergic have actually died as a result of inhaling the smoke.

Donald G. Crosby, a world-renowned toxicologist at the University of California, Davis, says that the toxic reaction created by the oils probably takes place in the first few minutes after contact, so washing yourself after a long day in the field probably won't do much good. Washing yourself immediately after exposure might be of some help, however, if you're close enough to facilities. Also, Crosby says that a hot shower taken later—as hot as you can stand it—can have the effect of overpowering the itching sensation for a few hours, and can also have the benefit of washing off any excess oils that haven't yet done their mischief.

If your clothes have come into contact with poison oak, they should be washed thoroughly before reuse, because the residual oils on the clothes can cause a reaction. Dogs seem to be protected from poison oak by their hair, but if you pet your dog after it's been in poison oak, you can catch it that way, too.

Professor Crosby says that susceptibility to poison oak varies among individuals, but that total immunity is a widely held but fallacious belief— a myth and a dangerous delusion.

Ticks. There was a time when ticks, although a nuisance, were not looked upon as a genuine danger. But that was before Lyme disease. Some cases of Lyme disease have shown up in California, although it does not appear to be as prevalent as in some Eastern states. According to *Time* magazine, California had 80 cases in 1996, whereas New York had 5,463.

If you're bitten by a tick, see your doctor and follow his/her advice. Some of the possible early symptoms of Lyme disease are fatigue, chills and fever, headache, muscle and joint pain, swollen lymph nodes, and a characteristic red rash surrounding the site of the bite.

The preventive action for ticks is the same as for poison oak: stay out of the bushes. Wear light-colored clothing (so you can spot ticks before they bite you), and wear long pants and a long-sleeved shirt. After a day in the field, inspect yourself carefully for crawling ticks. It also may help to spray your feet, ankles, and lower clothing with insect repellent, especially the kind containing DEET. Note that DEET dissolves some kinds of plastics (including your binoculars), should be kept away from the eyes, and that some people may have an allergic reaction to it.

Rattlesnakes. All but one of California's rattlesnakes occur only in the desert regions of Southern California. The exception is the western rattlesnake, which occurs throughout most of California. It can be found from sea level to 11,000 feet, but is most likely to be encountered in the dry foothill regions.

I have hiked and backpacked most of my life in California, covering thousands of miles, and have seen rattlesnakes only about 10 times. I have had them buzz right next to my feet, but have never been bitten, nor do I know anyone who has been bitten. Not many people who are bitten actually die as a result. (One source says there are about 7,000 venomous snake bites per year in the United States, but only about 15 to 25 deaths.) However, even if death does not occur, there may be other severe consequences, including tissue loss, residual nerve damage, and amputation.

The prevention is similar to that for ticks and poison oak: stay out of the bushes. This admonition also applies to long grass and to rocky places where you can't see where you are putting your feet. If clambering on rocks, don't put your hands in places where you can't see. Above all, be alert. Rattlesnakes don't always rattle before they strike.

If bitten, get to a doctor as soon as possible. Even better, get to a hospital emergency room if you can. Antivenin is more likely to be available there.

Bees and wasps. There are more deaths per year in the United States from the stings of bees and wasps than from rattlesnake bites. Millions of people get stung every year, and about 30 people die annually. Most of the deaths have been attributed to allergic reactions.

The publicity given to the so-called African killer bees in recent years have made people aware of the dangers of beestings. Killer bees have appeared in Southern California, but have not gotten as far as Northern California, although they may eventually. The problem with these bees is that they attack in swarms and inflict multiple stings.

Ordinary honeybees don't attack so aggressively. The kind of wasp called a yellow jacket, represents a more likely hazard than do other kinds of bees or wasps, because they often make their nests in the ground, and you might walk into one without knowing it. They also occasionally build their nests in tree branches.

Lightning. In most of California, lightning is fairly rare. In the high mountains, however, it occurs quite often in the summer. Above timberline, it represents a real danger. If you're above timberline and dark clouds begin to approach, get back among the trees as soon as you can. Don't get under an isolated tree or one that sticks prominently above its neighbors. Such trees act as the shortest routes between ground and sky for the lightning to follow. In a thick forest with trees of more or less the same height, the danger of lightning finding a path in your immediate vicinity is lessened. The best thing to do to protect yourself from lightning is to get inside the nearest car. Sit upright and keep your body away from the body of the car. It's important not to touch the inside of the car's body.

High-elevation exposure. Long exposure to sun at high elevations can be harmful. Unlike lightning, which generally gives you some warning, excessive exposure to the sun creeps up on you. Wear a hat and a long-sleeved shirt, and use sunscreen.

Mountain lions. On a strictly statistical basis, this is probably the least likely threat to your life you will ever face. Yet, mountain lion sightings and attacks have gained increasing publicity.

In all my years of hiking and camping in wilderness, I've never seen a mountain lion, although I've seen tracks. Nevertheless, from 1986 to 1995 nine attacks by mountain lions took place in California, two of them fatal; three of the attacks involved small children. To give some perspective to these figures, this represents a rate of 0.2 deaths per year, compared to 45,000 deaths per year in the United States from motor vehicle accidents.

Some of the recommendations of the California Department of Fish and Game are don't hike alone, keep children close to you, do not approach a lion, and don't turn your back on it. Speak loudly to it in a firm voice. Raise your arms high, and try to look big. Above all, don't run. The lion could mistake you for a deer and give chase.

Remember: Statistically speaking, you're much more likely to be bitten by a dog than by a mountain lion. If you are interested in further information, consult *Mountain Lion Alert* by Steven Torres (Falcon Publishing).

Black bears. Maybe I've never seen a mountain lion, but I've had far more encounters with black bears than I would have preferred. I've had them steal my food and bang against my tent cabin at night while fighting among themselves. One challenged me for the right-of-way on a trail (I yielded). I almost walked on a sleeping bear (both of us just about died from fright), and a mother bear came searching for me because I frightened her cubs. I have to say that I don't think my welfare was seriously threatened on any of these occasions, although I have to confess I was pretty concerned about what that mother bear was going to do.

Bears are strong animals and capable of inflicting serious injury. The best rule is to avoid them whenever possible. Some of the recommendations of the California Department of Fish and Game are don't feed a bear, keep a clean camp, don't approach a bear, and do not run. These rules apply to black bears, the most common kind. (Incidentally, so-called black bears are often brown.) Dealing with grizzly bears is a different matter, but California hasn't had any wild grizzlies since the 1920s. More information about traveling safely in bear country can be found in *Bear Aware* by Bill Schneider (Falcon Publishing).

Waves. Most people are not aware of the danger posed by big, unexpected waves, sometimes called killer waves. One rule is never turn your back on the ocean. Killer waves can appear out of nowhere, especially in winter, and have taken many lives. Caution is urged about going out on breakwaters, where the rocks are slippery and there is nowhere to run if a sudden big wave appears. Kenn Kaufman, in his book *Kingbird Highway,* tells of being washed off a jetty in Texas by a huge wave and nearly perishing.

Cliffs. It shouldn't be necessary to warn about cliffs, but people often fall off them. The warning is especially needed with respect to coastal sites. Informal trails seem to run everywhere at such locations, usually right along the cliff edges. And, of course, the ocean is constantly busy at undercutting cliffs, so those trails that look well used and safe may in fact be on the verge of collapse. The only good rule is to stay back from the edge.

Earthquakes. Some people from other regions have a great fear of earthquakes in California. Earthquakes do occur, of course; in fact, they make headline news when they do happen. But I've lived in California all my life, most of the time within striking range of the infamous San Andreas Fault, and have never been in a bad earthquake, although I've been rattled a couple of times. The likelihood of being in a bad earthquake is so small that the best thing to do is forget about it.

Crime. It is too bad that this topic comes up at all, but something must be said here. It is not likely that birders will be subjected to the kind of crime that results in personal injury, but some sites were deliberately omitted from this guide when I learned there might be a serious problem at those locations.

A more likely type of crime that birders may encounter is to find their cars broken into if they are left in remote parking lots. You should always be careful not to leave anything interesting or valuable in your car that can be seen from the outside. This is no guarantee against break-in, of course, because vandals obviously know that cars have trunks. Nevertheless, a break-in is more likely to occur if something valuable is in plain view, than if it is not.

Don't let all these safety precautions wear you down. The probabilities are very much on your side that you will have a wonderful, safe trip.

"California" Clapper Rail (federally listed endangered) at Palo Alto Baylands.

5. Birding Ethics

Everyone who enjoys birds and birding must always respect wildlife, its environment, and the rights of others. In any conflict of interest between birds and birders, the welfare of the birds and their environment comes first.

1   Promote the welfare of birds and their environment.

1(a) Support the protection of important bird habitat.

1(b) To avoid stressing birds or exposing them to danger, exercise restraint and caution during observation, photography, sound recording, or filming.

    Limit the use of recordings and other methods of attracting birds, and never use such methods in heavily birded areas, or for attracting any species that is Threatened, Endangered, or of Special Concern, or is rare in your local area.

    Keep well back from nests and nesting colonies, roosts, display areas, and important feeding sites. In such sensitive areas, if there is a need for extended observation, photography, filming or recording, try to use a blind or hide, and take advantage of natural cover.

    Use artificial light sparingly for filming or photography, especially for close-ups.

1(c) Before advertising the presence of a rare bird, evaluate the potential for disturbance to the bird, its surroundings, and other people in the area, and proceed only if access can be controlled, disturbance minimized, and permission has been obtained from private landowners. The sites of rare nesting birds should be divulged only to the proper conservation authorities.

1(d) Stay on roads, trails, and paths where they exist; otherwise keep habitat disturbance to a minimum.

2   Respect the law and rights of others.

2(a) Do not enter private property without the owner's explicit permission.

2(b) Follow all laws, rules, and regulations governing use of roads and public areas, both at home and abroad.

2(c) Practice common courtesy in contacts with other people. Your exemplary behavior will generate goodwill with birders and nonbirders alike.

3   Ensure that feeders, nest structures, and other artificial bird environments are safe.

3(a) Keep dispensers, water, and food clean and free of decay or disease. It is important to feed birds continually during harsh weather.

3(b) Maintain and clean nest structures regularly.

3(c) If you are attracting birds to an area, ensure the birds are not exposed to predation from cats and other domestic animals, or dangers posed by artificial hazards.

4   Group birding, whether organized or impromptu, requires special care.

Each individual in the group, in addition to the obligations spelled out in Items #1 and #2, has responsibilities as a Group Member.

4(a) Respect the interests, rights, and skills of fellow birders, as well as people participating in other legitimate outdoor activities. Freely share your knowledge and experience, except where code 1(c) applies. Be especially helpful to beginning birders.

4(b) If you witness unethical birding behavior, assess the situation, and intervene if you think it prudent. When interceding, inform the person(s) of the inappropriate action, and attempt, within reason, to have it stopped. If the behavior continues, document it, and notify appropriate individuals or organizations.

Group Leader Responsibilities (amateur and professional trips and tours).

4(c) Be an exemplary ethical role model for the group. Teach through word and example.

4(d) Keep groups to a size that limits impact on the environment and does not interfere with others using the same area.

4(e) Ensure everyone in the group knows of and practices this code.

4(f) Learn and inform the group of any special circumstances applicable to the areas being visited (e.g., no tape recorders allowed).

4(g) Acknowledge that professional tour companies bear a special responsibility to place the welfare of birds and the benefits of public knowledge ahead of the company's commercial interest. Ideally, leaders should keep track of tour sightings, document unusual occurrences, and submit records to appropriate organizations.

Reprinted by permission of American Birding Association

Two of the precepts involved in this code deserve some additional comment. These have to do with the birds' welfare and with the observance of private property rights.

No birder wants to damage the welfare of wild birds. Unfortunately, it is not always clear just where the boundary is located between acceptable and unacceptable behavior. For example, one of the principles says that birds should be observed and photographed without knowingly disturbing them in any significant way. The key word is *significant*. When we are walking down a trail and watching birds, we know that birds will flush from the undergrowth in response to our presence and fly farther down the trail. Is this significant, and therefore unacceptable? Some people seem to think so. They say that any flushing at all creates additional energy demands on birds and moves them closer to the edge of survival than they might otherwise be. However, lots of people, most of them nonbirders, also walk down those same trails and cause birds to flush. Flushing caused by birders is only a small fraction of the flushing that goes on constantly.

There is another principle in the code of ethics that says birders should avoid chasing or repeatedly flushing birds. In my view, that is the statement that provides the key to the issue. Repeated deliberate flushing could indeed cause unacceptable energy demands on birds, and should be avoided.

With respect to private property rights, it is a bit distressing to observe how often birders will trespass in order to see a bird they need for their life lists. But trespassing on private property is one of the major grievances that many property owners, especially those in rural areas, have against birders. The rule regarding trespassing on private property is simple: don't do it. Most of the sites in this book are in public ownership, so trespassing is not an issue. Wherever private property is involved, I have tried to call attention to that fact and urged that all viewing be done from the roadside. And, in suggesting places to park along the roadside, I have tried to suggest those that are not close to private residences. Many people get nervous when strangers park near their houses, and we birders don't need to get a major sector of the public down on us. We should also avoid blocking any gates, another grievance many property owners have.

Map Legend

Interstate	10	City or Town	○ Big Pine or Merced
US Highway	87 377	Campground	▲
State or County Road	36 CR 3808	Parking Area	Ⓟ
Forest Service Road	FR 224	Pass	‿
Controlled Access Highway with Interchange		Cabin or Building	■
Paved Road		Elevation	5,281 ft. X
Secondary Paved Road		Peak	
Gravel or Unimproved Road		Information/Visitor Center or Ranger Station	?
Birding Site	17	State/County/ International Boundary	NEVADA
Lake, Dam,River/Creek, Waterfall		Park/Refuge/Forest Boundary	
Bridge		Map Orientation	N
Marsh or Wetland			
Levee		Scale	0 0.5 1 Miles
Trail			
Railroad			

Other Symbols

Included in *California Wildlife Viewing Guide* (See page 4)

Area has at least one barrier-free trail

30

6. *Northern California's Best Birding Areas*

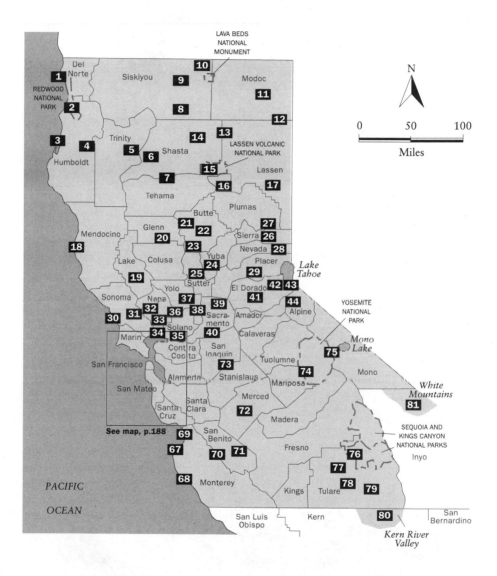

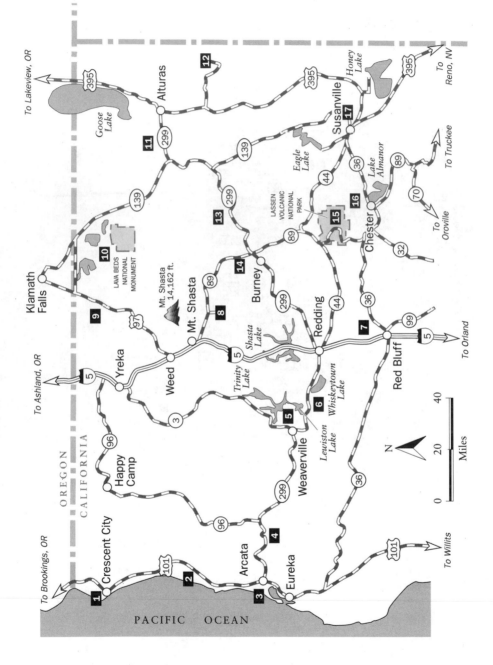

PACIFIC OCEAN

Redwood Coast to Modoc Plateau

The sites in this region create a journey through the top of California, from the coast to the high plateaus. Taken together, they form an 800-mile birding trail across the state (the sites in each region in this book are organized into "birding trails"), far removed both physically and spiritually from the urban areas of San Francisco and Los Angeles. The coast contains the finest redwoods in existence, and the plateau country has endless vistas dominated by the mighty presences of Mount Shasta and Lassen Peak.

The birding opportunities are unusual. The coastal sections give a chance to see such highly sought specialties as Marbled Murrelet, Tufted Puffin, Harlequin Duck, Rock Sandpiper, and Varied Thrush. The incomparable Klamath Basin has a million ducks, geese, and swans in late fall, plus the largest winter concentration of Bald Eagles in the lower 48 states. In the interior mountains you will have as good a chance of seeing birds such as Black Swift, Sage Grouse, Williamson's Sapsucker, Lewis's Woodpecker, and Townsend's Solitaire as anywhere in the country. And this is the region that many birds choose for breeding, including Wilson's Phalarope, White-faced Ibis, Willet, Common Snipe, Greater Sandhill Crane, and Yellow-headed Blackbird.

1 Crescent City

2 Prairie Creek Redwoods

3 Arcata and Humboldt Bay Region

4 Trinity River

5 Lewistown Lake

6 Tower House Historic District

7 Battle Creek

8 McCloud River Loop

9 Butte Valley

10 Klamath Basin

11 Modoc Plateau

12 Warner Mountains

13 Pit River Country

14 McArthur-Burney Falls Memorial State Park

15 Lassen Volcanic National Park

16 Lake Almanor

17 Eagle Lake and Honey Lake

1 Crescent City

Habitats: Sandy beach and mudflats, rocky headlands, coastal bay and lagoons, closed-cone pine forest, Douglas-fir forest.

Specialty birds: *Resident*—Pelagic Cormorant, Black Oystercatcher, Western Gull, Marbled Murrelet, Hutton's Vireo, Chestnut-backed Chickadee, Varied Thrush, Wrentit. *Summer*—Brown Pelican, Brandt's Cormorant, Heermann's Gull, Elegant Tern, Pigeon Guillemot, Tufted Puffin, Band-tailed Pigeon, Vaux's Swift, Allen's Hummingbird, Pacific-slope Flycatcher. *Winter*—Western and Clark's Grebes; Harlequin Duck; Bald Eagle; Black Turnstone; Surfbird; Rock Sandpiper; Mew and Glaucous-winged Gulls. *Migrant*—Pacific Loon, "Aleutian" Canada Goose, Wandering Tattler.

Other key birds: *Resident*—American Bittern; Sharp-shinned and Red-shouldered Hawks; Virginia Rail; Common Murre; Great Horned Owl; Black-capped Chickadee; Winter Wren; Golden-crowned Kinglet. *Summer*—Caspian Tern, Warbling Vireo, Swainson's Thrush, Common Yellowthroat, Wilson's Warbler. *Winter*—Red-throated and Common Loons; Tundra Swan; Canvasback; Ring-necked Duck; Black; White-winged; and Surf Scoters; Red-breasted Merganser; American Pipit; Fox Sparrow. *Migrant*—Pectoral Sandpiper, Red-necked Phalarope, Forster's Tern.

Best times to bird: April and May for breeding birds and spring migrants; October through April for wintering shorebirds, grebes, ducks, and some gulls.

Directions: Going either north or south on U.S. Highway 101, turn west on Front Street at the southern edge of the business district. Turn south (toward the water) at H Street, then go west on Howe Drive. Turn south onto A Street, park at the end of A Street near the lighthouse to check out the shore and the breakwater, then go north on A Street to Sixth Street and turn west to merge with Pebble Beach Drive. View **Castle Rock** from a parking lot about 2 miles north on Pebble Beach Drive. To get to **Point St. George,** continue north to the intersection with Washington Boulevard, and go to the end, where there is a parking lot. Walk north 0.5 mile to the beach, or take any of the trails to the left, to get to the rocky shore. Directions to Lake Earl and the mouth of the Smith River are given in the following sections.

The birding: Three "hot" birds people often come to Crescent City to find are Tufted Puffin, Rock Sandpiper, and Harlequin Duck. Tufted Puffins generally breed during April and May, and sit out in plain view on **Castle Rock,** but Castle Rock is a half-mile away, and the puffins can be seen only with a scope. Even then, you must look for a long time until you can make out little black specks with white heads sitting beside their burrows, along with zillions of Common Murres.

During spring and fall migration, watch for the endangered "Aleutian" Canada Goose, which is only about half the size of the largest subspecies of Canada Goose. (The "Aleutian" subspecies usually has a broad white band around the base of the neck. However, members of the "Cackling" subspecies, which is even smaller than the "Aleutian" subspecies, sometimes have narrow or incomplete white bands.) From late February to late April, thousands of "Aleutian" geese stage at Castle Rock and nearby areas, getting ready for their migration to their breeding grounds in the Aleutian Islands.

A short distance to the north of Castle Rock on Pebble Beach Drive is **Point St. George,** a classic place for Harlequin Ducks and Rock Sandpipers. Small flocks of Harlequin Ducks are sometimes present from October through April, puttering around in the pools among the rocks or in the surf; a few may be present in summer. Rock Sandpipers are rare, but this is one of the best places in California to see one. Other birds to look for are Brandt's Cormorant (summer), Black Oystercatcher (resident), Wandering Tattler (migration), Black Turnstone, and Surfbird (the last two are generally present from August to April). Also, look for flocks of Pacific Loons migrating offshore in spring and fall. At this time of year, when they are in breeding plumage, the backs of their heads and necks may look almost white. Marbled Murrelets and Pigeon Guillemots may be floating in the offshore waters, especially in late spring and summer. In winter, look for Western and Clark's Grebes, and Black, White-winged, and Surf Scoters. Some of the remarkable vagrants that have shown up here are Blue-footed Booby, White-collared Swift, and Red-headed Woodpecker.

While at Point St. George, don't overlook the "dickey birds." Wintering Golden-crowned Sparrows and resident White-crowned and Savannah Sparrows favor the grassy headlands.

In **Crescent City,** check the shore near Howe Drive and the breakwater for Rock Sandpipers in winter. Note, however, that Rock Sandpipers favor breakwaters that are washed with high waves, and such places can be dangerous. Also check the mouth of the small creek at the northeast edge of the city park near the swimming pool for gulls, ducks, and shorebirds. In May 1998, a Bristle-thighed Curlew was found near the lighthouse.

Go south on US 101 to **Anchor Way,** and drive to where you can look over the harbor. All sorts of birds may be here, including Red-throated Loon (winter), Heermann's Gull (summer), Mew Gull (fall and winter), and Western Gull. Harlequin Ducks sometimes are present. Other birds, that normally are associated with open coastline, such as Surf Scoter, Black Turnstone, and Surfbird (all fall and winter), and Pigeon Guillemot (March through September) may be found here. Look also for Common Loon, Double-crested Cormorant, and Red-breasted Merganser; Oldsquaws can be here in some winters. This is a good place to look for Elegant Terns, especially in warm-water years, and Forster's Terns in late August and September.

Another location of interest is the mouth of the **Smith River.** Go north from Crescent City on US 101 about 14.5 miles through the town of Smith River to Mouth of Smith River Road. Turn toward the ocean, go 0.3 mile to the end of the road, and park. When the river is running high, you will see a dramatic scene of conflict between the force of the river and the force of the ocean. It is hard to

1 Crescent City

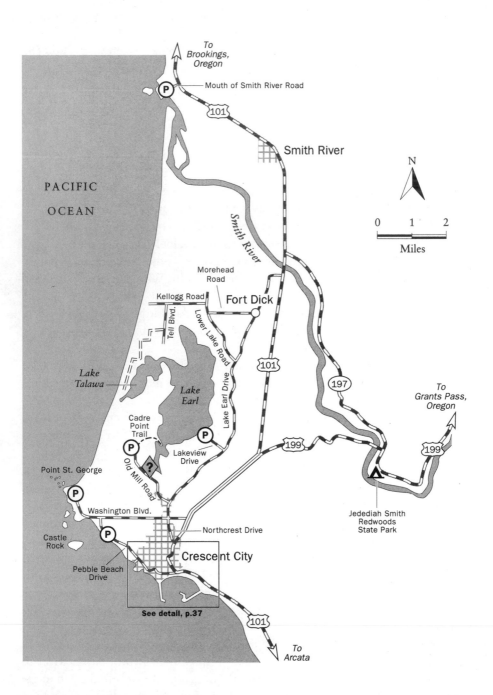

To Brookings, Oregon

P — Mouth of Smith River Road

101

Smith River

PACIFIC OCEAN

Smith River

N

0   1   2
Miles

Morehead Road

Kellogg Road

Fort Dick

Tell Blvd.

Lower Lake Road

101

197

To Grants Pass, Oregon

Lake Talawa

Lake Earl

Lake Earl Drive

Cadre Point Trail

P

P

Lakeview Drive

199

199

Old Mill Road

Point St. George

P

Washington Blvd.

Northcrest Drive

Jedediah Smith Redwoods State Park

Castle Rock

P

Crescent City

Pebble Beach Drive

See detail, p.37

101

To Arcata

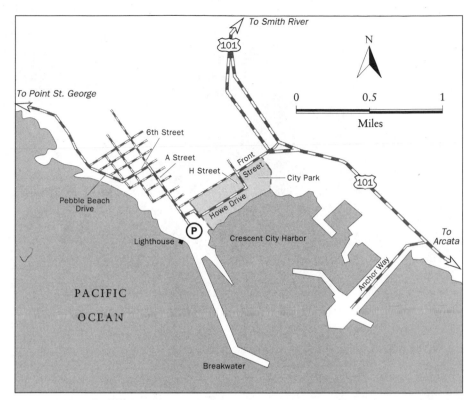

Crescent City detail.

predict just what might be here, but almost certainly there will be gulls, including western specialties such as Western Gull, Glaucous-winged Gull (September to May), and California Gull. Look also for Pelagic Cormorant, Brown Pelican (summer), and Caspian Tern (April to October).

To get to **Lake Earl,** from the junction of Washington Boulevard and Northcrest Drive in Crescent City, go north on Northcrest Drive 0.6 mile to Old Mill Road, turn left, and go 1.5 miles to the headquarters of the **Lake Earl Wildlife Area.** There is a parking lot just beyond the headquarters, and a trail that leads through the mixed conifer forest to Cadre Point (0.9 mile). The trail, mostly an old dirt road, leads through attractive coastal forest and emerges at the southern end of Lake Earl. In the forested areas look for resident Sharp-shinned Hawk, Band-tailed Pigeon, Great Horned Owl, Hutton's Vireo, Black-capped and Chestnut-backed Chickadees, Winter Wren, Golden-crowned Kinglet, and Varied Thrush, and for summer visitors such as Pacific-slope Flycatcher, Warbling Vireo, Swainson's Thrush, and Wilson's Warbler; Fox Sparrow is a winter visitor. In the brushy areas, residents such as Wrentits and California Quail are present, and Red-shouldered Hawks are in the more open areas. Watch for Allen's Hummingbird in spring and summer. At the end of the trail, near the lake, the shoreline consists

Birders at Point St. George.

mostly of marsh, with the lake visible at a distance; a scope is useful. Western Grebes have nested close to shore in this part of the lake, and Tundra Swans may be here in the winter. The marsh's resident birds include Virginia Rail, Marsh Wren, and Song Sparrow. In spring the vocalizations of Pied-billed Grebes and American Bitterns often can be heard. Look for Vaux's Swift and Common Yellowthroat in summer and American Pipit and Swamp Sparrow in winter.

To get to other parts of Lake Earl, return on Old Mill Road to Northcrest Drive and go north. (Northcrest Drive becomes Lake Earl Drive.) Lakeview Drive is 2.2 miles north of Old Mill Road. Turn west on Lakeview Drive and travel 0.7 mile to the end of the road and a parking lot that has limited views of the lake and lots of marsh. In the winter this part of the lake often has Canvasbacks as well as other wintering ducks such as Redheads, Ring-necked Ducks, and Greater Scaups. Bald Eagles are often seen here in January and February. The marshes have resident Pied-billed Grebes, American Bitterns, and Song Sparrows. Black Phoebes are widespread.

To get to **Lake Talawa,** return to the junction of Lakeview Drive and Lake Earl Drive, go 4.4 miles north on Lake Earl Drive to Fort Dick, and turn west on Morehead Road. Go 1.8 miles on Morehead Road, turn north on Lower Lake Road for 0.2 mile, and then west on Kellogg Road. Go 0.8 mile on Kellogg Road to Tell Boulevard, which is the entry to an abandoned subdivision, called Pacific Shores. The subdivision has many old, deteriorating roads, and it is easy to get lost. The county-maintained road is paved in places and graded gravel in others. Go 0.5 mile south on Tell Boulevard (paved), turn west on a well-graded gravel road, and south 0.2 mile later, at the T intersection. Follow the main road as it makes several right-angle turns until it ends 2.5 miles after the T intersection. Lake Talawa is visible from the lower reaches of the road, and in winter has many of the waterfowl listed previously. Sandpipers such as Pectoral, Western, Least, and others are found here in migration, as well as Red-necked Phalaropes. A couple of Eurasian Dotterels showed up here in September 1992. Flocks of Double-crested Cormorants often fly overhead to their roosting places inland.

General information: The Crescent City area has a great variety of habitats in a fairly compact region. There are offshore rookeries, rocky headlands, mixed conifer forests, sandy flats, lagoons, a protected harbor with a breakwater, and a redwood forest at Jedediah Smith Redwoods State Park. Redwood National Park officially begins at Crescent City and extends south to Prairie Creek Redwoods State Park.

ADDITIONAL HELP

NCA&G grid: Page 22, 2A, 2B.
Elevation: Sea level.
Hazards: Large, unexpected waves; ticks.
Nearest food, gas, lodging: Crescent City.
Camping: Jedediah Smith Redwoods State Park: 108 sites; RV dump station, on U.S. Highway 199, 9 miles east of Crescent City.
For more information: Lake Earl Wildlife Area; Jedediah Smith Redwoods State Park.

2 Prairie Creek Redwoods

Habitats: Redwood forest, stream, meadows.
Specialty birds: *Resident*—Marbled Murrelet, Spotted and Barred Owls, Steller's Jay, Chestnut-backed Chickadee, American Dipper, Varied Thrush. *Summer*—Band-tailed Pigeon, Vaux's Swift, Pacific-slope Flycatcher, Violet-green Swallow, Hermit Warbler. *Winter*—Townsend's Warbler.
Other key birds: *Resident*—Pileated Woodpecker, Gray Jay, Brown Creeper, Winter Wren, Golden-crowned Kinglet. *Summer*—Olive-sided Flycatcher, Warbling Vireo, Swainson's Thrush, Wilson's Warbler. *Winter*—Hermit Thrush.
Best times to bird: April through June for breeding birds. Predawn in April through June, for Marbled Murrelets.

Directions: Prairie Creek Redwoods is on U.S. Highway 101, about 35 miles south of Crescent City, or 41 miles north of Arcata. Exit from US 101 onto Newton B. Drury Scenic Parkway.

The birding: At one time, the Northern Spotted Owl was the most celebrated resident of these woods, but the owl has now had to move over for another celebrity—the Marbled Murrelet, a seabird that is related to the puffins and auklets. In treeless

2 Prairie Creek Redwoods

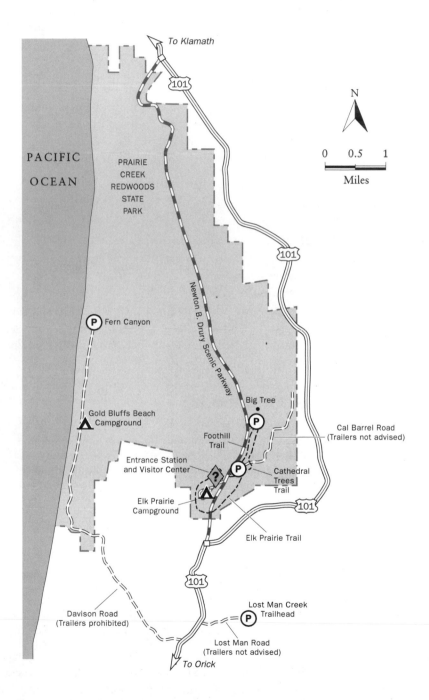

areas, such as in parts of Alaska, they build their nests on the ground, but in Northern California they build them high in old-growth redwoods and firs. From April through July they can be heard in the predawn hours as they fly from the ocean to their nesting sites. They are far more often heard than seen, and make a loud, strident series of *"keer!"* notes. It is best to be in place 45 minutes before sunrise (the "official" sunrise time, and not the time the sun comes up over the trees). Good places to watch for them are at Elk Prairie near the entrance station, and at the parking lot for the trailhead for **Lost Man Creek,** about 2.5 miles south of Elk Prairie (gravel access road, trailers not advised). Another location is at the **Big Tree** parking lot, about 1 mile north of Elk Prairie. It is sometimes even possible to hear them at dawn while lying in bed in the campground.

Murrelets are fast birds, flying up to 50 miles per hour, sometimes as low as 30 feet above the ground, but more often higher, up to 600 feet. Experienced Murrelet-watchers say that there is a possibility of confusion with the Vaux's Swift, which also occurs in the area. Swifts, of course, have long, thin, curved wings, whereas Murrelets have short wings and beat them with a rapid whir.

Also competing with the Spotted Owl for celebrity status is the Barred Owl, a somewhat recent arrival in the Northwest. Barred Owls are most often thought of as eastern birds, ranging into British Columbia and Washington, but they have expanded their range into Northern California. They were first detected in the state in 1981, with increasingly frequent reports since then, although they are still considered to be rare. Barred Owls resemble Spotted Owls but are larger. They have a distinctive call, often rendered as *"Who-cooks-for-you? Who-cooks-for you-all?"* In recent years, Barred Owls have been found along Cal Barrel Road and near the **Cathedral Trees Trail,** but can be difficult to locate if they are not calling. Barred and Spotted Owls occur in similar habitat, and the two have been known to interbreed.

All of the trails near the Elk Prairie Campground and entrance station lead through attractive redwood forests, sometimes next to meadows. Immediately adjacent to the entrance station and visitor center is a short, paved barrier-free trail called the **Redwood Access Trail.**

The most prominent birds in the forested areas are Steller's Jays and Chestnut-backed Chickadees. Often heard, but less often seen, are Varied Thrushes, which make a drawn-out eerie quavering call, first at one pitch and then usually repeated at a different pitch. Another typical bird of the coastal forest is the Swainson's Thrush (spring and summer), again more often heard than seen. The Swainson's song is a breezy series of flutelike whistles, rising upward in pitch. Look for residents such as Belted Kingfisher, Pileated Woodpecker, Common Raven, Bushtit, Brown Creeper, Winter Wren, Golden-crowned Kinglet, and Song and White-crowned Sparrows. Some summer visitors are Band-tailed Pigeon, Olive-sided and Pacific-slope Flycatchers, Warbling Vireo, Violet-green Swallow, and Hermit and Wilson's Warblers. Gray Jays occur here, but are uncommon to rare; they have been seen at the parking lot for the **Big Tree.** Look for them in Sitka spruce/redwood forests. Also, at the Big Tree parking lot look for the Pileated Woodpecker and Barred Owl. American Dippers have been seen in Lost Man Creek, below the parking area.

As has been pointed out by Stanley Harris in *Northwestern California Birds,* "winter replacements" take over for some of the summer visitors: The Hermit Thrush takes the place of the Swainson's Thrush, and Townsend's and Yellow-rumped Warblers replace Hermit and Wilson's Warblers.

General information: In the opinion of many, Prairie Creek Redwoods is the finest grove of redwoods in existence. At one time, US 101 passed right through the heart of the grove, but has now been routed around it via a freeway. The former US 101 is now known as the Newton B. Drury Scenic Parkway. Close to the southern border of the park is a beautiful large meadow known as Elk Prairie. Usually, a herd of Roosevelt elk can be seen grazing here.

ADDITIONAL HELP

NCA&G grid: Page 32, 3B.
Elevation: 200 feet.
Hazards: Rangers warn against getting too close to elk. Bears, mountain lions, and ticks are present.
Nearest food, gas, lodging: Orick; Klamath.
Camping: Elk Prairie: 75 sites; Gold Bluffs Beach: 25 sites, reached by 5 miles of gravel road (no trailers).
For more information: Prairie Creek Redwoods State Park.

3 Arcata and Humboldt Bay Region 🍴 ♿

Habitats: Sandy beach and mudflats, rocky headlands, coastal bays and lagoons, coastal scrub, Douglas-fir forest, freshwater marsh, stream, riparian woodland, pasturelands.

Specialty birds: *Resident*—Pelagic Cormorant, Wood Duck, White-tailed Kite, Peregrine Falcon, Black Oystercatcher, Anna's Hummingbird, Red-breasted Sapsucker, Chestnut-backed Chickadee, Varied Thrush, Wrentit. *Summer*—Brandt's Cormorant, Cinnamon Teal, Osprey, Heermann's Gull, Elegant Tern, Pigeon Guillemot, Tufted Puffin, Band-tailed Pigeon, Vaux's Swift, Allen's Hummingbird, Western Wood-Pewee, Pacific-slope Flycatcher, Cassin's Vireo, Violet-green Swallow. *Winter*—Western and Clark's Grebes; Harlequin Duck; Hooded Merganser; Eurasian Wigeon; Pacific Golden-Plover; Black Turnstone; Surfbird; Mew and Glaucous-winged Gulls. *Migrant*—Pacific Loon, Rufous Hummingbird.

Other key birds: *Resident*—American Bittern; Black-crowned Night-Heron; Common Merganser; Sharp-shinned and Cooper's Hawks; Virginia Rail; Common Murre; Barn Owl; Black-capped Chickadee; Winter Wren; Golden-crowned Kinglet. *Summer*—Green Heron; Caspian Tern; Olive-sided Flycatcher; Warbling Vireo; Purple Martin; Northern Rough-winged Swallow; Swainson's Thrush; Orange-crowned and Wilson's Warblers; American Goldfinch. *Winter*—Red-throated and Common Loons; Horned and Red-necked Grebes; Green-winged Teal; Ring-necked Duck; Greater Scaup; Black, White-winged, and Surf Scoters; Bufflehead; Red-breasted Merganser; Rough-legged Hawk; Merlin; Sora; Black-bellied and Semipalmated Plovers; Greater Yellowlegs; Willet; Marbled Godwit; Ruddy Turnstone; Sanderling; Long-billed Dowitcher; Bonaparte's Gull; Northern Shrike; American Pipit; Fox Sparrow. *Migrant*—Brant, Lesser Yellowlegs, Whimbrel, Red Knot, Short-billed Dowitcher, Parasitic Jaeger.

Best times to bird: For breeding birds, late April through June. For waterfowl, October through April.

Directions: See specific directions for each site.

The birding: Trinidad State Beach lies about 14.5 miles north of Arcata on U.S. Highway 101. After exiting US 101 at Trinidad, go west on Main Street to the T, and turn right on Stagecoach Road. The parking lot for the Elk Head Trail is about 0.8 mile north on Stagecoach Road (no fee, lock your car, and take valuables with you). The trail departs from the north end of the parking lot and leads through a lovely forest of alders and Sitka spruce to the rocky cliffs of Elk Head— about a 2-mile round trip. Some visible offshore islands, such as Green Rock, have nesting seabirds, especially thousands of Common Murres. Tufted Puffins have nested on the islands in some years. A scope is essential.

The forested section has resident Anna's Hummingbird, Chestnut-backed Chickadee, Winter Wren, Wrentit, Golden-crowned Kinglet, and Varied Thrush, and summer visitors such as Band-tailed Pigeon, Allen's Hummingbird, Olive-sided Flycatcher, Swainson's Thrush, and Wilson's Warbler. Rufous Hummingbird

3 Arcata and Humboldt Bay Region

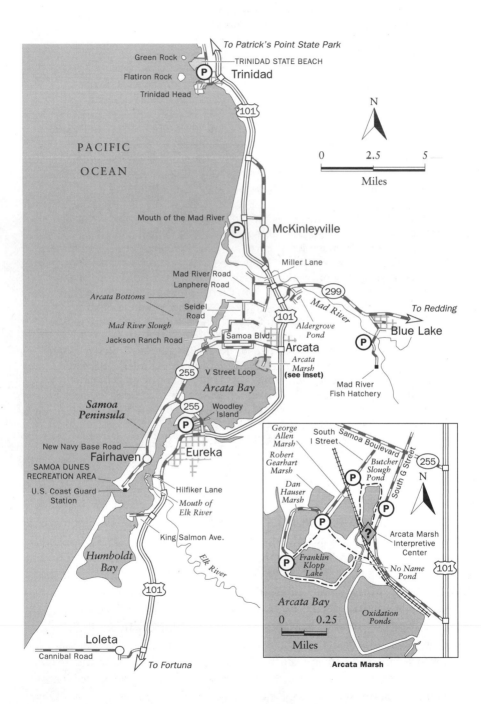

To Patrick's Point State Park

Green Rock
Flatiron Rock
Trinidad Head

TRINIDAD STATE BEACH
Trinidad

101

PACIFIC

OCEAN

N

0   2.5   5
Miles

Mouth of the Mad River

McKinleyville

Miller Lane

Mad River Road
Lanphere Road

Arcata Bottoms

Seidel
Road

299

Mad River

To Redding

Mad River Slough

Jackson Ranch Road

Samoa Blvd.

101

*Aldergrove
Pond*

Blue Lake

Arcata

*Arcata
Marsh*
(see inset)

Mad River
Fish Hatchery

255
V Street Loop

Arcata Bay

*Samoa
Peninsula*

255
Woodley
Island

New Navy Base Road

SAMOA DUNES
RECREATION AREA

U.S. Coast Guard
Station

Fairhaven

Eureka

Hilfiker Lane

*Mouth of
Elk River*

King Salmon Ave.

*Humboldt
Bay*

Elk River

101

Loleta

Cannibal Road

To Fortuna

*George
Allen
Marsh*

South
I Street

South Samoa Boulevard

*Robert
Gearhart
Marsh*

*Butcher
Slough
Pond*

255

N

*Dan
Hauser
Marsh*

Arcata Marsh
Interpretive
Center

*Franklin
Klopp
Lake*

*No Name
Pond*

101

Arcata Bay

0   0.25
Miles

*Oxidation
Ponds*

Arcata Marsh

is an uncommon spring migrant. On the rocky coast, in addition to the murres, look for Brandt's and Pelagic Cormorants, Black Oystercatcher, Black and Ruddy Turnstones, Surfbird, and Pigeon Guillemot.

The **Mouth of the Mad River** viewpoint lies about 1.3 miles south of the exit for Clam Beach County Park, on US 101. It is accessible only to southbound traffic. From the viewpoint, you look directly down on the sand bars at the mouth of the river, which may have shorebirds such as Black-bellied Plover, Sanderling, Dunlin, and dowitchers. Gulls favor this spot, and Caspian Terns are frequently seen here.

Aldergrove Pond is a delightful little pond tucked away in an unexpected location. From the junction of US 101 and California Highway 299 go east on CA 299 and exit at the first opportunity, which is Giuntoli Lane. Immediately turn right, go 0.1 mile to West End Road, and turn right. Go 0.2 mile to Aldergrove Road and turn left. The tiny parking lot lies about 0.2 mile down Aldergrove Road, on the left. Walk the short trail that leads along the edge of the pond for Green Heron, Wood Duck, Ring-necked Duck, Hooded Merganser, Belted Kingfisher, Marsh Wren, and Wilson's Warbler.

The large area called **Arcata Bottoms** is known for raptors such as White-tailed Kite, Rough-legged Hawk (winter), and Barn Owl, and for migrant sandpipers. From the junction of US 101 and California Highway 255 in Arcata, go west 1.5 miles on CA 255 to V Street, and turn left (south). This is the beginning of the **V Street Loop,** which will take you about 2 miles along a quiet rural road and eventually bring you back to CA 255 at Jackson Ranch Road. In the winter you can find large mixed flocks of blackbirds and starlings, as well as Bonaparte's, Mew, and Ring-billed Gulls. But this is also the time and location for the rare Pacific Golden-Plover. Also, Northern Shrikes (rare) are sometimes seen in winter. There are sloughs on both sides of the road that can have American and Eurasian Wigeons (the latter rare but regular in winter). Where Jackson Ranch Road intersects CA 255, continue straight and follow Jackson Ranch Road, which finally becomes Foster Avenue. Where Foster Avenue meets Seidel Road, turn north and go to Lanphere Road. Turn left (west) on Lanphere Road and go to the end. Extensive mudflats, part of **Mad River Slough,** lie along the road near the end, with shorebirds such as Killdeer, Semipalmated Plover, Western and Least Sandpipers, and Dunlin. Local birders check the fields carefully in this area in fall for rarities such as Mountain Plover and Buff-breasted Sandpiper. American Pipits occur commonly in winter in the coastal bottoms. In winter watch for such rarities as Black-and-white Warbler.

Arcata Marsh once was an abandoned landfill, but beginning in the 1970s, the city of Arcata embarked on a program of reclamation that has received international praise. The effluent from the nearby wastewater treatment plant is routed through a series of restored freshwater marshes before it is discharged into the bay. The greatest variety of birds occurs from mid-July (shorebirds begin to arrive) through winter until the end of April. More than 200 species of birds have been recorded here, including many rarities. Even river otters are sometimes spotted in the ponds. There are two main points of access: 1) Exit US 101 on Samoa Boulevard (CA 255), and go west to South I Street. Turn south and go about 1 mile to the end, where there is a parking lot and chemical toilets. 2) From Samoa Boulevard, turn south on South G Street and go about 0.5 mile to a parking lot on the west side of the street. The **Arcata Marsh Interpretive Center** (barrier-free trail) is nearby. Birds can be found in all the wetlands, but the area by Franklin Klopp Lake offers views of the lake and the north end of Arcata Bay.

The lake and marshes may have Gadwall, Cinnamon and Green-winged Teal, Greater Scaup, Ruddy Duck, egrets, and shorebirds such as Black-bellied Plover, Marbled Godwit, Red Knot, and dowitchers. Look for the "Eurasian" Green-winged Teal that occasionally occurs here. (The "Eurasian" form lacks the vertical white bar on the shoulder but has a horizontal white stripe along the scapulars.) On falling tides, the mudflats of **Arcata Bay** can have multitudes of shorebirds. The Christmas count of Marbled Godwits has sometimes been the highest in the nation. In the marshy areas, such as around No Name Pond and Butcher Slough Pond, look for Cinnamon Teal, Cooper's Hawk, Virginia Rail, Sora, and Marsh Wren. As the water drops in late summer, look for shorebirds as well as Peregrine Falcons and Merlins. In April and May look for Purple Martins, which are no-where common in California. Beware, however, that Purple Martins and European Starlings can somewhat resemble each other in flight, with their heavy bodied, broad-winged appearance. Fox and Golden-crowned Sparrows are common in winter. Also, in winter be sure to look for rarities such as Palm Warbler, Swamp Sparrow, and White-throated Sparrow.

Woodley Island can be reached by turning west from US 101 onto CA 255 in the northern end of Eureka. As you come to Woodley Island (0.6 mile) exit left and go past the marina to the end, where there is parking and a viewpoint. Typical birds are Common Loon, Western Grebe, Surf Scoter, Bufflehead, Red-breasted Merganser, Marbled Godwit, and Whimbrel. Mew and Glaucous-winged Gulls are here in the winter; Heermann's Gulls and Elegant Terns occur in late summer. From late spring to early summer, look northwest toward the grove of tall trees on the next island, where there is a rookery of Great and Snowy Egrets, Great Blue Herons, and Black-crowned Night-Herons.

Fairhaven is a well-known location for rare vagrants in spring (mid-May through June) and fall (end of August to mid-October). Some of this area's rarities are Black-billed Cuckoo; Cerulean, Golden-winged, Prairie, Blackpoll, and Magnolia Warblers; and Yellow-green, Red-eyed, and Philadelphia Vireos. Black-capped Chickadees occur here, and vagrant warblers sometimes accompany the chicka-dee flocks. Birders who have Fairhaven experience warn against the hordes of mosquitoes in spring, whereas fall is relatively mosquito-free. Also, if you intend to bird the area intensively, bushwhacking will be necessary, with the possibility of wet areas in spring.

To get to Fairhaven, continue on CA 255 west from Woodley Island 1.4 miles onto Samoa Peninsula, to the point where CA 255 bends sharply to the right, and New Navy Base Road comes in from the left. Go south on New Navy Base Road for 3.6 miles to Lincoln Avenue. There are four areas located south of Lincoln Avenue that have been given names by local birders—Horse Pasture, Airport Patch, Entrance Patch, and Cypress Patch.

Horse Pasture is the willow thicket extending southeast from the junction of New Navy Base Road and Lincoln Avenue. Airport Patch is another willow patch, 0.35 mile south of Horse Pasture. Park on the east side of the road; there is a fire hydrant here, but there is sufficient room to park without blocking access to the hydrant. The willow patch is on the west side of the road. *Do not trespass on the private property on the east side.* Entrance Patch is a small willow thicket 0.5 mile south of Airport Patch, opposite the entrance to the Samoa County Park Boat Ramp, on the west side of the road. Cypress Patch is 1.2 miles south of Entrance Patch, and consists of a grove of planted Monterey cypress and understory hardwoods (parking, picnic tables, and pit toilet). Keep to the right past the U.S. Coast Guard station and enter the Samoa Dunes Recreation Area (gate is locked 1 hour after sunset). Bear left at each intersection.[1]

Hilfiker Lane is on US 101, 3.4 miles south of the junction of US 101 and CA 255 in Eureka. Turn to the west and park next to the channel, the mouth of the Elk River. Check the open water for loons, Western and Clark's Grebe, Horned Grebe, Brant, and scoters. The sand flats at low tide should have shorebirds such as Black-bellied Plover, Marbled Godwit, Sanderling, and Western and Least Sandpipers. Elegant Terns show up August and September, and Parasitic Jaegers are sometimes seen during fall migration, harassing the terns.

King Salmon is an access point to the southern part of Humboldt Bay. Exit US 101 at King Salmon Avenue, about 6 miles south of the junction of US 101 and CA 255 in Eureka, go west 0.5 mile to where you can first see the bay, and park near the small park on the right. From here walk to the base of the breakwater and look across to the mouth of Humboldt Bay. Possible species here are Common, Pacific, and Red-throated Loons; Western and Clark's Grebes; Brant; Black, White-winged, and Surf Scoters; Red-breasted Merganser; and various gulls. Harlequin Duck and Oldsquaw (winter, both rare), King Eider (two records at this location), and Thick-billed Murre (one record) have been seen here. This is considered the most reliable local location for Red-necked Grebe and Black Scoter (winter, rare).

Loleta Bottoms lies about 6 miles south of King Salmon. Exit US 101 for Loleta, and turn west in Loleta on Cannibal Road. Many of the birds will be similar to those found at Arcata Bottoms, but this is a good place to look for Pacific Golden-Plover and Lapland Longspur in the winter (both rare).

Blue Lake lies about 5 miles east of the junction of US 101 and California Highway 299. Exit from CA 299 at Blue Lake, go 0.3 mile to Greenwood, and turn right where the sign reads "Central Blue Lake." Go 0.6 mile on Greenwood,

---

1 Many thanks to David Fix for material on Fairhaven.

turn left onto Railroad Avenue, and go a short distance to central Blue Lake. Turn right (south) on G Street, where a sign points to "Industrial Park" (G Street becomes Hatchery Road). Go past the industrial park. About 0.3 mile from central Blue Lake, you will cross the Mad River, and just beyond the bridge there is a large pullout on the right where you can park.

Some people call this the **Blue Lake Cottonwoods.** There is good riparian habitat here, although it is important to watch out for fast cars and poison oak. Black-capped and Chestnut-backed Chickadees; Sharp-shinned and Cooper's Hawks; Red-breasted Sapsucker; Downy Woodpecker; Pacific-slope Flycatcher; Western Wood-Pewee; Warbling and Cassin's Vireos; Orange-crowned and Wilson's Warblers; Song Sparrow; and American Goldfinch occur here. It has been claimed the Warbling Vireo says *"What's on the menu? Whattaya wanna order? Whattaya wanna eat?"*[2]

Walk back to the river and cross the bridge to get to the levee to see birds such as Common Merganser, White-tailed Kite, Greater Yellowlegs, Vaux's Swift, and Violet-Green Swallow.

From the Blue Lake Cottonwoods, continue on Hatchery Road about 1 mile to the entrance to the **Mad River Hatchery.** You can park near the office. Restrooms are at the opposite end of the parking lot. A barrier-free trail here leads to the river (follow the blue line). Along this trail is a dirt road to the left that leads through good birding habitat to some small ponds. Birds to look for are American Bittern, Green Heron, Black-crowned Night-Heron, Wood Duck, Osprey, Vaux's Swift, Belted Kingfisher, Allen's Hummingbird, Pacific-slope Flycatcher, Black Phoebe, Northern Rough-winged Swallow, and Wrentit.

General information: The Humboldt Bay region is one of the prime birding areas of the state. The Arcata Marsh Project is famous both for the excellent wildlife habitat that was created here, and for the variety of birds that can be seen. Each spring the city of Arcata sponsors a birding festival called Godwit Days. For more information, contact the city of Arcata.

ADDITIONAL HELP

NCA&G grid: Page 32, 2D; page 42, 3A, 2C.
Elevation: Sea level to 200 feet.
Hazards: Cliff edges, poison oak, ticks.
Nearest food, gas, lodging: Arcata; Eureka.
Camping: Patrick's Point State Park: 123 sites, 18 miles north of Arcata on US 101.
For more information: City of Arcata.

---

2 Thanks to R. J. Adams.

4 Trinity River

Habitats: Stream, foothill woodland, mixed conifer forest.
Specialty birds: *Resident*—Golden Eagle, Blue Grouse, Mountain Quail, White-headed Woodpecker, American Dipper, Townsend's Solitaire.
Summer—Osprey; Band-tailed Pigeon; Western Wood-Pewee; Hammond's, Dusky, Pacific-slope, and Ash-throated Flycatchers; Cassin's Vireo; Black-throated Gray and Hermit Warblers; Western Tanager; Black-headed Grosbeak.
Other key birds: *Resident*—Common Merganser, Ruffed Grouse, Purple Finch. *Summer*—Orange-crowned, Nashville, and Wilson's Warblers.
Best times to bird: April through July.

Directions: From the Blue Lake exit on California Highway 299, Berry Hill Summit lies about 22 miles east on CA 299. Turn right (south) on **Titlow Mountain Road** (paved), which exits just beyond the summit. Be sure your gas tank is full. Also, note that portions of this road may be blocked by snow until late spring. Forest Road 5N10 lies 6 miles from CA 299. Turn left on FR 5N10, which is gravel and patchy pavement. In 4.8 miles, FR 5N10 joins Friday Ridge Road (paved). Turn left on Friday Ridge Road, and rejoin CA 299 in about 12 miles. **Grays Falls Campground and Picnic Area** lies 4 miles east of the junction of CA 299 and Friday Ridge Road, on CA 299. There is much private land along this route, and birders should be careful not to trespass.

The birding: **Titlow Mountain Road** rises up to more than 4,000 feet, giving access to habitat with mountain birds such as Blue Grouse; White-headed Woodpecker (rare); Dusky and Hammond's Flycatchers; Townsend's Solitaire; Hermit Warbler; and Western Tanager. Mountain Quail and Band-tailed Pigeons inhabit these ridges, but are often difficult to find, although Mountain Quail may be heard calling in April and May. Spotted and Flammulated Owls have been found here but are even harder to find. At mid- and lower elevations look for Ruffed Grouse (rare) near meadows, hillside seeps, and streamside woodlands.

The **Trinity River Canyon** offers numerous opportunities to get off the highway for some birding, especially at the USDA Forest Service campgrounds along the route. **Grays Falls Campground and Picnic Area** is especially attractive, although it abounds with poison oak. The picnic area is on a wooded flat with lots of oaks, above the river. Look for Common Merganser; Osprey; Canyon Wren (rare); and American Dipper along the river, and California Quail; Western Wood-Pewee; Pacific-slope and Ash-throated Flycatchers; Cassin's Vireo; Steller's Jay; Nashville, Orange-crowned, Black-throated Gray, and Wilson's Warblers; Spotted Towhee; Black-headed Grosbeak; and Purple Finch in the woodlands. Overhead, watch for Golden Eagle and Common Raven.

General information: CA 299 is the most direct route in the northern part of the state from the coast to the interior valley. About 20 miles from Blue Lake, it climbs over Berry Hill Summit (2,859 feet), and then drops to the Trinity River at Willow Creek, at about 600 feet. From Willow Creek, the highway closely follows the

4 Trinity River

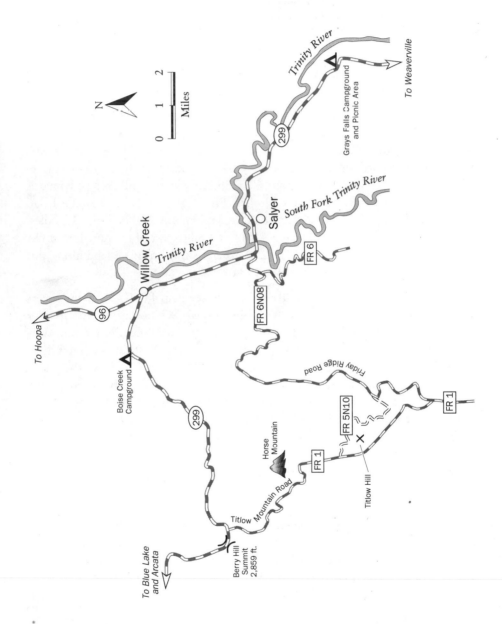

Trinity River most of the way to Weaverville, providing access to much attractive habitat.

ADDITIONAL HELP

NCA&G grid: Page 43, 5A, 7B; page 44, 1B.
Elevation: 200 to 4,000 feet.
Hazards: Poison oak, rattlesnakes, ticks.
Nearest food, gas, lodging: Willow Creek.
Camping: Grays Falls: 32 sites, 8 miles east of Willow Creek on CA 299. Boise Creek: 16 sites, 2 miles west of Willow Creek on CA 299.
For more information: Lower Trinity Ranger District.

5 Lewiston Lake ♙ ♿

Habitats: Freshwater marsh, lake, foothill woodland, mixed conifer forest.
Specialty birds: *Resident*—Wood Duck, Bald Eagle, Mountain Quail, Northern Pygmy-Owl, Anna's Hummingbird, Black Phoebe, Steller's Jay. *Summer*—Osprey, Cassin's Vireo. *Winter*—Hooded Merganser.
Other key birds: *Resident*—Common Merganser, Belted Kingfisher, Common Raven. *Summer*—Tree and Northern Rough-winged Swallows; Wilson's Warbler. *Winter*—Lesser Scaup, Bufflehead, Common and Barrow's Goldeneyes.
Best times to bird: April through June for breeding birds; late fall and early winter for wintering waterfowl.

Directions: From the junction of Trinity Dam Boulevard and U.S. Highway 299 near Lewiston, go 4 miles north on Trinity Dam Boulevard to Lewiston, and 2 miles farther to the beginning of the lake.

The birding: Lewiston Lake is not what one would normally think of as a birding "hotspot," but it is a pleasant place with good birding opportunities. The major attractions are Bald Eagles and Ospreys, both of which nest here. The shores attract marsh-loving birds such as Pied-billed Grebes, Great Blue Herons, and Red-winged Blackbirds, and Tree and Northern Rough-winged Swallows work the air above the lake. In winter the lake is home to American Wigeon, Lesser Scaup, Bufflehead, Common Goldeneye, and Barrow's Goldeneye (rare). Wood Ducks and Common Mergansers are resident. Hooded Merganser (rare in winter) has been seen in the river below the Trinity River Hatchery, and Northern Pygmy-Owl in the riparian area.

The lake is about 6 miles long, and the road runs close to the western shore. The campgrounds offer good birding if they are not crowded, but there are other places where you can get off the road and close to the shore. **Pine Cove** has a parking lot (fee), and a barrier-free trail that leads to picnic tables and a fishing platform, all of which adjoin a marshy area with Black Phoebes, Song Sparrows,

5 Lewiston Lake

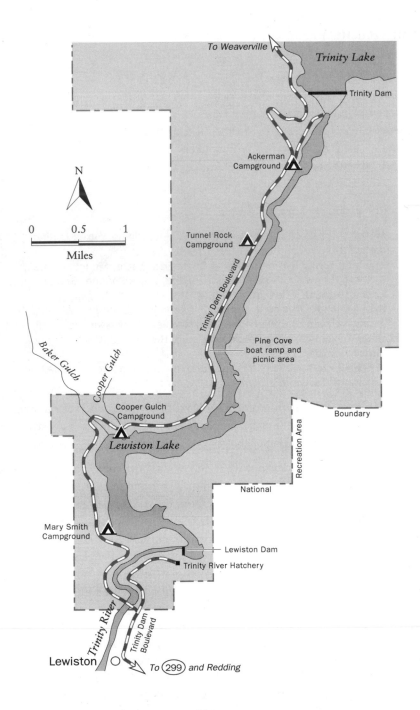

and the ever-present Mallards. Belted Kingfishers turn up anywhere there is water with fish in it, and Common Ravens may be overhead. The slopes above the lake have Mountain Quail.

Farther down the lake, **Cooper Gulch Campground** has a parking area that provides access to the **Baker Gulch Trail** (barrier-free). The trail leads to a delightful little rushing creek, where you may find Anna's Hummingbird, Cassin's Vireo, Steller's Jay, Song Sparrow, and Wilson's Warbler. The barrier-free portion of the trail ends at the creek, but the footpath continues along the lakeshore.

General information: Lewiston Lake is unusual for a reservoir because its level doesn't fluctuate. Its purpose is to provide a constant flow of water through the Clear Creek Tunnel, which delivers water to a power house at Whiskeytown Reservoir. As a result, it looks very much like a natural lake with some marshy shores.

ADDITIONAL HELP

NCA&G grid: Page 45, 6B, 6C.
Elevation: 2,000 feet.
Hazards: Poison oak, rattlesnakes, ticks.
Nearest food, gas, lodging: Lewiston.
Camping: Ackerman: 66 sites, 7 miles north of Lewiston, on Trinity Dam Boulevard; RV disposal station. Tunnel Rock: 6 sites, 6 miles north of Lewiston, on Trinity Dam Boulevard. Cooper Gulch: 5 sites, 3.3 miles north of Lewiston, on Trinity Dam Boulevard. Mary Smith: 18 sites (tent camping only), 2 miles north of Lewiston, on Trinity Dam Boulevard.
For more information: Weaverville Ranger District.

6 Tower House Historic District

Habitats: Stream, riparian woodland, mixed conifer forest, meadow.
Specialty birds: *Resident*—Steller's Jay; Bushtit; Wrentit; Spotted and California Towhees; Lesser Goldfinch. *Summer*—Western Wood-Pewee; Cassin's Vireo; Black-throated Gray and Hermit Warblers; Western Tanager; Black-headed Grosbeak; Lazuli Bunting; Bullock's Oriole.
Other key birds: *Resident*—Red-tailed Hawk, Common Raven. *Summer*—House Wren; Orange-crowned and Yellow Warblers; Yellow-breasted Chat. *Winter*—Cedar Waxwing.
Best times to bird: April through June.

Directions: The main entrance to the Whiskeytown Unit of the Whiskeytown-Shasta-Trinity National Recreation Area (administered by the National Park Service) is 7.5 miles west of Redding. Tower House Historic District is about 7.5 miles farther west, on California Highway 299 (parking, chemical toilets).

The birding: Take the paved trail from the parking area west across the footbridge on Clear Creek, then turn left to cross the bridge on Willow Creek, and turn right on the trail that parallels Willow Creek to the Tower Gravesite. On the return,

6 Tower House Historic District

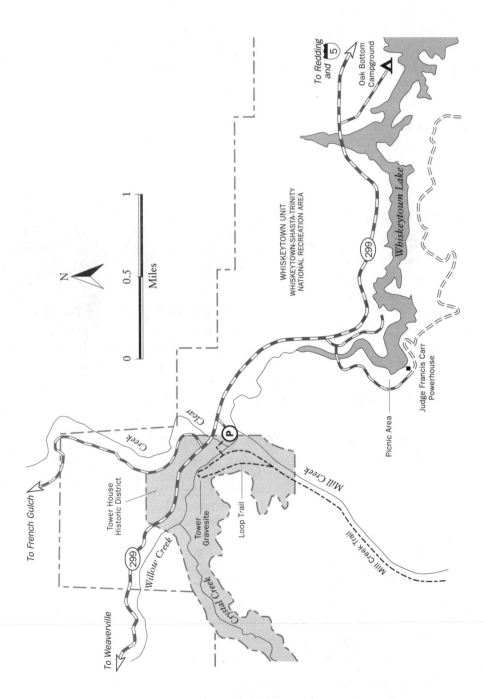

take the trail on the hillside that follows the old irrigation ditch to join the Mill Creek Trail, then return on Mill Creek Trail, a round trip of about 1 mile. This takes you through mixed habitats of riparian woodland, mixed conifer forest, and along the edge of an open meadow. It can be a delightful walk, especially in the spring before the weather gets hot, and when the birds are singing full force. However, beware the poison oak, which is abundant.

In the areas next to the stream, look for (or, more likely, listen for) Yellow-breasted Chats in late spring and summer. I heard three singing here along a section of Willow Creek about a half-mile long, in late May. Other spring and summer visitors are Western Wood-Pewee; Cassin's Vireo; House Wren; Orange-crowned, Yellow, Black-throated Gray, and Hermit Warblers; Western Tanager; Black-headed Grosbeak; Lazuli Bunting; and Bullock's Oriole. Common residents are Red-tailed Hawk; California Quail; Steller's Jay; Common Raven; Bushtit; Wrentit; American Robin; Spotted and California Towhees; and Lesser Goldfinch. Cedar Waxwings are winter visitors.

General information: Tower House Historic District is a part of the Whiskeytown-Shasta-Trinity National Recreation Area. It is a quiet retreat in attractive surroundings, away from the bustling crowds of boaters and swimmers on Whiskeytown Lake.

ADDITIONAL HELP

NCA&G grid: Page 45, 7C.
Elevation: 1,300 feet.
Hazards: Poison oak, rattlesnakes, and ticks. The National Park Service has posted a sign that reads, "Mountain lions have been encountered at close range in this area."
Nearest food, gas, lodging: Redding.
Camping: Oak Bottom: 101 walk-in tent sites, 22 RV sites between painted lines on paved parking area; RV dump station.
For more information: Whiskeytown Unit.

7 Battle Creek

Habitats: Freshwater marsh, stream, riparian woodland, foothill woodland, oak savanna.

Specialty birds: *Resident*—Wood Duck; Bald Eagle; Anna's Hummingbird; Acorn and Nuttall's Woodpeckers; Yellow-billed Magpie; Oak Titmouse; Western Meadowlark; Lesser Goldfinch. *Summer*— Osprey, Ash-throated Flycatcher, Western Kingbird, Black-headed Grosbeak. *Winter*—Ferruginous Hawk, Prairie Falcon, Lewis's Woodpecker, Mountain Bluebird, Golden-crowned Sparrow.

Other key birds: *Resident*—Red-shouldered Hawk, Sora, Belted Kingfisher, White-breasted Nuthatch, Bewick's Wren. *Summer*—Tree and Cliff Swallows; House Wren. *Winter*—Ruby-crowned Kinglet, Savannah Sparrow.

Best times to bird: April and May for breeding birds.

Directions: **From the north:** From the junction of Interstate 5 and Deschutes Road south of Anderson, go 2.3 miles east on Deschutes Road to Balls Ferry Road. Turn south and go 3 miles to Ash Creek Road, then turn east, go 1.2 miles to Gover Road, and turn south. Go 1.5 miles south on Gover Road (Gover Road becomes Jellys Ferry Road) to Coleman Hatchery Road (paved), turn east, and go 0.9 mile to Battle Creek Wildlife Area. (Coleman National Fish Hatchery lies 1 mile beyond Battle Creek Wildlife Area.) To continue to Paynes Creek Wetlands, from the junction with Coleman Hatchery Road go 11.7 miles south on Jellys Ferry Road, turn east on Bend Ferry Road (paved), and go 2.7 miles to Paynes Creek Wetlands. **From the south** from the junction of I-5 and California Highway 36 in Red Bluff, go 4 miles north on I-5 and exit at Jellys Ferry Road. Drive 2.6 miles north on Jellys Ferry Road, turn east on Bend Ferry Road (paved), and go 2.7 miles to Paynes Creek Wetlands. To continue to Battle Creek Wildlife Area, from the junction with Bend Ferry Road, go 11.7 miles north on Jellys Ferry Road to Coleman Hatchery Road (paved), turn east, and go 0.9 mile to Battle Creek Wildlife Area.

The birding: **Battle Creek Wildlife Area** has parking, restrooms, and a nature trail (about 1 mile round trip) that passes through riparian forest and along meadow edges. Resident woodland species such as California Quail; Nuttall's and Acorn Woodpeckers; Western Scrub-Jay; Tree Swallow; Oak Titmouse; Bushtit; White-breasted Nuthatch; and Bewick's and House Wrens are common, as are White-crowned and Golden-crowned Sparrows from October through April. For several years a pair of Ospreys have nested in the top of a tall dead tree near the western end of the loop trail. Not far away, adjacent to the trail, is a marsh that can have Wood Ducks and even a Sora (rare). Battle Creek has spawning salmon in the fall. Gnawed trees show that beavers are present, and otters have been seen.

Bald Eagles have nested in recent years near the fish hatchery. If the hatchery office is open, ask personnel where to stand to see the nest.

Paynes Creek Wetlands has less variety than Battle Creek but has been nicely outfitted by the Bureau of Land Management with parking, restrooms, and a

7 Battle Creek

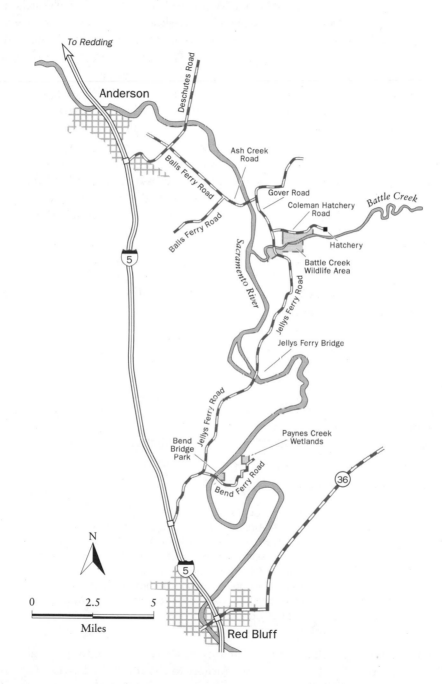

To Redding

Anderson

Deschutes Road

Balls Ferry Road

Ash Creek Road

Balls Ferry Road

Gover Road

Coleman Hatchery Road

Battle Creek

Hatchery

Battle Creek Wildlife Area

Sacramento River

Jellys Ferry Road

Jellys Ferry Bridge

Jellys Ferry Road

Bend Bridge Park

Paynes Creek Wetlands

Bend Ferry Road

5

36

N

0   2.5   5

Miles

5

Red Bluff

barrier-free trail to the wetlands, about 200 yards from the parking area. The surrounding area is oak savanna. The wetlands most likely will have egrets, herons, Mallards, and an occasional Black Phoebe, but the surrounding area has Anna's Hummingbird; Acorn and Nuttall's Woodpeckers; Ash-throated Flycatcher; Western Kingbird; White-breasted Nuthatch; Bewick's Wren; Savannah Sparrow; and Lesser Goldfinch. In winter there are sure to be Ruby-crowned Kinglets, and Golden-crowned and White-crowned Sparrows. This is meadowlark country, and the songs of Western Meadowlarks (even in winter) are constant.

Keep your eyes open for a Prairie Falcon. Also, Yellow-billed Magpies may pop up anywhere. At **Bend Bridge Park** (0.4 mile from Jellys Ferry Road, on Bend Ferry Road), pause a bit, provided the park isn't crowded, and enjoy the Sacramento River. The birds here are similar to those listed previously, with the addition of Red-shouldered Hawk, Belted Kingfisher, Black-headed Grosbeak, and zillions of Cliff Swallows that nest under the bridge. As you cross the Sacramento River on **Jellys Ferry Bridge** there is an Osprey nest on the top of the center span, which has been occupied in recent years. In winter look for Ferruginous Hawk, Lewis's Woodpecker, and Mountain Bluebird.

General information: Jellys Ferry Road doesn't have much traffic, and passes through oak savanna, crossing the Sacramento River several times. In spring the countryside is green and lush, but by late May the hills become brown in response to the state's hot and arid Mediterranean summer climate.

ADDITIONAL HELP

NCA&G grid: Page 56, 3A, 3C; page 57, 4A, 4B.
Elevation: 300 to 600 feet.
Hazards: Poison oak, rattlesnakes, ticks.
Nearest food, gas, lodging: Anderson; Red Bluff.
For more information: California Department of Fish and Game, Redding.

8 McCloud River Loop ♿

> **Habitats:** Stream, riparian woodland, mixed conifer forest.
> **Specialty birds:** *Resident*—Steller's Jay, Mountain Chickadee, American Dipper. *Summer*—Wood Duck; Osprey; Western Wood-Pewee; Willow and Pacific-slope Flycatchers; Cassin's Vireo; Hermit and MacGillivray's Warblers; Western Tanager; Black-headed Grosbeak.
> **Other key birds:** *Resident*—Cooper's Hawk. *Summer*—Spotted Sandpiper; Olive-sided Flycatcher; Warbling Vireo; Yellow and Wilson's Warblers; Chipping and Fox Sparrows.
> **Best times to bird:** Late April through June.

Directions: From McCloud, east of Mount Shasta City on California Highway 89, go 5.5 miles east on CA 89 to the turnoff to the south for **Fowlers Campground** and **Lower Falls** (paved). About 0.6 mile from CA 89, there is a fork (road

8 McCloud River Loop

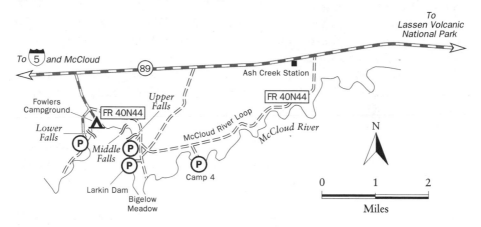

to the left is unpaved, labeled Forest Road 40N44). Go straight on the paved road and shortly come to another fork. The road straight ahead leads to **Fowlers Campground,** and the road to the right (paved) leads (in about 0.6 mile) to **Lower Falls.**

The birding: A barrier-free trail leads from **Fowlers Campground** downstream to Lower Falls (about 0.3 mile), and another trail leads upstream to Middle Falls (about 1 mile). **Lower Falls** is the best general birding area (picnic tables, restrooms). In May the trees and brushy flats can be alive with singing Olive-sided Flycatchers; Cassin's and Warbling Vireos; and Yellow Warblers. Hermit Warblers sing from invisible perches high in the pines. The trilled songs of Chipping Sparrows and Dark-eyed Juncos will give you practice in telling them apart. Look for Fox Sparrows in brushy areas. Look also for Pacific-slope Flycatcher; Mountain Chickadee; Brown Creeper; MacGillivray's and Wilson's Warblers; Western Tanager; and Black-headed Grosbeak. A gravel road extends a half-mile or so beyond the Lower Falls parking lot, giving access to good birding habitat.

Upper Falls offers similar birding opportunities to those at Lower Falls. To get there, return to FR 40N44 (unpaved), and follow it for about 1.2 miles to an unsigned fork. Take the fork to the right about 0.2 mile to Upper Falls parking area. The location of the falls is not well marked, but if you go downstream a short distance from the parking lot, you will be able to find a place where you can view the falls safely from the cliff top. The cliffs are vertical, and there is no guard rail. The Forest Service suggests that you check cliffs next to the falls to see if you can spot an American Dipper's nest, but I didn't see one.

To get to **Larkin Dam,** return to FR 40N44. About 0.2 mile farther there is a signed turnoff for Upper Falls, but when I was there the turnoff road was washed out and impassable. Beyond this turnoff about 0.2 mile there is a crossroad with a stop sign. Turn right and go about 0.3 mile to an access road to Larkin Dam, which is a tranquil spot with quiet water, willow thickets, picnic tables, restrooms, and a viewing platform. A short distance upstream, there has been an Osprey nest in the top of a tall dead tree.

The Larkin Dam area is a good place to look for Wood Ducks, as well as for Willow Flycatchers. Western Wood-Pewees also occur here but can be confused with Willow Flycatchers; neither species has conspicuous eye rings, and both have wing bars that sometimes are faint. Western Wood-Pewees generally have a slight crested look to the head, and if the bird sits up on a high perch and goes *"peeeer!"* it's a Western Wood-Pewee. Spotted Sandpipers, Belted Kingfishers, and Marsh Wrens occur here. Watch for Cooper's Hawks in the forested areas.

Back at the main loop road (FR 40N44), continue 0.8 mile to the access road to **Camp 4**, which lies about 0.3 mile down this road. Camp 4 (picnic tables, restrooms) is a nice site for birding, with the same species as mentioned previously. You often can have the place to yourself, with lots of room to walk about. Beyond the Camp 4 access road, the loop road (FR 40N44) continues about 3.5 miles to rejoin CA 89.

General information: The Forest Service has gone out of its way to improve the McCloud River Loop for wildlife viewing, especially at **Fowlers Campground and Lower Falls. Upper Falls** is worth a visit, although getting a good view of the falls is a bit difficult. Camping is not permitted at Upper Falls, Larkin Dam, or Camp 4.

ADDITIONAL HELP

NCA&G grid: Page 37, 5B, 6B.
Elevation: 3,400 feet.
Hazards: Rattlesnakes, ticks, steep cliffs.
Nearest food, gas, lodging: Mount Shasta City.
Camping: Fowlers: 38 sites, 5.5 miles east of Mount Shasta City on CA 89, and then south 0.6 mile.
For more information: McCloud Ranger District.

9 Butte Valley 🏚

Habitats: Freshwater marsh, lake, farm fields, sagebrush scrub.
Specialty birds: *Resident*—Bald and Golden Eagles; Prairie Falcon; Black-billed Magpie. *Summer*—Western and Clark's Grebes; Cinnamon Teal; Swainson's Hawk; Sandhill Crane; California Gull; Black Tern; Violet-green Swallow; Mountain Bluebird; Sage Thrasher; Brewer's Sparrow; Yellow-headed Blackbird. *Winter*—Greater White-fronted and Ross's Geese; Ferruginous Hawk.
Other key birds: *Resident*—Northern Shoveler, Lesser Scaup, Ruddy Duck, Common Raven, Horned Lark. *Summer*—Eared Grebe, Redhead, American Avocet, Forster's Tern, Vesper Sparrow. *Winter*—Snow Goose, Tundra Swan, Green-winged Teal, Bufflehead, Rough-legged Hawk.
Best times to bird: For breeding birds, April through July; for raptors, November through February.

9 Butte Valley

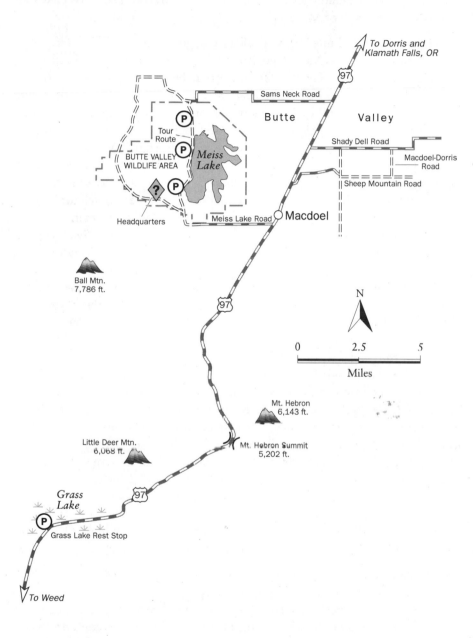

To Dorris and
Klamath Falls, OR

97

Sams Neck Road

Butte   Valley

Shady Dell Road

Macdoel-Dorris
Road

Sheep Mountain Road

Tour
Route

P

P

Meiss
Lake

P

BUTTE VALLEY
WILDLIFE AREA

Headquarters

Meiss Lake Road   Macdoel

Ball Mtn.
7,786 ft.

97

N

0   2.5   5

Miles

Mt. Hebron
6,143 ft.

Little Deer Mtn.
6,068 ft.

Mt. Hebron Summit
5,202 ft.

Grass
Lake

97

P

Grass Lake Rest Stop

To Weed

Directions: The small town of Macdoel is essentially the center of **Butte Valley.** Macdoel is on U.S. Highway 97, about 40 miles (50 minutes) north of Weed, and about 30 miles (40 minutes) south of Klamath Falls, Oregon. The **Grass Lake Rest Stop** is 18 miles south of Macdoel.

The birding: To get to **Butte Valley Wildlife Area,** go 0.4 mile south of Macdoel on US 97, and turn west on Meiss Lake Road. The pavement ends in 2.4 miles, and the road turns to gravel. The Wildlife Tour Route begins 4 miles from US 97, and extends about 5 miles through the heart of the wildlife area, much of it with marshes on one side, and Meiss Lake on the other. Herons and egrets are common, as are breeding Pied-billed and Eared Grebes; Gadwall; Mallard; Cinnamon Teal; Ruddy Duck; Ring-billed Gull; Forster's Tern; Marsh Wren; and Yellow-headed Blackbird. Tricolored Blackbird is worth checking for but is not present every year. One of the largest breeding colonies of California Gulls is located here. A small number of Sandhill Cranes breed on the wildlife area. Watch for Western and Clark's Grebes; Double-crested Cormorant; Wood Duck; Northern Shoveler; Redhead; Lesser Scaup; Killdeer; American Avocet; Violet-green Swallow; and Song Sparrow. Greater White-fronted, Snow, and Ross's Geese; Tundra Swan; Green-winged Teal; Bufflehead; and Bald Eagle winter here.

Butte Valley is well known for its raptors. Go north from Macdoel about 1 mile on US 97 to Sheep Mountain Road on the right, and follow Sheep Mountain Road until it begins to head due east. About 2.3 miles from US 97, you will come to a crossroads. Continue straight across, now on gravel, for another 3 miles, to the end of the public road. Then go north on Macdoel-Dorris Road 1 mile to Shady Dell Road (paved). This country, consisting mostly of farm fields, is a good area for Bald and Golden Eagles; Red-tailed Hawk; Prairie Falcon (uncommon); Common Raven; and Turkey Vulture. Keep your eyes open for Swainson's Hawk (summer). If you are here in winter, Ferruginous Hawk is a possibility, and Rough-legged Hawk is fairly common. Other birds to watch for are Black-billed Magpie, Horned Lark, Mountain Bluebird, Vesper Sparrow, and Western Meadowlark. Return to US 97 and go north 2.2 miles to Sams Neck Road and turn west. In the sagebrush areas, look for Sage Thrasher and Brewer's Sparrow.

The **Grass Lake Rest Stop** is a charming area, with a little trail from the parking area that leads to the edge of a fairly large wetlands. Sandhill Cranes can sometimes be seen here, and Black Terns have nested nearby.

General information: Butte Valley is a large valley lying at an elevation of about 4,200 feet. Much of the valley is occupied by Meiss Lake, which has been heavily diked and altered to create farmland and seasonal wetlands. The lake is now part of **Butte Valley Wildlife Area,** and to the north and east of the wildlife area is the **Butte Valley National Grassland,** a mix of public and private ownership.

ADDITIONAL HELP

NCA&G grid: Page 27, 4C, 6A.
Elevation: 4,200 feet.
Hazards: Sun exposure, rattlesnakes, ticks.
Nearest food, gas, lodging: Weed; Klamath Falls, Oregon.
For more information: Butte Valley Wildlife Area.

10 Klamath Basin 🏕

Habitats: Freshwater marsh, lake, sagebrush scrub, cliffs.
Specialty birds: *Resident*—Bald and Golden Eagles; Prairie Falcon; Black-billed Magpie; Canyon Wren; Western Meadowlark. *Summer*— Western and Clark's Grebes; White-faced Ibis; Cinnamon Teal; Sandhill Crane; Long-billed Curlew; Black Tern; Short-eared Owl; Say's Phoebe; Bank Swallow; Rock Wren; Tricolored and Yellow-headed Blackbirds; Bullock's Oriole. *Winter*—Greater White-fronted and Ross's Geese.
Other key birds: *Resident*—Canada Goose, Gadwall, American Wigeon, Northern Shoveler, Northern Pintail, Redhead, Canvasback, Lesser Scaup, Ruddy Duck, Loggerhead Shrike, Horned Lark. *Summer*—Eared Grebe; American White Pelican; Double-crested Cormorant; Black-crowned Night-Heron; Blue-winged Teal; Black-necked Stilt; American Avocet; Willet; Spotted Sandpiper; Common Snipe; Wilson's Phalarope; Caspian and Forster's Terns; Common Nighthawk; Marsh Wren; Savannah Sparrow. *Winter*—Snow Goose, Tundra Swan, Green-winged Teal, Rough-legged Hawk, Northern Shrike.
Best times to bird: Breeding birds from late April through June; migrating waterfowl from late October through November, and late March through April; Bald Eagles, December through February.

Directions: From the junction of California Highway 161 and U.S. Highway 97, go east on CA 161 about 10 miles to the entrance for the Auto Tour Route for **Lower Klamath Refuge.** To get to the **Visitor Center and Refuge Headquarters,** continue east about 7.5 miles on CA 161 and turn south on Hill Road. The visitor center lies 2.9 miles south on Hill Road. To get to the visitor center from the town of Tulelake, go west from CA 139 on East-West Road about 4.8 miles to Hill Road and turn south. The visitor center is 0.5 mile south on Hill Road. To get to the Auto Tour Route for **Tule Lake National Wildlife Refuge,** go south from the visitor center 4.7 miles.

The birding: The Klamath Basin is one of the most important bird areas in North America. In fall more than 1 million ducks, geese, and swans may be present in the peak month of November. Greater White-fronted Geese begin arriving in early September, whereas Snow and Ross's Geese come in early November. Tundra Swans are abundant in early winter. From December through February, the basin is famous for its gathering of Bald Eagles, which may number more than 1,000 in some years.

10 Klamath Basin

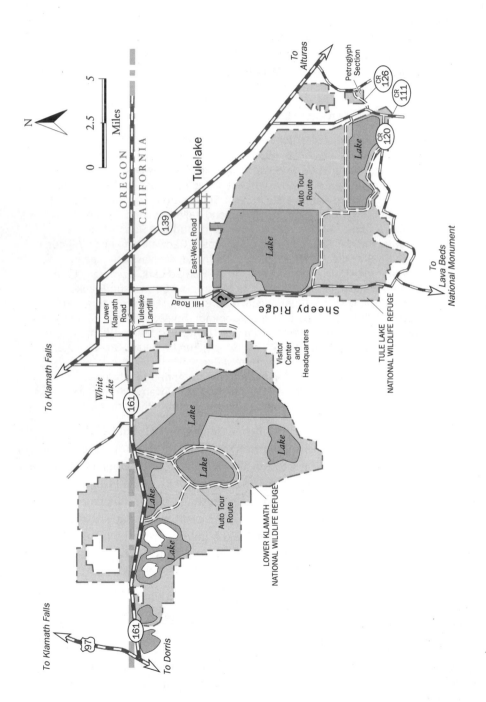

In spring and early summer large numbers of waterfowl and other birds breed in the refuges. It has been estimated that as many as 2,600 Canada Geese and 45,000 ducks are raised on the refuges each year, including Gadwall, American Wigeon, Mallard, Cinnamon Teal, Northern Shoveler, Northern Pintail, Green-winged Teal (rare as a breeder), Canvasback, Lesser Scaup, and Ruddy Duck. Some of the breeding birds that are sometimes hard to find in other locations in California can be found here, such as American White Pelican, White-faced Ibis, Blue-winged Teal (uncommon), Redhead, Sandhill Crane (uncommon), and Black Tern.

Common birds to be found in wet places are Western, Clark's, and Eared Grebes; Double-crested Cormorant; Great and Snowy Egrets; Black-crowned Night-Heron; Black-necked Stilt; American Avocet; Caspian and Forster's Terns; Marsh Wren; and Song Sparrow. Spotted Sandpiper, Long-billed Curlew, and Common Snipe are uncommon. Common Nighthawks may be overhead in summer.

Look for breeding Wilson's Phalaropes, especially in the shallow waters of **White Lake,** which is about 4 miles east of the entrance to Lower Klamath Refuge, and is visible from the shoulders of CA 161. Park well off the road, and watch for fast traffic. Phalaropes in California are seen most often in fall migration, when they show up in shades of gray and white instead of their gorgeous breeding plumage.

Another breeder is the Willet, a familiar shorebird that is most often seen on ocean beaches in the winter. At that time of year Willets are drab and gray all over (until they fly, that is, when their striking black-and-white wing pattern becomes visible). But here in the Klamath Basin, they are in their heavily mottled breeding plumage.

Tricolored Blackbirds, often difficult to find, can be found here in the marshes in summer. Look for the white border to the red patch, as opposed to a buffy border. Note, also, that the red shoulder patch on the Tricolored Blackbird may be covered up, so that only the white border is visible. Yellow-headed Blackbirds are common in the marshes, and Bullock's Orioles can pop up wherever there are trees.

The tour route for the **Lower Klamath Refuge** makes a loop from CA 161. Franklin's Gulls have nested at this refuge, but not on a regular basis. The tour route for the **Tule Lake Refuge** leads from its beginning on the road 4.7 miles south of the visitor center, and exits on the eastern side of the refuge. Along Sheepy Ridge, as you go south to the Tule Lake Auto Tour Route, check for nests of Red-tailed Hawk, Prairie Falcon, and Barn and Great Horned Owls. About halfway around the Tule Lake tour route, the route separates into two branches, the more southerly of which leads through some upland habitat. This is a good place for Short-eared Owls (uncommon), which often are visible in daytime.

Other birds to look for in dry habitats are California Quail; Say's Phoebe (uncommon in spring and fall); Loggerhead Shrike; Horned Lark; Rock and Canyon Wrens; Savannah and Vesper Sparrows; and Western Meadowlark. Occasionally

Northern Shrikes show up in the winter, and Black-billed Magpies might be anywhere.

To get to the **Petroglyph Section** from the point where the southerly branch of the Tule Lake Auto Tour Route exits onto County Road 120, go east about 1.6 miles to County Road 111, turn left (north) about 0.7 mile, cross some railroad tracks, and then turn immediately right (east) on County Road 126. In about 0.9 mile the road comes to the parking area for the Petroglyph Section. Breeding Prairie Falcons (uncommon) may be on the cliffs, visible from the parking lot. Look for an unusually abundant amount of "whitewash" on the cliff, just below the nesting cavity. Golden Eagles are uncommon in the area, and Rough-legged Hawks are fairly common in fall and winter.

There is a breeding colony of Bank Swallows (classified as threatened in California) that has been present for a number of years at the **Tulelake Landfill.** To get there, go south from CA 161 on Lower Klamath Road 0.4 mile to the entrance to the landfill. The road is paved to this point, and then turns to gravel past the entrance. If you go about 200 yards past the entrance, the colony is visible from the road. A large pile of earth within the landfill property has eroded away into steep banks, and Bank Swallows by the hundreds have constructed a tightly packed community of holes in the banks. Their continued presence may depend upon how well they tolerate the activities around them on the landfill property.

General information: There are six wildlife refuges in the Klamath Basin, three of which (Upper Klamath, Klamath Marsh, and Bear Valley) lie north of the border in Oregon, and are beyond the scope of this book. The three refuges in California are the Lower Klamath, Tule Lake, and Clear Lake. Lower Klamath and Tule Lake are the most accessible and provide outstanding birding opportunities.

Tule Lake and Lower Klamath NWRs have been classified as Globally Important Bird Areas because they provide habitat for more than 30 percent of the world's wintering population of Cackling Canada Goose, more than 20 percent of the world's breeding population of White-faced Ibis, nearly 1 percent of North America's wintering Bald Eagles, plus an incredible number of waterfowl.

ADDITIONAL HELP

NCA&G grid: Page 28, 1A, 3B.
Elevation: About 4,000 feet.
Hazards: Fast traffic on CA 161, rattlesnakes, ticks.
Nearest food, gas, lodging: Tulelake; Klamath Falls.
Camping: Lava Beds National Monument: 40 sites, about 20 miles south of the visitor center of the Tule Lake National Wildlife Refuge.
For more information: Klamath Basin National Wildlife Refuges.

11 Modoc Plateau

Habitats: Freshwater marsh, lake, juniper woodland, yellow pine forest, sagebrush scrub.

Specialty birds: *Resident*—Bald and Golden Eagles; Prairie Falcon; Black-backed Woodpecker; Black-billed Magpie; Mountain Chickadee; Cassin's Finch. *Summer*—Western and Clark's Grebes; Cinnamon Teal; Sandhill Crane; Black Tern; Gray Flycatcher; Cassin's Vireo; Juniper Titmouse; Mountain Bluebird; Sage Thrasher; Brewer's Sparrow; Yellow-headed Blackbird; Bullock's Oriole.

Other key birds: *Resident*—American Wigeon, Ring-necked Duck, Lesser Scaup, Ruddy Duck. *Summer*—Eared Grebe; American White Pelican; Gadwall; Redhead; Black-necked Stilt; American Avocet; Willet; Spotted Sandpiper; Common Snipe; Wilson's Phalarope; Caspian and Forster's Terns; Common Nighthawk; Olive-sided Flycatcher; Common Yellowthroat; Vesper and Lark Sparrows. *Winter*—Rough-legged Hawk.

Best times to bird: April through July, for breeding birds; November through March for most raptors.

Directions: For **Modoc National Wildlife Refuge:** From the junction of U.S. Highway 395 and California Highway 299 just north of Alturas, go south about 1 mile on US 395 to County Road 56, turn east, and go 0.6 mile to County Road 115. Go 1.5 miles south on CR 115, to the entrance to the wildlife refuge. For beginning of route through **Devils Garden,** from the junction of US 395 and CA 299 just north of Alturas, go west 3.5 miles on CA 299 to Forest Road 73. The access road for **Henski Wildlife Viewing Area** is 0.9 mile east of the junction of CA 139 and Lookout/Bieber Road, on the south side of CA 139.

The birding: The **Modoc National Wildlife Refuge's** Auto Tour Route (gravel) is about 2 miles long with access to a couple of short trails, but you often see more birds when you stay inside your car. Typical breeding water birds are Western, Clark's and Eared Grebes; Gadwall; American Wigeon; Cinnamon Teal; Redhead; Ring-necked Duck; Lesser Scaup; and Ruddy Duck. Some of the breeding shorebirds are Killdeer, Black-necked Stilt, American Avocet, Willet, Spotted Sandpiper, Common Snipe, and Wilson's Phalarope. Marsh Wrens make a constant chattering in the swamps, keeping company with Common Yellowthroats and Yellow-headed Blackbirds.

In addition to driving the Auto Tour Route, go south on CR 115 from the headquarters entrance, to the intersection with US 395, and back to Alturas on US 395. CR 115 has light traffic, but special care needs to be taken on US 395. Good views into many of the wetlands of the refuge can be had from these roads. Look for American White Pelican; Bald Eagle; Northern Harrier; Sandhill Crane; Caspian and Forster's Terns; and Common Nighthawk. In the drier areas you may find Mountain Bluebird and Black-billed Magpie. In areas with sagebrush, look for Sage Thrasher and Brewer's Sparrow, and in grassy areas for Vesper Sparrow. In winter, Rough-legged Hawks are often present.

11 Modoc Plateau

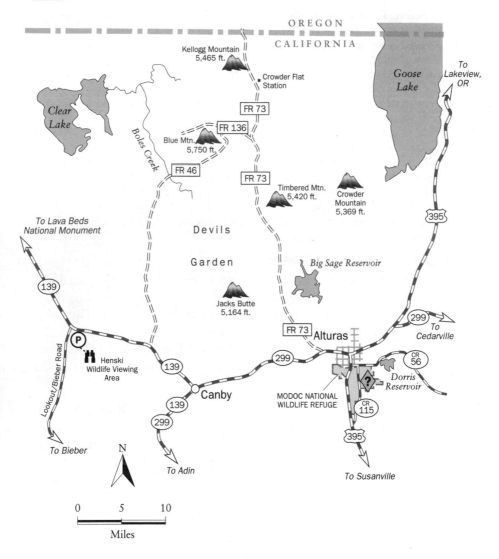

If you're game for driving 60 miles of dusty roads, try the **Devils Garden** area. This is high rocky plateau country, mostly covered with sagebrush and junipers. At first glance it seems inhospitable and waterless, but on an early spring morning it can be alive with birdsong. Go north 26 miles on FR 73 to Forest Road 136, then about 4 miles west on FR 136 to Forest Road 46, and then about 30 miles south to CA 139. The entire route consists of high-standard gravel roads.

The "special" bird here is the Gray Flycatcher, a bird of the Great Basin, and very much at home breeding in this sagebrush country. The songs of Western Meadowlarks come from all directions. Look for Golden Eagle; American Kestrel;

A Killdeer chick at Modoc National Wildlife Refuge.

Prairie Falcon; Cassin's Vireo; Mountain Chickadee; Juniper Titmouse (uncommon); Red-breasted Nuthatch; House Wren; Mountain Bluebird; Sage Thrasher; Lark, Brewer's, and Vesper Sparrows; and Cassin's Finch. Black-backed Woodpeckers are sometimes spotted in this country, especially in the region near Crowder Flat. At the point where FR 46 crosses Boles Creek, look for Spotted Sandpiper and Bullock's Oriole.

Henski Wildlife Viewing Area is worth a stop. The dirt access road is unmarked and a bit obscure, but there is a parking area just 50 yards from the main highway, and a gate. Walk beyond the gate among huge pines about 0.2 mile south to the lake, known as Henski Reservoir. In spring you might see Sandhill Crane, Spotted Sandpiper, Black Tern, Olive-sided Flycatcher (more likely heard than seen, with its trademark *"Quick! THREE beers!"* song), Mountain Chickadee, Western Bluebird, Chipping Sparrow, and Cassin's Finch.

General information: The Modoc Plateau is California's "big sky" country, a land of wide open spaces, vistas, and mountains. Dominant plants are sagebrush, juniper, and ponderosa pine. The dry sagebrush flats are interspersed with marshes and spring-fed rivers. It is a different kind of country, and considered part of the Great Basin.

ADDITIONAL HELP

NCA&G grid: Page 30, 1A, 3D.

Elevation: 4,400 to 4,900 feet.

Hazards: Rattlesnakes, ticks.

Nearest food, gas, lodging: Alturas.

Camping: Lava Beds National Monument: 40 sites; from the junction of CA 139 and Lookout/Bieber Road, go about 11 miles north on CA 139 to Lava Beds access road on the left, and then about 15 miles to the monument headquarters.

For more information: Modoc National Wildlife Refuge; Devils Garden Ranger District, for national forest information.

12 Warner Mountains

Habitats: Lake, mixed conifer forest, sagebrush scrub, meadow, subalpine zone.

Specialty birds: *Resident*—Wood Duck; Bald Eagle; Northern Goshawk; Blue Grouse; Red-breasted and Williamson's Sapsuckers; White-headed and Black-backed Woodpeckers; Steller's Jay; Clark's Nutcracker; Rock and Canyon Wrens; Townsend's Solitaire; Cassin's Finch. *Summer*— Swainson's Hawk; Calliope Hummingbird; Red-naped Sapsucker; Western Wood-Pewee; Hammond's, Dusky, Gray, Pacific-slope, and Cordilleran Flycatchers; Mountain Bluebird; MacGillivray's Warbler; Western Tanager; Green-tailed Towhee; Brewer's Sparrow; Black-headed Grosbeak; Lazuli Bunting. *Winter*—Ferruginous Hawk, Bohemian Waxwing.

Other key birds: *Resident*—Hairy Woodpecker, Gray Jay, Red-breasted Nuthatch, Golden-crowned Kinglet. *Summer*—Eared Grebe; American White Pelican; Warbling Vireo; Hermit Thrush; Yellow-rumped and Wilson's Warblers; Chipping and Fox Sparrows. *Winter*—Rough-legged Hawk.

Best times to bird: May through July; after mid-July, for higher elevations.

Directions: From the junction of U.S. Highway 395 and California Highway 299 just north of Alturas, go 18.6 miles south on US 395 to Likely. Turn east on Forest Road 64 (Jess Valley Road).

The birding: About 5 miles east of Likely on FR 64, you enter the canyon of the South Fork of the Pit River. Look and listen for Rock and Canyon Wrens. At about 9 miles from Likely is the junction of FR 64 and Forest Road 5, in **Jess Valley,** which is a great, flat, green valley surrounded by mountains. Turn to the south, on FR 64. In the spring, Jess Valley has great expanses of shallow water, with water birds such as Eared Grebe, Canada Goose, Wood Duck, Gadwall, American Wigeon, and sometimes American White Pelican and Sandhill Crane. The paved portion of FR 64 ends in 6.5 miles, at the turnoff to Blue Lake, which

12 Warner Mountains

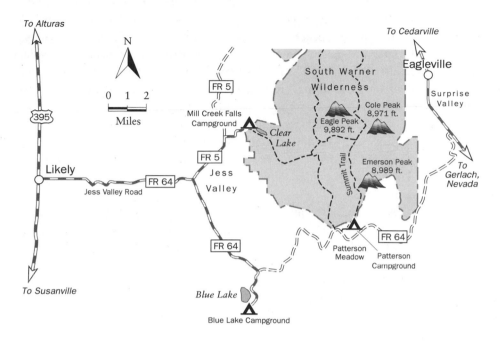

To Alturas

N

0 1 2
Miles

395

Likely

Jess Valley Road

FR 64

To Susanville

FR 5

Mill Creek Falls
Campground

*Clear
Lake*

FR 5

Jess
Valley

FR 64

Blue Lake

Blue Lake Campground

South Warner
Wilderness

Cole Peak
8,971 ft.

Eagle Peak
9,892 ft.

Emerson Peak
8,989 ft.

Summit Trail

Patterson
Meadow

Patterson
Campground

FR 64

To Cedarville

Eagleville

Surprise
Valley

To
Gerlach,
Nevada

is about 1 mile past the turnoff, and the campground 1 mile beyond that, on paved roads.

Blue Lake has breeding Red-breasted and Williamson's Sapsuckers; Cordilleran Flycatcher; Warbling Vireo; Steller's Jay; Mountain Chickadee; Red-breasted Nuthatch; Brown Creeper; Golden-crowned Kinglet; Hermit Thrush; American Robin, Yellow-rumped Warbler; Chipping Sparrow; Dark-eyed Junco; and Black-headed Grosbeak. Bald Eagles have been observed at the lake.

From the junction of the Blue Lake access road and FR 64, go east on FR 64 for 7.7 miles on good, well-graded gravel road to **Patterson Meadow,** where there is a small campground and guard station. This is a major trailhead for the South Warner Wilderness. Look for Mountain Bluebird in the high meadows, and in the sagebrush above the forested areas look for Gray Flycatcher; Green-tailed Towhee; Brewer's and Fox Sparrows; and Lazuli Bunting. Other birds are Dusky Flycatcher, Gray Jay, Clark's Nutcracker, Townsend's Solitaire, and Cassin's Finch.

A special bird that many people come to the Warner Mountains to see is the Cordilleran Flycatcher, which was split from Western Flycatcher a few years ago (Pacific-slope Flycatcher was the other outcome of this split). Beware, however, that Pacific-Slope and Cordilleran Flycatchers both occur in this region, and because the two species cannot be separated visually, you have to identify them by their calls. Listen for the smoothly connected, upwardly slurred *"suwheet!"* of the Pacific-slope, versus the two-syllable *"su-WHEET!"* of the Cordilleran, with the second syllable higher than the first. You should know, also, that some people searching for the Cordilleran Flycatcher in the Warners have reported hearing intermediate calls that they couldn't assign to either species. Another species of interest is Red-naped Sapsucker, which has been known to breed in the Warners.

From Patterson Meadow you can continue over the mountains to Eagleville, in **Surprise Valley** (31 miles). The road is gravel, steep, and narrow in places, and closed by snow until late spring. From Eagleville, the return through Cedarville to Alturas and US 395 is easy, over good paved roads. Swainson's Hawk occurs in Surprise Valley in summer. In late summer, check blackbird flocks for Bobolinks, which have occasionally bred here. In the winter the valley is a well-known place for Ferruginous and Rough-legged Hawks, and for Bald and Golden Eagles. Also, in winter, Bohemian Waxwings sometimes drift down into Surprise Valley from points farther north.

Back in Jess Valley, at the junction of FR 64 and FR 5, you can take the left-hand fork (FR 5) about 2 miles, and then turn right to go another 1.5 miles or so to **Mill Creek Falls Campground,** over a paved road. The falls and nearby **Clear Lake** can be reached via a short trail. Calliope Hummingbird and Wilson's and MacGillivray's Warblers occur along the creek and around Clear Lake. Instead of going to Mill Creek Falls, if you continue on FR 5 (good, well-graded gravel road), it will eventually lead you to Alturas in about 32 miles, through mixed conifer forest.

Black-backed Woodpeckers have been reported from this stretch, although they are by no means easy to find, often showing up suddenly when least expected. Northern Goshawks have been seen but are also hard to find—best bet is from August to October. Typical birds in this habitat are Blue Grouse, White-headed Woodpecker, Western Wood-Pewee, Hammond's Flycatcher, Steller's Jay, Mountain Chickadee, Red-breasted Nuthatch, Brown Creeper, Western Tanager, Chipping Sparrow, and Dark-eyed Junco.

General information: The Warner Mountains are perhaps the least-known mountains in California, an isolated range surrounded by sagebrush plateau country. The area houses a mixture of bird species, borrowing from the Cascades and Sierra Nevada to the west, from Oregon to the north, and from the Great Basin to the east. Most of the country is covered with mixed conifer forest, but there is much subalpine terrain leading up to the peaks.

ADDITIONAL HELP

NCA&G grid: Page 40, 3C; page 41, 5B, 6C.
Elevation: 4,400 to 7,200 feet.
Hazards: Protect yourself from excessive sun. Ticks and rattlesnakes are possible.
Nearest food, gas, lodging: Alturas.
Camping: Blue Lake: 48 sites, 16 miles east of Likely on FR 64, then 2 miles south on Blue Lake Road. Mill Creek Falls: 19 sites, 9 miles east of Likely on FR 64, then

2 miles north on FR 5, and 1.5 miles east on Mill Creek access road; Patterson: 5 sites, 16 miles east of Likely on FR 64 (paved), then 9 miles more on FR 64 (good gravel road).

For more information: Warner Mountain Ranger District.

13 Pit River Country

Habitats: Freshwater marsh, lake, sagebrush scrub.
Specialty birds: *Resident*—Sage Grouse, Short-eared Owl, Black-billed Magpie. *Summer*—Western and Clark's Grebes; White-faced Ibis; Cinnamon Teal; Osprey; Swainson's Hawk; Sandhill Crane; Long-billed Curlew; Black Tern; Bank Swallow; Yellow-headed Blackbird. *Winter*—Greater White-fronted and Ross's Geese; Bald Eagle; Ferruginous Hawk; Prairie Falcon.
Other key birds: *Resident*—Barn and Great Horned Owls; Loggerhead Shrike; Horned Lark. *Summer*—Eared Grebe, American White Pelican, American Bittern, Willet, Wilson's Phalarope, Forster's Tern, Common Yellowthroat. *Winter*—Tundra Swan, Snow Goose, Common Goldeneye, Common Merganser.
Best times to bird: April to July, for breeding species; January through March for most waterfowl; November to March for wintering raptors.

Directions: To get to **Ash Creek Wildlife Area,** from Bieber go 3.2 miles east on California Highway 299 to the wildlife area headquarters. To get to **Big Lake/ Ajumawi Lava Springs State Park,** turn north on Main Street in McArthur and go 3.6 miles on mostly gravel road to a parking lot (restrooms, boat launch) at the end of the road, adjacent to Big Lake. Signs mention McArthur Swamp, which borders the road on the west.

Birding information: A complete automobile loop around **Ash Creek Wildlife Area** can be made as follows: begin at the headquarters, go 4.4 miles east on CA 299 and turn north on County Road 428 (gravel); go 0.7 mile to Hunt Road, turn left, and go 2.2 miles to the end at **Wayman Barn** (parking). Subsequently, return on Hunt Road 1.7 miles and turn north on Wolters Road, which, after a couple of turns, becomes Elkins Lane; it is 3.2 miles to County Road 87, with a couple of viewing sites (parking) along the way. At CR 87 turn west and go 3.1 miles to a gravel road on the left that leads to the **Pilot Butte** viewing site (parking). Return to CR 87, go west 3.1 miles to the Lookout/Bieber Road (County Road 91), and then south 5.2 miles to a junction with CA 299.

The best wildlife viewing is at Pilot Butte and along the Lookout/Bieber Road. Near **Pilot Butte** parking area, look for Eared Grebe; Greater White-fronted, Snow, and Ross's Geese; Tundra Swan (these last four in the early spring, when they are marshaling for their northward migration); Cinnamon Teal and other waterfowl in the sloughs and ponds; Sandhill Crane; Willet; Long-billed Curlew; Western Kingbird; Loggerhead Shrike; Black-billed Magpie; Horned Lark; Savannah Sparrow; and Western Meadowlark. Be alert for Short-eared Owls, which sometimes hunt in the daytime. Also keep your eyes open for roosting Barn and Great Horned

13 Pit River Country

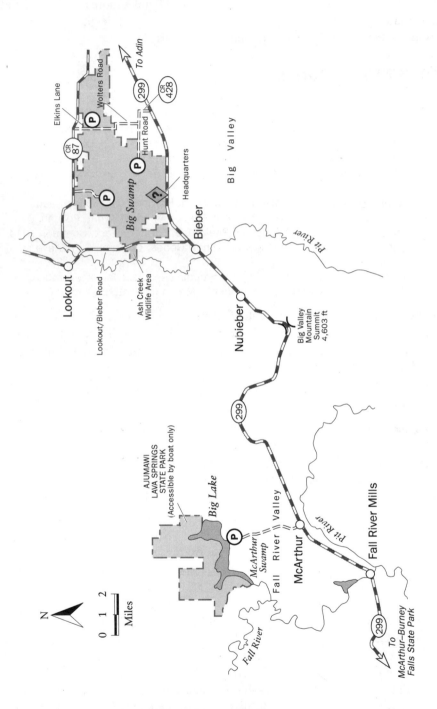

Owls in dense undergrowth. In the sagebrush areas, look for Sage Grouse (early morning hours are best). As a bonus, pronghorn antelope are often spotted here.

Some ponds and marshy areas along **Lookout/Bieber Road** can produce good birding. A few places where you can get off the road and park on a wide shoulder are 2.6 miles south of the junction of Lookout/Bieber Road and CR 87, and 3.1 miles south of the junction. The traffic moves fast, so caution is advised. Birds to look for here are American Bittern, White-faced Ibis, Cinnamon Teal, Common Goldeneye, Common Merganser, Wilson's Phalarope, Marsh Wren, Song Sparrow, and Yellow-headed Blackbird.

This open country can be good for raptors such as Bald Eagle, Ferruginous Hawk, and Prairie Falcon, especially from November through March. In spring Swainson's Hawks return from their wintering places in South America to breed here. Red-tailed Hawks are resident.

For full access to **Big Lake** a boat is needed; however, you can see lots of birds just by driving to the end of the road next to the boat launch and walking along the levee. **McArthur Swamp** lies west of the road. Look for American White Pelican; Cinnamon Teal; Northern Harrier; Forster's and Black Terns; and large numbers of Great Blue Herons, Great Egrets, and Double-crested Cormorants. Considerable numbers of Snow and Ross's Geese may move through during migration. Savannah and Song Sparrows; Common Yellowthroats; and Western Meadowlarks are almost certain to be present. On and around the lake, look for Western and Clark's Grebes (summer visitors); Osprey (common in summer); and Bald Eagle (uncommon in winter). Sandhill Cranes can be found in the wet meadows in summer.

There is a colony of Bank Swallows in **Fall River Mills,** next to CA 299, that has been there for years. It is on the north side of CA 299 as you enter town from the west, about 100 yards east of the bridge across the Fall River, directly opposite where Mechanic Street comes in. The bank is about 25 to 30 feet high, with many holes, although some of the holes have disappeared in recent years because of collapse. There is enough room to park off the road directly in front of the colony, next to the fence. You can watch the birds from your car, only about 50 feet away. They generally arrive by the latter part of April.

Personnel from the California Department of Fish and Game have stated that it is unusual for Bank Swallows to nest for a long time in one site because of the buildup of nest mites in their nesting holes. In the case of this particular site, which is owned by Fish and Game, the colony abandoned their holes the very next year after the site was purchased, possibly because of nest mites, but then returned to occupy the site for many consecutive years, but the site could be temporarily abandoned again.

General information: Ash Creek Wildlife Area is in the heart of Big Valley, with an elevation of about 4,100 feet. Big Lake/Ajumawi is a part of Fall River Valley with an elevation of about 3,300 feet. These two valleys are broad, flat plains lying along the drainage of the Pit River, separated by the Big Valley Mountains. Both Lassen Peak and Mount Shasta are visible from these valleys, rendering this region one of the most scenic in California.

ADDITIONAL HELP

NCA&G grid: Page 38, 3D; page 39, 4D, 6C.
Elevation: 3,300 to 4,100 feet.
Hazards: Rattlesnakes, ticks.
Nearest food, gas, lodging: Alturas; Burney.
Camping: McArthur–Burney Falls State Park: 128 sites; from McArthur, go 16 miles west on CA 299, and then 5.8 miles north on California Highway 89.
For more information: Ash Creek Wildlife Area.

14 McArthur–Burney Falls Memorial State Park

Habitats: Lake, stream, riparian woodland, mixed conifer forest, cliffs.
Specialty birds: *Resident*—Bald Eagle, Red-breasted Sapsucker, Steller's Jay, American Dipper. *Summer*—Osprey; Black Swift; Western Wood-Pewee; Cassin's Vireo; Black-throated Gray, Hermit, and MacGillivray's Warblers; Western Tanager; Black-headed Grosbeak.
Other key birds: *Resident*—White-breasted Nuthatch, Brown Creeper, Evening Grosbeak. *Summer*—Olive-sided Flycatcher; Nashville, Yellow, and Wilson's Warblers; Chipping Sparrow.
Best times to bird: Late April through June.

Directions: From the junction of California Highway 299 and California Highway 89, go 5.8 miles north on CA 89 to the park.

The birding: To the degree that anything in birding is guaranteed, this is almost a guaranteed place to see Black Swifts, which can be hard to find elsewhere in California. They generally arrive by the first week in May, and are gone by the first freeze of autumn. Stand at the lower viewpoint close to the falls and watch upward. They nest near the falls, behind the smaller streams of water. Look for the thin, boomerang-shaped wings. American Dippers also nest near the falls.

After viewing the swifts, walk downstream on the Falls Trail and come back up on the other side (about 300 feet elevation loss and gain). Watch for Belted Kingfisher and American Dipper in the creek, and for Red-breasted Sapsucker, Western Tanager, and Black-headed Grosbeak on the forested slopes. When you come back to the top of the falls, you can cross over to complete the round trip of about 1 mile, or climb up onto the flats and take the Pacific Crest Trail. This takes you away from the noise of the falls and into a different habitat, through open, sunny glades among the pines. This is the place for Western Wood-Pewee; White-breasted Nuthatch; Brown Creeper; Black-throated Gray, Hermit, and Nashville Warblers; and Chipping Sparrow. Olive-sided Flycatchers sing their *"Quick!*

14 McArthur–Burney Falls Memorial State Park

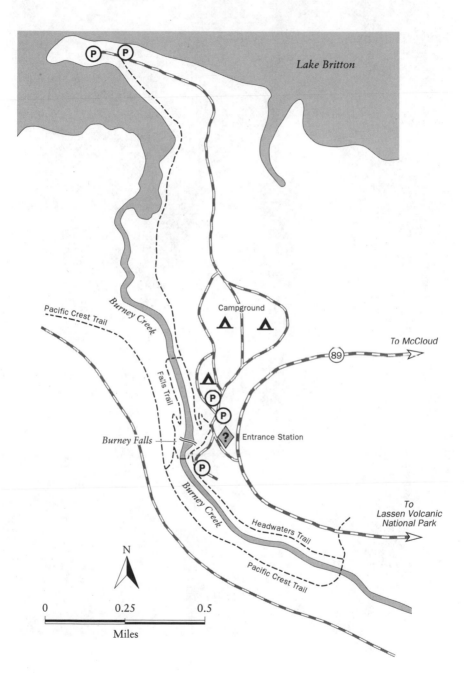

Lake Britton

Burney Creek

Pacific Crest Trail

Campground

Falls Trail

Burney Falls

Entrance Station

89

To McCloud

To Lassen Volcanic National Park

Burney Creek

Headwaters Trail

Pacific Crest Trail

N

0   0.25   0.5

Miles

Black Swifts nest at Burney Falls.

THREE beers!" song from the tops of trees, and Cassin's Vireos are constantly asking, *"are you there?"* and answering themselves, *"I am here."* Evening Grosbeaks may show up, but are unpredictable.

If you go to the upper footbridge and return by the Headwaters Trail, your round trip will be about 2 miles. The Headwaters Trail brings you close to the brushy patches near the creek, where you are likely to find Yellow, MacGillivray's, and Wilson's Warblers, and Spotted Towhee. Keep your eyes (and ears) open for an Osprey. Especially, listen for the loud chirping noise an Osprey makes, which sounds completely different from what you would expect for a large bird of prey.

A visit to Lake Britton could be worthwhile. It has picnickers and boats, but also has Ospreys and has had nesting pairs of Bald Eagles.

General information: Burney Falls is an eyeful, to say the least. This surely must be one of the loveliest waterfalls anywhere, and because it is fed by springs it is unusually constant in flow.

ADDITIONAL HELP

NCA&G grid: Page 38, 1D.
Elevation: 3,000 feet.
Hazards: Cliffs, rattlesnakes, ticks.
Nearest food, gas, lodging: Burney.
Camping: Campground at the state park, 128 sites. In summer, reservations are essential.
For more information: McArthur–Burney Falls Memorial State Park.

15 Lassen Volcanic National Park

Habitats: Lake, mixed conifer forest, meadow, subalpine zone.
Specialty birds: *Resident*—Williamson's Sapsucker; White-headed and Black-backed Woodpeckers; Clark's Nutcracker. *Summer*—Red-breasted Sapsucker; Western Wood-Pewee; Hammond's Flycatcher; Cassin's Vireo; MacGillivray's and Hermit Warblers; Western Tanager; Gray-crowned Rosy-Finch; Cassin's Finch.
Other key birds: *Resident*—Red-breasted and White-breasted Nuthatches; Golden-crowned Kinglet; Red Crossbill. *Summer*—Spotted Sandpiper; Common Nighthawk; Olive-sided Flycatcher; Warbling Vireo; Orange-crowned, Nashville, Yellow, and Wilson's Warblers; Chipping and Lincoln's Sparrows.
Best times to bird: May through August; the road from Manzanita Lake over the summit may be closed by snow until July.

Directions: The main highway through the center of Lassen from north to south is called the Lassen Park Road and is closed in winter. It constitutes the connecting link between the portions of California Highway 89 that lie north and south of the park. From Redding, via California Highway 44, it is about 47 miles (allow 1

15 Lassen Volcanic National Park

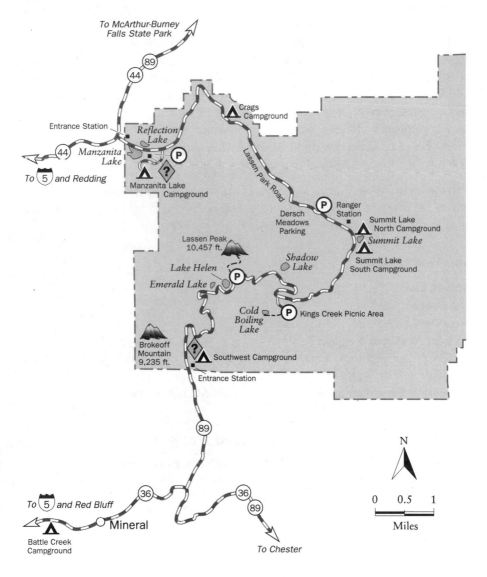

hour) to the north entrance. From Red Bluff, via California Highway 36, it is about 46 miles (allow 1 hour) to the junction with CA 89, and then 4.3 miles north on CA 89 to the south entrance.

The birding: The beginning point for most birders at Lassen Park is **Manzanita Lake** and neighboring **Reflection Lake,** partly because this area usually opens up before the summit road is cleared of snow. In early July Manzanita Lake gets lots of people, but earlier than that it can be quiet and peaceful. There is a trail along the edge of Manzanita Lake, and the **Lily Pond Nature Trail** (about 1 mile round-trip) begins near Reflection Lake. Typical resident birds in this area are White-headed Woodpecker; Steller's Jay; Common Raven; Mountain Chickadee; Red-breasted and White-breasted Nuthatches; Brown Creeper; and Red Crossbill. Summer visitors to look for are Common Nighthawk; Red-breasted Sapsucker; Olive-sided and Hammond's Flycatchers; Cassin's and Warbling Vireos; Western Tanager; Orange-crowned, Nashville, MacGillivray's, Hermit, and Yellow-rumped Warblers; and Cassin's Finch.

Manzanita Lake and the Lily Pond Nature Trail are places where Black-backed Woodpecker has been found, but it is uncommon at best, and often is missed. It has also been found (and frequently missed) at Crags Campground, Dersch Meadows, and Summit Lake.

Crags Campground, about 5 miles east of Manzanita Lake on the Lassen Park Road, is less heavily used than the popular campgrounds at Summit Lake and Manzanita Lake. Birding around the perimeter (beyond the last tents) can be pleasant nevertheless, and the **Lost Creek Organization Campground,** adjacent to the south, can be delightful at times when it is not in use by groups. The habitat is similar to that at Manzanita and Reflection lakes, and the birds listed for those areas can be expected here.

Dersch Meadows consists of a set of sparsely distributed meadows extending for a couple of miles along the east fork of Hat Creek. One of these meadows is bisected by the main road, about 1.5 miles north of Summit Lake (roadside marker number 39, with ample parking). It is a delightful spot, and a circuit of the meadow

Lassen Peak looms over Manzanita Lake.

edges can be enjoyable. Many of the species from all of the locations described above are here, because it is only about 1,000 feet higher. This is a location favored by Western Wood-Pewee; Mountain Chickadee; Red-breasted Nuthatch; Orange-crowned, Yellow, Yellow-rumped, and Wilson's Warblers; plus Chipping and Lincoln's Sparrows; and (of course) Dark-eyed Juncos. Black-backed Woodpeckers have sometimes been spotted along the fringes of the meadow.

Summit Lake, about 12 miles south of Manzanita Lake on the Lassen Park Road, is an attractive spot with campgrounds at both ends and a trail around the lake. The campgrounds tend to fill up early each day. Because of the presence of people, it is not as appealing to birders as are other places. Nevertheless, birds are present, such as Spotted Sandpiper, Williamson's Sapsucker, Steller's Jay, and Mountain Chickadee. It is a good idea to get outside the immediate environs of the campground, to get more birds. Black-backed Woodpecker has been seen in the vicinity.

At **Kings Creek Meadows,** about 4.5 miles south of Summit Lake on the Lassen Park Road (parking, picnicking, restrooms), the habitat changes somewhat, because you are at 7,400 feet elevation. The forest is more open, and there are many lodgepole pines and mountain hemlocks. From the parking lot, try the trail leading to **Cold Boiling Lake** (0.7 mile), which has a short, steep stretch at the beginning, but otherwise is fairly level. The most abundant birds will probably be Mountain Chickadee, Red-breasted Nuthatch, Yellow-rumped Warbler, and Dark-eyed Junco. Brown Creepers, Golden-crowned Kinglets, and Hermit Warblers also are around. This is the place to expect Clark's Nutcrackers, usually first detected because of their harsh, grating calls.

A hike to the top of **Lassen Peak** not only provides great views but also gives you a chance to see Gray-crowned Rosy-Finches, which breed here. The hike begins at the parking lot at the high point of the Lassen Park Road, at 8,512 feet. It is about 2.5 miles to the summit, with 2,000 feet elevation gain. It's not a difficult hike if you're in good shape, although many people find it a bit of a struggle because it's all in the open sun, and most of it has a grade of about 15 percent. Snow may remain on parts of the trail even into August.

General information: Lassen Volcanic National Park was set aside because of its volcano, Lassen Peak, which erupted explosively in 1915. What is often lost sight of is that it is also a place of wonderful forests, lakes, meadows, and subalpine slopes, still relatively undiscovered by many. The high standard road through the park reaches its high point near Lake Helen, just below timberline.

ADDITIONAL HELP

NCA&G grid: Page 48, 2D; page 58, 2A, 3A.
Elevation: 5,700 to 8,500 feet.
Hazards: At higher elevations, excessive exposure to sunlight and lightning strikes can be hazards; rattlesnakes and ticks are possibilities.

Nearest food, gas, lodging: Full services at Burney; gasoline and limited supplies available at Manzanita Lake.

Camping: Manzanita Lake: 179 sites, near the north entrance; RV disposal station. Crags: 45 sites, about 5 miles from the north entrance, on Lassen Park Road. Summit Lake: 46 sites at Summit Lake North, 48 sites at Summit Lake South, about 12 miles from Manzanita Lake. Southwest: 21 sites (walk-in), adjacent to the south entrance. Battle Creek (USDA Forest Service): 50 sites, on CA 36, about 2 miles west of Mineral.

For more information: Lassen Volcanic National Park.

16 Lake Almanor

Habitats: Lake, mixed conifer forest, meadows.

Specialty birds: *Resident*—Western and Clark's Grebes; Bald Eagle; Mountain Quail; Northern Pygmy-Owl; Williamson's Sapsucker; White-headed Woodpecker; Townsend's Solitaire; Cassin's Finch. *Summer*—Wood Duck; Cinnamon Teal; Osprey; Sandhill Crane; Western Wood-Pewee; Hermit and MacGillivray's Warblers; Western Tanager. *Winter*—Hooded Merganser.

Other key birds: *Resident*—Bufflehead, Common Merganser, Great Horned Owl, Gray Jay, Red-breasted Nuthatch, Evening Grosbeak. *Summer*—American White Pelican; Forster's Tern; Common Nighthawk; Warbling Vireo; Yellow and Wilson's Warblers; Chipping and Fox Sparrows. *Winter*—Common and Barrow's Goldeneyes.

Best times to bird: Late April through June for breeding birds.

Directions: Located about 75 miles east of Red Bluff, on California Highway 36 (allow 1.75 hours).

The birding: The best areas from the viewpoint of the birder are the CA36 **Causeway** and the area adjacent to the **North Arm.** Canada Geese nest in large numbers on the grassy flats near the causeway, and Sandhill Cranes have bred in the extensive meadows that appear when the water level is low enough. Excellent viewing is possible from the causeway, which contains both CA 36 and a railroad track. Park on the shoulder well off the road, and watch out for fast traffic. Watch out for trains, too, because the tracks are still in use.

In summer, Ospreys and Forster's Terns forage here. Western Grebes are common, and Clark's Grebes also occur, but Western Grebes generally outnumber Clark's. In some years Western Grebes have constructed their floating nests in shallow water near the causeway. American White Pelicans are sometimes visible, but do not nest here. Double-crested Cormorants, on the other hand, are fairly common nesters. Hooded Mergansers are usually present in winter, and Lake Almanor is one of the best places in the state to find them. Common Goldeneyes are common in winter, but Barrow's Goldeneyes are rare.

A good gravel road leaves CA 36 a short distance east of the causeway, and goes north for about 4 miles to **Last Chance Campground.** The road follows the

16 Lake Almanor

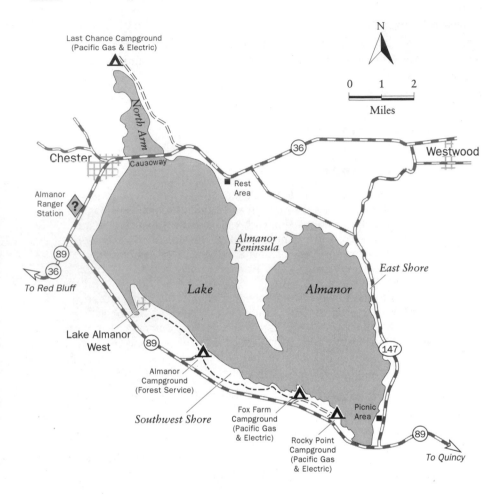

shore of the North Arm over much of this distance, giving you an opportunity to bird the meadows from your car. I saw Sandhill Cranes doing their breeding dance here. Look in the marshy areas for Wood Duck, Gadwall, Cinnamon Teal, Lesser Scaup, Bufflehead, and Common Merganser.

About midway between CA 36 and the campground there is a little valley and a small stream, with old dirt roads that provide foot access to good birding. Warbling Vireos, Mountain Chickadees, Hermit Warblers, Chipping Sparrows, Dark-eyed Juncos, and Cassin's Finches sing from the trees; MacGillivray's and Wilson's Warblers are in the bushes, and the "tin horn" sounds of Red-breasted Nuthatches are heard in the forest. Fox Sparrows are in brushy places, and Song Sparrows in the wet places. Canada Geese and Wood Ducks breed in the swamps in the little valley. (I saw a male Wood Duck perched 40 feet up in a dead tree here, presumably standing guard.) Steller's Jays are common, and a Western Tanager or a White-

Sandhill Cranes perform their breeding dance in the meadows at Lake Almanor.

headed Woodpecker may pop up any time. Lake Almanor often produces the highest count of White-headed Woodpeckers in the country during the annual Audubon Christmas Bird Count. Gray Jay is an uncommon to rare resident.

In the forested areas anywhere, look for Great Horned Owl, Northern Pygmy-Owl, Williamson's Sapsucker, Townsend's Solitaire (especially in the tops of trees), and Evening Grosbeak (irregular). In brushy areas, look and listen for Mountain Quail.

On the **Southwest Shore,** a paved, 9-mile hiking and biking trail is accessible from the day-use area of the Almanor Campground, and from the road leading to Fox Farm Campground. It provides access to mixed conifer forest, and in places gives an opportunity to bird the lakeshore. Ospreys and Bald Eagles are frequently seen.

On the **East Shore,** along California Highway 147, there are a few places where access is possible, although much of the lakeshore is private property. About 1.4 miles north from the junction of California Highway 89 and CA 147 there is a picnic area, and 5.3 miles north of the junction is a wide place where you can park close to the shore and scan the lake for Bald Eagles (uncommon in spring and summer, fairly common in fall and winter).

General information: Lake Almanor is an artificial lake created by Great Western Power Company in 1914. The name of the lake is a combination of the names of the daughters of a vice president of the company: **AL**ice, **MA**rtha, and Eli**NOR**e.

Today the lake is owned and operated by Pacific Gas and Electric (PG&E), primarily for power generation. During the peak summer months, PG&E tries to keep the lake level as high as possible, but later in the year the level drops. As a result of the water management, one can never be sure just where the shoreline will be.

ADDITIONAL HELP

NCA&G grid: Page 59, 5B, 6C.

Elevation: 4,500 feet.

Hazards: Fast traffic on the causeway, rattlesnakes, ticks.

Nearest food, gas, lodging: Chester.

Camping: Last Chance (PG&E): 25 sites, about 4 miles on good gravel road north from CA 36, paved interior roads. Almanor (USDA Forest Service): 101 sites, about 5.6 miles south of the junction of CA 36 and CA 89. Fox Farm (PG&E): 30 sites, about 9 miles south of the junction of CA 36 and CA 89. Rocky Point (PG&E): 20 sites, about 10 miles south of the junction of CA 36 and CA 89.

For more information: Almanor Ranger District.

17 Eagle Lake and Honey Lake 🛉

Habitats: Freshwater marsh, lake, juniper woodland, sagebrush scrub.
Specialty birds: *Resident*—Bald Eagle, Sage Grouse, Lewis's Woodpecker, Pinyon Jay, Black-billed Magpie, Pygmy Nuthatch, Townsend's Solitaire. *Summer*—Western and Clark's Grebes; Cinnamon Teal; Osprey; Dusky Flycatcher; Rock Wren; Mountain Bluebird; Sage Thrasher; Brewer's and Sage Sparrows; Yellow-headed Blackbird. *Winter*—Ferruginous Hawk, Prairie Falcon.
Other key birds: *Resident*—Common Merganser. *Summer*—Eared Grebe; American White Pelican; Redhead; Virginia Rail; Sora; Black-necked Stilt; American Avocet; Willet; Spotted Sandpiper; Caspian and Forster's Terns; Common Nighthawk; Loggerhead Shrike; Blue-gray Gnatcatcher; Common Yellowthroat. *Winter*—Northern Shrike.
Best times to bird: May to July; March and April for Sage Grouse.

Directions: To get to **Eagle Lake,** from the junction of California Highway 36 and County Road A-1 (3 miles west of Susanville), go 13.5 miles north on CR A-1 to the lake. To get to **Honey Lake,** from the junction of CA 36 and U.S. Highway 395 about 3.5 miles southeast of Susanville, go 14.7 miles east on US 395 to Mapes Road, and turn south 1.7 miles to Fish and Game Road. The headquarters of Honey Lake Wildlife Area is 1 mile east on Fish and Game Road (chemical toilets, sign-in required). For directions to other locations, see below.

The birding: The southern end of **Eagle Lake** has a lot of recreational development. The marina at **Gallatin Beach,** 1.5 miles from CR A-1 on Gallatin Road (parking, restrooms), is the natural place to begin. In May, before the boaters arrive in force, the harbor behind the breakwater can be full of American White Pelicans, Western

17 Eagle Lake and Honey Lake

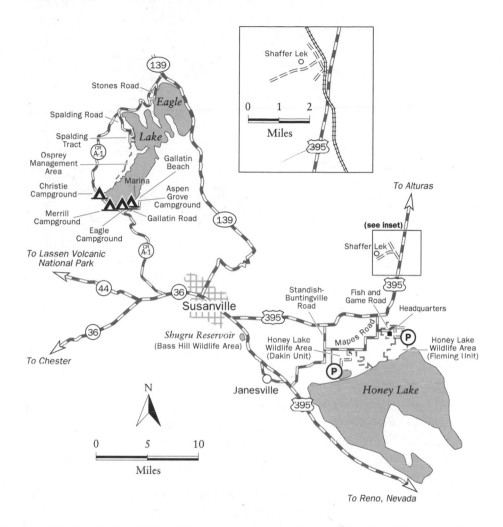

and Clark's Grebes (Clark's is much rarer than Western), and California Gulls. Both Ospreys and Bald Eagles are fairly common. Keep your eye open for Common Nighthawks, which might be darting about in full daylight, uttering their nasal *"peent! peent!"* flight calls. A paved path starts at the west edge of the parking lot at Gallatin Beach and extends along much of the southern lakeshore. A pair of Ospreys have nested near here in recent years less than 0.3 mile from the parking lot.

Much of the western shore of Eagle Lake is closed to entry during spring and summer, because it is prime Osprey nesting territory. From the junction of CR A-1 and Gallatin Road, continue north on CR A-1 about 13 miles to Spalding Road. (The entire route around the lake, including CR A-1 and CA 139, consists of paved highways.) Take Spalding Road into **Spalding Tract.** It deadends at The

American White Pelicans at Eagle Lake. The bird on the right has a fibrous plate on its upper mandible, typical of breeding White Pelicans.

Strand, which parallels the shore for about 1.5 miles. Look here for Western, Clark's, Pied-billed and Eared Grebes, plus Caspian and Forster's Terns and Yellow-headed Blackbird.

From the junction of CR A-1 and Spalding Road, continue north 5.7 miles to Stones Road, which loops down fairly close to the lake and then returns to CR A-1. Look for California Quail and Mountain Bluebird, and be alert for Bald Eagles and Ospreys. Throughout the area in winter, look for Ferruginous Hawks and Prairie Falcons.

CR A-1 comes to CA 139 about 22 miles from your beginning at Gallatin Beach. From this junction at the north end, CA 139 runs south along the **eastern shore** of the lake for about 7 miles, before heading overland to Susanville. Some of the best birding can be along this 7-mile section, although safe pullouts are scarce in some places. Eared Grebes can be numerous here. Look also for Western and Clark's Grebes, as well as Canada Geese, Common Mergansers, Ruddy Ducks, Spotted Sandpipers, and Yellow-headed Blackbirds. Away from the lake, look for species that favor drier locations, such as Dusky Flycatcher, Black-billed Magpie, Pygmy Nuthatch, Rock Wren, Blue-gray Gnatcatcher, and Townsend's Solitaire. Pinyon Jay is a good possibility.

From the headquarters of **Honey Lake Wildlife Area,** which is located in the **Fleming Unit** (see directions above), go about 100 yards beyond the headquarters buildings to a sign that reads "Fish Pond," and turn right. It is about 0.3 mile on a dirt road to a parking area by a pond, which may hold Cinnamon Teal (summer),

Blue-winged Teal (rare in summer), Redhead (uncommon), and Gadwall. Virginia Rail, Sora, and Common Yellowthroat are rare to uncommon in summer. Pied-billed Grebes are resident, and their loud *"cow-cow-cow-cow-uh, cow-uh"* calls can be heard in spring.

If you turn left instead of right at the Fish Pond sign, it is 0.9 mile on a gravel road to a parking lot. From here, you have an almost unlimited view south across the lake to the Diamond Mountains. Among the water birds to expect in breeding season are Western and Clark's Grebes. These two are usually present in more or less equal numbers at Honey Lake, whereas Western greatly outnumbers Clark's at most locations. Other common breeders are American Wigeon; Gadwall; Cinnamon and Green-winged Teal; Mallard; Northern Pintail; Northern Shoveler; and Ruddy Duck. Canvasback, Redhead, Ring-necked Duck, and Lesser Scaup are uncommon breeders.

Back at the junction of Mapes Road and Fish and Game Road, follow Mapes Road to the south. It makes a sharp right-angle turn after 1 mile, and at 2 miles intersects Capezzoli Lane. Turn sharply left, and after 0.9 turn sharply right. Throughout these turns, the road retains its name of Mapes Road, which intersects Galeppi Road 2.4 miles after Capezzoli Lane. The road to here is paved, but becomes gravel after this junction. Turn left and enter the **Dakin Unit.** The check-in station comes at 0.3 mile, and at 1.1 miles, turn right, go 1.1 miles to a T junction, and turn left 0.4 mile to a parking lot. California and Ring-billed Gulls and Caspian Terns nest on the islands offshore, and Franklin's Gull has been seen with regularity. There are ponds close to the road along the way. Look for Black-crowned Night-Heron (mostly a summer visitor), various waterfowl, Willet (summer visitor), and Long-billed Dowitcher (migrant). Throughout the area, watch for Northern Harriers, which are common residents. A rarity to look for in the area in winter is American Tree Sparrow. Bald Eagle is uncommon in winter.

When leaving the area, go west 2.7 miles on Mapes Road from its junction with Galeppi Road, to Standish-Buntingville Road, turn left and go 5.3 miles to US 395. The access road to **Janesville** is 0.7 mile to your right, on the way back to Susanville. Turn left into Janesville, and follow Main Street for 2.5 miles through the center of town, after which you rejoin US 395. Janesville is an excellent place for Lewis's Woodpeckers, which are likely to occur in the trees in town; be sure to check the telephone poles and crossbars. Another place to look is in the Janesville Cemetery, 1.7 miles after leaving US 395. Turn right on Cemetery Lane, go 0.1 mile to the cemetery, and park. Besides Lewis's Woodpecker, you are likely to find Acorn Woodpecker, Steller's Jay, and Pygmy Nuthatch.

When you come to US 395 again, turn left toward Susanville and go 3.2 miles to Shugru Reservoir, which is a part of **Bass Hill Wildlife Area.** There is a wide place next to the road, adjacent to the reservoir, where you can park. There may be many gulls here, especially California, Ring-billed, and Herring, but there also may be grebes, ducks, and shorebirds.

Good places to see Sage Grouse are often hard to find, and leks (open areas where the males strut and display in spring) that have been active in the past have often become inactive. There is a lek north of Honey Lake that has remained active for years, where you may observe the grouse without disturbing them. This is the **Shaffer** (SHAY-fer) **Lek**. To get there, from the junction of CA 36 and US 395 south of Susanville, go 20.6 miles east and north on US 395 to a railroad crossing (see detail map). Exactly 1 mile past the railroad crossing there is an obscure dirt road on the left. You can tell you are approaching the dirt road because there is a small white building nearby, next to the railroad track. The dirt road can be badly rutted, with many holes and rough places, and is best traversed by a high-clear-ance vehicle. **In wet weather it is impassable!** After turning on this road, go 0.2 mile to cross the railroad again, pass an obscure dirt road on the left, and, after 0.7 mile from the highway, turn left on a fairly prominent dirt road. Go 0.75 mile on this road and stop next to an obscure fire ring on the left. Since rocks are easily removed, there is no assurance this ring will stay there, so watch your odometer, and stop after 0.75 mile. Look to your right (north) about 150 yards to an open area, fairly free of brush, but littered with many boulders. This is the lek. The birds here seem to be fairly oblivious to the presence of cars on the road, and even to the sight of people getting out of their cars. However, you should stay next to the road and not attempt to approach the birds because they will surely leave if you do. If disturbed often enough, they could desert the lek. This exact sequence of events has happened at some other leks, so the continued existence of this one depends upon how careful people are. The birds are close enough to be seen easily with binoculars, but a spotting scope helps.

Usually, people are advised to reach the vicinity of a Sage Grouse lek before dawn, preferably in March, and generally this is good advice. However, I visited this lek well after dawn in the middle of April, and there were 16 grouse there, 14 of them males displaying in all their finery.

Some other birds to look for in this sagebrush country are Loggerhead (com-mon resident) and Northern (uncommon winter visitor) Shrikes, Sage Thrasher (mostly, in summer), and Brewer's and Sage Sparrows (both summer visitors).

General information: Eagle and Honey lakes are unusual— neither one has a natu-ral outlet, although Eagle Lake apparently has some subsurface flow out to the east. The western shore of Eagle Lake lies in pine forest and its eastern shore is in junipers and sagebrush, so it could be said that the lake lies right on the border of the Great Basin. Its waters are fairly alkaline and support a special set of aquatic species, including trophy-size trout. Honey Lake is a region of interior drainage, and in times of prolonged drought it may go completely dry.

During February and March as many as 30,000 geese and 20,000 ducks may be on the Honey Lake Wildlife Area. Many of these remain to nest, so certain areas are closed to entry during the nesting season from March 1 to about the middle of May. During hunting season (early October to the middle of January), the gates are open on Saturdays, Sundays, and Wednesdays, which are hunt days, but entry is permitted only with a valid hunting permit. On the other four days of the week during hunting season the gates are closed, but entry is permitted on foot from the parking lots (no permit necessary).

ADDITIONAL HELP

NCA&G grid: Page 50, 1D, 2C; page 60, 2A, 4B; page 61, 4B, 5A.

Elevation: 3,900 to 5,100 feet.

Hazards: Rattlesnakes, ticks.

Nearest food, gas, lodging: Susanville.

Camping: Aspen Grove: 26 sites, 1.5 miles east of CR A-1 on Gallatin Road, tent camping only. Eagle: 45 sites, 0.8 mile east of CR A-1 on Gallatin Road. Merrill: 181 sites, 0.9 mile west of Gallatin Road on CR A-1; RV dump station. Christie: 69 sites, 3.1 miles west of Gallatin Road on CR A-1.

For more information: Eagle Lake Ranger District, Honey Lake Wildlife Area.

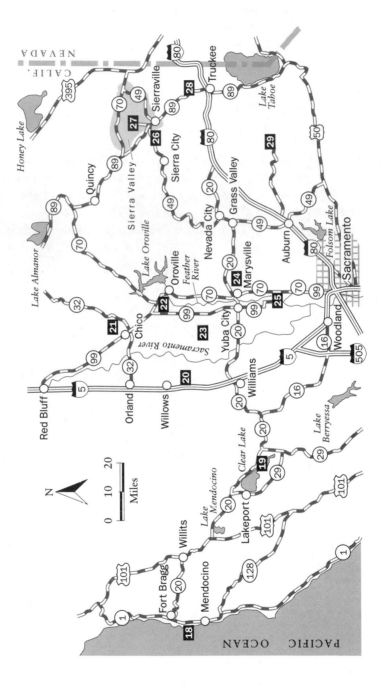

Mendocino Coast to Sierra Valley

This birding trail, like the one described in the Redwood Coast to Modoc Plateau region, cuts across the state, on the way passing through the center of the Sacramento Valley. Even though there are fewer redwoods, the coastline at Mendocino is perhaps even more scenic than it is to the north. Hollywood seems to think so, anyway—movie producers have often selected this locale when they needed a spectacular background.

The Sacramento Valley is one of the premier regions in the world for winter concentrations of waterfowl. The Sacramento National Wildlife Refuge and Gray Lodge Wildlife Area are located here, and are thought of as two of the crown jewels of the refuge system. In winter, the flocks of Snow Geese and Ross's Geese can fill the sky, and these are two of the best places in California to see the rare Eurasian Wigeon. Also, you have now moved into the range of the Yellow-billed Magpie, found only in California. The valley contains remnant sections of riparian forest, mostly extirpated elsewhere in the state, with birds such as Western Yellow-billed Cuckoo, Black-headed Grosbeak, and Bullock's Oriole. Surrounding the valley are the foothills, which provide prime habitat for Acorn and Nuttall's Woodpeckers, Oak Titmouse, Western Bluebird, and Lesser Goldfinch.

Farther east, you enter the Sierra Nevada. The Yuba Pass and Yuba River region is considered by many to offer some of the best birding in the state, with highly sought specialties such as Mountain Quail, Black-backed Woodpecker, Calliope Hummingbird, American Dipper, and Cassin's Finch.

18 Mendocino Coast

19 Clear Lake

20 Sacramento Refuge Complex

21 Chico

22 Oroville

23 Gray Lodge Wildlife Area

24 Spenceville Wildlife Area and District 10

25 Bobelaine Audubon Sanctuary

26 Yuba Pass

27 Sierra Valley

28 Donner Country

29 Mosquito Ridge

18 Mendocino Coast ♿ 👁

Habitats: Sandy beach and mudflats, rocky headlands, coastal bays and lagoons, coastal scrub, closed-cone pine forest, redwood forest; mixed conifer forest, freshwater marsh, riparian woodland.

Specialty birds: *Resident*—Peregrine Falcon, Black Oystercatcher, Hutton's Vireo, Chestnut-backed Chickadee, Pygmy Nuthatch, Wrentit. *Summer*—Brown Pelican, Osprey, Heermann's Gull, Pigeon Guillemot, Allen's Hummingbird, Pacific-slope Flycatcher, Hermit Warbler. *Winter*— Pacific Loon; Black Turnstone; Surfbird; Rock Sandpiper; Mew and Glaucous-winged Gulls; Varied Thrush; Townsend's Warbler. *Migrant*— Wandering Tattler.

Other key birds: *Resident*—Red-shouldered Hawk, Spotted Sandpiper, Common Murre, Gray Jay, Winter Wren, Pine Siskin. *Summer*—Olive-sided Flycatcher, Warbling Vireo, Swainson's Thrush, Wilson's Warbler. *Winter*—Red-throated and Common Loons; Whimbrel.

Best times to bird: April through June for breeding birds; October through March for most gulls; end of July through October for shorebirds.

Directions: All directions are from the junction of California Highway 1 and California Highway 20, just south of Fort Bragg. **MacKerricher State Park** is about 5 miles north on CA 1. **Mendocino Coast Botanical Gardens** is 0.8 mile south on CA 1. **Jug Handle State Reserve** is 3.3 miles south on CA 1. **Point Cabrillo Reserve** is 4.5 miles south on CA 1 to Point Cabrillo Drive, then right on Point Cabrillo Drive, and 1.7 miles to the entrance. **Russian Gulch State Park** is 6.2 miles south on CA 1. **Mendocino** and **Mendocino Headlands State Park** are reached by turning on Lansing Street, about 7.2 miles south on CA 1. **Van Damme State Park** is about 10 miles south, on CA 1.

The birding: MacKerricher State Park has a delightful barrier-free trail that leads to Laguna Point where there is a lookout platform. It can be productive at high tide to scan the "loafing rocks" to the north. Typical birds on the rocky headlands are Black Oystercatcher (resident), Willet, Whimbrel, Spotted Sandpiper, Black Turnstone, Surfbird (the last five species in winter), and Wandering Tattler (uncommon fall migrant). A special bird to look for in winter here is Rock Sandpiper, although it is rare, generally with only one bird present.

Look for Double-crested, Brandt's, and Pelagic Cormorants. Belted Kingfisher might be found perched on the rocks at the surf's edge. Gulls abound, with Western Gull as a year-round resident, Heermann's Gulls in late summer and fall, and Mew, California, Herring, and Glaucous-winged-Gulls in winter. Look for Red-throated, Pacific, and Common Loons, mostly in fall and winter, but especially watch for flocks of migrating Pacific Loons in spring. Brown Pelicans should be here in late summer. Ospreys may be present in summer, and Common Murres may be offshore any time of year.

In the forested areas look for resident Red-shouldered Hawk, California Quail, Steller's Jay, and Pygmy Nuthatch. A trail extends entirely around Lake Cleone,

18 Mendocino Coast

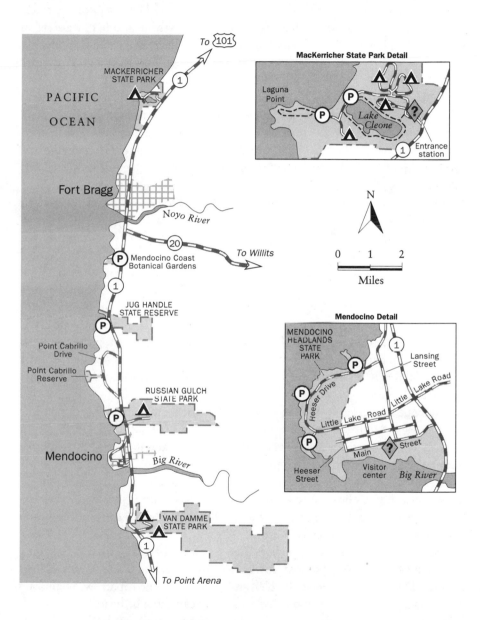

MACKERRICHER
STATE PARK

PACIFIC

OCEAN

To 101

1

MacKerricher State Park Detail

Laguna
Point

P

P

Lake
Cleone

1 Entrance
station

?

Fort Bragg

Noyo River

20 To Willits

P Mendocino Coast
Botanical Gardens

1

N

0   1   2
Miles

JUG HANDLE
STATE RESERVE

P

Point Cabrillo
Drive

Point Cabrillo
Reserve

RUSSIAN GULCH
STATE PARK

P

Mendocino

Big River

Mendocino Detail

MENDOCINO
HEADLANDS
STATE
PARK

P

1

Lansing
Street

P

Heeser Drive

Little Lake Road

Little Lake Road

P

Main Street

?

Heeser
Street

Visitor
center

Big River

VAN DAMME
STATE PARK

1

To Point Arena

part of it a boardwalk that penetrates a dense alder swamp, where flycatchers, vireos, and warblers might be expected during breeding season. Typical resident birds are Chestnut-backed Chickadee and Bushtit.

Mendocino Coast Botanical Gardens (fee, book shop) is a delightful place, mostly because of its extensive gardens that are penetrated by a network of trails, leading to the rocky coastline. The birds are similar to those at other locations on the coast. This is a good place to look for Anna's (resident) and Allen's (spring and summer) Hummingbirds, resident birds such as Downy Woodpecker, and summer visitors such as Pacific-slope and Olive-sided Flycatchers.

Jug Handle State Reserve (parking, picnic tables, chemical toilets) gives access to the **Ecological Staircase Nature Trail.** The trail leads out to Jug Handle Bay, and then goes back under CA 1 and up the canyon, traversing a series of stepped plateaus on the way (the "staircase"), and leading eventually to the Pygmy Forest, a round trip of about 5 miles. The "steps" are ancient marine terraces, each one 100,000 years older than the one that came before it as you proceed inland. The **Headlands Loop** portion of this trail is only about 0.5 mile round trip. The birds are similar to those mentioned for the two previous areas.

Point Cabrillo Reserve can be entered only on foot; public access is allowed during daylight hours. The entrance is rather hidden and must be watched for carefully. No parking is permitted along the entrance road; you must park on Point Cabrillo Drive wherever you can find enough space on the shoulder. It is about a half-mile walk along the paved entrance road to the old lighthouse at Point Cabrillo. The access road may have American Kestrels, and Savannah, Song, White-crowned (resident), and Golden-crowned (winter) Sparrows, plus other birds that love open country with scattered bushes. Common Ravens are likely. At the point the seabirds and shorebirds are similar to those described for MacKerricher State Park.

Many people feel that **Russian Gulch State Park** is the premier location on the coast. It has not only spectacular headlands but also a delightful walk up the **Fern Canyon Trail.** The trail is actually an old paved road, and it goes all the way to a waterfall 2.3 miles upstream. The trail is also used by bicycles and is generally barrier free. The canyon was clearcut more than 100 hundred years ago but has grown back. It gives little evidence of its clearcut past, although if you look carefully it is evident that none of the trees are very old. One of the most common birds in spring and summer is Wilson's Warbler; also look for Warbling Vireo. Residents are Hutton's Vireo, Steller's Jay, Chestnut-backed Chickadee, Pygmy Nuthatch, Winter Wren, Spotted Towhee, and Pine Siskin. Some winter visitors are Varied Thrush, Townsend's Warbler, and Golden-crowned Sparrow. Swainson's Thrush is a summer visitor, and its ethereal song can often be heard.

On the headlands at Russian Gulch there is a short trail that leads to the cliffs and around the **Blow Hole,** a collapsed sea cave with a tunnel leading to the ocean through which the waves surge. California Quail are often in the forest edges next to the headlands. Black Phoebes can be found here as well as elsewhere along the

The Mendocino coast at Russian Gulch State Park.

coast. Don't be surprised if a Peregrine Falcon goes sailing by, because they nest in the region.

The town of **Mendocino** is a remarkable place. On one side of Main Street is a row of souvenir shops and upscale restaurants; on the other is open habitat leading to the ocean. The open habitat belongs to **Mendocino Headlands State Park,** and it is laced with trails. (Be careful here because there are many abrupt cliffs that are undercut in places.) Be prepared for Wrentits in the coastal scrub, and from the cliffs opposite the main part of town it is sometimes possible to watch breeding Pigeon Guillemots at fairly close range on the nearby sea stacks.

Van Damme State Park is similar to Russian Gulch State Park, but is larger. It has Gray Jays, just about at the southern limit of their range on the Pacific Coast, and Hermit Warblers in summer.

General information: The Mendocino coast is one of the most scenic locations in California. Whenever Hollywood wanted a beautiful rocky coast background for a movie, Mendocino seems to have been the choice. *Frenchman's Creek, Johnny Belinda, The Russians Are Coming! The Russians Are Coming!,* and *Murder, She Wrote* have used this area as background. Although spring and fall climates are superb, summers can have fog, and count on rain in winter.

ADDITIONAL HELP

NCA&G grid: Page 73, 5A, 5B.
Elevation: Sea level.
Hazards: Poison oak, rattlesnakes,ticks.
Nearest food, gas, lodging: Fort Bragg; Mendocino.
Camping: MacKerricher State Park: 153 sites, 5 miles north of Fort Bragg on CA 1; RV dump station. Russian Gulch State Park: 30 sites, 2 miles north of Mendocino on CA 1. Van Damme State Park: 74 sites, 3 miles south of Mendocino on CA 1.
For more information: Mendocino Coast State Parks.

19 Clear Lake 🚹 ♿

Habitats: Freshwater marsh, lake, stream, riparian woodland, oak savanna.
Specialty birds: *Resident*—Western and Clark's Grebes; Wood Duck; Osprey; White-tailed Kite; Western Screech-Owl; Northern Pygmy-Owl; Nuttall's Woodpecker; Hutton's Vireo; Oak Titmouse; Western Bluebird; Wrentit; California Thrasher; Lesser Goldfinch. *Summer*—Western Wood-Pewee, Western Kingbird, Black-headed Grosbeak. *Winter*—Lewis's Woodpecker, Say's Phoebe.
Other key birds: *Resident*—Green Heron; Black-crowned Night-Heron; Cooper's and Red-shouldered Hawks; Wild Turkey; Virginia Rail; Sora; Barn and Great Horned Owls; White-breasted Nuthatch; Bewick's Wren. *Summer*—Common Yellowthroat, Wilson's Warbler. *Winter*—American White Pelican.
Best times to bird: All year; April to June is best for breeding birds.

Directions: **Anderson Marsh State Historic Park** is on California Highway 53, 0.6 mile north of the junction of CA 53 and California Highway 29 in Lower Lake (fee, parking, chemical toilets). The parking lot is open Wednesday through Sunday, 10 A.M. to 5 P.M. To get to **Clear Lake State Park,** go south on CA 29 from Lakeport about 3 miles to the point where California Highway 175 comes in from the west, turn off CA 29, go east 1 short block, turn right on Soda Bay Road, and go about 6.1 miles to the park entrance. From the south, leave CA 29/175 at the exit for Kelseyville. Go through Kelseyville on State Street, which joins Gaddy Lane, and meets Soda Bay Road about 3 miles after leaving CA 29/175. Turn right; it's about 1 mile to park entrance.

The birding: Even though the lake is heavily developed, the section surrounding **Anderson Marsh State Historic Park** has retained much of its natural flavor. The **Cache Creek Nature Trail,** with a return on the **Anderson Flats Trail,** provides access to several different habitats, with the first 0.5 mile barrier free. The complete loop is about 2 miles round trip.

To get to Cache Creek, which is the outlet for Clear Lake, walk through the farmyard past the historic buildings. If the gate to the parking lot is closed, it is permissible to park outside (without blocking the gate) and walk the trails. The

19 Clear Lake

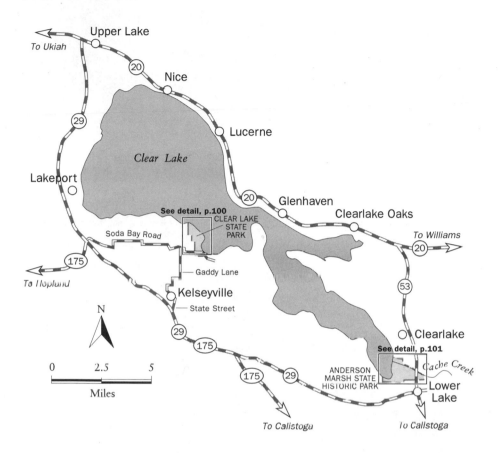

trail crosses an open field and then penetrates the riparian area. The barrier-free portion terminates at a viewing platform. The continuation of the trail runs for a short way along the bank of the creek, then next to a slough, and across more grassy fields to an oak-studded ridge containing a low rocky point called Ridge Point, from which a small portion of Anderson Marsh is visible. However, unless it is a wet year, the part of the marsh you can see won't appear marshy at all, but will look like a dry meadow. The return route to the parking lot is directly across the grassy open area called Anderson Flats. Signs are posted in the area warning about rattlesnakes. Also, poison oak abounds.

Look for resident Wild Turkey, Red-shouldered Hawk, Nuttall's Woodpecker, Black Phoebe, Hutton's Vireo, and White-breasted Nuthatch in the wooded areas, and Green Heron, Black-crowned Night-Heron, Wood Duck, Belted Kingfisher, Common Yellowthroat, and Song Sparrow in the wet areas. Summer visitors are Western Wood-Pewee and Wilson's Warbler. The marshes contain Virginia Rail and Sora (both uncommon). In areas of thick vegetation, be alert for roosting Barn and Great Horned Owls.

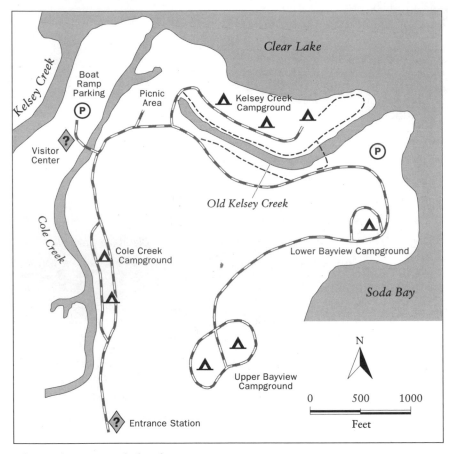

Clear Lake State Park detail.

In open areas look for White-tailed Kite, Red-tailed Hawk, American Kestrel, Say's Phoebe (winter), and Western Kingbird (summer). In the scattered oaks near Ridge Point, you can expect Cooper's Hawk, Lewis's Woodpecker (rare, winter), Acorn Woodpecker, Oak Titmouse, Western Bluebird, and Lesser Goldfinch.

Clear Lake State Park is more heavily used than Anderson Marsh, but can also provide attractive birding, such as at Kelsey Creek Campground. Park in the picnic area, go back to the main access road, and follow it toward the east along the edge of Old Kelsey Creek. There are likely to be Belted Kingfishers here, as well as Green Herons.

Cross the footbridge into the campground and follow the trail out to the point. From there, you can look across the mouth of Old Kelsey Creek to the other side, where there has been an Osprey nest in recent years. Generally there will be one or more Ospreys around somewhere in the summer (rare in winter). Turkey Vultures are likely to be abundant. The point gives a good view of the lake, and you should look for Western and Clark's Grebes, which nest at the lake and sometimes are

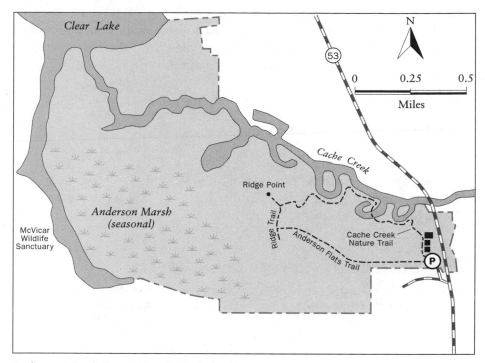

Clear Lake

53

N

0   0.25   0.5
Miles

Cache Creek

Ridge Point

McVicar
Wildlife
Sanctuary

Anderson Marsh
(seasonal)

Ridge Trail

Anderson Flats Trail

Cache Creek
Nature Trail

P

Anderson Marsh State Historic Park detail.

present in considerable numbers. Pied-billed Grebes are common, as are Mallards and hybrids of Mallards. In winter, look for American White Pelican.

From the point, you can return either by going directly back through the campground or taking a trail back along Old Kelsey Creek on the campground side of the creek. Birds to look for are residents such as California Quail (often in the campground), Red-shouldered Hawk (listen for the strident *"keer! keer! keer!"*), Anna's Hummingbird, Nuttall's Woodpecker, Bushtit, Bewick's Wren, Western Bluebird, California Thrasher, and Spotted and California Towhees, and summer visitors such as Wilson's Warbler and Black-headed Grosbeak. Wrentits can often be heard on the hillside above the campground. Western Screech-Owl, Great Horned Owl, and Northern Pygmy-Owl are resident, and at night in the campground you may be able to hear them.

Winter and spring can be attractive times for birding at Clear Lake. Some of the common winter visitors are Ruby-crowned Kinglet, and Golden-crowned and White-crowned Sparrows.

General information: Clear Lake is the largest body of fresh water lying entirely within California. It is heavily used for boating and fishing, and virtually its entire shore is lined with homes and resorts. It has a mild climate most of the year, but temperatures can reach 100 degrees F in the summer.

ADDITIONAL HELP

NCA&G grid: Page 75, 6D; page 84, 1A.
Elevation: 1,300 feet.
Hazards: Poison oak, rattlesnakes, ticks.
Nearest food, gas, lodging: Lakeport.
Camping: Campgrounds in Clear Lake State Park, 147 sites, RV disposal station.
For more information: Clear Lake State Park.

20 Sacramento Refuge Complex ii

Habitats: Freshwater marsh, riparian woodland, valley grassland.
Specialty birds: *Resident*—White-faced Ibis, Wood Duck, Cinnamon Teal, White-tailed Kite, Nuttall's Woodpecker, Yellow-billed Magpie, Tricolored Blackbird. *Summer*—Western Kingbird, Bullock's Oriole. *Winter*—Greater White-fronted and Ross's Geese; Eurasian Wigeon; Bald Eagle; Peregrine Falcon.
Other key birds: *Resident*—American White Pelican; American and Least Bitterns; Black-crowned Night-Heron; Blue-winged Teal; Redhead; Ring-necked Pheasant; Virginia Rail; Sora; Common Moorhen; Black-necked Stilt; Barn and Great Horned Owls; Loggerhead Shrike. *Summer*—American Avocet, Blue Grosbeak. *Winter*—Eared Grebe; Snow Goose; Tundra Swan; Green-winged Teal; Canvasback; Ring-necked Duck; Bufflehead; Sharp-shinned and Cooper's Hawks; Merlin; Greater and Lesser Yellowlegs; Common Snipe; Long-eared Owl; American Pipit; Lincoln's Sparrow.
Best times to bird: November through April.

Directions: From the junction of Interstate 5 and California Highway 20 in Williams, it is 17 miles north on I-5 to the turnoff for **Sacramento National Wildlife Refuge.** Turn east and almost immediately turn north on County Road 99W. Go 1.5 miles to the entrance of the refuge (parking, restrooms, visitor center). For **Colusa National Wildlife Refuge,** from the junction of I-5 and CA 20 in Williams, go 6.3 miles east on CA 20 to entrance to the refuge.

The birding: **Sacramento National Wildlife Refuge** has a 6-mile auto tour route (gravel) that gives access to several ponds and marshes. There is also a nature trail called the **Wetlands Walk,** about 2 miles round trip.

The auto tour route has long views across some of the ponds, and there is a barrier-free viewing platform. In the ponds, look for resident Pied-billed Grebe

20 Sacramento Refuge Complex

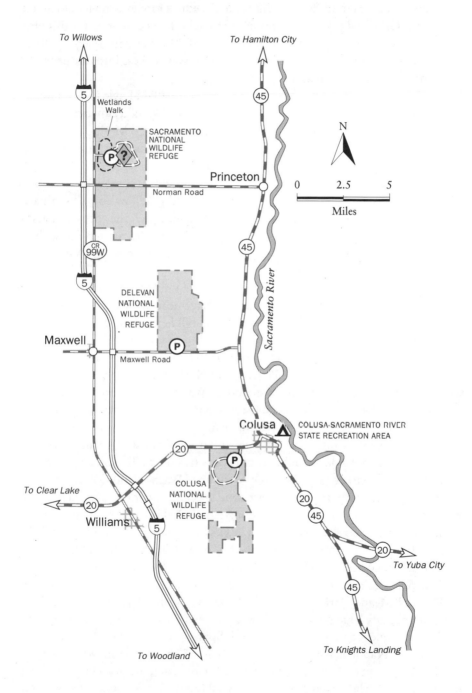

To Willows

To Hamilton City

5

Wetlands
Walk

SACRAMENTO
NATIONAL
WILDLIFE
REFUGE

45

P ?

Princeton

N

0   2.5   5

Miles

Norman Road

CR
99W

45

5

DELEVAN
NATIONAL
WILDLIFE
REFUGE

Sacramento River

Maxwell

P

Maxwell Road

Colusa

COLUSA-SACRAMENTO RIVER
STATE RECREATION AREA

20

P

To Clear Lake

COLUSA
NATIONAL
WILDLIFE
REFUGE

20

20

45

Williams

5

20

To Yuba City

45

To Woodland

To Knights Landing

and Ruddy Duck. The following are winter visitors: Eared Grebe; Greater-White-fronted, Snow, and Ross's Geese; Tundra Swan; American Wigeon; Green-winged Teal; Canvasback; and Bufflehead. Eurasian Wigeon is rare in winter, but regular. Here and at Gray Lodge Wildlife Area may be the best places to look for this bird. Gadwall, Blue-winged Teal (rare), Cinnamon Teal, Northern Shoveler, Northern Pintail, and Redhead (uncommon) are residents; however, these birds are generally less numerous in summer than in winter.

From the viewing platform look for raptors such as Bald Eagle (uncommon in winter), White-tailed Kite, Northern Harrier, Red-tailed Hawk, American Kestrel, Peregrine Falcon (uncommon in winter, rare in summer), and Merlin (rare in winter). In particular, scan the trees to the east for perching Peregrines. A scope helps. In spring and fall look for American White Pelican.

Many of the ponds have mudflats that attract shorebirds such as Black-necked Stilt; American Avocet; Greater and Lesser (uncommon) Yellowlegs; Western and Least Sandpipers; Dunlin; and Long-billed Dowitcher. Check the edges of marshy growth for Common Snipe. In August and September rare shorebirds such as Solitary, Semipalmated, Baird's, or Pectoral Sandpipers may show up. White-faced Ibis is a resident.

American Bittern, Virginia Rail, Sora, and Common Moorhen might be found in the extensive marshes. In particular, as you drive near the marshes, check carefully to see if a bittern is "hiding" there, with its bill held straight up in the air to resemble the surrounding marsh growth. Least Bitterns are possible, but uncommon to rare. Egrets and Black-crowned Night-Herons are common, and other marsh-loving birds such as Black Phoebe, Marsh Wren, and Song and Lincoln's (winter) Sparrows are almost sure to be around. Watch for Tricolored Blackbirds— nesting colonies of as many as 10,000 birds have occurred at these refuges, although they shift in location from year to year.

The **Wetlands Walk** takes you through a mixture of marshes, small ponds, and some riparian woodland. Nuttall's Woodpecker (resident), Tree Swallow (mostly in summer), Ruby-crowned Kinglet, Yellow-rumped Warbler, and Golden-crowned and White-crowned Sparrows (the last four species, in winter) are likely in the areas with trees and bushes. In winter Long-eared Owl is a possibility (very rare), and so are Sharp-shinned and Cooper's Hawks (uncommon). In spring Blue Grosbeaks and Bullock's Orioles arrive to breed. Wood Duck, Ring-necked Duck, and Bufflehead should be looked for in the small ponds. In the more open areas, check for Western Kingbird (spring and summer), Loggerhead Shrike, Yellow-billed Magpie, Western Meadowlark, and Brown-headed Cowbird. The upland areas support a surprisingly large population of Ring-necked Pheasants, and the short grass should have American Pipits and Savannah Sparrows in winter.

At **Colusa National Wildlife Refuge,** there is a 3-mile auto tour route (gravel), with much the same species as listed above for the Sacramento refuge (parking, chemical toilets). The **Wetlands Discovery Trail** (about 1 mile round trip) begins at the parking lot and runs between a canal and slough surrounded by trees, crosses the canal on a footbridge, and returns on the opposite side of the canal. This is a good place to watch for Wood Ducks as well as Barn and Great Horned Owls that roost in the trees or other heavy growth.

General information: There are six refuges in the Sacramento National Wildlife Refuge Complex: Sacramento, Colusa, Delevan, Sutter, Butte Sink, and Sacramento River (Llano Seco Unit) national wildlife refuges. The two units described here have the best access.

The Central Valley is considered to be the single most important wintering site for waterfowl in the Pacific Flyway. In winter 2 million ducks and a half million geese may be present in the valley, and in November and December, the thousands of Snow Geese moving across the sky is one of the most breathtaking sights in nature. Most of the world's population of Ross's Geese spend the winter in the Central Valley. Beavers, otters, and muskrats frequent the waterways.

ADDITIONAL HELP

NCA&G grid: Page 77, 4A.
Elevation: 100 feet.
Hazards: Poison oak, rattlesnakes, ticks.
Nearest food, gas, lodging: Williams; Willows.
Camping: Colusa–Sacramento River State Recreation Area: 22 sites, in Colusa, near the junction of CA 20 and California Highway 45.
For more information: Sacramento National Wildlife Refuge Complex.

21 Chico

Habitats: Lake, stream, riparian woodland, valley grassland.
Specialty birds: *Resident*—Wood Duck, Nuttall's Woodpecker, Hutton's Vireo, Yellow-billed Magpie, Oak Titmouse, Western Bluebird, Phainopepla, Spotted Towhee, Rufous-crowned Sparrow, Lesser Goldfinch. *Summer*—Yellow-billed Cuckoo, Western Wood-Pewee, Ash-throated Flycatcher, Western Kingbird, Bank Swallow, Black-headed Grosbeak, Bullock's Oriole. *Winter*—Northern Pygmy-Owl, American Dipper. *Migrant*—Rufous Hummingbird, Black-throated Gray Warbler.
Other key birds: *Resident*—Red-shouldered Hawk, Great Horned Owl, White-breasted Nuthatch, Bewick's Wren, Lark Sparrow, American Goldfinch. *Summer*—Common Yellowthroat. *Winter*—Fox and Lincoln's Sparrows. *Migrant*—Warbling Vireo; Orange-crowned and Wilson's Warblers.
Best times to bird: All year.

Directions: For **Bidwell Park:** From the junction of California Highway 99 and California Highway 32 in Chico, go east on CA 32 for 0.1 mile and turn left on Fir Street. Follow signs for "Bidwell Park Info Center." As you make the turn on Fir Street it becomes East Eighth Street. Go 0.8 mile on East Eighth Street to **Bidwell Park Information Center** and **Chico Creek Nature Center.**

21 Chico

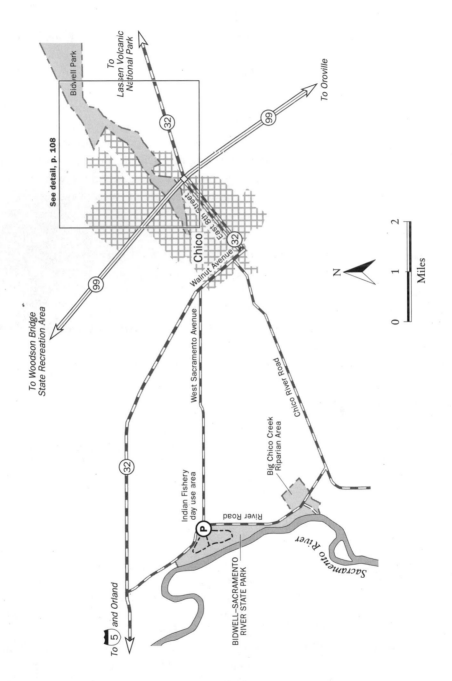

To Lassen Volcanic National Park

To Oroville

Bidwell Park

See detail, p. 108

32

99

Chico

East 8th Street

32

Walnut Avenue

99

To Woodson Bridge State Recreation Area

West Sacramento Avenue

Chico River Road

Big Chico Creek Riparian Area

32

Indian Fishery day use area

River Road

Sacramento River

BIDWELL–SACRAMENTO RIVER STATE PARK

To 5 and Orland

N

0 1 2

Miles

For **Bidwell–Sacramento River State Park:** From the junction of CA 99 and CA 32 in Chico, go west on East Eighth Street 1.8 miles, follow CA 32 as it turns sharply right onto Walnut Avenue, and after 1 mile turn left on West Sacramento Avenue. Go 4.5 miles to River Road, turn right and then immediately left, into the **Indian Fishery Day Use Area** (chemical toilet).

The birding: For **Bidwell Park,** the place to begin is at the Bidwell Park Information Center (closed Mondays). From there, if you come back out to East Eighth Street, return 0.1 mile toward Chico, and reenter the park, you will come to the **Cedar Grove Nature Trail**, which is also called the **World of Trees Nature Trail.** (Restrooms are available inside the nature center, and also near the nature trail about 150 yards west of the parking lot.)

The World of Trees Nature Trail is about 0.5 mile round trip and is barrier free. Resident birds to expect here are Red-shouldered Hawk (uncommon); Anna's Hummingbird; Acorn and Nuttall's Woodpeckers; Hutton's Vireo (uncommon); Western Scrub-Jay; Oak Titmouse; Bushtit; Spotted and California Towhees; and House Finch. Rufous Hummingbird and Wilson's Warbler are likely in migration.

To get to the opposite side of Big Chico Creek, starting from the World of Trees Nature Trail, take South Park Drive (one way) to Manzanita Avenue, turn left to cross the creek, immediately turn left again on Vallombrosa Avenue, and after 0.3 mile turn left again onto **North Park Drive** (one way). This is an area of huge valley oaks and sycamores (and lots of poison oak). There are parking spots along the road, picnic tables, and trails leading through the woods. Look for Western Wood-Pewee, House Wren, Black-headed Grosbeak, and Bullock's Oriole in spring and summer, and for Ruby-crowned Kinglet, and Fox, Lincoln's, Golden-crowned, and White-crowned Sparrows in winter. Residents are Great Horned Owl, Downy Woodpecker (uncommon), White-breasted Nuthatch, Bewick's Wren, Song Sparrow, Brown-headed Cowbird, and American and Lesser Goldfinches.

To get to **Upper Park,** follow South Park Drive to Manzanita Avenue as described above, go northwest about 0.6 mile to Wildwood Avenue, go 0.3 mile and turn right onto Upper Park Road. It is about 1.3 miles to a gate (closed on Sundays and Mondays, but you can walk on the road) and a parking lot near Horseshoe Lake (chemical toilets). There may be waterfowl on the lake, but in the general area there also may be resident California Quail; Black Phoebe; Yellow-billed Magpie; Western Bluebird; Phainopepla; Rufous-crowned and Lark Sparrows; and Western Meadowlark. Common summer visitors are Tree, Barn, and Cliff Swallows, and Western Kingbird. In winter check for Northern Pygmy-Owl in the riparian area, and American Dipper along the creek.

At **Bidwell–Sacramento River State Park,** near the parking area at Indian Fishery Day Use Area, a pond and two loop trails lead through the riparian forest. Typical resident birds here and elsewhere in the riparian sections are Wood Duck; Red-shouldered Hawk; Acorn, Nuttall's, and Downy Woodpeckers; Black Phoebe; Western Scrub-Jay; Oak Titmouse; White-breasted Nuthatch; Bewick's Wren;

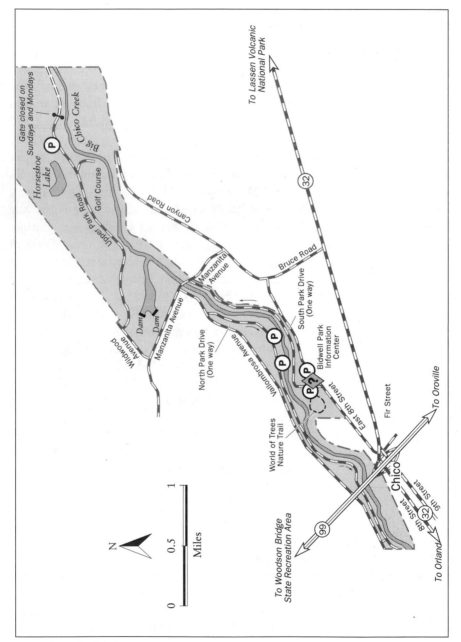

Bidwell Park detail.

Spotted Towhee; and Lesser Goldfinch. Some summer visitors are Ash-throated Flycatcher, House Wren, Common Yellowthroat, Black-headed Grosbeak, and Bullock's Oriole. Yellow-billed Cuckoos are occasionally heard here in June and July in the dense riparian forests. The cuckoos are classified as state-listed endangered, and there are only a few pairs along the entire river, so it is highly unlikely you will see one.

From the junction of River Road and West Sacramento Avenue, go south 1.7 miles on River Road to a dirt access road on the right that leads through the **Big Chico Creek Riparian Area**. When the access road is too muddy the gate will be closed, but you can walk in. Parking is prohibited on the west side of River Road, but is permitted in the wide areas on the east side. The property on both sides of the road is owned by the state park. It is only about 0.4 mile to the Sacramento River along the dirt access road, through mature riparian forest. The birds are the same as those listed for the Indian Fishery Day Use Area, with the possibility of Forster's Terns in spring or fall working along the open river. Also, Bank Swallows may be foraging over the river in summer, because they nest in the area.

Both Bidwell Park and Bidwell–Sacramento River State Park are excellent for migrants—late April and early May for spring migrants, and September for fall migrants. Some migrants to look for are Rufous Hummingbird (spring), Warbling Vireo, and warblers such as Orange-crowned, Nashville, Yellow, Black-throated Gray, Townsend's, MacGillivray's, and Wilson's, as well as Western Tanager.

General information: Bidwell Park is a huge city park of 3,600 acres, extending along Big Chico Creek for 10 miles from the heart of the city of Chico into the foothills. It has traditional city park areas, swimming beaches, a golf course, a nature trail, and miles of riparian habitat. Bidwell–Sacramento River State Park is primarily intended to preserve a section of the riparian forest that still remains along the Sacramento River.

ADDITIONAL HELP

NCA&G grid: Page 67, 7B.
Elevation: 300 feet.
Hazards: Poison oak, rattlesnakes, ticks.
Nearest food, gas, lodging: Chico.
Camping: Woodson Bridge State Recreation Area: 46 sites, 18 miles north of Chico on CA 99, and then 3 miles west on South Avenue.
For more information: Chico Creek Nature Center; Bidwell–Sacramento River State Park.

22 Oroville

Habitats: Lake, stream, riparian woodland, valley grassland.
Specialty birds: *Resident*—Golden Eagle, Western Bluebird, Phainopepla, Lesser Goldfinch. *Summer*—Black-chinned Hummingbird, Western Kingbird. *Winter*—Western and Clark's Grebes; Osprey; Bald Eagle; Ferruginous Hawk; Prairie Falcon; Mew, Glaucous-winged, and Thayer's Gulls; Say's Phoebe.
Other key birds: *Resident*—Loggerhead Shrike, American Goldfinch. *Winter*—Common and Barrow's Goldeneyes; Bufflehead; Common Merganser; Cooper's and Rough-legged Hawks; Merlin.
Best times to bird: November through March.

Directions: For the **Feather River Parkway,** from the junction of California Highway 70 and California Highway 162 in Oroville, go north 0.6 mile on CA 70 to Montgomery Street, then east on Montgomery 0.8 mile to Huntoon Street; turn left for 1 block and drive up onto the levee, which has a paved road on top (there are broad shoulders for parking). A paved bike trail extends in both directions.

To get to **Nelson Avenue,** return to Montgomery Street, turn left, and go 0.4 mile to Washington Avenue; turn left and cross the Feather River. Washington Avenue becomes Table Mountain Boulevard; follow it for 0.7 mile to Nelson Avenue, and turn west. **North Thermalito Forebay** appears after about 3 miles. Continue on Nelson Avenue through open foothill country for about 2.2 miles beyond the forebay (road becomes gravel) to Wilbur Road, and turn left. It is 1.8 miles to CA 162. Turn right on CA 162. It is 0.9 mile, on the left, to the part of **Oroville Wildlife Area** that is adjacent to Thermalito Afterbay (parking, restrooms), and 0.5 mile more to the causeway across Thermalito Afterbay.

To get to **South Thermalito Forebay** (operated by Lake Oroville State Recreation Area), go west from CA 70 about 3 miles on Grand Avenue to the entrance (fee, restrooms).

The birding: The paved bike path along the **Feather River Parkway** offers a variety of birding experiences. In the fall when the salmon are running, it is a good place to see Osprey and a variety of gulls, including Mew, Thayer's, and Glaucous-winged. In winter look for Common and Barrow's (rare) Goldeneyes, and Common Merganser, as well as egrets and herons. The trees and bushes along the river support common residents such as Anna's Hummingbird, Black Phoebe, Oak Titmouse, Bushtit, Bewick's Wren, Western Bluebird, and Lesser and American Goldfinches. Western Kingbird (common) and Black-chinned Hummingbird (uncommon) are present in spring and summer, and Cooper's Hawk and Phainopepla are uncommon residents. Tree Swallows are present year-round, although their numbers are reduced in winter. Red-breasted Mergansers, rare inland, have occasionally shown up here.

The route along **Nelson Avenue** crosses North Thermalito Forebay and takes you into rolling, grassy foothills—raptor country. Ferruginous and Rough-legged Hawks, and Prairie Falcons are rare to uncommon in winter. Golden Eagles are

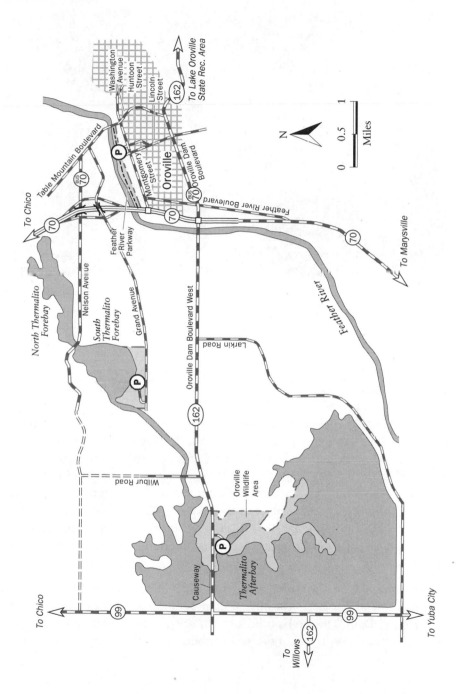

Western Grebe.

rare residents; Bald Eagles are spotted more frequently than Goldens in winter. Northern Harrier and American Kestrel are common residents, and Merlin is a rare winter visitor. Western Meadowlark is common year-round, Say's Phoebe is uncommon in fall and winter, and Common Raven is an uncommon resident. Waterfowl may be present on North Thermalito Forebay.

Thermalito Afterbay often has waterfowl in winter, including an occasional Common Loon. The parking lot at the **Oroville Wildlife Area** (this is only a small portion of the wildlife area) gives close views of water birds on an arm of the lake, as well as land birds like Loggerhead Shrike, sparrows, and goldfinches. At the causeway it is possible to park on the side of the road (wide shoulders, but watch for fast traffic on CA 162) and scan the lake for Western and Clark's Grebes; Double-crested Cormorant; Northern Pintail; Bufflehead; American Coot; and other water-oriented birds, mostly in winter. **South Thermalito Forebay** offers similar viewing.

General information: The Oroville Dam lies just 5 miles upstream from the city of Oroville, and at 770 feet is the highest dam in the United States, slightly higher than Hoover Dam. The forebay and afterbay are part of the electrical generation system. Feather River is one of the major tributaries of the Sacramento River.

ADDITIONAL HELP

NCA&G grid: Page 68, 1D, 2D; page 78, 1A, 2A.
Elevation: 175 feet.
Hazards: Poison oak, rattlesnakes, ticks.
Nearest food, gas, lodging: Oroville.
Camping: Lake Oroville State Recreation Area: Coyote (Loafer Creek Area): 137 sites; RV dump station, on CA 162, 8.5 miles east of Oroville. Bidwell Canyon: 70 sites with full hook-ups, 7 miles east of Oroville on CA 162, then l.6 miles north on Kelly Ridge Road.
For more information: Lake Oroville State Recreation Area.

23 Gray Lodge Wildlife Area

Habitats: Freshwater marsh, riparian woodland.
Specialty birds: *Resident*—Wood Duck, Cinnamon Teal, White-tailed Kite, Burrowing Owl, Nuttall's Woodpecker, Yellow-billed Magpie, California Towhee. *Winter*—Greater White-fronted and Ross's Geese; Eurasian Wigeon; Sandhill Crane.
Other key birds: *Resident*—American and Least Bitterns; Northern Harrier; Cooper's and Red-tailed Hawks; Ring-necked Pheasant; Virginia Rail; Sora; Common Moorhen; Great Horned Owl; Loggerhead Shrike; Common Yellowthroat. *Summer*—Blue Grosbeak. *Winter*—Snow Goose, Green-winged Teal, Ring-necked Duck, Bufflehead, Common Goldeneye, American Pipit, Orange-crowned Warbler, Lincoln's Sparrow.
Best times to bird: November through April.

Directions: From the junction of California Highway 99 and California Highway 20 in Yuba City, go 9.4 miles north on CA 99 to Pennington Road in Live Oak, then travel 8 miles west (Pennington Road makes many turns, eventually becoming North Butte Road) to Almond Orchard Road. Go north 1.7 miles on Almond Orchard Road (which changes its name to Pennington Road as it crosses the county line) to the entrance to Gray Lodge Wildlife Area on the left. (Note that there are two different roads, in two different counties, bearing the name Pennington Road.) From the entrance it is 2.4 miles to the parking lot (lot number 14, fee, chemical toilets). Approaching from the north on CA 99, turn west in the center of Gridley on Sycamore Street. Go west on Sycamore Street about 6 miles to Pennington Road, and then south about 3 miles to the entrance.

The birding: The nature trail (paved, barrier free) begins at the parking lot and goes about 0.3 mile to a viewing platform. The trail runs next to a marsh that contains mostly American Coots and Common Moorhens, although there are other marsh dwellers such as American Bittern; Virginia Rail; Sora; Marsh Wren; Common Yellowthroat; Song and Lincoln's Sparrows; and Red-winged Blackbird. Least Bittern is a breeder but is seldom seen.

23 Gray Lodge Wildlife Area

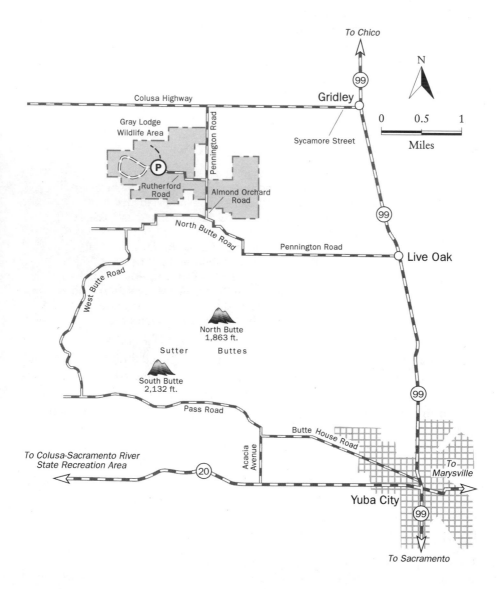

In the woodlands bordering the trail, in winter look for Ruby-crowned Kinglet, Yellow-rumped Warbler, and Golden-crowned and White-crowned Sparrows. Nuttall's and Downy Woodpeckers; Yellow-billed Magpie; and California Towhee are year-round residents.

From the viewing platform a large mixture of waterfowl is usually visible. In late fall and winter, especially in November and December, there often will be large numbers of Snow Geese, and thousands may suddenly roar into the air, responding to some sudden impulse. Ross's Geese are typically mixed in with the Snow Geese.

Other waterfowl are Greater White-fronted Goose; Wood Duck; Gadwall; American Wigeon; Mallard; Cinnamon and Green-winged Teal; Northern Shoveler; Northern Pintail; Ring-necked Duck; Lesser Scaup; Bufflehead; and Common Goldeneye. Wood Ducks, especially, have increased in the area because of an active nesting box program. Be sure to scan the wigeons for Eurasian Wigeon— they are rare, but this is one of the best places to see them in California. Typical raptors are White-tailed Kite, Northern Harrier, Red-tailed Hawk, and American Kestrel, but there is always the possibility of a Cooper's Hawk or Bald Eagle. The area around the entrance may have Burrowing Owl.

An auto tour route (3 miles round trip, gravel) originates from the parking lot. Watch for Ring-necked Pheasant, Great Horned Owl, Killdeer, Black Phoebe, Loggerhead Shrike (uncommon), American Pipit, Orange-crowned Warbler, Savannah Sparrow, and Western Meadowlark. Blue Grosbeak is a summer visitor. Be alert overhead for Sandhill Cranes, which spend the winter foraging in nearby fields.

General information: Gray Lodge is an attractive area, with a mix of habitats. It doesn't have as many places where you can look across expanses of water as at Sacramento National Wildlife Refuge, but it has more riparian habitat. If the weather is not foggy, a dominant nearby feature is the Sutter Buttes. The buttes are the remnants of an ancient volcano that once stood on the site, and are the only interruption in the general flatness of the Central Valley for its entire length.

ADDITIONAL HELP

NCA&G grid: Page 77, 7B.
Elevation: 100 feet.
Hazards: Ticks, rattlesnakes, and poison oak.
Nearest food, gas, lodging: Yuba City; Gridley.
Camping: Colusa–Sacramento River State Recreation Area: 22 sites, in Colusa, near the junction of CA 20 and California Highway 45.
For more information: Gray Lodge Wildlife Area.

24 Spenceville Wildlife Area and District 10

Habitats: Riparian woodland, farm fields, valley grassland, foothills woodland, oak savanna.

Specialty birds: *Resident*—White-faced Ibis, Black Rail, Western Screech-Owl, Nuttall's Woodpecker, Hutton's Vireo, Yellow-billed Magpie, Oak Titmouse, Western Bluebird, Rufous-crowned Sparrow, Lesser Goldfinch. *Summer*—Black-chinned Hummingbird, Ash-throated Flycatcher, Western Kingbird, Violet-green Swallow, Black-headed Grosbeak, Lazuli Bunting, Bullock's Oriole, Lawrence's Goldfinch. *Winter*—Bald Eagle, Lewis's Woodpecker, Red-breasted Sapsucker, Says' Phoebe. *Migrant*—Rufous Hummingbird, Hammond's Flycatcher.

Other key birds: *Resident*—Cooper's and Red-shouldered Hawks; Wild Turkey; White-breasted Nuthatch; Lark Sparrow. *Summer*—Orange-crowned Warbler. *Winter*—Tundra Swan; Greater Yellowlegs; Fox and Lincoln's Sparrows. *Migrant*—Wilson's Warbler.

Best times to bird: For breeding songbirds, April through June; for wintering waterfowl and raptors, November through March.

Directions: To get to **Spenceville Wildlife Management and Recreation Area** from the junction of California Highway 70 and California Highway 20 in Marysville, go about 20 miles east on CA 20 to a point 1.3 miles beyond Smartville, and turn south on Smartville Road at the sign for "Beale Air Force Base." After about 1 mile, turn left at the junction of Smartville Road and Hammonton-Smartville Road; after 4.5 miles, turn left again, on Waldo Road (gravel). **Waldo Bridge** (called by some, the Iron Bridge) is 1.8 miles from the turn, on Waldo Road. To reach Waldo Bridge from the south, at Sheridan on California Highway 65 turn east on Riosa Road in Sheridan, and turn north after 1 block onto Camp Far West Road. Follow this road about 7 miles to the junction with McCourtney Road at Camp Far West Reservoir. Turn left to go across the dam. Just after crossing the dam, you will come to a junction at which Camp Far West Road appears to go both left and right, but you are now in a different county (Yuba County) than on the opposite end of the dam (Placer County), and the road called Camp Far West Road is not the same as the one you followed from Sheridan. Turn right, following Camp Far West Road around the reservoir, and continue about 3.9 miles beyond the dam (changes to gravel), to a junction with Long Ravine Road. Continue straight ahead on Long Ravine Road 1.6 miles to a junction with Spenceville Road, keep left on Spenceville Road, and continue 0.5 mile to Waldo Bridge.

To get to the area known as **District 10** (a name belonging to the local irrigation district) from the junction of CA 70 and CA 20 in Marysville, go about 6 miles north on CA 70 to Woodruff Lane, and turn right. Follow Woodruff Lane, as it jogs right and then left, for 3.4 miles, to where it joins with Matthews Lane. You can go north on Matthews Lane (narrow shoulders, poor parking) for 3.5 miles to Ramirez Lane. From the junction of Woodruff Lane and Matthews Lane, it is 1.6 miles east on Woodruff Lane to CA 20. The entire region is known as District 10.

24 Spenceville Wildlife Area and District 10

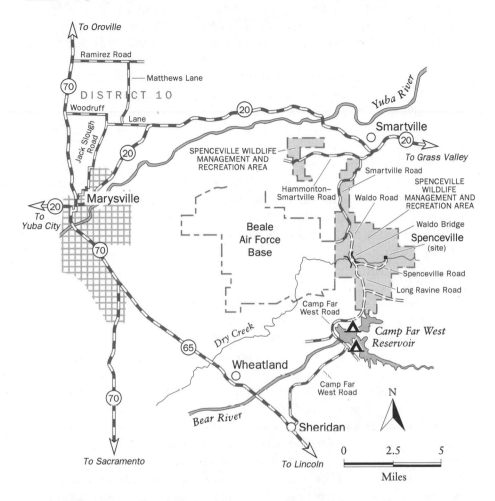

The birding: **Spenceville Wildlife Management and Recreation Area** is an area of rolling foothills, grassy slopes, and oak savanna. It is delightful in its own right, especially in spring, but has become celebrated in birding circles because of its unusual population of Black Rails. Normally, one thinks of Black Rails in association with flatland marshes. In California they were thought to occur only in scattered locations along the coast, around the San Francisco Bay, in the Imperial Valley, and on the lower Colorado River. Thus, it was a surprise to discover, only a few years ago, that there was an apparently resident population in the foothills, mostly in Yuba County. Since the rails require moist places, usually with cattails, they occur only in places that have a permanent source of water. In most cases, the necessary water is supplied by the irrigation ditches that wind through the foothills. This situation has resulted in speculation that the rails have begun occurring here in reasonable numbers only since the ditches were constructed.

Most of the known Black Rail locations are either on private property or are at sensitive research sites; however, there is one site where they might be observed without causing undue intrusion. Park at **Waldo Bridge** on the north side (wide shoulders). Squeeze through the gate to the east (this is public land), and follow the horse trail about 200 yards east, to a small tributary that flows into Dry Creek from the north. The tributary is essentially a narrow band of marsh, extending perhaps 0.7 mile upstream and surrounded by a fence to keep out cattle. There is a rough, informal trail running near the tributary on the slope above the marsh, and by following this trail, you can easily see into all parts of the marsh. Experts on Black Rails recommend that you do not actually walk into the marsh, because predators such as raccoons and coyotes tend to follow human trails to see what they might lead to. Great care should be taken at this site so that we are not responsible for driving away the few rails that are believed to breed here.

Your chance of actually seeing a Black Rail is just about zero. Even researchers who spend a considerable amount of time investigating Black Rails seldom see them, because they are small and skilled at remaining hidden. However, you might be able to hear one. They sometimes call spontaneously in the month of June, either early in the morning or just before sunset, and not only just at night, contrary to what some field guides say. The common call is usually described as a rapid *"kik-kee-doo,"* repeated at intervals. Another call resembles a harsh grating sound. Since the Black Rail is classified as state-listed threatened, it is contrary to the ABA Code of Birding Ethics to use tape recordings to attract them.

Quite aside from the Black Rails, Spenceville is an appealing place in its own right. You can squeeze past (or climb) the gates anywhere that it is posted as public land, and wander across the foothills. An especially attractive place is at the end of Spenceville Road. From the Waldo Bridge, go south 0.5 mile on Waldo Road to its junction with Spenceville Road, then east on Spenceville Road 2 miles to the end of the road, adjacent to the site of historic **Spenceville.**

Spenceville is marked by some large piles of mine tailings. You can cross Dry Creek here on an old concrete bridge and walk in either direction along an old dirt road, now closed to vehicles. There is another old road at the east of the Spenceville site that skirts the fence surrounding the site and leads north into attractive habitat. Or, at the end of Spenceville Road, where it is blocked by huge boulders, you can cross Dry Creek on an old wooden bridge (decaying, and with at least one hole large enough for a person to fall through), and continue on Spenceville Road (closed to vehicles) upstream along Dry Creek.

Some of the common resident birds are Cooper's and Red-shouldered Hawks; Western Screech-Owl; Anna's Hummingbird; Acorn and Nuttall's Woodpeckers; Hutton's Vireo; Yellow-billed Magpie; Oak Titmouse; Bushtit; White-breasted Nuthatch; Bewick's Wren; Western Bluebird; Rufous-crowned and Lark Sparrows; Western Meadowlark; and Lesser Goldfinch. Wild Turkeys have been introduced and are widespread in the foothills.

Common summer visitors are Black-chinned Hummingbird, Ash-throated Flycatcher, Western Kingbird, Violet-green Swallow, Orange-crowned Warbler, Black-headed Grosbeak, Lazuli Bunting, and Bullock's Oriole. Lawrence's Goldfinch is an uncommon summer breeder.

In migration, look for Rufous Hummingbird, Hammond's Flycatcher, and Wilson's Warbler. Some common winter visitors are Ruby-crowned Kinglet, and Fox and Lincoln's Sparrows; uncommon ones are Red-breasted Sapsucker and Say's Phoebe. Lewis's Woodpecker is sometimes seen in winter, but is rare and irregular. Once in a while a Long-eared Owl has been found nesting in the live oak woodlands.

The rice fields in **District 10** attract ducks and geese in winter when they are flooded, and this in turn attracts Bald Eagles. Watch for them, not only overhead but also perched in trees or even sitting on one of the low levees surrounding the rice fields. Northern Harriers are common residents.

Also, where flooded fields occur, look for wintering shorebirds such as Greater Yellowlegs and Dunlin. White-faced Ibis may show up any time of year, although they are not known to have nested recently in this area. They have, however, nested in the Sacramento Valley and are known to shift their nesting locations from year to year, so they could repeat as nesters in the future.

District 10 is known to be one of the better places to see Tundra Swans. Those who bird the district on a regular basis say they are almost always to be found here in November or December each year.

General Information: This site is a mix of two kinds of habitat: rolling foothill country and flat agricultural rice fields. The two flow smoothly together into a bit of unspoiled rural California.

ADDITIONAL HELP

NCA&G grid: Pages 78, 2C, 4D; page 79, 4C, 4D.
Elevation: 100 to 400 feet.
Hazards: Poison oak, rattlesnakes, ticks.
Nearest food, gas, lodging: Marysville.
Camping: Camp Far West Lake (reservations needed, see Appendix F): North Side, 76 sites, plus 10 with full hook-ups; 9 miles northeast from Sheridan, on Camp Far West Reservoir; RV dump station; open all year. South Side: 67 sites; 8 miles northeast from Sheridan, on Camp Far West Reservoir; closed in winter. Nevada County Fairgrounds: in Grass Valley, 32 miles east of Marysville on CA 20, then 0.5 mile southwest on McCourtney Road; enter at Gate 4; 132 sites on grass under mature pines, 24 with hook-ups; RV dump station; reservations recommended in summer and on holiday weekends (see Appendix F).
For more information: Spenceville Wildlife Management and Recreation Area.

25 Bobelaine Audubon Sanctuary

Habitats: Stream, riparian woodland.

Specialty birds: *Resident*—Wood Duck, Nuttall's Woodpecker, Yellow-billed Magpie, Western Bluebird. *Summer*—Western Wood-Pewee, Ash-throated Flycatcher, Black-headed Grosbeak, Bullock's Oriole. *Migrants*—Willow Flycatcher; Black-throated Gray and MacGillivray's Warblers; Western Tanager.

Other key birds: *Resident*—Green Heron, Red-shouldered Hawk, Great Horned Owl, White-breasted Nuthatch, Bewick's Wren. *Winter*—Common Merganser. *Migrants*—Orange-crowned, Nashville, Yellow, and Wilson's Warblers.

Best times to bird: April through June, and September through November. July and August are usually pretty hot, and in the winter the preserve can be closed by flooding.

Directions: From Sacramento, go north about 20 miles on California Highway 70/99 to where the two highways split. Follow CA 99 about 6.8 miles to Laurel Avenue, turn east, and go 0.7 mile to sign that reads "End of Public Road," and then 0.1 mile farther to a parking lot (chemical toilet). The sanctuary is open from sunrise to sunset for viewing wildlife.

The birding: The sanctuary has an extensive trail system, kept mowed by the managers of the preserve. Huge oaks, sycamores, and cottonwoods are draped with festoons of grapevines. There are also many white skeletons of trees that are the result of a fire that ran through the sanctuary in 1992.

The main trail, **Center Trail,** begins in the parking lot, leads up onto the west levee for about 0.3 mile, and then goes down into the heart of the preserve. About 0.7 mile from the beginning, a short spur trail leads to the **Rivers Overlook.** As you look out over the Feather River from this spot, it is easy to imagine that you are seeing the river the way it was in the past. From the Rivers Overlook a good return route is to continue a short distance to an unsigned junction with the **Otter Trail,** which leads back through an especially nice part of the forest that seems to have been relatively untouched by the fire. The round trip is about 1.5 miles.

The birds that like forests and brushy thickets are the ones most evident here. Common residents are Red-shouldered Hawk; California Quail; Mourning Dove; Great Horned Owl; Anna's Hummingbird; Acorn, Nuttall's, and Downy Woodpeckers; Oak Titmouse; Bushtit; White-breasted Nuthatch; Bewick's Wren; Western Bluebird; Spotted and California Towhees; and House Finch. In the more open areas, especially as you are approaching on the entrance road, look for Yellow-billed Magpie. The ponds and sloughs almost always have Pied-billed Grebe, Great Blue Heron, Belted Kingfisher, and Black Phoebe, and may have Double-crested Cormorant, Wood Duck, and Green Heron, all of which are resident. On the Feather River, there may be Common Mergansers in the winter.

Summer visitors are Western Wood-Pewee, Ash-throated Flycatcher, House Wren, Black-headed Grosbeak, and Bullock's Oriole. Some of the migrants are Willow Flycatcher; Western Tanager; and Orange-crowned, Nashville, Yellow,

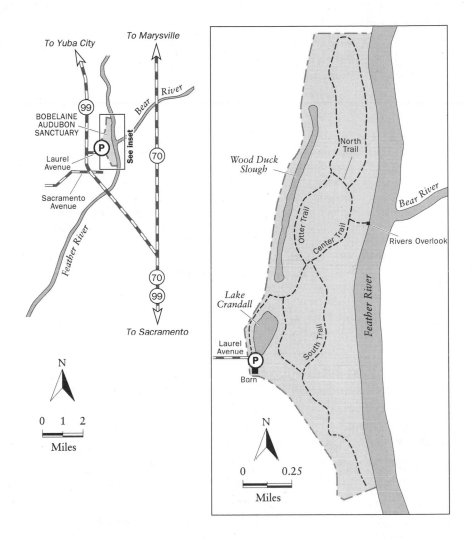

Black-throated Gray, MacGillivray's, and Wilson's Warblers. In the past, Yellow-billed Cuckoos nested here, but not recently. In winter Ruby-crowned Kinglets and sparrows such as Golden and White-crowned all return in force, beginning about October.

General information: Bobelaine is 430 acres of riparian forest, owned by the National Audubon Society and managed by the Sacramento Audubon Society. Signs warn against the possibility that limbs from trees killed in the 1992 fire may break off with no warning, or even that an entire tree may fall.

ADDITIONAL HELP

NCA&G grid: Page 86, 2A.
Elevation: 40 feet.
Hazards: Poison oak, rattlesnakes, ticks, falling branches.
Nearest food, gas, lodging: Yuba City.
For more information: National Audubon Society—*California*

Yuba Pass

Habitats: Lake, stream, mixed conifer forest, meadow.
Specialty birds: *Resident*—Blue Grouse; Mountain Quail; Band-tailed Pigeon; Northern Pygmy-Owl; Red-breasted and Williamson's Sapsuckers; White-headed and Black-backed Woodpeckers; American Dipper; Townsend's Solitaire; Cassin's Finch. *Summer*—Anna's and Calliope Hummingbirds; Western Wood-Pewee; Hammond's Flycatcher; Hermit and MacGillivray's Warblers; Western Tanager; Green-tailed Towhee.
Other key birds: *Resident*—Hairy Woodpecker, Red-breasted Nuthatch, Golden-crowned Kinglet, Pine Grosbeak, Red Crossbill, Pine Siskin, Evening Grosbeak. *Summer*—Olive-sided Flycatcher; Warbling Vireo; Nashville, Yellow-rumped and Wilson's Warblers; Chipping, Fox, and Lincoln's Sparrows.
Best times to bird: April through July.

Directions: From Sierra City, on California Highway 49, **Yuba Pass** is 13.2 miles east on CA 49 (parking, restrooms). For **Sand Pond** and **Lower Sardine Lake,** go east on CA 49 from Sierra City about 7 miles to **Bassett's Station,** turn north on Gold Lake Road, go 1.3 miles, and turn west on the Packer Lake Road to Sand Pond and Sardine Lake (parking, restrooms). **Salmon Creek Campground** is 1.5 miles from Bassett's Station, on Gold Lake Road.

The birding: Yuba Pass is well known as one of the better places to seek Black-backed Woodpecker; however, this bird is elusive and notoriously difficult to find, and many people have wound up disappointed. Check dead trees with loose bark, and watch for trees with nesting holes in them. Such trees also are used by Northern Pygmy-Owls, several species of woodpeckers, and Mountain Chickadees.

A walk for a mile or so along the dirt road to the north of the pass leads through good habitat. Some of the area has been logged, but is coming back and is attractive to Wilson's and Yellow-rumped Warblers, and Fox Sparrow. Birds such as Williamson's Sapsucker; Hairy Woodpecker; Western Wood-Pewee; Olive-sided and Hammond's Flycatchers; Mountain Chickadee; Red-breasted Nuthatch; Brown Creeper; Golden-crowned Kinglet; Townsend's Solitaire; Hermit Warbler; Western Tanager; Chipping Sparrow; Cassin's Finch; and Pine Siskin may be anywhere in the forested portions.

In the spring, Blue Grouse can be heard going *"vroom! vroom!"* at a distance, and Mountain Quail cry out their loud *"quark!"* calls from nearby brushy slopes.

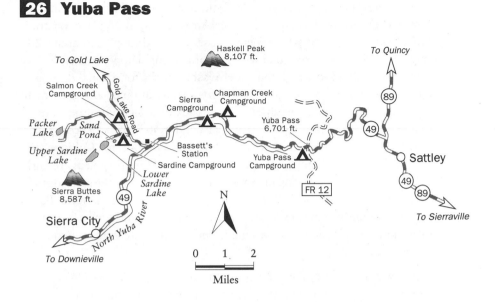

Pine Grosbeaks have been seen here, but are fairly rare and elusive. Red Crossbills and Evening Grosbeaks also show up from time to time, but these are irruptive and unpredictable.

It is worthwhile to check around the campground and the adjacent meadow. Nesting trees for Black-backed Woodpecker and Northern Pygmy-Owl have been reported in the past next to the meadow, and Lincoln's Sparrows and Wilson's Warblers have nested in the bushes.

Sand Pond has an interpretive trail and boardwalk (about 1 mile round trip), but it is too rough to be considered barrier free. About half of the trail leads through a marshy flat with many dead trees. The remainder passes through typical Sierran forest, with birds such as Western Wood-Pewee; Warbling Vireo; Steller's Jay; Nashville and Yellow-rumped Warblers; Song and Fox Sparrows; and Dark-eyed Junco. The piercing calls of Mountain Quail can be heard in the spring, coming from the nearby manzanita slopes.

Salmon Creek Campground can have good birding in late May and early June just after the snow has mostly melted, and before the campground begins filling up with campers. It is especially good at this time of year because the willows have not yet come out in full leaf, and the birds can be seen easily. The willow flats along the creek adjacent to the campground can have summer visitors such as Western Wood-Pewee; Warbling Vireo; Yellow, Yellow-rumped, MacGillivray's, and Wilson's Warblers; Western Tanager; Green-tailed Towhee; and Fox Sparrow. The nearby forest has residents such as Red-breasted Sapsucker and White-headed Woodpecker.

The section of the **North Yuba River** paralleling CA 49 from Sierra City to Bassett's Station has rocky sections and waterfalls, offering the kind of habitat preferred by American Dippers. Beginning about 3 miles from Sierra City, and for the next mile, the road comes close to the river. An especially good place to park is at 3.1 miles from Sierra City, where there is a short paved loop road about 200 yards long on the left side of the road with lots of parking. Dippers generally like to stick near whitewater, so watch the water-washed rocks for a small dark gray bird foraging along. A dipper frequently will fly a short distance along a stream between foraging stops, and sometimes may plunge out of sight into the water.

The store at **Bassett's Station** (cafe, store, gas, and motel; open all year) generally has hummingbird feeders out, and is a good place to look for Calliope (uncommon) and Anna's Hummingbirds in summer. Rufous Hummingbirds are fairly common in July and August during migration. The feeders are on the second story, so it is necessary to view the birds from the parking lot in front of the store. Band-tailed Pigeons are fairly common in the surrounding trees, and Steller's Jays are everywhere. There is a large public parking lot below the store at the junction, as well as public restrooms.

General information: CA 49 climbs from 4,100 feet at Sierra City to 6,700 feet at Yuba Pass, paralleling the North Yuba River all the way. At the pass there is a dirt road to the north that doesn't get a lot of traffic and thus is attractive to birders. There is also a road to the south, which is a high-standard gravel road (Forest Road 12), but this road gets a good deal of traffic and is less appealing to birders.

ADDITIONAL HELP

NCA&G grid: Page 70, 3D.
Elevation: 4,100 to 6,700 feet.
Hazards: Fast traffic, rattlesnakes, ticks.
Nearest food, gas, lodging: Sierra City; Bassett's Station.
Camping: Yuba Pass: 20 sites, 13.7 miles east of Sierra City, on CA 49. Chapman Creek: 29 sites, 9.9 miles east of Sierra City, on CA 49. Sierra: 16 sites, 9.1 miles east of Sierra City, on CA 49. Sardine: 29 sites, 7 miles east of Sierra City on CA 49 to Bassett's Station, then turn north on Gold Lake Road 1.3 miles and turn west on the Packer Lake Road to Sardine Lake. Salmon Creek: 32 sites, 7 miles east of Sierra City on CA 49 to Bassett's Station, then 1.5 miles north on Gold Lake Road.
For more information: Downieville Ranger District.

27 Sierra Valley

Habitats: Freshwater marsh, sagebrush scrub, meadow.
Specialty birds: *Resident*—Black-billed Magpie. *Summer*—White-faced Ibis, Cinnamon Teal, Sandhill Crane, Mountain Bluebird, Sage Thrasher, Brewer's Sparrow, Yellow-headed Blackbird. *Winter*—Ferruginous Hawk.
Other key birds: *Resident*—Horned Lark. *Summer*—American White Pelican, Black-crowned Night-Heron, Redhead, Ruddy Duck, Virginia Rail, Sora, Black-necked Stilt, American Avocet, Willet, Common Snipe, Wilson's Phalarope, Common Nighthawk, Vesper Sparrow.
Best times to bird: April through June.

Directions: From the junction of California Highway 49 and California Highway 89 in Sierraville, go 3.9 miles west on CA 49/89 to Sattley, and turn north on Westside Road, which later becomes County Road A-23. Go north on Westside Road 10.6 miles to **Marble Hot Springs Road** (sandy dirt road, shown as Dyson Lane on some maps); there are some electrical transformers just north of the intersection). Turn east on Marble Hot Springs Road. From Portola, go east 3.9 miles on California Highway 70 to CR A-23 and turn south. Go 4.7 miles to Marble Hot Springs Road.

The birding: Most of the birds of interest are associated with the marshes, and **Marble Hot Springs Road** is the best place to be, especially where the road crosses the streams that join to become the Middle Fork of the Feather River. Marble Hot Springs Road (about 3 miles long) is sandy and not especially dusty. Best of all, it has little traffic. In breeding season (late April through June), being in the marshes in the early morning is a wonderful experience. The Marsh Wrens are chattering, the Willets are "singing," the Common Snipes are winnowing overhead, the White-faced Ibises are squawking, and the Yellow-headed Blackbirds are groaning out their love songs and sounding very much as if they were being strangled to death. All of the above birds breed here, as do Black-crowned Night-Herons, Gadwalls, Northern Pintails, Cinnamon Teal, Redheads, Ruddy Ducks, Black-necked Stilts, American Avocets, and Wilson's Phalaropes.

Sandhill Cranes are fairly common breeders, but a scope is probably going to be necessary to pick them out at a distance. American White Pelicans may be present, but do not breed here. Virginia Rails and Soras are uncommon breeders, and are more likely to be heard than seen. Willets and Common Snipes, on the other hand, often stand right up on the tops of fenceposts in plain view. In the sagebrush sections, Horned Lark, Savannah Sparrow, and Western Meadowlark are common. Sage Thrasher and Brewer's and Vesper Sparrows are less common. The best way to identify a distant Brewer's Sparrow is by its buzzy, lengthy song, which sometimes goes on so long it appears the bird must run out of breath. A Black-billed Magpie or a Mountain Bluebird could turn up anywhere. Red-winged and Brewer's Blackbirds are abundant.

 Sierra Valley

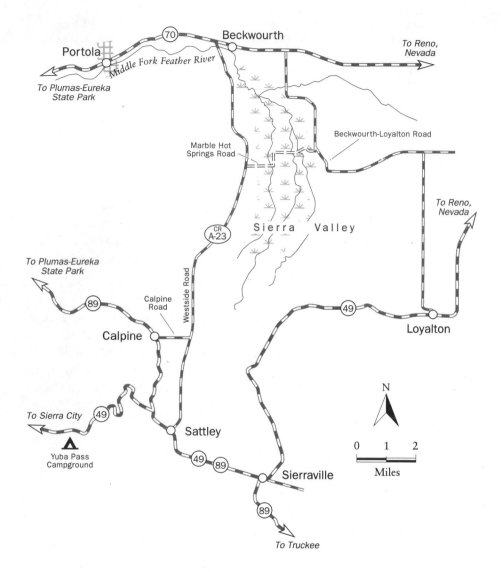

Anywhere in the valley it is worthwhile to keep an eye on the sky for Common Nighthawk (summer), and for raptors. In winter this is a good place for Ferruginous Hawk.

General information: Sierra Valley is an unusual place—a vast, high mountain valley rimmed with forested mountains. The valley floor is not completely flat, but is slightly undulating, creating expanses of marsh alternating with sagebrush. It is not quite Great Basin country, and not quite mountain country, but shares characteristics of both regions.

Common Snipe at Sierra Valley. It's not clear whether this bird is one-legged, or is merely holding one leg up into its belly feathers.

ADDITIONAL HELP

NCA&G grid: Page 71, 5C.

Elevation: 5,000 feet.

Hazards: Fast traffic, rattlesnakes, ticks.

Nearest food, gas, lodging: Portola.

Camping: Yuba Pass: 20 sites, 6 miles west of the junction of CA 49 and CA 89 west of Sattley, at Yuba Pass, on CA 49. Plumas-Eureka State Park: 67 sites; from the junction of CA 70 and CA 89 west of Portola, go about 0.8 mile south on CA 89, turn west on County Road A-14, and go 5 miles to the park.

For more information: Sierraville Ranger District.

28 Donner Country

Habitats: Stream, riparian woodland, mixed conifer forest, sagebrush scrub, meadow.

Specialty birds: *Resident*—Williamson's Sapsucker, White-headed Woodpecker, Pygmy Nuthatch, American Dipper. *Summer*—Calliope Hummingbird; Western Wood-Pewee; Willow and Hammond's Flycatchers; Hermit Warbler; Western Tanager; Green-tailed Towhee.

Other key birds: *Resident*—Hairy Woodpecker, Dark-eyed Junco. *Summer*—Spotted Sandpiper; Warbling Vireo; Yellow-rumped Warbler; Chipping and Fox Sparrows.

Best times to bird: Late April through July.

28 Donner Country

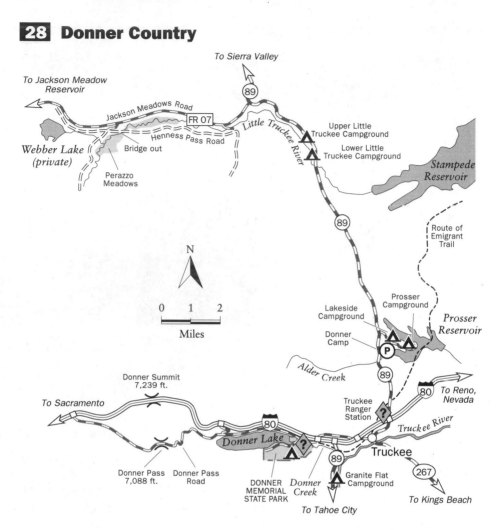

Directions: Donner Memorial State Park is on Interstate 80, about 105 miles (2 hours) east of Sacramento, and about 1 mile west of the "west junction" of I-80 and California Highway 89, adjacent to Donner Lake. Note that CA 89 intersects I-80 twice, once just to the west of Truckee (the "west junction") and once just to the east of Truckee (the "east junction"). Exit from I-80 at a sign that reads "Donner State Park," and go west 0.3 mile on Donner Pass Road to the park entrance (parking, restrooms, no fee to view the Donner Monument or walk the nature trail). To get to **Donner Camp** from Donner Memorial State Park, take I-80 east about 3 miles to where CA 89 goes north toward Sierraville (the "east junction"). Donner Camp is about 2.8 miles north of I-80 on CA 89, and is marked by a USDA Forest Service sign reading "Donner Camp Historical Site." To get to **Perazzo Meadows,** go north for about 14 miles on CA 89 from I-80, and turn left (west) on Forest Road 07 (Jackson Meadows Road, paved); the turnoff for Perazzo Meadows is about 5.4 miles west.

The birding: From the front of the museum next to the parking lot at **Donner Memorial State Park,** walk to the south on the nature trail. The trail leads past the site of one of the cabins of the Donner Party, crosses Donner Creek, and returns through the meadows. Steller's Jay, Mountain Chickadee, American Robin, Yellow-rumped Warbler, Song Sparrow, and Dark-eyed Junco are the most visible species, but others are Calliope Hummingbird; White-headed and Hairy Woodpeckers; Western Wood-Pewee; Hammond's Flycatcher; Warbling Vireo; Hermit Warbler; and Chipping Sparrow.

The habitats at **Donner Camp** are somewhat different from those at the state park. Many of the birds are the same, but there is a lot of sagebrush near Donner Camp, attractive habitat for Green-tailed Towhees and Fox Sparrows. Look also for Williamson's Sapsucker, Western Wood-Pewee, and Pygmy Nuthatch. There is a barrier-free loop trail here with sections of boardwalk, about 0.7 mile round trip.

Perazzo Meadows is one of the places in California where Willow Flycatcher is known to nest. The area around the meadows offers some attractive birding, but one of the problems is that much of the land is under private ownership and thus is off-limits to birders. However, some of the land is owned by the USDA Forest Service as is described later.

The sign for Perazzo Meadows is on FR 07 about 5.4 miles west of CA 89. Turn left at the sign onto a gravel road, and descend toward the river. In 0.7 mile the road comes to a junction (referred to herein as "the crossroads") with the old

Donner Camp, where Green-tailed Towhees and Fox Sparrows frequent the sagebrush.

129

Henness Pass Road. The roads leading to the areas of greatest birding interest are the ones to the left and straight ahead. The one to the right leads up the canyon, away from the river, and eventually rejoins FR 07.

If you take the road to the left, in about 0.5 mile you will come to the Little Truckee River. The land on both sides of the road belongs to the USDA Forest Service, but just before the river it changes to private ownership. At the time this guide went to press, the bridge across the river was washed out (it might have been rebuilt since then). When I was there, an American Dipper was building a nest in the framework of the ruined bridge. Willow Flycatchers nest in the nearby willows, and Western Wood-Pewee, Warbling Vireo, Western Tanager, and Chipping Sparrow (all summer visitors) are in the nearby woods.

Back at the crossroads, if you take the road straight ahead and then turn left in about 100 yards on a dirt road (passable for ordinary cars if not too muddy), you will come to the river in about 0.2 mile. From this point downstream to just before the ruined bridge is all USDA Forest Service land. Here you can walk easily in an open forest, near the meadows. It is possible to remain just within the forest margin, or on the meadows' dry, gravelly edges, and get good views without having to venture into the easily damaged meadows themselves. Birds to look for, besides the Willow Flycatcher, are Yellow Warbler, and Song and White-crowned Sparrows in the willows, Spotted Sandpiper along the marshy edges, and Mountain Chickadee, Yellow-rumped Warbler, Chipping Sparrow, and Cassin's Finch in the woods.

General information: Most people have heard of the tragedy of the Donner party of 1846, and probably know that they camped near Donner Lake. They had been delayed by controversy and bad luck, and when they tried to cross the summit in late October they were turned back by deep snow, and were forced to camp for the winter. Most of the party were at Donner Lake, but some, such as the Donners themselves, couldn't make it that far and had to stop a few miles back along the trail near Alder Creek. The latter is the location now known as Donner Camp. Both groups endured frightful hardships, and some of them finally resorted to cannibalism. Of the 87 original members of the party, 40 died.

ADDITIONAL HELP

NCA&G grid: Page 81, 4A, 6B.
Elevation: 5,900 feet.
Nearest food, gas, lodging: Truckee.
Camping: Donner Memorial State Park: 154 sites. Granite Flat: 74 sites, 1.5 miles south of I-80, on CA 89. Lakeside: 30 undesignated sites, 3.6 miles north of I-80 on CA 89, then 1 mile east on paved access road; gravel interior roads. Prosser: 29 sites, 3.6 miles north of I-80 on CA 89, then 1.5 miles east on paved access road; deteriorating pavement on interior roads. Lower Little Truckee: 15 sites, 11.1 miles north of I-80 on CA 89; gravel interior roads. Upper Little Truckee: 26 sites, 11.7 miles north of I-80 on CA 89; gravel interior roads.
For more information: Donner Memorial State Park; Truckee Ranger District.

29 Mosquito Ridge

Habitats: Yellow pine forest, mixed conifer forest.
Specialty birds: *Resident*—Blue Grouse, Spotted Owl, Acorn Woodpecker. *Summer*—Flammulated Owl, Common Poorwill, Western Wood-Pewee, Hermit Warbler, Western Tanager, Black-headed Grosbeak.
Other key birds: *Resident*—Northern Saw-whet Owl; Red-breasted and White-breasted Nuthatches; Winter Wren; Golden-crowned Kinglet. *Summer*—Hermit Thrush, Nashville Warbler.
Best times to bird: May through early June.

Directions: From junction of Interstate 80 and California Highway 49 in Auburn, go 1.7 miles east on I-80 to the Foresthill exit. Go east on Foresthill Road 16.5 miles to Mosquito Ridge Road in Foresthill, and turn right, toward French Meadows. Travel 17.5 miles east on Mosquito Ridge Road (Forest Road 96) to **Little Oak Flat Road** on the right. (Note the milepost markers, on paddle-shaped signs along the road.) This is a one-way dirt road that leads to Little Oak Flat in about a mile. For **Placer County Big Trees Grove,** continue on Mosquito Ridge Road for 6.7 miles, and follow the signs to Big Trees Grove.

The birding: Flammulated Owl is a "jinx bird" for many people, which means it can be difficult to locate. I tried five different places in California where they allegedly could be found, without success. Then I discovered that, in some circles, Mosquito Ridge is "famous" for Flammulated Owl. I went there on a still night in early June, and heard three along the dirt road leading to **Little Oak Flat,** one of them right by the road. One trouble with Flammulated Owls is that they don't seem to respond well to taped calls.

The thing to do is to drive along the dirt road slowly after dark, stopping frequently to listen for their call, a long series of low, mellow hoots. It is wise to get acquainted with this road while it is still daylight, rather than attempting to travel it for the first time in the dark. Also, if the road is muddy, it would be better not to go at all. A further problem is that construction crews have created high, abrupt water-barriers of heaped-up earth in the road, which could cause low-clearance cars to bottom out.

Flammulated Owls have also been reported on Mosquito Ridge Road itself, between Little Oak Flat and the Placer County Big Trees Grove. In addition, Blue Grouse and Common Poorwill have been spotted on this road, because it has relatively little traffic compared with other roads (I saw a Blue Grouse at dusk standing in the middle of the road). Northern Saw-whet Owls have been found along the road at the upper end, near Big Trees Grove.

Little Oak Flat, at about 4,000 feet, has ponderosa pines and black oaks, so the birds here are those associated with this kind of habitat. Flammulated Owls like it and so do Acorn Woodpeckers, Western Wood-Pewees, Western Scrub-Jays, White-breasted Nuthatches, American Robins, Dark-eyed Juncos, and Black-headed Grosbeaks.

29 Mosquito Ridge

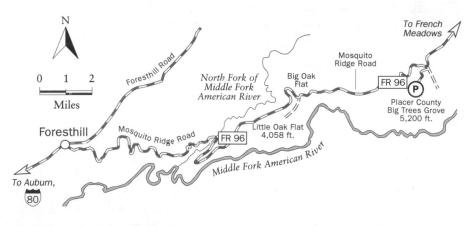

The **Placer County Big Trees Grove,** at about 5,200 feet, has Spotted Owl; Steller's Jay; Red-breasted Nuthatch; Winter Wren; Golden-crowned Kinglet; Townsend's Solitaire; Nashville, Yellow-rumped, and Hermit Warblers; and Western Tanager. Chestnut-backed Chickadees have been seen here, but are more common along the coast. When I was there last, it was just at dusk in early June, and Hermit Thrushes were singing everywhere in the forest.

General information: Mosquito Ridge Road is a paved, two-way road, with many curves, and often traverses steep mountainsides. Mosquito Ridge is a narrow, high ridge in a land of deep canyons and steep mountainsides. Little Oak Flat appears almost out of place, out on the sharp end of Mosquito Ridge. The Placer County Big Trees Grove is the northernmost grove of giant sequoias, and contains only six mature trees. The next grove of giant sequoias is 50 miles to the south, at Calaveras Big Trees State Park.

ADDITIONAL HELP

NCA&G grid: Page 80, 3D.
Elevation: 4,000 to 5,200 feet.
Hazards: Poison oak, rattlesnakes, and ticks.
Nearest food, gas, lodging: Auburn.
Camping: French Meadows: 75 sites, 36 miles east of Foresthill on Mosquito Ridge Road.
For more information: Foresthill Ranger District.

Black-headed Grosbeak.

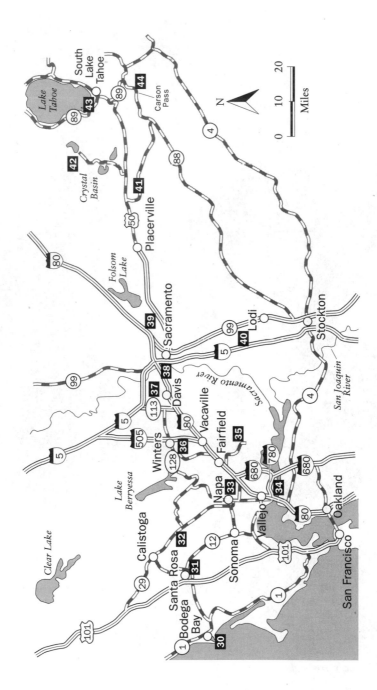

Bodega Bay to Lake Tahoe

The birding sites of Bodega Bay may not be as famous as those of Monterey and Point Reyes, but many people regard them as their equal. The main reason is that the Bay has many kinds of habitats located closely together—cliffs, ocean, bays, and mudflats. At times, the birds show up in amazing numbers. Bodega Bay lies at one end of the birding trail belonging to this region and Lake Tahoe, a world-class attraction in anybody's book, lies at the other. Bodega Bay is one of the best places in the state to observe shorebirds, loons, and other water birds at close range. It also has a long list of pelagic species.

Inland, the lower Sacramento Valley has some of the heaviest concentrations of Yellow-billed Magpies, White-tailed Kites, and Swainson's Hawks to be found anywhere. Both Grizzly Island and Vic Fazio Yolo Wildlife Areas have been declared Globally Important Bird Areas because of their wintering waterfowl. Yolo County is one of the few places in the state where the rare Mountain Plover can be found with reasonable regularity, and Woodbridge Road has thousands of wintering Sandhill Cranes.

Besides Lake Tahoe, the mountains have the lovely Crystal Basin, one of the better places to find White-headed Woodpecker, Black-throated Gray Warbler, Hermit Warbler, and Lazuli Bunting. The trail ends at the spectacular Carson Pass, with Blue Grouse, Clark's Nutcracker, Mountain Chickadee, and Pine Grosbeak.

30 Bodega Bay and the Sonoma Coast

31 Annadel State Park

32 Napa Valley

33 Skyline Wilderness Park

34 Benicia State Recreation Area

35 Grizzly Island and Suisun Marsh

36 Lake Solano and Putah Creek

37 Yolo Farmlands

38 Vic Fazio Yolo Wildlife Area

39 American River

40 Cosumnes River Preserve and Woodbridge Road

41 Sly Park

42 Crystal Basin

43 Lake Tahoe

44 Carson Pass and Hope Valley

30 **Bodega Bay and the Sonoma Coast** 🏛 ♿

Habitats: Pelagic, sandy beach and mudflats, rocky headlands, coastal bays and lagoons, coastal scrub.

Specialty birds: *Resident*—Brandt's and Pelagic Cormorants; White-tailed Kite; Peregrine Falcon; Snowy Plover; Black Oystercatcher; Cassin's Auklet. *Summer*—Black-footed Albatross, Brown Pelican, Cinnamon Teal, Osprey, Heermann's Gull, Elegant Tern, Pigeon Guillemot, Tufted Puffin. *Winter*—Pacific Loon; Western and Clark's Grebes; Laysan Albatross; Short-tailed and Black-vented Shearwaters; Fork-tailed Storm-Petrel; Wandering Tattler; Long-billed Curlew; Black Turnstone; Surfbird; Rock Sandpiper; Mew, Thayer's, and Glaucous-winged Gulls; Ancient and Marbled Murrelets; Rhinoceros Auklet. *Migrant or postbreeding visitor*—Pink-footed, Flesh-footed, and Buller's Shearwaters; Ashy and Black Storm-Petrels; Sabine's Gull; Xantus's and Craveri's Murrelets.

Other key birds: *Resident*—Black-crowned Night-Heron, Common Murre. *Summer*—Sooty Shearwater; Leach's Storm-Petrel; Caspian and Forster's Terns. *Winter*—Red-throated and Common Loons; Horned, Red-necked, and Eared Grebes; Northern Fulmar; Brant; Green-winged Teal; Greater and Lesser Scaups; Black, White-winged, and Surf Scoters; Bufflehead; Common Goldeneye; Red-breasted Merganser; Merlin; Black-bellied and Semipalmated Plovers; Greater Yellowlegs; Whimbrel; Marbled Godwit; Ruddy Turnstone; Sanderling; Long-billed Dowitcher; Black-legged Kittiwake. *Migrant*—Red-necked and Red Phalaropes; South Polar Skua; Pomarine, Parasitic, and Long-tailed Jaegers; Common and Arctic Terns; Short-billed Dowitcher.

Best times to bird: August through November for most pelagic birds. Most waterfowl are present from November to April. Most species of shorebirds are here August through March.

Directions: The name Bodega Bay is applied both to the town and to the bay that lies outside the sand spit that houses Doran Park. The shallow bay that lies adjacent to the town of Bodega Bay is called Bodega Harbor. The name "Bodega" applies to the small town just off California Highway 1, about 5 miles southeast of Bodega Bay. The town of Bodega Bay lies on CA 1, about 25 miles west of U.S. Highway 101 (allow 45 minutes). To get there from Santa Rosa, go west on California Highway 12 through Sebastopol, follow Bodega Highway to the town of Bodega, and then to CA 1. At the junction with CA 1, turn right to reach Bodega Bay.

The birding: To get to what is called the **West Side,** go 0.9 mile north of the town of Bodega Bay on CA 1, and turn left (west). After 0.3 mile, you will intersect Bay Flat Road. **Porto Bodega** lies straight ahead. Bay Flat Road extends to the right, becomes Westshore Road, and runs along the west side of Bodega Harbor.

The road along the west side runs close to the shore. It has bicycle paths on both sides, so it is important when parking not to obstruct these paths. At several points along the way are large dirt parking areas. The northern end of the harbor often has Red-throated, Pacific, and Common Loons; American Wigeon; Mallard;

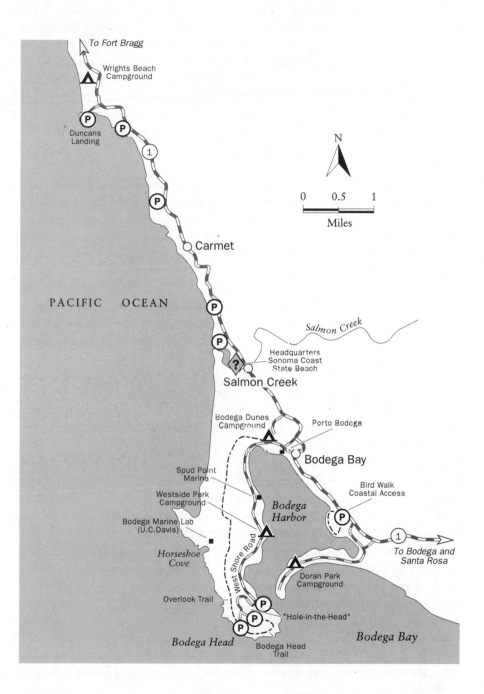

To Fort Bragg

Wrights Beach
Campground

Duncans
Landing

1

N

0   0.5   1

Miles

Carmet

PACIFIC   OCEAN

Salmon Creek

Headquarters
Sonoma Coast
State Beach

?

Salmon Creek

Bodega Dunes
Campground

Porto Bodega

Bodega Bay

Spud Point
Marina

Westside Park
Campground

Bird Walk
Coastal Access

Bodega Marine Lab
(U.C.Davis)

*Bodega
Harbor*

*Horseshoe
Cove*

West Shore Road

To Bodega and
Santa Rosa

Doran Park
Campground

Overlook Trail

"Hole-in-the-Head"

Bodega Head

Bodega Head
Trail

Bodega Bay

Northern Pintail; Green-winged Teal; Greater and Lesser Scaups; Bufflehead; Common Goldeneye; Red-breasted Merganser; Ruddy Duck, American Coot; and Pied-billed, Horned, Red-necked, Eared, Western, and Clark's Grebes. Black, White-winged, and Surf Scoters can be found here. Hundreds of Brant sometimes gather on the mudflats during migration and in winter. Thousands of shorebirds are often present, especially Marbled Godwits and Willets, along with Killdeer; Semipalmated and Black-bellied Plovers; Greater Yellowlegs; Whimbrel; Long-billed Curlew; Ruddy Turnstone; Sanderling; Western and Least Sandpipers; Dunlin; Long-billed and Short-billed Dowitchers; and occasionally a Red Knot. There are usually Great Blue Herons around, and Great and Snowy Egrets. Among the rarities that have turned up in the harbor are Arctic Loon, Emperor Goose, Steller's Eider, and Oldsquaw.

Naturally, there are lots of gulls. The more common ones are Heermann's, Mew, Ring-billed, California, Herring, Thayer's, Western, and Glaucous-winged. Most of them are primarily winter visitors, but the Western Gull breeds here, and Heermann's Gulls show up in late summer and fall, with a few remaining through winter. Brown Pelicans are common in late summer and fall, and American White Pelicans sometimes turn up.

Spud Point Marina is located on the west side, 1.3 miles from CA 1. Just beyond the marina is a gravel parking area near a concrete walkway that partly encircles the boat basin. The walkway allows for close looks at many kinds of birds, especially loons. On one occasion a Cassin's Auklet was found inside the boat basin.

Westside Park (campground) lies about 0.5 mile beyond Spud Point. Just beyond the campground is a large dirt parking area next to the harbor from which extensive mud flats can be scanned at low tide. Shorebirds of all kinds work these flats, and at times it seems as if every Marbled Godwit in California must be here. When shorebirds are present, watch for the possibility of a Merlin.

Bodega Marine Laboratory, operated by the University of California at Davis, lies about 0.5 mile beyond Westside Park. Entrance is restricted, but special tours are available one day a week, as posted on the gate.

Hole-in-the-Head is 3.2 miles from CA 1 (parking, pit toilets). In the 1950s, a major utility company excavated a hole at this location, which was intended to hold a nuclear power plant. However, the Nuclear Safeguards Committee refused to issue a permit for the plant, on the grounds that it was too close to the San Andreas Fault, which runs directly through Bodega Harbor. Today the hole is filled with water, and is part of Sonoma Coast State Beach. It gets its name because it is located on Bodega Head. Hole-in-the-Head usually has ducks and gulls, and Black-crowned Night-Herons often roost in the bushes. The willows just to the south of the "hole" act as a migrant trap, and vagrants from the east often turn up here. The trees around the entrance to the Bodega Marine Laboratory often also have vagrants.

Bodega Head is at the end of the road, about 3.7 miles from CA 1 (parking, pit toilets). This is a popular whale-watching spot in winter, when the California gray whales are migrating. But it is also popular with birders because of the alcids (auks, murres, puffins, and guillemots) that often congregate offshore. Shearwaters can sometimes be seen during strong offshore winds, and this is an excellent location for rock-loving Black Oystercatcher; Wandering Tattler; Ruddy and Black Turnstones; and Surfbird. Black Oystercatchers are year-round residents; the other four are winter visitors. Once in a while, a Rock Sandpiper turns up here in winter.

The alcids most likely to be seen are Common Murre, Pigeon Guillemot, and Rhinoceros Auklet; Marbled and Ancient Murrelets are also possible, but less likely. The only alcid that breeds here is the Pigeon Guillemot, readily recognized by its white wing patches and vivid red legs.

All three Pacific Coast cormorants—Pelagic, Brandt's, and Double-crested— breed along the Sonoma Coast, and are resident year-round. Pelagic and Brandt's Cormorants stick to salt water, and are Pacific Coast specialties, but Double-crested Cormorants occur from coast to coast, and frequently nest near fresh water. The Pelagic Cormorant, especially, is a major breeder on the Sonoma Coast. In the spring, the white patches on the flanks of this otherwise all black bird make it stand out from the others.

A trail about a mile long extends around the head. The trail leads along the cliffs, and you must watch carefully, because in places the cliffs are undercut. More sensational views of rocky headlands and crashing surf can hardly be found anywhere. The trail extends among bushes that afford singing perches for Song, White-crowned, and Savannah Sparrows, all of which are resident. Golden-crowned Sparrows are winter visitors.

The most common raptors are Red-tailed Hawks, which often float on motionless wings when there is a strong wind blowing. Northern Harriers also are common, with Ospreys, White-tailed Kites, and Peregrine Falcons less common.

The area generally referred to as the **Sonoma Coast** extends up CA 1 north of Bodega Bay for about 10 miles, running close to the shore in many places. Almost the entire section lies within Sonoma Coast State Beach. There are many "pocket" beaches along this section of coast, as well as rocky headlands. The birding opportunities and species to be found are similar to those at Bodega Head.

To get to **Doran Beach Regional Park,** go 1 mile south of Bodega Bay, and then follow signs (fee, parking, restrooms, campground). The access road runs near Doran Park Marsh, which usually has ducks and egrets; Cinnamon Teal is a resident.

Doran Park lies on a sand spit separating Bodega Bay from Bodega Harbor. At the extreme end of the spit is a rock jetty that protects the channel leading into the harbor. Close looks at birds can be had along the harbor side of the sand spit where the channel meets the harbor. Buffleheads, grebes, and scoters seem to favor the channel, and shorebirds are often on the flats. Red-necked Grebe (rare) has occurred here.

On the ocean side of the sand spit is a long, curving beach with gentle surf. Loons often lie in this protected bay in winter, and Forster's and Caspian Terns work the surf in summer and fall. Snowy Plovers (uncommon) are here year-round.

A short distance north of the access road to Doran Park is **Bird Walk Coastal Access,** which is a barrier-free trail running along levee tops surrounding dredge disposal ponds (fee, parking, chemical toilets). The trail is about 0.7 mile round trip and gives great views of the harbor. However, you are farther from the birds here than in many places along the west side and on the sand spit at Doran Park.

Pelagic trips leave from **Porto Bodega.** Go 0.9 mile north of Bodega Bay on CA 1, and then 0.3 mile left on the road toward Westside Park. Bodega Bay is becoming more and more known for pelagic (deepwater) trips. A major destination, when the weather permits, is Cordell Bank, which lies about 20 miles offshore. Some species regularly sighted are Black-footed Albatross; Pink-footed, Buller's, and Sooty Shearwaters; and Ashy Storm-Petrel. Seen less often are Flesh-footed, Short-tailed, and Black-vented Shearwaters, and Laysan Albatross. Still less frequent are Fork-tailed, Leach's, and Black Storm-Petrels; and Marbled, Xantus's, and Craveri's Murrelets. Northern Fulmar and Black-legged Kittiwake show up irregularly.

Pomarine and Parasitic Jaegers; Sabine's Gull; and Elegant, Common, and Arctic Terns are often seen in fall. Long-tailed Jaeger and South Polar Skua are spotted less often. Red and Red-necked Phalaropes are common during spring and fall migration. Occasionally a Tufted Puffin appears. In the extremely rare category are two "gadfly petrels," Murphy's and Cook's Petrels. Although these are rare, they appear to be regular along the California coast. Some extreme rarities that have shown up are Great-winged and Dark-rumped Petrels, and Light-mantled Sooty Albatross.

Not all target species will be seen on any given trip, of course, partly because they occur in different seasons. The bar charts in Chapter 8 will help in determining which species are likely to show up in certain seasons. It will probably take several boat trips before you see all the species you are after.

For more information on pelagic trips, contact Shearwater Journeys, an organization that has been offering pelagic trips for many years, and also conducts pelagic trips out of Monterey and Santa Cruz. A newer organization, Mollymawk Offshore Adventures, is now also offering pelagic trips out of Bodega Bay. (See Appendix A for addresses and telephone numbers of both organizations.)

General information: From a birder's point of view, there is hardly any other place where such a variety of birds can be seen (mostly in winter), and at reasonably close range. On weekends and during vacation periods, the roads and parking areas can be crowded, because Sonoma Coast is California's second most popular state park (Old Town San Diego is number one). But during the week in winter you can have the place almost to yourself, and that is when the birds are at their best. One of Bodega Bay's claims to fame is that it was the site for the Alfred

Hitchcock thriller *The Birds,* released in 1963. Some of the shots were taken in Bodega Bay, and others were taken in the nearby village of Bodega.

Bodega Bay has been classified as a Globally Important Bird Area because it is an important migrant stopover and wintering area for waterbirds and shorebirds, and also because California Black Rail and Snowy Plover have been recorded there.

ADDITIONAL HELP

NCA&G grid: Pages 92, 93, 4B.
Elevation: Sea level.
Hazards: Poison oak, ticks.
Nearest food, gas, lodging: Bodega Bay.
Camping: Wrights Beach: 30 sites, 6.5 miles north of Bodega Bay on CA 1. Bodega Dunes: 98 sites, 1.5 miles north of Bodega Bay on CA 1; RV dump station. Westside Park: 48 sites, 1.8 miles from CA 1 on west side of Bodega Harbor. Doran Park: 134 sites, about 1 mile south of Bodega Bay on CA 1; RV dump station.
For more information: Sonoma Coast State Beach; Doran Beach Regional Park; Shearwater Journeys; Mollymawk Offshore Adventures.

31 Annadel State Park

Habitats: Mixed redwood and Douglas-fir forest, freshwater marsh, lake, foothill woodland.
Specialty birds: *Resident*—Nuttall's Woodpecker, Hutton's Vireo, Chestnut-backed Chickadee, Western Bluebird, Lesser Goldfinch. *Summer*—Western Wood-Pewee; Pacific-slope and Ash-throated Flycatchers; Cassin's Vireo; Violet-green Swallow; Black-throated Gray Warbler; Black-headed Grosbeak; Lazuli Bunting; Bullock's Oriole.
Other key birds: *Resident*—Cooper's and Red-shouldered Hawks; Wild Turkey; Virginia Rail; Great Horned Owl; Hairy and Pileated Woodpeckers; Winter Wren; Hermit Thrush; Purple Finch. *Summer*—Olive-sided Flycatcher; Warbling Vireo; Swainson's Thrush; Orange-crowned, Yellow, and Wilson's Warblers.
Best times to bird: April through July for breeding species.

Directions: Go east on California Highway 12 from Santa Rosa, turn right (south) at Mission Boulevard, left on Montgomery Drive, and right on Channel Drive, watching for signs for Annadel State Park (fee).

The birding: W. P. Richardson Trail, a 5-mile round trip to **Lake Ilsanjo,** takes you through Douglas-fir forest, meadows, and mixed oak woodland. The trail begins at the northwest corner of the parking lot at the end of Channel Drive. You can use the Steve's "S" Trail for the return.

31 Annadel State Park

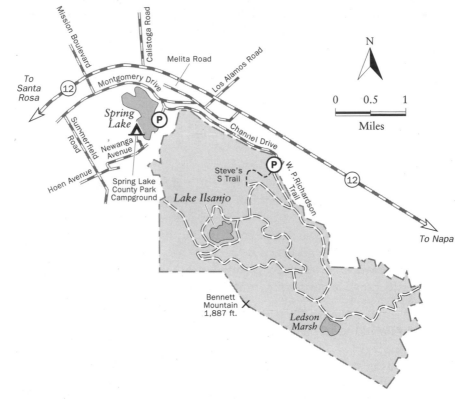

The forested portion is a good place to find resident Great Horned Owl; Pileated and Hairy Woodpeckers; Steller's Jay; Brown Creeper; Winter Wren; Hermit Thrush; and Purple Finch, and summer breeders such as Olive-sided and Pacific-slope Flycatchers; Western Wood-Pewee; and Cassin's Vireo.

In more open areas, look for resident birds such as Red-shouldered and Cooper's Hawks; Acorn and Nuttall's Woodpeckers; Oak Titmouse; Chestnut-backed Chickadee; Bushtit; Bewick's Wren; Western Bluebird; and Lesser Goldfinch, and summer breeders such as Ash-throated Flycatcher; Orange-crowned and Black-throated Gray Warblers; Black-headed Grosbeak; and Lazuli Bunting. Dark-eyed Juncos and California and Spotted Towhees are common.

Birds that favor riparian habitats are resident Downy Woodpecker, Black Phoebe, and Hutton's Vireo, and summer breeders such as Warbling Vireo; Tree and Violet-green Swallows; Swainson's Thrush; Yellow and Wilson's Warblers; and Bullock's Oriole.

Lake Ilsanjo is a pleasant spot bordered by marsh that has Pied-billed Grebes, Mallards, Ruddy Ducks, and Virginia Rails. In the oak woodland on the way to the lake, be sure to look for Wild Turkeys.

General information: Annadel State Park has 35 miles of trails in a 5,000-acre "wilderness at your doorstep" on the eastern edge of populous Santa Rosa. It is a delightful place, with mature forest on the north-facing slope, even including a few small groves of redwoods. Much of it is oak woodland, considered to be the best example of this kind of forest in public ownership. Be warned, however, that the park sees heavy use by horses and bicycles.

ADDITIONAL HELP

NCA&G grid: Page 93, 7A.
Elevation: 350 to 1,000 feet.
Hazards: Poison oak, rattlesnakes, ticks.
Nearest food, gas, lodging: Santa Rosa.
Camping: Spring Lake County Park; from the junction of Mission Boulevard and Montgomery Drive, turn west on Montgomery Drive, then left at Summerfield Road, and follow signs; open only on weekends in winter.
For more information: Annadel State Park; Spring Lake County Park.

32 Napa Valley 🏛

Habitats: Redwood forest, Douglas-fir forest, lake, riparian woodland.
Specialty birds: *Resident*—Western and Clark's Grebes; Wood Duck; Osprey; Golden Eagle; Western Screech-Owl; Northern Pygmy-Owl; Spotted Owl; Nuttall's Woodpecker; Hutton's Vireo; Chestnut-backed Chickadee; Rock Wren; Western Bluebird; Wrentit; Rufous-crowned Sparrow; Lesser Goldfinch. *Summer*—Pacific-slope and Ash-throated Flycatchers; Cassin's Vireo; Black-throated Gray Warbler; Black-headed Grosbeak. *Winter*—Bald Eagle, Say's Phoebe, Varied Thrush.
Other key birds: *Resident*—Red-shouldered Hawk, Wild Turkey, Northern Saw-whet Owl, Pileated Woodpecker, Winter Wren, Lark Sparrow. *Summer*—Olive-sided Flycatcher; Warbling Vireo; Orange-crowned, Yellow, and Wilson's Warblers; Yellow-breasted Chat; Chipping Sparrow. *Winter*—Fox Sparrow.
Best times to bird: Winter for most birds; April through July for summer breeders.

Directions: Napa Valley extends for about 30 miles along California Highway 29; from Napa to Calistoga. For directions to individual sites, see the following descriptions.

The birding: To get to **Bothe–Napa Valley State Park:** From the junction of California Highway 12/121, California Highway 12/29, and California Highway 29/121 southwest of Napa, go about 24 miles north on CA 29 to the park entrance on the

32 Napa Valley

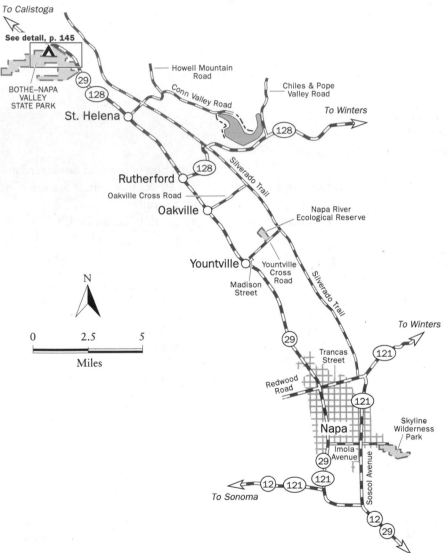

To Calistoga

See detail, p. 145

BOTHE–NAPA
VALLEY
STATE PARK

29
128

St. Helena

Howell Mountain
Road

Conn Valley Road

Chiles & Pope
Valley Road

To Winters

128

Rutherford

128

Oakville Cross Road

Oakville

Silverado Trail

Napa River
Ecological Reserve

Yountville

Yountville
Cross
Road

Madison
Street

Silverado Trail

N

0   2.5   5
Miles

29

Trancas
Street

121

To Winters

Redwood
Road

121

Skyline
Wilderness
Park

Napa

Imola
Avenue

Soscol Avenue

29

12   121

121

To Sonoma

12
29

To Vallejo

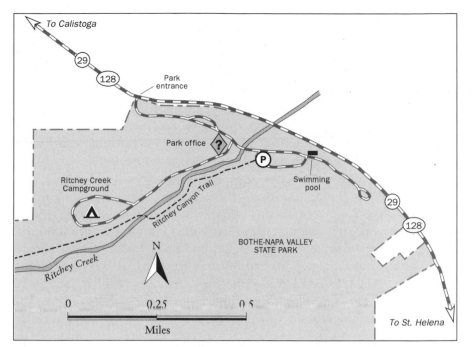

Bothe–Napa Valley State Park detail.

left (fee, parking, restrooms). The big attractions here are Spotted Owl and Pileated Woodpecker. To find these birds, it is generally necessary to hike up the canyon on the Ritchey Canyon Trail, in the mixed Douglas-fir and redwood forest. Because there are only five to six pairs of Pileated Woodpeckers and only one pair of Spotted Owls, take care not to cause any disturbance. The place to look for Spotted Owl is near the redwood flat about 2 miles up the Ritchey Canyon Trail.

Some other residents are Western Screech-Owl, Northern Pygmy-Owl, Northern Saw-whet Owl, Nuttall's Woodpecker, Hutton's Vireo, Steller's Jay, Chestnut-backed Chickadee, Winter Wren, Wrentit, Spotted Towhee, and Lesser Goldfinch. Varied Thrush, Fox Sparrow, and Pine Siskin (irregular) are winter visitors, and Olive-sided and Ash-throated Flycatchers; Cassin's and Warbling Vireos; Black-throated Gray and Wilson's Warblers; Chipping Sparrow; and Black-headed Grosbeak are summer breeders.

To get to the **Napa River Ecological Reserve,** from the junction of CA 12/121, CA 12/29, and CA 29/121 southwest of Napa, go 10.8 miles north on CA 29 to the Madison Street turnoff into Yountville. Turn right (east) and go 0.2 mile to Yount Street, jog left and then right onto Yountville Cross Road. Go 1 mile to Napa River Ecological Reserve on the left (parking, chemical toilet). The reserve has a delightful loop trail about 1 mile long that leads through a riparian forest. Take the trail across the field, over the levee, and into the riparian area (follow the arrows). Walk upstream about 50 yards and watch carefully for the trail, which goes down into the riverbed and across a narrow footbridge. The area may be flooded at high water.

This is a spot that regularly gets Yellow-breasted Chats in the breeding season. Look for Nuttall's Woodpecker, Chestnut-backed Chickadee, Oak Titmouse, Bushtit, and California and Spotted Towhees among the resident birds, and Pacific-slope Flycatcher, Cassin's Vireo, and Orange-crowned and Yellow Warblers among the summer breeders. Wood Ducks are present occasionally.

Lake Hennessey: From Rutherford, at the junction of CA 29 and California Highway 128, go 2.8 miles east on CA 128 to the junction with Silverado Trail. CA 128 goes to the right, and then immediately left, to take you to the south shore of the lake. There are turnouts along CA 128, and a boat launching ramp about 3 miles from Silverado Trail (fee, parking, restrooms). To go to the north shore from the junction of CA 128 and Silverado Trail, turn left on Silverado Trail and go 3.2 miles to Howell Mountain Road. Turn right (east) and go 1.1 miles to Conn Valley Road, then turn right and go about 3 miles to a small bridge that crosses the inlet stream to the lake. A gate on the right gives access to a dirt road (open for hiking) that runs along the west shore of the lake. If you continue on Conn Valley Road, after about 1 mile you will come to the end. There is also a gate here, and a dirt road (open for hiking) runs along the north shore (no fee, unless you plan to fish or launch a boat). The only parking is on wide dirt shoulders.

The **west shore** is well wooded. Look for Red-shouldered Hawk; Nuttall's and Pileated Woodpeckers; Bushtit; Wrentit; Spotted and California Towhees; and Golden-crowned Sparrow (winter).

From the end of Conn Valley Road, the path along the **north shore** gives good views of the lake. The lake usually has Ruddy Ducks and Western and Clark's Grebes. In winter it may have Bald Eagles and Bonaparte's Gulls. On the dry slopes you may find Rock Wren and Rufous-crowned Sparrow, both resident. Golden Eagles occasionally soar over the ridges, and Ospreys work the lake.

The road along the **south shore** gives views of the lake from various wide pullouts and finally intersects Chiles and Pope Valley Road about 4 miles from Silverado Trail (the lake ends in another 0.5 mile). Wild Turkey, Say's Phoebe, Western Bluebird, and Lark Sparrow occur in this area.

General information: Napa Valley is renowned worldwide for its wines. North of the city of Napa, the wineries line the road from Yountville to Calistoga, and the crowds are heavy on holidays and weekends. However, excellent birding opportunities also exist in Napa Valley, sometimes only a short distance from the bustling tourists.

ADDITIONAL HELP

NCA&G grid: Page 84, 1D; page 94, 2A.
Elevation: 300 to 1,000 feet.
Hazards: Rattlesnakes, poison oak, ticks.
Nearest food, gas, lodging: Napa.
Camping: Ritchey Creek Campground, Bothe–Napa Valley State Park: 50 sites, 24 miles north of Napa on CA 29.
For more information: Bothe–Napa Valley State Park; Napa River Ecological Reserve, Department of Fish and Game (Yountville).

33 Skyline Wilderness Park

Habitats: Lake, riparian woodland, foothill woodland, chaparral.
Specialty birds: *Resident*—Golden Eagle, Band-tailed Pigeon, Western Screech-Owl, Northern Pygmy-Owl, Nuttall's Woodpecker, Steller's Jay, Oak Titmouse, Wrentit, California Thrasher. *Summer*—Lazuli Bunting. *Winter*—Varied Thrush.
Other key birds: *Resident*—Red-shouldered Hawk, Wild Turkey, Belted Kingfisher, White-breasted Nuthatch. *Winter*—Cooper's Hawk.
Best times to bird: November through March for wintering species; April through July for breeding species.

Directions: At the junction of California Highway 29 and California Highway 29/ 121 southwest of Napa, go east about 1.5 miles on CA 121 to Soscol Avenue. Continue straight across Soscol Avenue and go 1.3 miles to the park entrance (fee, parking, restrooms).

The birding: Skyline Park has about 25 miles of trail, most of which are open to horses and bicycles. The **Main Trail** is about 5 miles round trip, with 600 feet elevation gain. Besides offering good birding opportunities, the trail is noted for its wildflower displays in the spring.

The Main Trail departs from the southwest corner of the parking lot, and soon passes the Martha Walker Garden. A small pond near the garden has had Wood Ducks on it. Birders are welcome to enjoy both the garden and pond. The trail heads for an opening in the fence called the Corridor. Visitors should not enter the sidegates along the Corridor, because the areas on both sides belong to the Napa State Hospital.

There are small ponds on both sides of the Corridor that may have Black Phoebes and Wood Ducks. The oaks along here can abound with small birds such as White-breasted Nuthatch; Ruby-crowned Kinglet; California Towhee; White-crowned and Golden-crowned Sparrows; and Dark-eyed Junco. White-throated Sparrow (rare) has occurred here in winter.

Beyond the corridor the forest is more open. This is a good place for Nuttall's and Acorn Woodpeckers; Steller's Jay; and Western Scrub-Jay. Gray squirrels abound.

33 Skyline Wilderness Park

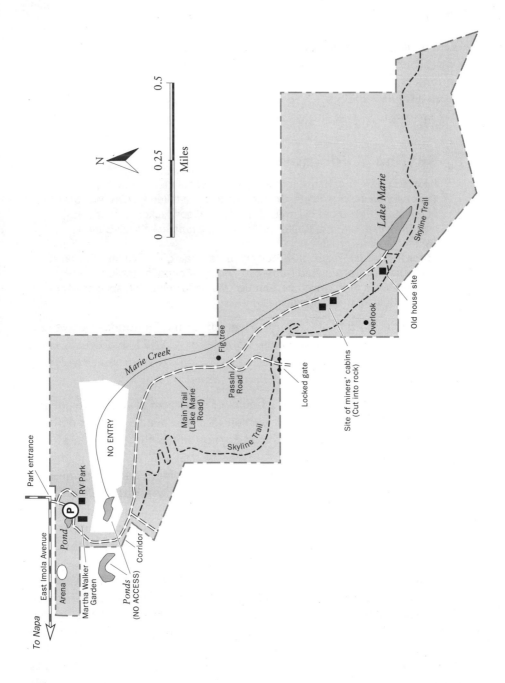

The trail ascends into the open, and about a mile from the beginning, passes into a valley with chaparral on the slopes. The songs of Wrentits and the calls of California Quail are heard here. Flocks of Band-tailed Pigeons have been seen, although they are nomadic and may not occur every year. Also, look for Anna's Hummingbird, Bushtit, Bewick's Wren, California Thrasher, and Spotted Towhee.

The trail enters a shaded forest with oaks and California bay laurels. This is Varied Thrush habitat (winter), although they can be common one year and absent the next. Oak Titmice are common. Red-shouldered and Cooper's Hawks, and Western Screech-Owls occur here. At one point there are several large recesses carved into the rock, which reportedly were once roofed over and used by miners.

Lake Marie provides a tranquil spot for hikers and birders to rest on a bench overlooking the lake. Mallards, American Coots, and Pied-billed Grebes seem to be the most common occupants, with an occasional Belted Kingfisher. Lazuli Bunting (summer) and Northern Pygmy-Owl have been found at the upper end of the lake, and Wild Turkeys might pop up anywhere.

An alternative route for your return is via the Skyline Trail, which at one point gives a view of San Pablo Bay and Mount Tamalpais. Turkey Vultures and Common Ravens will probably be soaring in the sky. Golden Eagles nest in the nearby mountains and are occasionally seen.

General information: Skyline Wilderness Park lies only a mile or so from the busy thoroughfares of Napa. The part of the park adjacent to the entrance is managed for intensive recreation, with horse arenas, an archery range, RV park, and picnic grounds. (Open Monday through Thursday from 9 A.M. to 5 P.M.., and Friday through Sunday from 8 A.M. to 5 P.M.)

ADDITIONAL HELP

NCA&G grid: Page 94, 4B.
Elevation: 200 to 1,000 feet.
Hazards: Signs warn against wild pigs, rattlesnakes, poison oak, and ticks.
Nearest food, gas, lodging: Napa.
Camping: RV park on-site; tent camping in spring and summer. Bothe–Napa Valley State Park: 50 sites, 24 miles north of Napa on CA 29.
For more information: Skyline Park Citizen's Association.

34 Benicia State Recreation Area

Habitats: Coastal bays and lagoons, salt marsh, coastal scrub.
Specialty birds: *Resident*—White-tailed Kite; Black and Clapper Rails.
Summer—Brown Pelican, Allen's Hummingbird. *Winter*—Western and
Clark's Grebes.
Other key birds: *Resident*—American Bittern, Black-crowned Night-
Heron, Northern Harrier, Virginia Rail, Sora, Loggerhead Shrike, Marsh
Wren. *Summer*—Common Yellowthroat. *Winter*—Spotted Sandpiper,
Lincoln's Sparrow.
Best times to bird: November to March for grebes, most waterfowl, and
wintering sparrows; April to July for breeding songbirds.

Directions: From the junction of Interstate 80 and Interstate 780 in Vallejo, take I-780 east 2.7 miles to the exit for Columbus Parkway. Get off the interchange, turn right, and immediately turn left into the main entrance for **Benicia State Recreation Area** (fee, parking, restrooms). For the **east parking area,** get back onto I-780 going east, and exit at the first interchange onto Military West. At the stop sign, turn right and then immediately turn right again, to the parking area (fee, parking, no restrooms).

The birding: Turn right after the main entrance, go to T intersection and turn left toward **Dillon Point** (parking, restrooms). From this point it is possible to scope the bay for Western and Clark's Grebes, and for rafts of ducks. Eurasian Wigeon, Tufted Duck, Oldsquaw, and Barrow's Goldeneye have been seen here. You can also descend the steps to a trail along the edge of the bay that goes to Dillon Point, about 0.2 mile. Terns and Brown Pelicans occur in spring and summer, and Spotted Sandpiper may be present in winter. Check any trees for roosting Black-crowned Night-Herons.

East parking area. Views into the bay can be had from here, plus close views of birds working the shore. There is a bicycle trail, and a footpath begins at the southwestern corner of the parking lot, goes out past the marsh, and rejoins the bicycle path (about 0.7 mile round trip). Here you might see American Bittern, Clapper Rail, Virginia Rail, and Sora. Black Rails occur here, although they are difficult to see.

At almost any time of year the chatter of Marsh Wrens can be heard. Anna's Hummingbird, California Towhee, and Song Sparrow are resident, and Allen's Hummingbird and Common Yellowthroat are summer visitors. In winter Lincoln's, Golden-crowned, and White-crowned Sparrows are present. White-tailed Kite, Northern Harrier, Red-tailed Hawk, and American Kestrel can occur anywhere and any time of year. Watch for Loggerhead Shrikes, which are declining in some parts of the country.

General information: Benicia State Recreation Area sits where the flow from the Sacramento–San Joaquin river system meets the incoming tides from San Pablo Bay. The sheltered Southampton Bay adjoins the strait, and provides a resting place for grebes and rafts of ducks in winter.

34 Benicia State Recreation Area

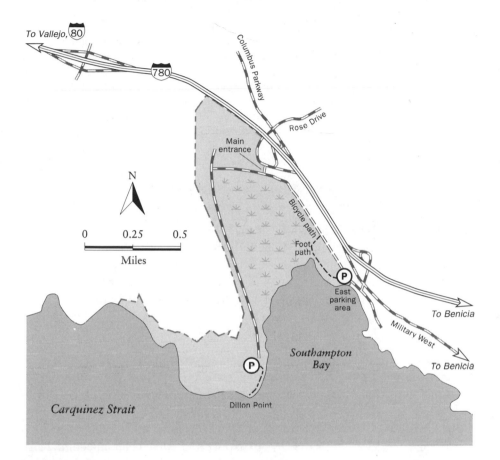

ADDITIONAL HELP

NCA&G grid: Page 94, 4D.
Elevation: Sea level.
Hazards: Rattlesnakes, ticks; poison oak is possible.
Nearest food, gas, lodging: Vallejo.
For more information: Silverado District, California State Parks.

35 Grizzly Island and Suisun Marsh 🍴

Habitats: Coastal bays and lagoons, coastal scrub, salt marsh, freshwater marsh.

Specialty birds: *Resident*—White-tailed Kite; Golden Eagle; Black and Clapper Rails; Short-eared Owl; Western Meadowlark; Lesser Goldfinch. *Summer*—Cinnamon Teal; Allen's Hummingbird. *Winter*—Prairie and Peregrine Falcons; Long-billed Curlew; Tricolored Blackbird.

Other key birds: *Resident*—Eared Grebe, American Bittern, Northern Harrier, Virginia Rail, Sora, Common Moorhen, Black-necked Stilt, American Avocet, Horned Lark. *Summer*—Common Yellowthroat. *Winter*—Tundra Swan; Green-winged Teal; Canvasback; Redhead; Ring-necked Duck; Greater and Lesser Scaups; Common Goldeneye; Rough-legged Hawk; Merlin; Greater Yellowlegs; American Pipit; Lincoln's Sparrow.

Best times to bird: November to March for most waterfowl; April to July for breeding birds.

Directions: For **Peytonia Slough Ecological Reserve,** from the junction of Interstate 80 and California Highway 12 near Fairfield, go 3 miles east on CA 12 to the exit for Suisun City. Get in the right-hand lane and turn right on Lotz Way. Go 1 block, turn left on Main Street, go 0.6 mile to the stop sign at Cordelia Street, and turn left. Go 1 block to Kellogg Street, turn right, go to the end of the paved road, and turn left into a parking lot (no fee, restrooms). For directions to Hill Slough, Rush Ranch, and Grizzly Island, see the following sections.

The birding: A trail begins at the southeastern corner of the parking lot next to **Peytonia Slough Ecological Reserve.** It goes about 0.5 mile to the intersection of Peytonia Slough and Suisun Slough, through habitat that consists mostly of shrubs and weedy growth. About halfway down the main trail a trail branches to the right, crosses a footbridge, and leads into the marsh proper. Typical resident birds are White-tailed Kite, Northern Harrier, Clapper Rail, Anna's Hummingbird, Black Phoebe, Western Meadowlark, and Lesser Goldfinch. Marsh Wrens are abundant, and their bubbling and squeaking noises are everywhere. Look for Allen's Hummingbird in spring and summer, beginning in February. During Audubon Christmas Bird Counts, this general area has often produced the largest numbers in the nation for White-tailed Kite, Northern Harrier, and Black and Virginia Rails. Since there are Black Rails here, you might think you could actually see one, but the marsh growth is too heavy. Palo Alto Baylands (page 238) offers a better opportunity, but even there it is not a sure thing.

For **Hill Slough Wildlife Area,** start from the junction of the Suisun City exit and CA 12, go east on CA 12 for 1.1 miles and exit right (south) onto Grizzly Island Road. About 1 mile from the exit, there are dirt parking areas on both sides of the road, and a chemical toilet.

The footpath that leads through a gate in the fence and along the levee is a good place for Common Yellowthroat and Song, Lincoln's, Golden-crowned, and White-crowned Sparrows. The top of the levee provides good views into the ponds

35 Grizzly Island and Suisun Marsh

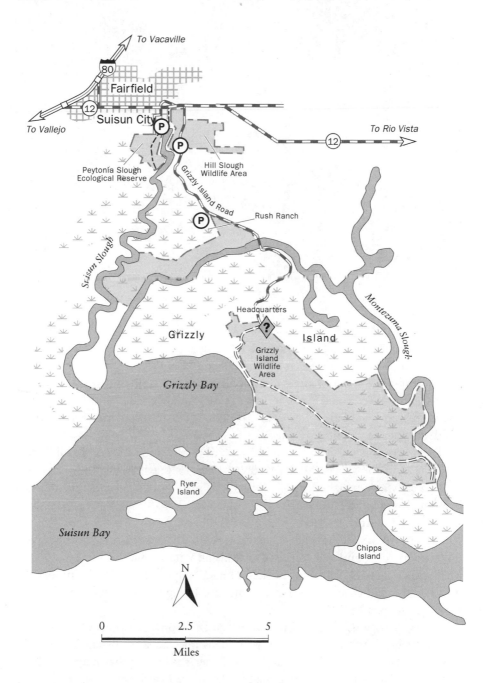

Male Ruddy Duck.

for Eared Grebe; American Wigeon; Blue-winged (rare), Cinnamon, and Green-winged Teal; Northern Shoveler; Northern Pintail; Canvasback, Redhead (uncommon); Ring-necked Duck; Greater and Lesser Scaups; Common Goldeneye; and Ruddy Duck. Also watch for American Bitterns and Merlins. Least Bittern (rare) has been seen here. Snow Geese and Tundra Swans are sometimes seen as are Golden Eagles and Prairie Falcons.

Rush Ranch is on Grizzly Island Road, about 1.5 miles beyond Hill Slough (parking, restrooms). The **Marsh Trail**, 2.2 miles long, passes near both freshwater and saltwater marshes. Birds along the Marsh Trail are similar to those at Peytonia Slough and Hill Slough.

The headquarters for **Grizzly Island Wildlife Area** is on Grizzly Island Road, 9 miles from CA 12 (fee, parking, chemical toilets). The pavement ends just beyond the headquarters, and a gravel road extends another 8 miles to the end, next to Montezuma Slough. Visitors are asked to park only in the marked parking lots. Access to the wildlife area is restricted to hunters during the hunting season (broadly speaking, August to February).

Along Grizzly Island Road there are ponds in some locations where various ducks, coots, egrets, and Common Moorhens may be seen. Black-necked Stilts and American Avocets occur year-round. Other shorebirds that may be present are Killdeer, Greater Yellowlegs, Long-billed Curlew, Least Sandpiper, Dunlin, and Long-billed Dowitcher. The open country is ideal for Horned Larks, American Pipits, Western Meadowlarks, and blackbirds. Tricolored Blackbirds occur, but are uncommon. White-tailed Kites are fairly common, as are Red-tailed Hawks and Northern Harriers. Short-eared Owls are frequently seen and have been known to breed here. This is a good place to see Ferruginous and Rough-legged Hawks in winter, and Peregrine and Prairie Falcons occasionally are spotted.

General information: Grizzly Island Wildlife Area, Peytonia Slough Ecological Reserve, and Hill Slough Wildlife Area add up to about 14,000 acres, but they constitute only a fraction of the vast wetlands in the area, collectively called Suisun Marsh. The Suisun Marsh, at 84,000 acres, is the largest estuarine marsh in the U.S. In 1998, it was declared to be a Globally Important Bird Area because it "provides habitat for globally significant numbers of wintering Northern Pintails, continentally significant numbers of wintering California Clapper Rails, and nationally significant numbers of American Wigeons and Northern Shovelers, in addition to migrating shorebirds." It has been estimated that 250,000 ducks are present in winter. In addition to the birds, there is a resident herd of tule elk. River otters are sometimes visible in the ditches and sloughs.

ADDITIONAL HELP

NCA&G grid: Page 95, 6C.
Elevation: Sea level.
Hazards: Ticks.
Nearest food, gas, lodging: Fairfield.
For more information: Grizzly Island Wildlife Complex; Rush Ranch Education Council.

36 Lake Solano and Putah Creek

Habitats: Lake, stream, riparian woodland, foothill woodland, chaparral.
Specialty birds: *Resident*—Wood Duck; Golden Eagle; Mountain Quail; Western Screech-Owl; Northern Pygmy-Owl; White-throated Swift; Black-chinned Hummingbird; Nuttall's Woodpecker; Western Scrub-Jay; Yellow-billed Magpie; Oak Titmouse; Bushtit; Rock and Canyon Wrens; Western Bluebird; Wrentit; California Thrasher; Phainopepla; Spotted Towhee; Rufous-crowned and Sage Sparrows; Lesser Goldfinch. *Summer*— Common Poorwill; Pacific-slope and Ash-throated Flycatchers; Black-headed Grosbeak; Bullock's Oriole; Lawrence's Goldfinch. *Winter*— Hooded Merganser, Osprey, Red-breasted Sapsucker, Varied Thrush.
Other key birds: *Resident*—Green Heron, Red-shouldered Hawk, Great Horned Owl, White-breasted Nuthatch, American Goldfinch. *Summer*— Northern Rough-winged Swallow, Blue-gray Gnatcatcher, Yellow-breasted Chat. *Winter*—Double-crested Cormorant; Bufflehead; Common and Barrow's Goldeneyes; Common Merganser; Cooper's Hawk; Greater Yellowlegs.
Best times to bird: All year; April to July best for breeding species; November to March best for waterfowl.

36 Lake Solano and Putah Creek

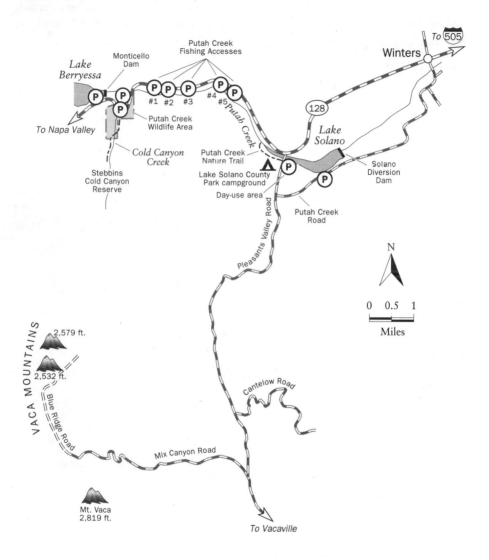

Directions: From the junction of Interstate 505 and California Highway 128, go west on CA 128 to Winters, then 4.1 miles beyond Winters to the junction with Pleasants Valley Road. Lake Solano County Park lies just across the bridge to the south. The day-use area is to the left (east) of Pleasants Valley Road (fee, parking, restrooms), and the campground is to the right (west). To get to the Putah Creek Fishing Accesses (fee), when coming from Winters, continue straight ahead on CA 128.

The birding: Park in the lot next to the day-use area at **Lake Solano County Park** (fee), and bird the grassy area downstream. There will be an abundance of people on weekends, but during the week in the off-season, you will almost have the place to yourself. There is a lot of mistletoe in the trees, and this attracts Phainopeplas, resident here in small numbers. Double-crested Cormorants roost in the trees directly across the creek. Common Goldeneyes and Common and Hooded Mergansers can often be spotted in winter on the quiet waters downstream from the day-use area. A scope is useful.

After birding the day-use area, cross the road to the campground and take the **Putah Creek Nature Trail,** which runs along the creek about 0.7 mile. Cooper's Hawk; Nuttall's Woodpecker; Red-breasted Sapsucker; Black Phoebe; Oak Titmouse; Bushtit; Western Bluebird; California and Spotted Towhees; and American Goldfinch are often found here. Green Herons are sometimes in the creek, and in the winter there may be Hooded Mergansers, Barrow's Goldeneyes, and Wood Ducks on the water. Beavers are present in the creek but are seldom seen, although river otters are sometimes spotted.

During the Audubon Christmas Bird Count of 1995, the Putah Creek area gained national prominence (of a sort) when it produced the highest count of Western Scrub-Jays (848) of any area in the nation. The area also has produced the highest national counts for Northern Pygmy-Owl (1995) and Lesser Goldfinch (1996, 1997).

To get to a different part of **Lake Solano,** from the park entrance go south on Pleasants Valley Road 1 mile to Putah Creek Road. Turn left (east) on Putah Creek Road and go about 1 mile to a large dirt parking area on the right-hand side. The broad reach of Lake Solano lies just across the road. In the winter, many species of ducks take up residence here, such as Hooded Mergansers and Wood Ducks (resident). Also, keep your eyes open for Ospreys. In summer Tree and Northern Rough-winged Swallows work over the lake surface. At times when the water is low, extensive mudflats are exposed that attract shorebirds, especially Greater Yellowlegs.

To continue up **Putah Creek,** from the junction of Pleasants Valley Road and CA 128, go west on CA 128. There are five **public fishing accesses** along the next 4 miles, some with picnic tables and chemical toilets (fee). Some of the fishing accesses are closed in winter, but you can park along the road and walk in, unless they are flooded.

The best accesses for birding are numbers 3, 2, and 1. These lie 2.5 miles, 3.3 miles, and 3.4 miles, respectively, from the junction with Pleasants Valley Road. Common resident birds are California Quail, Great Horned Owl, Acorn and Nuttall's Woodpeckers, and Lesser Goldfinch. Less common residents are Red-shouldered Hawk, Golden Eagle, Western Screech-Owl, and Northern Pygmy-Owl. Lewis's Woodpecker and Varied Thrush have sometimes been present in winter, but are irregular. Golden-crowned and White-crowned Sparrows, and Ruby-crowned Kinglet are abundant in winter. Pacific-slope and Ash-throated Flycatchers, Black-headed Grosbeak, and Bullock's Oriole are fairly common summer breeders.

Red-breasted Sapsucker.

Black-chinned Hummingbird is an uncommon breeder, and Yellow-breasted Chat is a rare breeder.

Just after crossing the bridge over Putah Creek (4.7 miles from Pleasants Valley Road) there is a large dirt area to the right (a part of the Putah Creek Wildlife Area), which is the parking area for **Monticello Dam** (no fee, no restrooms). The western edge of the parking lot is bordered by Cold Canyon Creek. If the water is not too high, you can pick your way down the steep bank, rock-hop across the creek, and climb the other side. Watch for rattlesnakes and loose rocks. From here, a broad, easy path extends for about 0.2 mile and ends below Monticello Dam. Common Mergansers and Common Goldeneyes are often in the quiet water below the dam. If the flow from the dam is not too powerful, there may be Rock and Canyon Wrens among the rocks on either side of the creek. Check the dry rocky slopes for Rufous-crowned Sparrow. In most winters, an American Dipper takes up residence under the nearby highway bridge.

Stebbins Cold Canyon Reserve parking area is 0.1 mile farther along CA 128, and is really just a wide place on the right side of the road. Stebbins Cold Canyon Reserve is one of the units of the University of California Natural Reserve System (no fee, no restrooms). It is open to the public, which makes it unusual, since most U.C. natural reserves are open only to researchers and student classes.

From the parking area, cross the road (taking care, because this is a curve with restricted visibility), go to the gate on the opposite side, and take the path upstream. The path crosses a portion of the Putah Creek Wildlife Area, and then enters Stebbins Cold Canyon Reserve. Be sure to sign in. The trail goes upstream for a mile or so, but is difficult in places because of landslides. Also, watch for poison oak. The birds are typical of oak/chaparral habitat, such as California Thrasher, Spotted and California Towhees (all resident), and Black-headed Grosbeak (summer). You are almost guaranteed to hear Wrentits in this chaparral country. Their loud song, consisting of a descending series of whistles that speed up toward the end (sometimes referred to as a "bouncing Ping-Pong ball song") can generally be heard all year.

Many people continue on up CA 128 to Monticello Dam, where there are parking areas close to the top. White-throated Swifts can frequently be seen from here, especially in spring and summer. They often nest in the cliffs above the parking area.

To get a look (or perhaps only a listen) at Common Poorwill, go south on Pleasants Valley Road about 7.2 miles from Lake Solano County Park, to **Mix Canyon Road.** This road leads to the crest of the Vaca Mountains and into the chaparral country where Mountain Quail, Common Poorwill, Blue-gray Gnatcatcher, and Sage Sparrow reside. Near the 1.4 milepost on Mix Canyon Road, where the creek goes under the road, Lawrence's Goldfinches have nested. The road is narrow, winding, and steep, but is paved all the way to the top (4.7 miles), after which it levels off into a gravel road. The road runs through chaparral along the crest, providing stunning views of the valleys on both sides. Wrentits sing everywhere. If you get there just about sunset, you can hear the Common Poorwills giving their loud song, especially in May, sounding like a shortened version of the eastern Whip-poor-will's song. If you are lucky you may get a look at one sitting in the road after dark, its eyes reflecting your headlights like a couple of live coals. It is advisable to use low gear in coming back down the steep road.

Yellow-billed Magpies occur in the open country adjacent to Putah Creek, but only occasionally do they show up in the riparian zone. Most often, magpies are found in nearby fields and orchards.

General information: This section of Putah Creek is not what you would expect in the inner coastal ranges of California. It is a clear, rushing stream that flows at about the same rate all year long because of the releases from Monticello Dam. Just downstream from Lake Solano County Park is a diversion dam, which creates Lake Solano. Putah Creek and environs have been classified as a Nationally Important Bird Area because of Yellow-billed Magpie, a species endemic to California.

ADDITIONAL HELP

NCA&G grid: Page 85, 5D; page 95, 5A.
Elevation: 150 to 2,300 feet.
Hazards: Rattlesnakes, poison oak, ticks.
Nearest food, gas, lodging: Vacaville; Davis.
Camping: Lake Solano County Park: 66 sites, on Pleasants Valley Road, 0.2 mile south of CA 128. Call for reservations (see Appendix F).
For more information: Lake Solano County Park.

37 Yolo Farmlands

Habitats: Farm fields, valley grassland.
Specialty birds: *Resident*—White-tailed Kite, Burrowing Owl, Yellow-billed Magpie, Tricolored Blackbird, Western Meadowlark. *Summer*—Swainson's Hawk. *Winter*—Ferruginous Hawk; Prairie and Peregrine Falcons; Mountain Plover; California Gull; Short-eared Owl.
Other key birds: *Resident*—Cattle Egret, Northern Harrier, Red-tailed Hawk, American Kestrel, Ring-necked Pheasant, Barn Owl, Loggerhead Shrike, Horned Lark. *Summer*—Northern Rough-winged Swallow. *Winter*—Rough-legged Hawk; Merlin; American Pipit; Savannah and White-crowned Sparrows.
Best times to bird: For Burrowing Owl, very early morning or late afternoon. For Short-eared Owl, dusk. For Swainson's Hawk, April to September. For Ferruginous and Rough-tailed Hawks, Prairie Falcon, and Mountain Plover, November through March.

Directions: For a general birding loop, from Interstate 505 take the exit for County Road 29A and go east to County Road 99. Go north on County Road 99 to

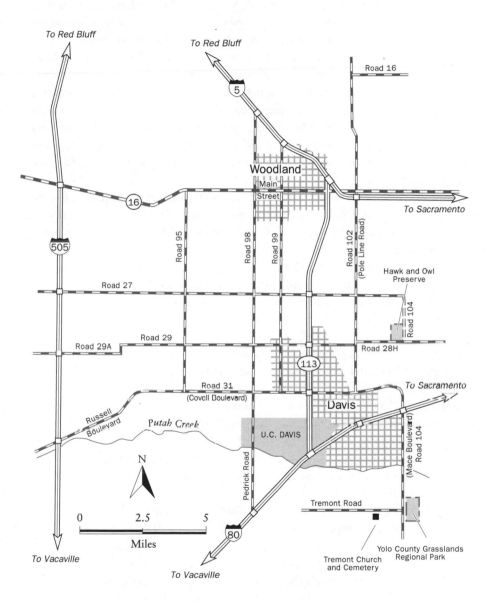

To Red Bluff

To Red Bluff

Road 16

5

Woodland

Main
Street

To Sacramento

16

Road 95

Road 98

Road 99

Road 102
(Pole Line Road)

505

Hawk and Owl
Preserve

Road 27

Road 104

Road 29A

Road 29

Road 28H

Road 31
(Covell Boulevard)

113

To Sacramento

Davis

U.C. DAVIS

(Mace Boulevard)
Road 104

Russell
Boulevard

Putah Creek

N

Pedrick Road

Tremont Road

0   2.5   5

Miles

80

Yolo County Grasslands
Regional Park

Tremont Church
and Cemetery

To Vacaville

To Vacaville

County Road 27, and return west, to I-505. County Roads 95 and 98 offer alternate connecting routes. See the following site descriptions for other directions.

The birding: Roads 27, 29, 29A, 31, 95, 98, 99, and 102 (see map) all offer rural birding opportunities. However, Roads 31, 98, and 102 carry fairly heavy traffic, so the other roads are quieter, with better opportunities to see birds. Appropriate places to pull off and stop safely are scarce, so be careful when stopping.

Swainson's Hawks have been extirpated in much of their former range in California. They need nesting sites in tall trees, usually in riparian areas, and foraging territory nearby with low-growing plants. Their breeding range in California is now concentrated in the Central Valley, with disjunct populations in the northeastern part of the state, and in Inyo and Mono counties. In summer they are easy to find in Yolo County, but in winter almost the entire population migrates to Mexico and South America, except for a small group that has overwintered in the Delta in recent years.

The lower Sacramento Valley is one of the major places in the United States for wintering Red-tailed Hawks, American Kestrels, and Western Meadowlarks, as shown by Audubon Christmas Bird Count records. White-tailed Kites are frequently seen, and Northern Harriers appear to be everywhere. A few Ferruginous Hawks, Rough-legged Hawks, Merlins, and Prairie and Peregrine Falcons turn up every winter, although they are rare. There also are huge mixed flocks of blackbirds in winter, with an occasional Tricolored Blackbird among them.

Great and Snowy Egrets are common residents, and the number of Cattle Egrets seems to be increasing. These rural roads also are good places to see Loggerhead Shrikes. Flocks of Horned Larks and American Pipits forage in the fields in winter, and Savannah and White-crowned Sparrows are common in the weedy fence rows.

Mountain Plovers have been seen (December to February) near the intersection of Roads 102 and 16. You must park well off the road (the traffic on Road 102 is fast and heavy) and scan the plowed fields, looking for "clods of dirt that move." A scope is helpful. However, many people have gone to this location and failed to see the plovers, because they move around a lot and may be way out in the center of a field. It pays to search all the rural roads in this vicinity.

Populations of Mountain Plovers have seriously declined in the last 25 years, and the bird has been proposed for listing as a threatened or endangered species. It is believed that about 80 percent of the population spends the winter in California, with nearly a quarter of them in the Central Valley. In a census taken in 1998, 2,663 birds were counted, with the two largest flocks containing about 250 birds each. One of these flocks was the one in Yolo County (described in this section), the other was in the Imperial Valley.

Short-eared Owls can often be seen at dusk in winter at the **Hawk and Owl Preserve,** managed cooperatively by the Hunt-Wesson Cannery and Yolo Audubon Society. The preserve is on the north side of Road 28H, 2 miles east of Road 102, at the junction of Roads 28H and 104. There are a few places where you can park well off Road 28H, which gets lots of traffic, or along Road 104, which is gravel and less traveled than Road 28H. The Hawk and Owl Preserve is a large grassy area with many sprinkler heads, where the Hunt-Wesson cannery disposes of its wastewater. The water causes the grass to grow, which attracts rodents, which in turn attract raptors, especially White-Tailed Kites, Northern Harriers, and Barn and Short-eared Owls (in winter, just after sunset, these owls can often be seen flying about like huge moths). There is also a large population of Ring-necked Pheasants at the preserve and in the surrounding region. Because the Yolo County Land Fill is next door, there are many gulls here, mostly Ring-billed, California, and Herring.

Burrowing Owls can often be seen at **Yolo County Grasslands Regional Park.** From the junction of Interstate 80 and Mace Boulevard east of Davis, go south on Mace Boulevard (it becomes Road 104) 3.8 miles to the park entrance on the left (east). Turn into the park and go 0.2 mile, to a sign that reads "Home of the Sacramento Valley Soaring Society; Burrowing Owl Habitat—Do Not Disturb" (no fee, chemical toilet). Park near the sign and look about 100 to 150 yards to the northeast to a patch of disturbed earth surrounded by mown grass. There are usually a couple of Burrowing Owls, plus many ground squirrels, near the disturbed earth. They are more likely to be visible in the early morning or late afternoon, but sometimes are out in the middle of the day. More Burrowing Owls are in the surrounding fields but they are harder to see because of the tall grass and weeds.

Tremont Road, which is directly opposite the entrance to the regional park, leads to the **Tremont Church and Cemetery,** 0.5 mile on the left. Barn Owls sometimes roost in the dense cypress trees in the cemetery. Horned Larks are usually in the adjoining fields in winter.

Yellow-billed Magpie is one of the few true endemic (meaning, found nowhere else) birds in California, and the Central Valley is their stronghold. In driving the rural roads of Yolo County you are virtually certain to encounter them. In particular, look along Road 98 both north and south of Road 31 for a mile or two. While traveling the roads, watch for swallows in spring and summer, especially Tree, Northern Rough-winged, Barn, and Cliff.

General information: Many rural areas in Northern California offer good birding on farmlands, and Yolo County is no exception. One thing to note in this particular region is that many of the crops are low growing and offer attractive foraging opportunities for Swainson's Hawk, a state-listed threatened species.

ADDITIONAL HELP

NCA&G grid: Page 85, 7D.

Elevation: 50 feet.

Hazards: Fast road traffic.

Nearest food, gas, lodging: Davis; Woodland.

For more information: Davis Chamber of Commerce; Woodland Chamber of Commerce.

38 Vic Fazio Yolo Wildlife Area 🏕

Habitats: Freshwater marsh, riparian woodland, valley grassland.
Specialty birds: *Resident*—White-faced Ibis, Western Meadowlark. *Summer*—Cinnamon Teal, Western Kingbird, Yellow-headed Blackbird, Bullock's Oriole. *Winter*—Greater White-fronted and Ross's Geese; Sandhill Crane; Long-billed Curlew; Short-eared Owl; Tricolored Blackbird.
Other key birds: *Resident*—Eared Grebe; American Bittern; Black-crowned Night-Heron; Ruddy Duck; Northern Harrier; Barn and Great Horned Owls; Horned Lark; Loggerhead Shrike; Marsh Wren; Red-winged and Brewer's Blackbirds; American Goldfinch. *Summer*—Black-necked Stilt, American Avocet, Blue Grosbeak. *Winter*—American White Pelican; Snow Goose; Tundra Swan; Gadwall; Northern Shoveler; Northern Pintail; Canvasback; Merlin; Greater Yellowlegs; Common Snipe; American Pipit; Savannah and Lincoln's Sparrows.
Best times to bird: November through January for wintering waterfowl.

Directions: From Davis, go east about 6 miles on Interstate 80 and exit for East Chiles Road. At East Chiles Road (also called Road 32B) turn left (east) and go 0.2 mile to a gravel access road on the right, which climbs to the top of the levee. Turn left through the gate on top of the levee, and down into the Yolo Bypass. From Sacramento, take the frontage road exit off I-80 at the west end of the causeway, turn right at a stop sign, go back under I-80, and turn left at the gravel access road leading onto the levee. If the bypass is flooded, the entrance gate will be closed.

The birding: The **Auto Tour Route** (4 miles round trip) takes you near several of the ponds and marshes, and is open all year unless the bypass is flooded. In the winter there can be tens of thousands of ducks and geese present. Sometimes large flocks of Tundra Swans are here.

The geese mostly are White-fronted, Canada, and Snow, with Ross's Geese mixed in with the flocks of Snow Geese. The best place for spotting a Ross's Goose is in a flock of Snow Geese flying overhead. Look for birds that are substantially smaller than the others. Flocks of American White Pelicans and Sandhill Cranes are seen overhead fairly often, although the cranes are seldom spotted on the ground. Northern Pintails are the most abundant ducks in winter, but Gadwalls, Mallards, Northern Shovelers, and Canvasbacks can also be present in large

38 Vic Fazio Yolo Wildlife Area

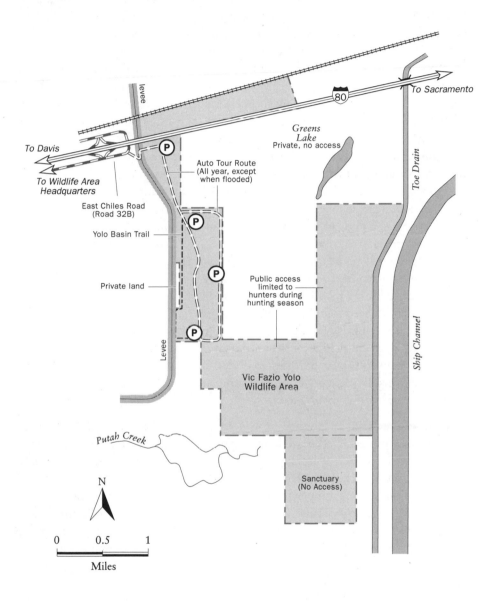

numbers. So can California Gulls. In breeding season most of the birds are Mallards and Cinnamon Teal, but Eared Grebes are also present. Ruddy Ducks and Marsh Wrens are resident.

Some of the most prominent birds are Great and Snowy Egrets, and Great Blue Herons. An American Bittern can occasionally be spotted winging over the marshes. Black-crowned Night-Herons are common but generally are not highly visible because of their nighttime foraging habits. However, huge daytime roosts have been observed in the Yolo Bypass just north of the wildlife area. White-faced Ibis are frequently seen here, as well as Black-necked Stilt, American Avocet, both regular breeders, and nonbreeding shorebirds such as Greater Yellowlegs; Long-billed Curlew; Western and Least Sandpipers; Dunlin; Long-billed Dowitcher; and Common Snipe. Western Kingbird, Blue Grosbeak, and Bullock's Oriole are usually present during breeding season, and Loggerhead Shrike, Song Sparrow, and American Goldfinch are resident. Look for Savannah, Lincoln's, and White-crowned Sparrows in winter, and check for Yellow-headed Blackbirds in summer. Snowy Plovers nested here in 1998, but probably do not do so on a regular basis.

The bypass is a good place for raptors. The most common are Red-tailed Hawks and Northern Harriers, but American Kestrels also are present, and once in a while a Merlin may appear in winter. Don't forget to look for Great Horned and Barn Owls, which often roost in what trees there are. Long-eared Owls (rare) have been spotted roosting in willows in winter along the edges of the bypass. Short-eared Owls have been found in the marshy areas.

Open-country birds abound in winter. Huge mixed flocks of blackbirds may be working over the fields, consisting mostly of Red-winged and Brewer's, but often with many European Starlings as well. Check the flocks carefully for Tricolored Blackbirds. Flocks of Western Meadowlarks are common in winter, as are Horned Larks and American Pipits.

General information: At the time of its completion in 1997, the Vic Fazio Yolo Wildlife Area was the largest wetlands restoration project in the western United States. It consists of 3,700 acres lying entirely within the Yolo Bypass, which is a flood control project constructed by the U.S. Army Corps of Engineers. In flood years the wildlife area is completely submerged; in others, it receives no floodwaters at all. Vic Fazio Yolo Wildlife Area has been classified as a Globally Important Bird Area because it provides habitat for a globally significant number of waterfowl, continentally significant numbers of Least Sandpipers and Northern Pintails, and nationally significant numbers of Canvasbacks, Dunlin, and American White Pelicans.

The Yolo Basin Foundation helps to provide interpretive services and field trips for the wildlife area. In February each year, the foundation sponsors a major wildlife celebration, headquartered in Davis, called California Duck Days. (For information, see California Duck Days in Appendix A.)

ADDITIONAL HELP

NCA&G grid: Page 86, 2D.
Elevation: 30 feet.
Nearest food, gas, lodging: Davis.
For more information: Vic Fazio Yolo Wildlife Area.

39 American River ⚔

Habitats: Stream, riparian woodland, foothill woodland.
Specialty birds: *Resident*—Wood Duck; White-tailed Kite; Acorn and Nuttall's Woodpeckers; Yellow-billed Magpie; Phainopepla; Lesser Goldfinch. *Summer*—Ash-throated Flycatcher, Black-headed Grosbeak, Bullock's Oriole. *Winter*—Mew, California, Thayer's, and Glaucous-winged Gulls
Other key birds: *Resident*—Green Heron, Red-shouldered Hawk, Wild Turkey, Great Horned Owl, White-breasted Nuthatch, Northern Mockingbird. *Summer*—Orange-crowned Warbler. *Winter*—Bufflehead, Common Goldeneye, Common Merganser, Greater Yellowlegs, Lincoln's Sparrow.
Best times to bird: September through May.

Directions: To get to the **Effie Yeaw Nature Center,** from the junction of U.S. Highway 50 and Watt Avenue east of Sacramento, go 1.1 miles north on Watt Avenue, and turn right on Fair Oaks Boulevard. Go about 2.9 miles east to Van Alstine Avenue, then right 0.3 mile to California Avenue. Turn left and go 0.2 mile to Tarshes Drive, then turn right, following signs to Ancil Hoffman Park–Effie Yeaw Nature Center (fee, parking, restrooms, visitor center).

For Ambassador Park, from Watt Avenue go 7 miles east on US 50 to Sunrise Boulevard, then 0.6 mile north on Sunrise Boulevard to Coloma Road. Turn left, go 0.9 mile to Elmanto Drive, then right 0.2 mile to Ambassador Drive. The **Elmanto Access** lies directly ahead (fee, parking, chemical toilet, open 5 A.M. to 9 P.M.). To get to **Ambassador Park** (an unofficial name for the area), instead of going straight ahead at Ambassador Drive, turn right and go 0.2 mile to a parking area (open 5:30 A.M. to 8 P.M.).

For **Upper Sunrise** and **Lower Sunrise,** go 0.8 mile north on Sunrise Boulevard from the junction of Sunrise Boulevard and Coloma Road to South Bridge Street; turn right and go 0.4 mile to a parking area next to the river (fee, restrooms, open 5 A.M. to 9 P.M.). This is Upper Sunrise. You can go an additional 1.4 miles upstream on a park road that parallels the river. To get to Lower Sunrise, instead of going to the parking area, turn left under Sunrise Boulevard to a large parking area (restrooms). From here, Sunrise Boulevard can be reentered for southbound traffic only. There is another parking area near the river about 0.3 mile downstream.

For the **Nimbus Fish Hatchery,** from Sunrise Boulevard go 3.2 miles east on US 50 to Hazel Avenue, then 0.3 mile north on Hazel Avenue to Gold Country

39 American River

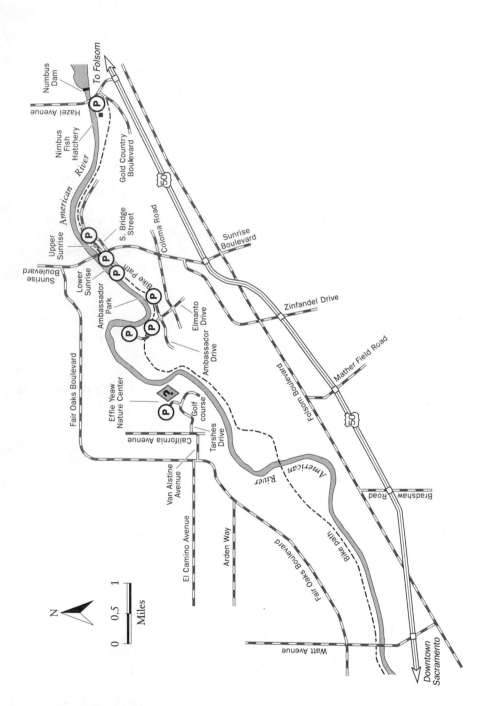

Boulevard. Turn left and then immediately turn right on Nimbus Road into the parking lot for the fish hatchery.

The birding: The birds in all the following areas are likely to be much the same, depending, of course, upon habitat. Resident birds in the wooded areas are California Quail; Red-shouldered Hawk; Great Horned Owl; Acorn, Nuttall's and Downy Woodpeckers; Western Scrub-Jay; Oak Titmouse; Bushtit; White-breasted Nuthatch; Bewick's Wren; Spotted and California Towhees; and Lesser Goldfinch. Fairly common spring and summer breeders are Ash-throated Flycatcher, Orange-crowned Warbler, Black-headed Grosbeak, and Bullock's Oriole. Beginning in October, winter visitors such as Ruby-crowned Kinglet, Yellow-rumped Warbler, and Golden-crowned and White-crowned Sparrows show up in force. Lincoln's Sparrows appear at about the same time but are less numerous.

In more open areas, look for residents such as Red-tailed Hawk, Anna's Hummingbird, Black Phoebe, Yellow-billed Magpie, Northern Mockingbird, and Song Sparrow. Belted Kingfishers will be wherever there is water, and quiet waters may hold Wood Ducks.

Here's something else to look for in places where you can see directly down into the river—spawning salmon. The salmon run begins in mid-October and continues into December. If the river is not running too high, you can see them spawning in the shallows, especially near the Nimbus Fish Hatchery.

Effie Yeaw Nature Center: Effie Yeaw (pronounced YAW) was a conservationist and teacher who was instrumental in the establishment of the American River Parkway. The visitor center has exhibits, books, and a few live birds on display in cages. On the trails that traverse the natural area outside, the most abundant birds are likely to be Western Scrub-Jay and Acorn and Nuttall's Woodpeckers. There is also a resident flock of Wild Turkeys.

Ambassador Park: This is a local name for the lovely grove of trees, mostly oaks, bordering the river in this stretch. From the parking area two paths lead to the river. The paved path on the downstream side of the parking lot leads to the river and bike path in about 100 yards. The rather obscure path on the upstream side (an old road, partly paved) leads directly into a grove of large trees, and in about 0.2 mile comes to a green lawn adjacent to the river and bike path. The oak grove's resident birds include Acorn and Nuttall's Woodpeckers, Western Scrub-Jay, and Oak Titmouse, and may also have migrant flycatchers and warblers, especially in September.

Birding from the bike path can be a bit of a hassle, but a horse trail between the bike path and the river allows you to get away from the bikes and closer to the river where you can usually see Great Blue Herons, Great and Snowy Egrets, Double-crested Cormorants, Belted Kingfishers, Killdeer, and gulls. In September and October winter visitors such as Greater Yellowlegs, Bufflehead, Common Goldeneye, and Common Merganser show up. Check the river in winter for rarities such as Barrow's Goldeneye and Hooded Merganser.

Lower Sunrise: From the parking lot, a maintenance road runs close to the river, to the next parking area about 0.3 mile downstream. The trail is used by horses, but is closed to bicycles. It offers a rather quiet opportunity (at least in midweek) to find many of the woodland birds that are in Ambassador Park, and gives frequent opportunities to check the river.

The area near the **Nimbus Fish Hatchery** can have lots of gulls in winter, mostly Ring-billed, California, and Herring, but also Bonaparte's, Mew, Thayer's, and Glaucous-winged. Glaucous Gull is rare. From the hatchery you can walk downstream on a fairly good informal trail along the bank of the river. In about 0.5 mile the trail joins the paved bike path. In this area, the country is open, with small trees, mostly live oaks, scattered about. This is a good place for White-tailed Kite. Phainopeplas often perch right in the tops of trees, which makes them easy to spot. The bike path can be used to return to the fish hatchery, where the access road to the hatchery meets Gold Country Boulevard.

General information: The American River Parkway extends 30 miles along the American River from Folsom Lake to Discovery Park, where the American joins the Sacramento River. (Less than half the parkway is included here.) It is used heavily by rafters, kayakers, fishermen, joggers, horseback riders, and bicyclists. According to parkway rules, bicyclists have priority on the designated bike paths. Pedestrians are supposed to walk to one side, on the shoulders.

ADDITIONAL HELP

NCA&G grid: Page 86, 4D; page 87, 5C.
Elevation: 100 feet.
Hazards: Poison oak, rattlesnakes, ticks, and the river, which claims lives every year.
Nearest food, gas, lodging: Sacramento; Folsom.
For more information: Sacramento County Regional Parks.

40 Cosumnes River Preserve and Woodbridge Road 🏕 ♿

Habitats: Freshwater marsh, riparian woodland.

Specialty birds: *Resident*—Wood Duck, Cinnamon Teal, White-tailed Kite, Nuttall's Woodpecker, Yellow-billed Magpie, Western Bluebird, Wrentit, Tricolored Blackbird. *Summer*—Swainson's Hawk; Pacific-slope and Ash-throated Flycatchers; Western Kingbird; Black-headed Grosbeak; Lazuli Bunting; Bullock's Oriole. *Winter*—Greater White-fronted Goose, Sandhill Crane. *Migrant*—Black-throated Gray, Townsend's, and MacGillivray's Warblers; Western Tanager.

Other key birds: *Resident*—American Bittern, Green Heron, Black-crowned Night-Heron, Red-shouldered Hawk, Common Moorhen, Black-necked Stilt, Great Horned Owl, Horned Lark, White-breasted Nuthatch, Marsh Wren, American Goldfinch. *Summer*—American Avocet, Common Yellowthroat, Blue Grosbeak. *Winter*—American White Pelican, Tundra Swan, Green-winged Teal, Ring-necked Duck, Greater Yellowlegs, Common Snipe, Ruby-crowned Kinglet, American Pipit, Lincoln's Sparrow. *Migrant*—Warbling Vireo; Orange-crowned, Yellow, and Wilson's Warblers.

Best times to bird: April through July for breeding birds; April to October for Swainson's Hawks; September for fall migrants; November through March for most waterfowl; November through February for Sandhill Cranes.

Directions: From Sacramento, go about 22 miles south on Interstate 5, exit at Twin Cities Road (allow 25 minutes), and go east 1 mile to Franklin Road. Go south on Franklin Road 1.3 miles to the parking lot for **Willow Slough Trailhead** on the left, 1.5 miles to the parking lot for **Lost Slough Boardwalk** (chemical toilet) on the right, and 1.7 miles to the **Visitor Center** on the left. To get to **Woodbridge Road,** from the junction of Twin Cities Road and I-5, go south about 7 miles on I-5 to Peltier Road. After exiting I-5, turn left to go under the freeway, and immediately turn right on Thornton Road. Go south on Thornton Road, parallel to the freeway, to Woodbridge Road, and turn west, back under the freeway. Travel 2.5 miles to the parking area on the south side of the road.

The birding: The **Lost Slough Boardwalk** takes you into marshes that have waterfowl and shorebirds in season (open from 10 A.M. to 4 P.M. daily, from September through May, and weekends only, from June through August). Only a portion of the trail (about 1 mile round trip) is actually on a boardwalk, and this portion is barrier free. The full loop, totaling about 1.5 miles, takes you along the edges of the waterfowl ponds, but waterfowl have a habit of taking off when people get too close, so it may be just as effective to look into these ponds from the edge of Franklin Road opposite the visitor center. Some residents are Pied-billed Grebe; Great Blue Heron; Great and Snowy Egrets; Black-crowned Night-Heron; Mallard; Cinnamon Teal; Ruddy Duck; Common Moorhen; Killdeer; Black-necked Stilt; Belted Kingfisher; Black Phoebe; Marsh Wren; and Song Sparrow. Winter

40 Cosumnes River Preserve and Woodbridge Road

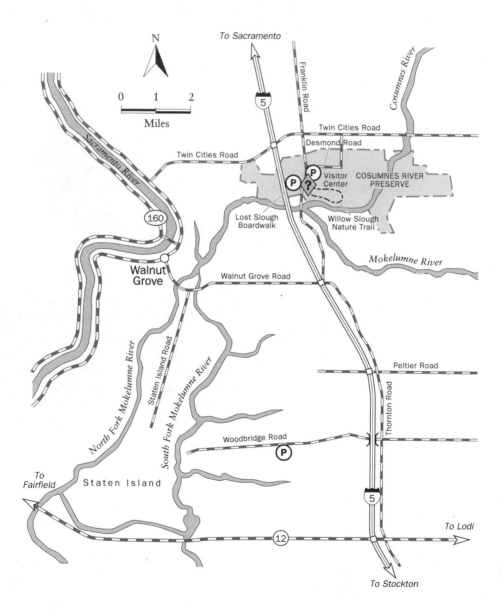

N

To Sacramento

0   1   2
Miles

5

Franklin Road

Cosumnes River

Twin Cities Road

Desmond Road

Twin Cities Road

Sacramento River

160

Visitor Center

COSUMNES RIVER PRESERVE

P

P

?

Lost Slough Boardwalk

Willow Slough Nature Trail

Mokelumne River

Walnut Grove

Walnut Grove Road

North Fork Mokelumne River

Staten Island Road

South Fork Mokelumne River

Peltier Road

Thornton Road

Woodbridge Road

P

To Fairfield

Staten Island

5

To Lodi

12

To Stockton

visitors are Tundra Swan (November through January), Greater White-fronted Goose, Gadwall, American Wigeon, Northern Shoveler, Northern Pintail, Green-winged Teal, and Ring-necked Duck.

Winter shorebirds include Greater Yellowlegs; Western and Least Sandpipers; Dunlin; Long-billed Dowitcher (sometimes in large flocks); and Common Snipe. American Avocets breed here in spring but are scarce in winter. Look for Sandhill Cranes from November through February. If you don't find them here, then try Woodbridge Road (described later).

Open-country raptors are White-tailed Kite, Northern Harrier, Red-tailed Hawk, and American Kestrel (all resident), and Swainson's Hawk (April to October). Other open-country birds include Horned Lark, American Pipit, Savannah Sparrow (all winter visitors), and Western Meadowlark (resident). Blackbirds abound, and so do Brown-headed Cowbirds. Look for Tricolored Blackbirds in flocks of mixed blackbirds in winter. Nesting colonies of Tricoloreds are possible, but the species is notorious for shifting its nesting locations from year to year. American White Pelicans show up from time to time, and Double-crested Cormorants are almost sure to be somewhere.

The **Willow Slough Nature Trail** (open every day during daylight hours) is about 3.3 miles round trip and takes you through willow thickets, restored wetlands, and riparian forest. You may want to take along mosquito repellent. In wet winters the trail can become flooded and inaccessible. Resident birds are Green Heron, Wood Duck, Red-shouldered Hawk, California Quail, Great Horned Owl, Nuttall's Woodpecker, Western Scrub-Jay, Yellow-billed Magpie, Oak Titmouse, Bushtit, White-breasted Nuthatch, Bewick's and House Wrens, Western Bluebird, Wrentit, Spotted Towhee, House Finch, and American Goldfinch. Fairly common summer breeders are Pacific-slope and Ash-throated Flycatchers; Common Yellowthroat; Black-headed and Blue Grosbeaks; Lazuli Bunting; and Bullock's Oriole. Warbling Vireo; Black-throated Gray, Townsend's (rare), MacGillivray's, and Wilson's Warblers; and Western Tanager are uncommon to rare in spring (April, May) and fall (September) migration; they don't breed here. A few Orange-crowned and Yellow Warblers are seen during the breeding season, but more commonly are seen in spring and fall migration. Common winter visitors are Ruby-crowned Kinglet; Yellow-rumped Warbler; Lincoln's, Golden-crowned, and White-crowned Sparrows; and Dark-eyed Junco.

You can see waterbirds and shorebirds from the shoulders of **Desmond Road**, which intersects Franklin Road just north of the parking area for Willow Slough Nature Trail.

Woodbridge Road is one of the better places in California to view Sandhill Cranes in winter. There are two subspecies in California—the Greater (about 5 feet tall) and the Lesser (about 4 feet tall). About 25,000 Lesser Sandhill Cranes and 6,000 Greater winter in California. Almost all of those at Woodbridge Road are Greaters, and they are classified as "state-listed threatened." Greater Sandhill Cranes nest primarily in eastern Oregon and northeastern California, whereas

Lessers go to Alaska and Siberia. From the parking lot it frequently is possible to spot Sandhills grazing in the fields to the south (a scope helps), but they also may be seen in the fields anywhere bordering Woodbridge Road. At dusk flocks of cranes fly in to roost in the Woodbridge Ecological Reserve just north of Woodbridge Road, and their haunting calls as they circle for a landing are among the wonderful sounds in nature.

General information: The Cosumnes River Preserve contains nearly 10,000 acres, and is owned by a group of organizations, including The Nature Conservancy, Bureau of Land Management, and Ducks Unlimited. Much of the preserve is riparian forest, but there are also areas managed for wintering waterfowl and migrating shorebirds. The preserve has been classified as a Globally Important Bird Area because of its wintering populations of Greater and Lesser Sandhill Cranes.

ADDITIONAL HELP

NCA&G grid: Page. 96, 3C.
Elevation: Barely above sea level.
Hazards: Poison oak, ticks.
Nearest food, gas, lodging: Stockton; Lodi.
For more information: Cosumnes River Preserve.

41 Sly Park 🏃

Habitats: Lake, stream, mixed conifer forest.
Specialty birds: *Resident*—Mountain Quail; White-headed and Pileated Woodpeckers; American Dipper. *Summer*—Osprey, Western Wood-Pewee, Pacific-slope Flycatcher, Cassin's Vireo, Black-throated Gray Warbler, Western Tanager, Black-headed Grosbeak, Bullock's Oriole, Lesser Goldfinch. *Winter*—Bald Eagle, Western Bluebird. *Migrant*—Rufous Hummingbird.
Other key birds: *Resident*—Common Merganser, Cooper's Hawk, Spotted Sandpiper, Hairy Woodpecker, Winter Wren, Yellow-rumped Warbler. *Summer*—Olive-sided Flycatcher; Orange-crowned, Nashville, Yellow, and Wilson's Warblers; Purple Finch. *Winter*—Ring-necked Duck, Common Goldeneye, Fox Sparrow.
Best times to bird: April through July; November to February for Bald Eagles.

Directions: From Placerville on U.S. Highway 50, go about 13.5 miles east on US 50 to Pollock Pines and turn south on Sly Park Road. It is about 4 miles to the entrance to **Sly Park Recreation Area.**

The birding: During the summer the park teems with people; however, in midweek in late spring, you can have the place almost to yourself. At such times birding can be good almost anyplace, including in the campground areas. There are three trails of interest—the Miwok Trail, the Liberty Trail, and the trail to Park Creek.

41 Sly Park

The **Miwok Trail** is about 0.5 mile round trip, and runs close to a small stream in a mixed forest. Resident birds to look for are Cooper's Hawk (uncommon); Hairy, White-headed, and Pileated Woodpeckers; Mountain Chickadee; Winter Wren; Ruby-crowned Kinglet; Yellow-rumped Warbler; and, of course, Steller's Jay. Mountain Quail may be heard calling from the slopes in spring. Summer visitors are Olive-sided and Pacific-slope Flycatchers; Western Wood-Pewee; Cassin's Vireo; Orange-crowned, Yellow, Black-throated Gray, and Wilson's Warblers; Western Tanager; and Purple Finch.

To get to the **Liberty Trail,** park at the parking lot for the Stonebraker Boat Launch and pick up the trail at the far end of the lot. Bear right, to take the lakeside trail, which leads to the Chimneys. Return via the road through the Hilltop Campground, which passes near the Liberty Tree. From here the Liberty Trail goes down the shallow draw and back to the Stonebraker parking lot.

Resident birds on this trail include Bewick's Wren, Spotted Towhee, Western Bluebird (fairly common in fall and winter), and summer visitors such as Nashville Warbler, Black-headed Grosbeak, Bullock's Oriole, and Lesser Goldfinch. In fall and winter look for Fox Sparrow. On the lake you may see Osprey, Common Merganser, and Canada Goose (all three breed here), as well as Ring-necked Duck and Common Goldeneye. Along the shore look for Spotted Sandpiper, and in winter for Bald Eagle.

The trail to **Park Creek** can be accessed from near the group camps. The creek and surrounding area might produce an American Dipper (uncommon) or a Rufous Hummingbird in fall.

General information: Sly Park surrounds Jenkinson Lake, a water supply reservoir constructed by the Bureau of Reclamation. The area around the lake is well forested, and because of its elevation (3,500 feet) it has less snowfall than do higher elevations. It is open all year. When the water level is high, it is an attractive lake, but in drought years the water can drop drastically by the end of summer.

ADDITIONAL HELP

NCA&G grid: Page 88, 3C.
Elevation: 3,500 feet.
Hazards: Rattlesnakes, ticks.
Nearest food, gas, lodging: Pollock Pines; Placerville.
Camping: Campground at park, 159 sites; RV dump station.
For more information: Sly Park Recreation Area.

42 Crystal Basin 🏕 ♿

Habitats: Lake, stream, mixed conifer forest, extensive burned areas coming back into brush.
Specialty birds: *Resident*—Bald Eagle, Northern Goshawk, Blue Grouse, Mountain Quail, White-headed Woodpecker, Townsend's Solitaire. *Summer*—Osprey; Calliope Hummingbird; Western Wood-Pewee; Hammond's Flycatcher; Cassin's Vireo; Hermit, Black-throated Gray, and MacGillivray's Warblers; Western Tanager; Green-tailed Towhee; Black-headed Grosbeak; Lazuli Bunting.
Other key birds: *Resident*—Common Merganser; Hairy and Pileated Woodpeckers; Red-breasted Nuthatch; Golden-crowned Kinglet; Dark-eyed Junco. *Summer*—Olive-sided Flycatcher; Warbling Vireo; Nashville, Yellow-rumped and Wilson's Warblers; Chipping and Fox Sparrows.
Best times to bird: April through July.

Directions: The road into Crystal Basin, Forest Road 3, called Ice House Road, leaves U.S. Highway 50 about 20 miles east of Placerville (allow 30 minutes) and leads north. It is a good, paved, two-lane road, but it carries a considerable amount of traffic. Be alert for logging trucks. When stopping, make sure that you do not trespass on lands that are posted. The mileages given for the various sites are measured from US 50.

The birding: Cleveland Fire—Beginning about 1 mile from US 50, and for the next 7.2 miles, you will pass through the burned area left by a fire in 1992, which covered approximately 22,000 acres. The trees and brush are coming back, and provide habitat for lots of birds.

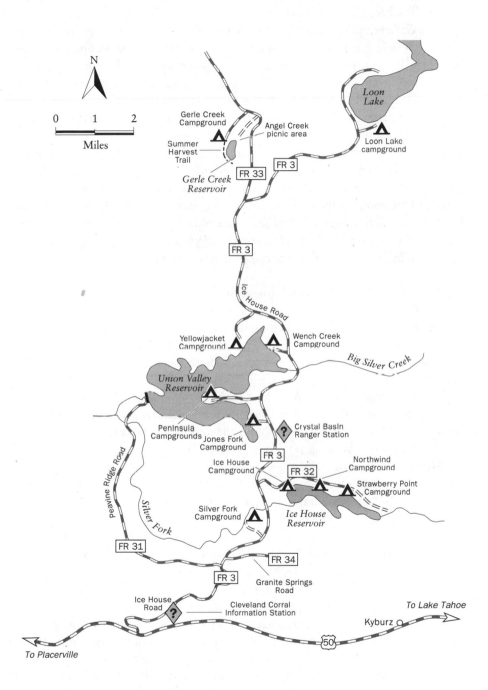

N

0   1   2
Miles

Loon Lake

Gerle Creek
Campground

Angel Creek
picnic area

Loon Lake
campground

Summer
Harvest
Trail

*Gerle Creek
Reservoir*

FR 33   FR 3

FR 3

Ice House Road

Yellowjacket
Campground

Wench Creek
Campground

Big Silver Creek

*Union Valley
Reservoir*

Peavine Ridge Road

Peninsula
Campgrounds

Jones Fork
Campground

Crystal Basin
Ranger Station

FR 3

Ice House
Campground

Northwind
Campground

FR 32

Strawberry Point
Campground

Silver Fork

Silver Fork
Campground

*Ice House
Reservoir*

FR 31

FR 34

FR 3

Granite Springs
Road

Ice House
Road

Cleveland Corral
Information Station

To Lake Tahoe

Kyburz

50

To Placerville

About 3 miles from US 50 is the **Cleveland Corral Information Station** (parking, restrooms). In this area are Mountain Quail, House Wren, Wilson's Warbler, Spotted Towhee, Lazuli Bunting, and House Finch.

The **Granite Springs Road,** Forest Road 34, at 6.7 miles, goes to the east. About 0.3 mile out this road, a small colony of Black-throated Sparrows was found in 1997, far removed from their usual desert habitat. How permanent the colony may be remains to be seen. This is also a good place for Mountain Quail, Green-tailed Towhee, Fox Sparrow, and Lazuli Bunting.

At 7.2 miles from US 50, you will come to the top of the ridge, and at 7.9 miles there is a large pullout on the left where you can park. You are still in the burned area, but there are many brushy spots that are attractive to birds. Walk downhill a couple of hundred yards to the north, especially to the draw that has a lot of greenery. This is a good place for Green-tailed Towhee. Fox Sparrows also occur here, and the songs of these two species sound enough alike to cause confusion. Look for Lazuli Buntings, which seem to like to perch in the branches of the trees killed by the fire, and for Anna's Hummingbirds, Spotted Towhees, and Chipping Sparrows. In the brush in the bottom of the draw, you might find MacGillivray's Warblers.

The dirt road to **Silver Fork Campground** is on the left, about 8.7 miles from US 50 (0.3 mile to the campground from Ice House Road). On weekends the campground is usually full, but during the week—if it is not heavily occupied—it is an attractive area for birding. Numerous informal trails lead to the creek. Red-breasted Nuthatches seem to be ever present, with their *"ank-ank-ank"* sounding in the forest. This is a good place for flycatchers, and for MacGillivray's Warbler in the bushes along the creek. Also, look for Mountain Quail, Calliope Hummingbird, Western Wood-Pewee, Olive-sided Flycatcher, Warbling and Cassin's Vireos, Steller's Jay, Mountain Chickadee, Nashville and Black-throated Gray Warblers, and Black-headed Grosbeak.

The road to **Ice House Reservoir** (Forest Road 32) is 10.4 miles from US 50. It leads to the reservoir, three campgrounds, and a picnic area. The turnoff for the picnic area is 1.1 miles from the junction with Ice House Road. The forest around the picnic area offers good birding for Hairy Woodpecker; Western Wood-Pewee; Cassin's Vireo; Mountain Chickadee; Brown Creeper; Golden-crowned Kinglet; Hermit and Yellow-rumped Warblers; Western Tanager; and Chipping and Fox Sparrows. The loud *"Quick! THREE beers!"* of Olive-sided Flycatchers is heard frequently from the treetops in the spring.

Back on Ice House Road, at 14.4 miles, the paved road to the left leads to the **Peninsula** area and two campgrounds. It is 0.8 mile to a parking lot serving a boat launching area. The peninsula is narrow, so you can easily access the shore of **Union Valley Reservoir** on both sides. Canada Geese sometimes hang out here, and Ospreys and Bald Eagles are occasionally seen over the lake. A pair of eagles has nested somewhere around the lake since 1986, and up to 10 eagles are either here or at Ice House Reservoir during the winter. The forest hereabouts has Mountain Chickadees, Dark-eyed Juncos, and an occasional Hermit Warbler. Common Mergansers and Buffleheads have been seen on the lake.

Big Silver Creek comes at 15.9 miles, on Ice House Road. Just after you cross the creek, there is a group camping area on the left. If the camp is not in use by a group, especially in early season, it can be an attractive area for birding along Big Silver Creek. Look for birds such as Hairy, White-headed, and Pileated Woodpeckers; Western Wood-Pewee; Hammond's Flycatcher; Warbling Vireo; Steller's Jay; Townsend's Solitaire; and American Robin.

The turnoff to **Loon Lake** comes at 23.3 miles. The road that intersects at right angles from the right is actually the continuation of Ice House Road (FR 3); in 4.8 miles you will come to Loon Lake (another reservoir), which is heavily used by boaters.

The road straight ahead changes number, from FR 3 to Forest Road 33, and leads to Gerle (pronounced GUR-lee) Creek Reservoir and Gerle Creek Campground. At the 24.5-mile point, a dirt road takes off to the left, and goes to **Angel Creek Picnic Area** (parking, restrooms).

The paved turnoff to **Gerle Creek Campground** comes at the 26.1-mile point, on the left. At the entrance to the campground there is a sign for the Gerle Creek Interpretive Trail, which runs parallel to Gerle Creek. Northern Goshawk has been seen in this area.

At the far end of the campground, next to **Gerle Creek Reservoir,** is a parking area and picnic tables, marking the beginning of the **Summer Harvest Trail** (barrier free for about half its length). The trail runs for about 0.7 mile along the edge of Gerle Creek Reservoir. Some of the trail passes through open forest, but in places it traverses swampy areas lined with bracken fern. Typical birds include Steller's Jay, Mountain Chickadee, Red-breasted Nuthatch, and MacGillivray's Warbler. Canada Geese have nested on an island in the reservoir.

General information: Crystal Basin is an attractive area. About half of the basin is in private hands, a legacy of railroad-building days. Sacramento Municipal Utility District (known familiarly as SMUD) has three reservoirs in the basin (Ice House Reservoir, Union Valley Reservoir, and Loon Lake). In winter the main roads are kept open by SMUD, except during major storms when they may be closed. Tire chains are advisable in the mountains in winter.

ADDITIONAL HELP

NCA&G grid: Page 89, 5A, 5B.
Elevation: 3,300 to 6,400 feet.
Hazards: Fast traffic on roads, high-elevation sun exposure, rattlesnakes, ticks.
Nearest food, gas, lodging: Pollock Pines; Placerville.

Camping: Ice House: 83 sites, 10.4 miles from US 50 on Ice House Road, and then 1.1 miles east on FR 32; RV dump station. Northwind: 10 sites, 10.4 miles from US 50 on Ice House Road, and then 2.2 miles east on FR 32 (no fee, no water). Strawberry Point: 10 sites, 10.4 miles from US 50 on Ice House Road, and then 2.8 miles east on FR 32 (no fee, no water). Jones Fork: 10 sites, 13.2 miles from US 50, on Ice House Road (no fee, no water). Peninsula area: 14.4 miles from US 50, on Ice House Road. Fashoda: 30 sites, tent camping only. Sunset: 131 sites, RV dump station. Wench Creek: 100 sites, 16.6 miles from US 50 on Ice House Road. Yellowjacket: 40 sites, 18.7 miles from US 50 on Ice House Road, and then 1.3 miles west on spur road; RV dump station. Gerle Creek: 50 sites, 23.3 miles from US 50 on Ice House Road, and then 4.5 miles on FR 33. Loon Lake: 53 sites, 27.7 miles from US 50 on Ice House Road, and then 0.4 mile east on spur road; RV dump station.

For more information: Eldorado Information Center (USDA Forest Service); Pacific Ranger District.

43 Lake Tahoe 🚹 ♿

Habitats: Freshwater marsh, lake, stream, mixed conifer forest, meadow.

Specialty birds: *Resident*—Blue Grouse, White-headed Woodpecker, Pygmy Nuthatch, Cassin's Finch. *Summer*—Osprey, Calliope Hummingbird, Western Wood-Pewee, Western Tanager, Black-headed Grosbeak. *Winter*—Bald Eagle. *Migrant*—Rufous Hummingbird.

Other key birds: *Resident*—Common Merganser, Killdeer, Hairy Woodpecker, Red-breasted Nuthatch, Golden-crowned Kinglet, Red Crossbill, Evening Grosbeak. *Summer*—Common Snipe; Forster's Tern; Olive-sided Flycatcher; Warbling Vireo; Yellow and Yellow-rumped Warblers; Chipping Sparrow.

Best times to bird: April to July.

Directions: From the junction of U.S. Highway 50/California Highway 89 and CA 89 in South Lake Tahoe, go 3.4 miles north on CA 89 to a crossroads. The road to the right (north) goes to Tallac Historic Site; Fallen Leaf Road, to the left, goes to Fallen Leaf Campground (0.6 mile from the junction) and to a dirt parking area for **Fallen Leaf Lake Trail** (0.8 mile from the junction). The road to the **Lake Tahoe Visitor Center** is 0.1 mile farther on CA 89.

The birding: At the **Lake Tahoe Visitor Center** (parking, restrooms), take the barrier-free **Lake of the Sky Trail** to Tallac Point (about 1 mile round trip). The trail runs on a low ridge through pines and scattered sagebrush, overlooking the marshy flats where Taylor Creek joins Lake Tahoe. From Tallac Point you can walk along the sand spit to the mouth of the creek, detouring around sunbathers on the way. Birds to look for are Western Wood-Pewee, Steller's Jay, Mountain Chickadee, Pygmy Nuthatch, Western Tanager, and Chipping Sparrow in the forest, and Osprey,

43 Lake Tahoe

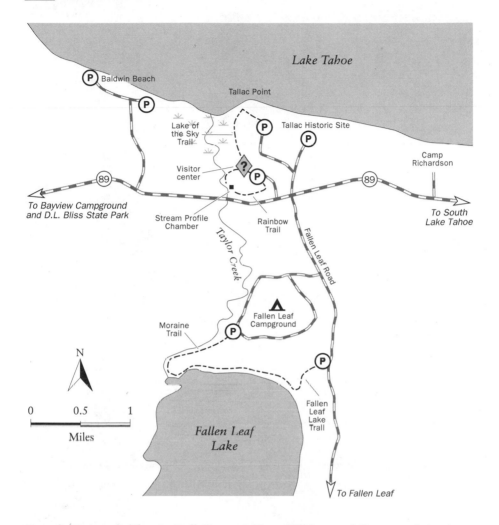

Canada Goose, California Gull, Forster's Tern, Killdeer, and Common Snipe (rare and irregular) in and above the marshy flats. Look for Common Mergansers on the lake. From October 15 to March 15, the area of the flats is closed to public access because it is a gathering ground for Bald Eagles.

From the visitor center, take the **Rainbow Trail,** which makes a loop through the meadows adjacent to Taylor Creek and gives access to the **Stream Profile Chamber.** From the chamber you can look through a glass pane into a pond in the creek, to see trout and other underwater life. Look for Calliope Hummingbirds, which breed here, and Rufous Hummingbirds, which do not, but migrate south from their breeding grounds beginning in July. Look also for Warbling Vireo, Tree Swallow, and Yellow Warbler.

Lake Tahoe is an immense gem of the Sierra Nevada.

From the dirt parking area on the Fallen Leaf Road, take the **Fallen Leaf Lake Trail** to the lake, which is about 1 mile round trip. The trail leads through meadows, aspen groves, and pine/fir forest, climbs over a glacial moraine, and arrives at the lake (gravelly beach). Some birds to look for here are White-headed and Hairy Woodpeckers; Western Wood-Pewee; Olive-sided Flycatcher; Warbling Vireo; Mountain Chickadee; Red-breasted Nuthatch; Golden-crowned Kinglet; Yellow-rumped Warbler; Black-headed Grosbeak; Cassin's Finch; Red Crossbill; and Evening Grosbeak, the latter two being erratic and unpredictable. Listen for the *"vroom! vroom! vroom!"* of Blue Grouse in spring.

The Fallen Leaf Lake Trail is also accessible from the Fallen Leaf Campground, where it is called the **Moraine Trail.** There is a parking area (day-use fee) at the southwestern corner of the campground, near sites 73 and 74.

General information: Lake Tahoe is one of the gems of the Sierra Nevada. The portion of the lake on the southwestern corner is almost all under the ownership of the USDA Forest Service. Fallen Leaf Lake is another gem, and is often overlooked because it lies off to one side of the highway. Mount Tallac (9,735 feet) rises directly above the lake, and displays a snowy cross on its face in spring and early summer. Taylor Creek, which runs between Fallen Leaf Lake and Lake Tahoe, is a spawning site for runs of kokanee salmon in fall.

ADDITIONAL HELP

NCA&G grid: Page 89, 7A.
Elevation: 6,300 feet.
Hazards: Rattlesnakes, ticks.
Nearest food, gas, lodging: South Lake Tahoe.
Camping: Fallen Leaf: 205 sites, 3.4 miles north of South Lake Tahoe on CA 89, then 0.6 mile west on Fallen Leaf Road. Bayview: 10 sites, 7.8 miles north of South Lake Tahoe on CA 89. D. L. Bliss State Park: 168 sites, 11 miles north of South Lake Tahoe on CA 89.
For more information: Lake Tahoe Basin Management Unit

44 Carson Pass and Hope Valley

Habitats: Lake, lodgepole–red fir forest, sagebrush scrub, subalpine zone.

Specialty birds: *Resident*—Blue Grouse, Williamson's Sapsucker, Steller's Jay, Clark's Nutcracker, Mountain Chickadee, Townsend's Solitaire, Cassin's Finch. *Summer*—Prairie Falcon, Dusky Flycatcher, Mountain Bluebird, Hermit Warbler, Green-tailed Towhee. *Migrant*—Hammond's Flycatcher, MacGillivray's Warbler.

Other key birds: *Resident*—Great Horned Owl, Hairy Woodpecker, Dark-eyed Junco, Pine Grosbeak, Pine Siskin. *Summer*—Warbling Vireo; Yellow-rumped Warbler; Chipping, Fox, Lincoln's, and White-crowned Sparrows. *Migrant*—Orange-crowned Warbler.

Best times to bird: June through September.

Directions: Carson Pass is about 55 miles east of Jackson (allow 2 hours), on California Highway 88 (parking, restrooms, information station open in season). Hope Valley is about 7 miles east of Carson Pass, on CA 88. **Luther Pass** is on California Highway 89, 2.6 miles north of the junction of CA 88 and CA 88/89.

The birding: The hike from **Carson Pass to Frog Lake** is about a mile one way, with 300 feet of elevation gain. **Winnemucca Lake** is 1.5 miles farther, with another 200 feet of elevation gain. The first portion is through open forest, but near Frog Lake the country becomes subalpine, and you'll have sensational views of Round Top.

The trail is popular, especially on weekends, so it helps to start out early. After you reach subalpine territory you can move off the trail and avoid the crowds. If you go after Labor Day, especially in midweek, you can have things pretty much to yourself. In the Sierra, this is generally the best time of year.

The "trademark bird" of these elevations is the Clark's Nutcracker, which almost always can be heard making its raucous cry somewhere. There is a possibility of encountering a flock of Pine Grosbeaks, but they are elusive and unpredictable. Other characteristic birds are Dusky Flycatcher, Mountain Chickadee, Mountain Bluebird, Townsend's Solitaire (the last two, uncommon), Yellow-rumped Warbler, Lincoln's Sparrow (wet places in willow thickets), Dark-eyed Junco, and Cassin's Finch. Blue Grouse are sometimes encountered along the trail.

Red-tailed Hawks are usually soaring overhead, at least until the snows arrive and they are driven downslope. Prairie Falcon is uncommon; look for the identifying dark areas in the "armpits."

Check the willow thickets for Orange-crowned and MacGillivray's Warblers, which normally breed at lower elevations, but in late summer after breeding is over drift upslope. Also in late summer, migrants such as Willow and Hammond's Flycatchers move through.

Other birds to look for are Williamson's Sapsucker, Hairy Woodpecker, Steller's Jay, Common Raven, Brown Creeper, House Wren, Hermit Warbler, White-crowned Sparrow, and Pine Siskin. In brushy areas, check for Green-tailed Towhee and Fox Sparrow.

44 Carson Pass and Hope Valley

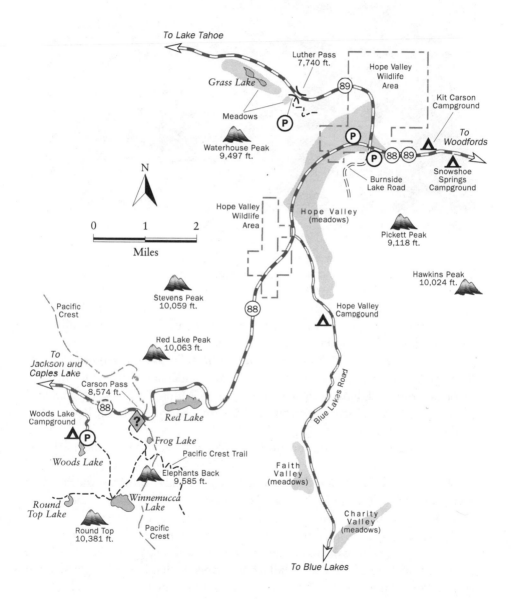

To Lake Tahoe

Luther Pass
7,740 ft.

Hope Valley
Wildlife
Area

Grass Lake

89

Kit Carson
Campground

To
Woodfords

Meadows

Waterhouse Peak
9,497 ft.

88 89

N

0   1   2
Miles

Hope Valley
Wildlife
Area

Burnside
Lake Road

Snowshoe
Springs
Campground

Hope Valley
(meadows)

Pickett Peak
9,118 ft.

Hawkins Peak
10,024 ft.

Stevens Peak
10,059 ft.

88

Hope Valley
Campgound

Pacific
Crest

Red Lake Peak
10,063 ft.

To
Jackson and
Caples Lake

Carson Pass
8,574 ft.

88

Woods Lake
Campground

?

Red Lake

Blue Lakes Road

Frog Lake

Woods Lake

Pacific Crest Trail

Elephants Back
9,585 ft.

Faith
Valley
(meadows)

Round
Top Lake

Winnemucca
Lake

Round Top
10,381 ft.

Pacific
Crest

Charity
Valley
(meadows)

To Blue Lakes

185

Round Top, near Carson Pass.

In **Hope Valley**, in addition to the foregoing birds, look for Great Horned Owls. They have been heard hooting at night in the Hope Valley Campground. The California Department of Fish and Game owns portions of Hope Valley and manages them as the **Hope Valley Wildlife Area.** Thus, the land in the valley is a mixture of ownership by Fish and Game, and the USDA Forest Service. At the junction of CA 88 and CA 88/89, the road to Burnside Lake (gravel) heads south. If you go a quarter mile or so and park, you can wander at will through a delightful open forest, with birds such as Warbling Vireo, Mountain Chickadee, Yellow-rumped Warbler, Chipping Sparrow, and Cassin's Finch. American Robins and Dark-eyed Juncos are common.

About 0.2 mile west of the junction of CA 88 and CA 88/89, on the north side of the road, is one of the access points to the Hope Valley Wildlife Area. There is ample parking by an old gate. Walk around the gate, and stroll across the meadow on the remains of the old Luther Pass Highway, to the West Fork of the Carson River. Birds are similar to those mentioned in the preceding paragraph.

Luther Pass and the adjacent meadows at **Grass Lake** make a delightful stop. Park at the pass, west of the road near the big boulders. The old Luther Pass Road leads off from here and down the hill toward Hope Valley. It is an easy walk, and you can go as far as you like. You probably won't see anyone else. The birds are similar to those already mentioned.

General information: Carson Pass (8,574 feet) offers access to beautiful subalpine country. As a result, it is extremely popular, partly because it is a trailhead for the

Mokelumne Wilderness. This part of the Sierra crest was where the first winter crossing of the Sierra Nevada took place, in February 1844, by a party led by John C. Fremont and Kit Carson, a crossing in which they all nearly perished. As you stand on the crest near Frog Lake and look toward the east, you can persuade yourself that this is the exact place where Fremont and Carson crossed, rather than at the modern Carson Pass where the highway now goes. The terrain east of Frog Lake appears to be a much better route than the steep slopes near Carson Pass itself.

Hope Valley, in the opinion of some, is the second most beautiful mountain valley in the Sierra Nevada, surpassed only by Yosemite Valley. In June, with the green of its huge meadow valley and the snowy peaks behind, it may very well come up to the brag. In mid-October, the aspens blaze into yellow and gold, offering what is probably the best display of autumn color in California.

ADDITIONAL HELP

NCA&G grid: Page 90, 1B, 1C.
Elevation: 7,100 to 9,000 feet.
Hazards: Exposure to high-elevation sun, lightning.
Nearest food, gas, lodging: South Lake Tahoe.
Camping: Hope Valley; 20 sites, 1.6 miles south of CA 88 on Blue Lakes Road; gravel interior roads. Kit Carson: 12 sites, 1.2 miles east of the junction of CA 88 and CA 88/89, on CA 88/89. Snowshoe Springs: 13 sites, 1.8 miles east of the junction of CA 88 and CA 88/89, on CA 88/89; no trailers. Woods Lake: 25 sites, 1.8 miles west of Carson Pass on CA 88, then 2 miles south on paved local access road. Caples Lake: 35 sites, 4 miles west of Carson Pass on CA 88.
For more information: East of Carson Pass—Carson Ranger District; west of Carson Pass—Amador Ranger District.

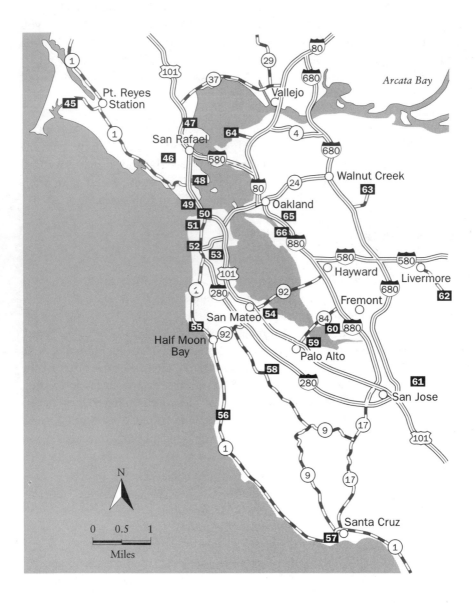

San Francisco Bay Area

The San Francisco Bay is remarkable from a birding viewpoint, because it has many outstanding birding sites in spite of its being a major metropolitan area. The birding trail here is a loop that begins at Point Reyes and wraps around the bay. There are many sites right in the city, some of them so close to the airport that a person with only a few hours to spare could still manage to get in a little birding.

The bay itself is the centerpiece, and provides a chance for specialties such as Black Rail, California Clapper Rail, Burrowing Owl, Least Tern, and Black Skimmer. But there is also the hinterland, such as at Mines Road and Del Puerto Canyon, where the land seems so remote that it might be in another country. The bottom line is that the Bay Area is one of the most beloved birding areas in the U.S.

45 Point Reyes

46 Mount Tamalpais

47 Las Gallinas Wildlife Ponds

48 Richardson Bay Audubon Center and Sanctuary

49 Marin Headlands

50 Presidio

51 Golden Gate Park

52 Lake Merced

53 San Bruno Mountain

54 Foster City

55 Pillar Point

56 San Mateo Coast

57 Santa Cruz

58 Skyline Boulevard

59 Palo Alto Baylands and Shoreline at Mountain View

60 Don Edwards San Francisco Bay National Wildlife Refuge

61 Alum Rock Park

62 Mines Road and Del Puerto Canyon

63 Mount Diablo

64 Point Pinole Regional Shoreline

65 Lake Merritt

66 Martin Luther King Jr. Regional Shoreline

45 Point Reyes 🏕 ♿

Habitats: Sandy beach and mudflats, dunes, rocky headlands, coastal bays and lagoons, coastal prairie, coastal scrub, closed-cone pine forest, Douglas-fir forest, salt marsh, freshwater marsh, riparian woodland.

Specialty birds: *Resident*—Brandt's and Pelagic Cormorants; Wood Duck; Snowy Plover; Black Oystercatcher; Western Gull; Rhinoceros Auklet; Band-tailed Pigeon; Spotted Owl; Hutton's Vireo; Steller's Jay; Chestnut-backed Chickadee; Bushtit; Pygmy Nuthatch; Western Bluebird; Wrentit; Tricolored Blackbird; Western Meadowlark. *Summer*—Brown Pelican, Cinnamon Teal, Osprey, Heermann's Gull, Elegant Tern, Pigeon Guillemot, Allen's Hummingbird, Western Wood-Pewee, Pacific-slope Flycatcher, Violet-green Swallow, Black-headed Grosbeak, Bullock's Oriole. *Winter*—Pacific Loon; Western and Clark's Grebes; Eurasian Wigeon; Peregrine Falcon; Pacific Golden-Plover; Wandering Tattler; Long-billed Curlew; Black Turnstone; Mew, Thayer's, and Glaucous-winged Gulls; Red-breasted Sapsucker; Varied Thrush; Townsend's Warbler; Golden-crowned Sparrow.

Other key birds: *Resident*—Double-crested Cormorant; Red-shouldered Hawk; Forster's Tern; Common Murre; Barn, Great Horned, and Northern Saw-whet Owls; Common Raven; Horned Lark; Winter and Marsh Wrens; Hermit Thrush; Common Yellowthroat; Savannah, Song, and White-crowned Sparrows; Purple Finch; Pine Siskin. *Summer*—Caspian Tern; Olive-sided Flycatcher; Warbling Vireo; Purple Martin; Swainson's Thrush; Orange-crowned, Yellow, and Wilson's Warblers; Grasshopper Sparrow; American Goldfinch. *Winter*—Red-throated and Common Loons; Horned, Eared, and Red-necked Grebes; Black, White-winged, and Surf Scoters; Bufflehead; Sharp-shinned and Cooper's Hawks; Virginia Rail; Sora; Greater Yellowlegs; Ruddy Turnstone; Common Snipe; Swamp and White-throated Sparrows. *Migrant*—Red-necked Phalarope; Palm, Blackpoll, and Black-and-white Warblers; American Redstart; Lapland Longspur.

Best times to bird: All year is good; November through March for most waterfowl; April through June for breeding birds; August to October for shorebirds; May through June, and September through October for vagrant land birds.

Directions: From the junction of U.S. Highway 101/California Highway 1 and CA 1 north of the Golden Gate Bridge, take CA 1 north about 26 miles to Olema (allow 60 to 90 minutes). The Bear Valley visitor center is about 0.5 mile west of Olema, on Bear Valley Road. Point Reyes Station is 2 miles beyond Olema, on CA 1.

The birding: The **Outer Peninsula** is the part of the Point most people head for first. From Point Reyes Station, go 0.2 mile south on CA 1 and turn west on Sir Francis Drake Boulevard. It is 13.9 miles to the Drakes Beach road, then 4.1 miles farther to the Chimney Rock road, and 1 mile more to the end of the road at the parking lot for the lighthouse (restrooms). On winter weekends when the whale-watchers are out in force, this parking lot and the one for Chimney Rock may be full, and

45 Point Reyes

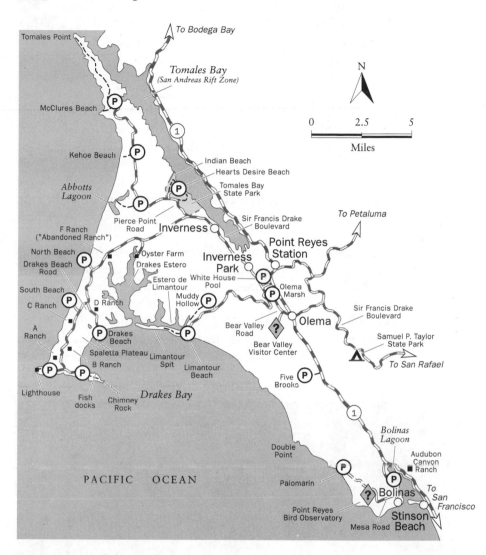

you could find yourself shunted off by the park rangers to South Beach until space opens up.

It is a 0.4-mile walk from the parking lot to the **lighthouse.** Vagrants such as Magnolia and Prairie Warblers and American Redstart have shown up here, mostly in September and October, either in the cypress trees near the lighthouse, or in the bushes below the path. From the Point itself, many seabirds usually can be seen, although you are very high above them. Common Murres are resident breeders. There often are scores of Brown Pelicans flying about or perched on the rocks during the summer. With luck, you might spot a Parasitic Jaeger, Northern Fulmar, or Sooty Shearwater, all of which occasionally show up this close to shore.

From the intersection with the Chimney Rock road, it is 0.8 mile on a narrow paved road to the parking lot for **Fish Docks** and **Chimney Rock** (chemical toilet). The term Fish Docks applies not only to the docks on the bay but also to the adjacent water and land areas. In winter the bay is likely to have loons, Western and Clark's Grebes, and scoters. King Eider and Oldsquaw (both rare) have shown up here. The trees and bushes near the parking lot can have Swainson's Thrush (summer), White-crowned Sparrow (resident), American Goldfinch (resident), and vagrant warblers in the spring and fall; Townsend's Warbler is a winter visitor. The large trees east of the house (private) near the parking lot have had nesting Great Horned Owls. To the west of the parking lot (200 to 300 yards) is a gully choked with willows, called **New Willows,** reached by walking partway down the road and then taking an informal trail along the steep slope. Vagrants have sometimes been seen here.

The trail to **Chimney Rock** is about 1.5 miles round trip. In spring Savannah Sparrows serenade you from the grassy tufts. The viewpoint at the end is protected by a fence (the cliffs are steep and undercut), but you can get excellent views of residents such as Brandt's and Pelagic Cormorants, Black Oystercatcher, Common Murre, Rhinoceros Auklet, and Western Gull. In summer Brown Pelican, Pigeon Guillemot, Osprey, Heermann's Gull, and Elegant Tern show up. In winter look for Mew, California, Thayer's, and Glaucous-winged Gulls; Black, White-winged,

Heermann's Gull.

and Surf Scoters; Wandering Tattler; and Ruddy and Black Turnstones. Rarely, Tufted and Horned Puffins appear.

Migrant traps: Most of the outer peninsula is rolling grassland, but here and there are clumps of trees, mostly cypress that act as magnets in the fall for eastern migrants that have somehow misdirected themselves and wound up on the Pacific Coast. They get funneled out onto the long peninsula of Point Reyes and often take shelter in these small groves. Subsequently, if they continue to follow their misoriented internal compasses, they fly out over the Pacific Ocean and perish. The Farallon Islands, 20 miles southwest of Point Reyes, get an unusual number of eastern vagrant land birds.

The **Historic "A" Ranch** (Nunes Ranch) has a clump of cypress next to the farm buildings that often has migrants such as Blackpoll Warbler. Park well away from the farm buildings, making sure you don't block any gates, and stay among the trees, away from the houses. The **Historic "B" Ranch** (Mendoza Ranch) has some trees along the main road that sometimes have migrants. Again, park away from the farm buildings, and do not block the gates.

Access to the **Spaletta Plateau** is 0.6 mile south from the **Historic "C" Ranch** (Spaletta Ranch). A pedestrian passage has been provided next to the gate. The grasses are kept short by grazing cattle, and the area attracts rare birds such as Pacific Golden-Plover, Buff-breasted Sandpiper, Palm Warbler, and Lapland Longspur. Access to the **Spaletta Slop Ponds** can be had by going through the gate just to the northeast of the Historic "C" Ranch (leaving the gate as you found it) and walking across the fields to two ponds a quarter of a mile or so below the farmhouses. These ponds have been good for shorebirds.

From the junction of the main road with the Drakes Beach road, it is 1.5 miles to the parking lot at **Drakes Beach** (restrooms, picnicking, visitor center, and cafe open on weekends). As you enter the parking area there is a grove of trees on the right next to the **Francis Drake Monument.** Vagrants have shown up here, and Barn and Great Horned Owls have sometimes roosted. About 100 yards beyond the monument, on the northwest edge of the parking lot, a short trail through the bushes leads to a pond. Mostly, the pond has gulls on it, but also has had various grebes and waterfowl. Look in the bushes for warblers, vireos, and sparrows. From the beach in front of the visitor center, it is about a half-mile hike along the beach to the east to Horseshoe Pond. Gadwalls have nested here, and beginning in August this is a good place for shorebirds. Hundreds of Red-necked Phalaropes have been observed here during migration. Also, look for Caspian Tern (summer) and Forster's Tern (resident).

About 0.9 mile down the Drakes Beach road from its junction with the main road, is the **Historic "D" Ranch;** 0.3 mile south of the ranch is a gate on the east side with a pedestrian passage next to it. Park off the road without blocking the gate, and walk through the gate about 200 yards to the east. Lapland Longspurs, Chestnut-collared Longspurs, and Snow Buntings (all rare) have been seen here.

The **Historic "F" Ranch** (the Abandoned Ranch) has a fairly good-sized grove, and there are no farm buildings here. Rarities such as Bay-breasted Warbler and Rose-breasted Grosbeak have turned up here, but they very well can show up at any of the migrant traps on the Point.

Throughout this grassy open country, keep an eye out for flocks of Tricolored Blackbirds; they breed in the region, but shift their breeding sites from year to year. The male Tricolored has a pure white chevron below the red shoulder patch, whereas male Red-winged Blackbirds have a buffy patch, or sometimes no patch. Frequently, the red patch on a Tricolored may be covered up, so that only the white chevron is visible (the white chevron may be tinged with buff in the fall). Another bird to look for in this grassy country in breeding season is Grasshopper Sparrow. Northern Harrier, Horned Lark, Western Meadowlark, and Common Raven are residents. Extreme rarities such as Smith's Longspur and Eurasian Dotterel have shown up on these pasturelands.

The turnoff for **Tomales Bay State Park** (Pierce Point Road) is about 6.3 miles from Point Reyes Station on Sir Francis Drake Boulevard. Drive 1.2 miles along Pierce Point Road to the entrance for Tomales Bay State Park (fee), and from there, 1.3 miles down to **Hearts Desire Beach** (parking, restrooms), then take the trail north from the parking lot to **Indian Beach** (1 mile round trip). In spring there should be Warbling Vireo, Swainson's Thrush, and Wilson's Warbler. In winter look for Cooper's Hawk, Varied Thrush, and Golden-crowned Sparrow. Brown Creeper, Bewicks' Wren, Hermit Thrush, and Spotted and California Towhees are resident.

Tomales Bay State Park has been a good place to see Spotted Owl. There was one pair that was easily observed, and the owls often would sit directly overhead oblivious to the presence of people. In 1995 the male disappeared, and the female recruited a new mate. The following year the female disappeared, and only a month later the newly recruited male was found with an injured wing. Attempts were made to rehabilitate it, but the bird was very ill, and it died. However, the rangers at the park believe the nesting area will be reoccupied. Maybe by the time you read this, it will already have happened, so here are the directions. After you get to Indian Beach (see preceding directions), take the dirt road to the left, away from the beach, for 0.1 mile to an old dirt road on the right. Go up this road a short distance to a junction with another dirt road, and check the trees in the area. If you do find an owl, the rangers ask that you please do not do anything to disturb it.

Another place where Spotted Owls have been found, but not in a location where they are so easily observed, is in the canyon above Pebble Beach. To get there, park at the Hearts Desire Beach parking lot, and hike south 0.5 mile to Pebble Beach, on the Johnstone Trail. Just before you get to Pebble Beach, the Johnstone Trail cuts off to the right. The trail to the left leads to the beach (there is a pit toilet about 30 yards down this trail, on the left). If you continue on the Johnstone Trail a few hundred yards, you will be in the general area where the owls have been found. These owls, however, have not been known to take up perches over the trail the way they have at the location near Indian Beach.

There is a dead tree with an Osprey nest in it, about 300 yards up the Johnstone Trail from Pebble Beach, which has been occupied in recent years. Because the Ospreys become very agitated when people walk below their nest, it is probably best not to linger.

The parking lot for **Abbotts Lagoon** (restrooms) is 3.3 miles along Pierce Point Road from the junction with Sir Francis Drake Boulevard. It is a 1.5-mile walk to the lagoon, and another 0.5 mile to the beach. The first half mile or so is barrier free. Abbotts Lagoon is good beginning in early August for shorebirds, such as Greater Yellowlegs; Sanderling; Western and Least Sandpipers; Dunlin; and rarities such as Baird's and Pectoral Sandpipers. Snowy Plovers nest in the dunes nearby. Also, loons and other water birds make extensive use of the lagoon. A rare Arctic Loon was here in 1991. A small flock of Mute Swans is sometimes present, but Mute Swan has not yet been added to the California list as a self-sustaining wild species. (An official "California Bird List" is maintained by the California Bird Records Committee of the Western Field Ornithologists.)

The trailhead for **Kehoe Beach** (parking on road shoulders, pit toilets) is at 5.3 miles along Pierce Point Road. It is about 0.7 mile to the beach by trail, leading past a marsh. Marsh Wrens and blackbirds are at the marsh, Swainson's Thrushes and Wilson's Warblers are in the willows, and American Goldfinches and Wrentits are on the hillsides. Kehoe Beach is broad and scenic, with the usual shorebirds, terns, and gulls. A Bristle-thighed Curlew was at Kehoe Beach in May 1998, in the company of some Whimbrels.

Pierce Point Road ends 9.1 miles from the main road at the parking lot for McClures Beach and Tomales Point. Tomales Point is a 4.7-mile hike one way, with magnificent views both of the ocean and of Tomales Bay. A large herd of tule elk roams here.

Close to the bottom of Tomales Bay is **White House Pool**, 0.6 mile from the junction with CA 1, on Sir Francis Drake Boulevard (parking, restrooms). A short trail leads along a nearby slough. Birds that might be seen here are resident Black Phoebe, Hutton's Vireo, Chestnut-backed Chickadee, Bushtit, Winter Wren, Western Bluebird, Common Yellowthroat, Song Sparrow, and Purple Finch. In summer look for Allen's Hummingbird; Western Wood-Pewee; Pacific-slope Flycatcher; Warbling Vireo; Violet-green Swallow; Swainson's Thrush; Orange-crowned; Yellow, and Wilson's Warblers; Black-headed Grosbeak; Bullock's Oriole; and American Goldfinch, and in winter for Bufflehead, Virginia Rail, Ruby-crowned Kinglet, and even a rare Swamp Sparrow.

About 0.4 mile south of White House Pool, on Bear Valley Road, the road to Limantour goes to the west 5.8 miles to Muddy Hollow (parking), and then 1.6 miles more to Limantour Beach (parking, pit toilets). From the Muddy Hollow parking lot, a trail leads down **Muddy Hollow** and in about 1.8 miles comes to Limantour Beach. The habitat along the Muddy Hollow Trail is primarily riparian, with birds such as Red-shouldered Hawk; California Quail; Anna's and Allen's Hummingbirds; Belted Kingfisher; Downy Woodpecker; Black Phoebe; Hutton's and Warbling Vireos; Bushtit; Bewick's Wren; Wrentit; Swainson's Thrush; Orange-crowned, Yellow, and Wilson's Warblers; and Golden-Crowned and White-crowned Sparrows. Check for winter rarities such as Black-and-white Warbler and White-throated Sparrow.

From the **Limantour Beach** parking lot, a trail goes to the beach, the first part of which is barrier free. Just before the trail arrives at the dunes it splits into three parts. The part straight ahead enters loose sand and goes to the beach; the trail to the left (east) is paved for about 300 yards and then disappears in the sand; and the trail to the right (west) runs along Limantour Spit between the dunes and Estero de Limantour. The estero can be an excellent place for shorebirds in migration, and waterfowl in winter. Look for Virginia Rail, Marsh Wren, and Common Yellowthroat in the marshes, and Black-bellied Plover, Greater Yellowlegs, Willet, Long-billed Curlew, and Elegant Tern on the flats. Ospreys sometimes perch near the marshes, and a Peregrine Falcon might show up. Cinnamon Teal is a summer breeder.

The opposite end of the Muddy Hollow Trail begins at the Limantour Beach parking lot. The trail runs along the border of the marshes belonging to Estero de Limantour before coming to a line of trees that mark the edge of a good-sized pond, which may have American Wigeon and Gadwall, as well as egrets. The area is also well supplied with poison oak.

From the junction of Bear Valley and Limantour roads, it is about 0.1 mile south on Bear Valley Road to a gravel road on the east side leading to **Olema Marsh.** It is 0.1 mile to a parking area and an overlook where you can view the marsh. Common Snipe, Virginia Rail, and Sora might be found here in winter. Swamp Sparrows (rare) have been seen here a number of times in winter.

The **Headquarters and Visitor Center** are 1.2 miles south of Olema Marsh, on Bear Valley Road. There are picnic tables here, and a barrier-free trail called the **Earthquake Trail.**

About 3.5 miles south of Olema on CA 1 is the gravel entrance road to **Five Brooks,** which is a major trailhead (parking, restrooms). About 100 yards from the parking lot is a small pond surrounded by willows and poison oak. A trail encircles the pond (about 0.7 mile round trip). The best access comes at the beginning, where an opening offers a good view into the pond. Birds that have been known to breed here and in the immediate area are Wood Duck; Band-tailed Pigeon; Northern Saw-whet Owl; Anna's and Allen's Hummingbirds; Red-breasted Sapsucker (rare breeder); Olive-sided and Pacific-slope Flycatchers; Western Wood-Pewee; Hutton's and Warbling Vireos; Steller's Jay; Violet-green Swallow; Chestnut-backed Chickadee; Pygmy Nuthatch; Western Bluebird; Swainson's Thrush; Wrentit; Yellow and Wilson's Warblers; Purple Finch; Pine Siskin; and American Goldfinch.

South of Olema on CA 1, at 5.6 miles, a road branches to the west just before Bolinas Lagoon. The road leads to the small town of Bolinas, but there is no sign. Along this road, 1.1 miles from the turnoff, is a limited amount of shoulder parking on the east side of the road, giving access to a trail leading to **Pine Gulch Creek** (owned by Marin County Open Space District). Look for Sharp-shinned Hawk, Downy Woodpecker, Purple Martin (irregular), flycatchers, vireos, and warblers. Unfortunately this trail has a tendency to become overgrown, so at times it may be traversable for only a short distance.

Farther on, at 0.1 mile from Pine Gulch Creek, you will come to a junction with Horseshoe Hill Road. Turn left, go 0.5 mile to Mesa Road, and turn right. A sign reads "Point Reyes Bird Observatory." After 3.4 miles, the road turns to gravel, and 0.5 mile more is **Point Reyes Bird Observatory (PRBO)**. The end of the road is 0.7 mile beyond PRBO, at the Palomarin Trailhead.

Wrentit and White-crowned Sparrow, as well as others, have been investigated in depth at PRBO. Visitors are welcome, 9 A.M. to 5 P.M. daily. The **Fern Canyon Nature Trail** begins about halfway down the parking lot, and leads into lots of good bird habitat. The trail can get rather overgrown and is steep in spots. After going to the bottom of Fern Canyon, it is possible to continue up the opposite side and come out at the main road, but this requires walking back along the road and coping with the dust of passing cars.

Some resident birds here are California Quail; Hutton's Vireo; Western Scrub-Jay; Steller's Jay; Chestnut-backed Chickadee; Bushtit; Bewick's and Winter Wrens; Wrentit; Spotted and California Towhees; and White-crowned Sparrow. Some summer breeders are Pacific-slope Flycatcher, Warbling Vireo, Swainson's Thrush, Wilson's Warbler, and Black-headed Grosbeak.

From the junction of CA 1 and the road to Bolinas, it is 1 mile south on CA 1 to the **Audubon Canyon Ranch,** the location of one of the best-known Great Blue Heron/egret rookeries in the state. (Open weekends and holidays from mid-March to mid-July; donation requested.) The birds build their nests in the tops of redwood trees. From the parking lot, a moderately steep but short trail leads to an observation point on a ridge, where you can look directly out at the nesting birds.

CA 1 runs next to the eastern shore of **Bolinas Lagoon** for about 3.5 miles. There are numerous wide areas where you can pull off and park and scan the lagoon for water birds (a scope is useful), and the nearby flats for shorebirds. Little Stint (very rare) has been seen here. Rafts of waterfowl reside on the lagoon in the winter months, sometimes including the rare Eurasian Wigeon.

General information: Point Reyes is legendary with birders, both for its many breeding species and for its lengthy list of fall vagrants. Virtually the entire peninsula is part of the Point Reyes National Seashore, operated by the National Park Service.

Much of the seashore consists of treeless coastal prairie, with herds of dairy cattle. The dairy ranches are owned by the National Park Service but are operated as private enterprises. Birders may go through farm gates and cross the fields, but should avoid the immediate vicinity of the farm residences. In all cases, gates must be left as you found them, and you should not park so as to block any gates. In many places, special pedestrian passages have been provided next to the farm gates. Birders should avoid interfering with the cattle, or with any of the other farming operations. The rangers warn that cattle are unpredictable and could charge a person on foot.

The high "spine" of the peninsula is typical Douglas-fir forest, but toward the northern end the forest becomes dominated by Bishop pines. There are no red-woods on Point Reyes, even though there are many of them just over the ridge at Samuel P. Taylor State Park.

The long fiordlike Tomales Bay occupies the location of the San Andreas Fault zone, and CA 1 from Point Reyes Station to Stinson Beach runs directly along the fault zone.

ADDITIONAL HELP

NCA&G grid: Page 93.
Elevation: Sea level to 600 feet.
Hazards: Poison oak, rattlesnakes, ticks, undercut cliffs.
Nearest food, gas, lodging: Olema; San Rafael.
Camping: Samuel P. Taylor State Park: 60 sites, about 5 miles east of Olema on Sir Francis Drake Boulevard.
For more information: Point Reyes National Seashore.

46 Mount Tamalpais ♚ ♿

> **Habitats:** Coastal scrub, redwood forest, Douglas-fir forest, lake, riparian woodland, oak savanna.
> **Specialty birds:** *Resident*—Band-tailed Pigeon, Western Screech-Owl, Spotted Owl, Nuttall's Woodpecker, Hutton's Vireo, Steller's Jay, Chestnut-backed Chickadee, Pygmy Nuthatch, Western Bluebird, Wrentit, Rufous-crowned Sparrow, Lesser Goldfinch. *Summer*—Allen's Hummingbird; Western Wood-Pewee; Pacific-slope and Ash-throated Flycatchers; Cassin's Vireo; Violet-green Swallow; Black-throated Gray and Hermit Warblers; Black-headed Grosbeak; Lazuli Bunting; Bullock's Oriole. *Winter*—Townsend's Warbler.
> **Other key birds:** *Resident*—Great Horned Owl, Northern Saw-whet Owl, Pileated Woodpecker, Red-breasted Nuthatch, Winter Wren, Golden-crowned Kinglet, Hermit Thrush, Purple Finch, Pine Siskin. *Summer*—Olive-sided Flycatcher; Warbling Vireo; Swainson's Thrush; Orange-crowned and Wilson's Warblers; Chipping Sparrow.
> **Best times to bird:** All year; April through June for breeding species; October through April for winter residents.

Directions: From the junction of U.S. Highway 101 and California Highway 1 north of Sausalito, go 3.3 miles northwest on CA 1 to a road on the right leading

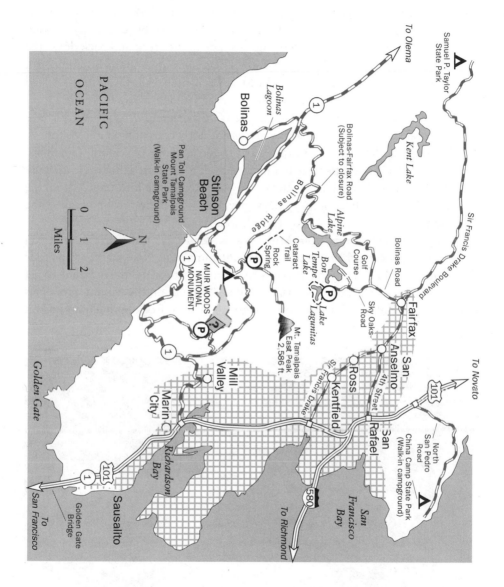

to Muir Woods and Mount Tamalpais. Travel 0.8 mile on this road to the turnoff for Muir Woods on the left. **Muir Woods** is 1.5 miles down the road (fee, parking, restrooms, visitor center, cafe). Muir Woods is a day-use area and closes at sunset.

The birding: Muir Woods opens at 8 A.M., and by 10 o'clock the tour buses start to roll in, but during that short period you can get some nice birding in, by walking the paved trail (barrier free) that goes up one side of the creek and back down the other. Some resident birds are Spotted Owl (uncommon), Anna's Hummingbird, Pileated Woodpecker (uncommon), Hutton's Vireo, Steller's Jay, Chestnut-backed Chickadee, Bushtit, Winter Wren, Brown Creeper, Golden-crowned Kinglet, Spotted Towhee, and Purple Finch. Black-headed Grosbeak and Wilson's Warbler are summer residents, and Townsend's Warbler is a fairly common winter visitor.

Even though Spotted Owls are present in the canyons of Mount Tamalpais, such as at Muir Woods, they are not often seen. It is estimated that there are only 25 to 30 pairs in all of Marin County. They seek out dense forest away from the more public areas. On cool foggy days they are likely to be roosting high in the trees, but on warm days they may roost lower.

To get to **Rock Spring** from Muir Woods, return 1.5 miles up the road you came down, to rejoin the main road to Mount Tamalpais. Note that RVs and tour buses are not allowed to return up this road, but must use a different route to get back to CA 1, as directed by signs. Continue 4.4 miles on the Mount Tamalpais road, turn right at Pan Toll junction, and go 1.4 miles to Rock Spring (parking, pit

A path skirts the trunks of ancient trees at Muir Woods.

toilets; road open 7 A.M. to 9 P.M.). This is a popular trailhead on weekends, but is quieter during the week.

Several trails originate at Rock Spring. The lands to the north belong to the Marin Municipal Water District and are open to the public during daytime hours. In fact, virtually the entire north slope of Mount Tamalpais belongs to the water district, and is laced with trails.

The **Cataract Trail,** which goes down a gentle valley, through rocky glens, open glades, and Douglas-fir forest, is highly recommended. Signs read, "Do not ride, carry, or walk bikes on this trail." On Mount Tamalpais, the fire roads, of which there are many, are open to bicycles, but the foot trails are not.

You can walk as far as you like on the Cataract Trail, which connects into the general trail system. Typical birds are resident Band-tailed Pigeon; Great Horned Owl; Northern Saw-whet Owl; Western Screech-Owl; Anna's Hummingbird; Acorn Woodpecker; Hutton's Vireo; Chestnut-backed Chickadee; Oak Titmouse; Red-breasted, White-breasted, and Pygmy Nuthatches; Bushtit; Bewick's Wren; Western Bluebird; Orange-crowned Warbler; Spotted and California Towhees; Dark-eyed Junco; Lesser Goldfinch; and Pine Siskin. Townsend's Warbler is a fairly common winter visitor, whereas Hermit Thrush is an uncommon resident. Regular summer visitors are Allen's Hummingbird; Western Wood-Pewee; Olive-sided and Ash-throated Flycatchers; Cassin's and Warbling Vireos; Violet-green Swallow; Swainson's Thrush; Black-throated Gray and Hermit Warblers; Chipping Sparrow; Black-headed Grosbeak; and Lazuli Bunting. Golden-crowned Sparrow and Ruby-crowned Kinglet are winter visitors.

To get to **Lake Lagunitas** from Rock Spring, take the road (open 9 A.M. to 9 P.M.) to the west, which runs along the crest of Bolinas Ridge (the road to the east from Rock Spring goes about 3 miles to the summit of Mount Tamalpais). The only word to describe the road along Bolinas Ridge is "spectacular." In many locations you can look almost straight down to Stinson Beach, Bolinas Lagoon, and the Pacific Ocean.

At 3.8 miles from Rock Spring you will come to a junction with the Bolinas-Fairfax Road, which runs a twisty narrow course from CA 1 to Fairfax, and is subject to closure. Your average speed here will be about 15 to 20 miles per hour. From the junction, it is 7.8 miles to a gate that marks the end of the controlled section, and a golf course. Watch closely here because 0.9 mile beyond the golf course, on the right, is Sky Oaks Road, which leads in 2 miles to Lake Lagunitas.

To get to **Lake Lagunitas** from US 101, exit at San Rafael and go west on Fourth Street, following signs for Fairfax. In San Anselmo, your route joins Sir Francis Drake Boulevard. It is 3.8 miles from US 101 to the center of Fairfax, where you must turn left to get to Broadway, which runs parallel to Sir Francis Drake Boulevard, turn right to Broadway, and then turn left on Bolinas Road in the center of Fairfax. From there it is 1.5 miles to Sky Oaks Road. Lake Lagunitas is 2 miles more, at the end of Sky Oaks Road.

At Lake Lagunitas (fee) there is a large parking area, picnic tables, and restrooms. From the parking area, the dam is 200 yards or so directly up the valley. A dirt road on the left takes you to the dam, and there is a trail (a fire road) all around the lake, a round trip of about 2 miles. The habitats vary from open forest, to oak savanna on the north side of the lake, to cool redwood groves on the south.

Birds to look for at Lake Lagunitas, besides many already listed for other locations on Mount Tamalpais, are Acorn and Nuttall's Woodpeckers; Black Phoebe; Wrentit; Spotted and California Towhees, and in the drier areas, Rufous-crowned Sparrow (uncommon). Bullock's Oriole (summer) has nested in the area, and Golden-crowned Sparrow and Ruby-crowned Kinglet are common winter visitors.

General information: Marin County has to be one of the most breathtakingly beautiful places in the country. Besides the spectacular views of the Golden Gate (see the description for Marin Headlands), there are also the magnificent groves at Muir Woods, the road along Bolinas Ridge, and, of course, Point Reyes. One problem is that *everyone* wants to go to Marin County on the weekends. You can beat the game by getting out early, or by going during the week if you can.

ADDITIONAL HELP

NCA&G grid: Page 104, 1A.
Elevation: 100 to 2,000 feet.
Hazards: Poison oak, ticks, rattlesnakes.
Nearest food, gas, lodging: San Rafael; Mill Valley.
Camping: Samuel P. Taylor State Park: 60 sites, about 11 miles west of Fairfax on Sir Francis Drake Boulevard. Pan Toll Campground: 16 walk-in sites, in Mount Tamalpais State Park. China Camp State Park: 31 walk-in sites, 3 miles east of US 101 on North San Pedro Road.
For more information: Mount Tamalpais State Park; Muir Woods National Monument.

47 Las Gallinas Wildlife Ponds 🏃

Habitats: Freshwater marsh, valley grassland, wastewater ponds.
Specialty birds: *Resident*—White-tailed Kite. *Summer*—Cinnamon Teal, Elegant Tern, Allen's Hummingbird. *Winter*—Western and Clark's Grebes; Eurasian Wigeon; Long-billed Curlew; Mew Gull.
Other key birds: *Resident*—Black-necked Stilt; Barn and Great Horned Owls. *Summer*—Caspian and Forster's Terns. *Winter*—American White Pelican; Canvasback; Bufflehead; Common Goldeneye; Black-bellied and Semipalmated Plovers; American Avocet; Greater Yellowlegs; Whimbrel; Marbled Godwit; American Pipit. *Migrant*—Wilson's and Red-necked Phalaropes.
Best times to bird: August to October for shorebirds; October through March for most waterfowl and sparrows.

47 Las Gallinas Wildlife Ponds

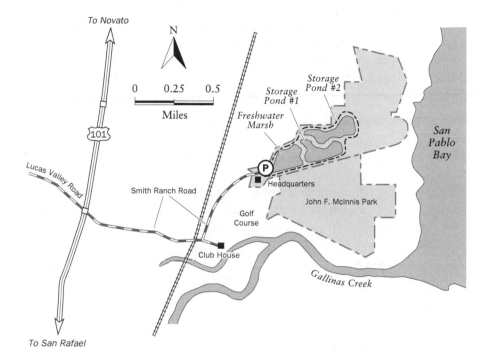

Directions: Go 3.5 miles north on U.S. Highway 101 from the center of San Rafael to the exit for Smith Ranch Road, and then east 0.6 mile to McInnis Park entrance, turning left just after crossing the railroad track. Go 0.7 mile to headquarters of Las Gallinas Valley Sanitary District, following signs for "Wildlife Ponds." Bear left into the parking lot. The ponds are open seven days a week sunrise to sunset.

The birding: Birders are welcome to walk the tops of the dikes throughout the area. The route shown as a dashed line on the map is recommended because it encircles the main ponds, providing a round trip of about 2 miles.

Cinnamon Teal are regular nesters, and small numbers of Gadwall, Northern Pintail, and Northern Shoveler also breed. In October other waterfowl begin to arrive, such as American Wigeon, Canvasback, Bufflehead, Common Goldeneye, and Ruddy Duck. Eurasian Wigeon is rare, but shows up most winters. Tufted Duck is even rarer. In winter also look for Western and Clark's Grebes; Double-crested Cormorant; American White Pelican; and Mew and California Gulls. In summer Caspian and Forster's Terns may be present, and Elegant Tern appears in August and September.

If the water in any of the ponds is shallow enough, check for Black-necked Stilt, American Avocet, Greater Yellowlegs, Black-bellied Plover, Willet, Long-billed

Curlew, and Marbled Godwit in fall. In spring and fall migration, look for Semi-palmated Plover, Whimbrel, and Wilson's and Red-necked Phalaropes.

Other birds around the ponds and in the nearby fields include residents such as Great and Snowy Egrets; White-tailed Kite; Anna's Hummingbird; Barn and Great Horned Owls; Belted Kingfisher; Black Phoebe; Marsh Wren; and Song Sparrow. In spring and summer, look for Allen's Hummingbird, and from October through March, for American Pipit, Ruby-crowned Kinglet, and Golden-crowned and White-crowned Sparrows.

General information: Birders often gravitate to wastewater treatment ponds because they know good birds are to be found there. The 20-acre freshwater marsh/pond at Las Gallinas has water up to 6 feet deep in the center, and several small islands that give some security to nesting and roosting waterfowl. Storage ponds numbers 1 and 2 fluctuate in level because of water management requirements. There are open views of bay marsh to the east, all the way to Mount Diablo. Mount Tamalpais looms over the ponds just to the south.

ADDITIONAL HELP

NCA&G grid: Page 94, 1D.
Elevation: Sea level.
Hazards: Ticks; rattlesnakes are possible.
Nearest food, gas, lodging: San Rafael.
Camping: Samuel P. Taylor State Park: 60 sites, 15 miles west of San Rafael on Sir Francis Drake Boulevard.
For more information: Las Gallinas Valley Sanitary District.

48 Richardson Bay Audubon Center and Sanctuary

Habitats: Sandy beach and mudflats, coastal bay, coastal scrub, freshwater marsh.
Specialty birds: *Resident*—Anna's Hummingbird; Chestnut-backed Chickadee; Wrentit; Spotted and California Towhees; Lesser Goldfinch. *Summer*—Heermann's Gull, Elegant Tern, Allen's Hummingbird, Pacific-slope Flycatcher, Bullock's Oriole. *Winter*—Pacific Loon; Western and Clark's Grebes; Long-billed Curlew; Black Turnstone; Mew, Thayer's, and Glaucous-winged Gulls.
Other key birds: *Resident*—Downy Woodpecker, Bewick's Wren, American Goldfinch. *Summer*—Caspian and Forster's Terns; Orange-crowned and Wilson's Warblers. *Winter*—Red-throated and Common Loons; Greater and Lesser Scaups; Surf Scoter; Bufflehead; Common Goldeneye; Red-breasted Merganser; Black-bellied and Semipalmated Plovers; Greater Yellowlegs; Marbled Godwit; Sanderling; Hermit Thrush; Fox Sparrow. *Migrant*—Yellow Warbler.
Best times to bird: All year; September through April for most water birds.

48 Richardson Bay Audubon Center and Sanctuary

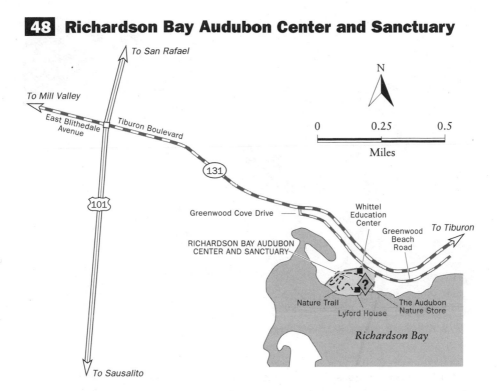

Directions: From the junction of U.S. Highway 101 and California Highway 131 (Tiburon Boulevard), go east 0.9 mile on CA 131 to Greenwood Cove Drive and turn right. Immediately turn left and go 0.3 mile to Richardson Bay Audubon Center and Sanctuary. Greenwood Cove Drive turns into Greenwood Beach Road shortly before the Audubon Center.

The birding: For such a small area, the sanctuary has a remarkable variety of habitats. Birds to be seen on the near waters of Richardson Bay, primarily in winter, include Red-throated, Pacific, and Common Loons; Western and Clark's Grebes; Double-crested Cormorant; Canvasback; Redhead (rare); Greater and Lesser Scaups; Bufflehead; and Ruddy Duck. The winter concentrations of Western and Clark's Grebes are especially noteworthy. Western Gulls are resident, whereas Mew and Glaucous-winged Gulls show up in winter. Look for Heermann's Gulls and Elegant Terns in late summer. Forster's Terns are present most of the year, but are rare in winter.

The beaches and mudflats may have many different kinds of shorebirds, mostly in winter, but a western specialty to look for here is Black Turnstone. Black Phoebes are usually found near water, and resident land birds are Anna's Hummingbird, Western Scrub-Jay, Chestnut-backed Chickadee, Bushtit, Bewick's Wren, Wrentit, Northern Mockingbird, and Spotted and California Towhees. Look for Allen's Hummingbird in spring and early summer. Ruby-crowned Kinglet and Golden-crowned and White-crowned Sparrows are winter visitors.

Black Turnstone.

In the wooded areas, look for resident Downy Woodpecker and Lesser and American Goldfinches, and check near the pond for Song Sparrow. Bullock's Oriole and Orange-crowned and Wilson's Warblers are summer visitors, and Yellow Warbler is a migrant.

General information: The center and sanctuary, owned and operated by National Audubon Society—California, has a magnificent setting on the edge of Richardson Bay, with a charming old Victorian home called the Lyford House. The sanctuary has 11 acres of land and 900 acres of tidal bay waters. A nature trail (about 0.5 mile) winds up over a hill and back near a small pond. **The Audubon Nature Store** features an extensive selection of books on natural history. The santuary has been classified as a Nationally Important Bird Area because it provides habitat for nationally significant numbers of California Gulls and Western Grebes, plus large numbers of migrating and wintering waterfowl.

ADDITIONAL HELP

NCA&G grid: Page 104, 2A.
Elevation: Sea level to 100 feet.
Hazards: Poison oak, ticks.
Nearest food, gas, lodging: Mill Valley.
Camping: Samuel P. Taylor State Park: 60 sites, 15 miles west of San Rafael on Sir Francis Drake Boulevard.
For more information: Richardson Bay Audubon Center.

49 Marin Headlands 🏃

Habitats: Rocky headlands, coastal bays and lagoons, coastal scrub, riparian woodland, chaparral.

Specialty birds: *Resident*—Chestnut-backed Chickadee; Wrentit. *Summer*—Brown Pelican; Osprey; Heermann's Gull; Caspian and Elegant Terns. *Winter*—Peregrine Falcon.

Other key birds: *Resident*—Turkey Vulture; Northern Harrier; Red-shouldered and Red-tailed Hawks; American Kestrel; White-crowned Sparrow; American Goldfinch. *Winter*—Canvasback, Bufflehead. *Migrant*—Sharp-shinned, Cooper's, and Broad-winged Hawks; Merlin; Red-necked Phalarope.

Best times to bird: September through November for raptors on fog-free days from 10 A.M. to 3 P.M. (peak times); for most other birds, fall and winter.

Directions: Going north on U.S. Highway 101/California Highway 1, just after crossing Golden Gate Bridge, take the exit for Sausalito and Golden Gate National Recreation Area, turn left at the stop sign off the exit, then turn right onto Conzelman Road immediately before the entrance leading back onto the Golden Gate Bridge. Going south on US 101/CA 1 from the junction of US 101 and CA 1, it is about 3.8 miles to the exit for Sausalito and Golden Gate National Recreation Area, which comes just before the Golden Gate Bridge. Turn right onto Conzelman Road where you see the signs for Marin Headlands. Follow Conzelman Road (no RVs, trailers, or busses) 1.7 miles to the beginning of a one-way road. Park in spaces on the left side of the road (chemical toilets are in an old artillery tunnel). Go just beyond the tunnel to where a paved fire road goes steeply up the hill and a sign reads "Hawk Hill."

The birding: From the parking on Conzelman Road, hike all the way to the very crest of **Hawk Hill,** a distance of perhaps 0.2 mile, with a bit of climbing. On a Saturday or Sunday in September and October, there may be 200 or more people on Hawk Hill watching for raptors. This means that after about 10 A.M. on a weekend, parking becomes difficult. The average numbers of birds passing per hour for the most common species are Red-tailed Hawk, 12.2; Turkey Vulture, 10.6; Sharp-shinned Hawk, 6.2; Cooper's Hawk, 4.3 (1995 figures).

Average number of sightings per season, from 1989 to 1995			
Turkey Vulture	3,881	Swainson's Hawk	4
Osprey	66	Red-tailed Hawk	5,954
White-tailed Kite	31	Ferruginous Hawk	17
Bald Eagle	2	Rough-legged Hawk	6
Northern Harrier	445	Golden Eagle	15
Sharp-shinned Hawk	3,980	American Kestrel	507
Cooper's Hawk	1,872	Merlin	88
Northern Goshawk	1	Prairie Falcon	7
Red-shouldered Hawk	212	Peregrine Falcon	50
Broad-winged Hawk	124	Unidentified (1995)	2,162

49 Marin Headlands

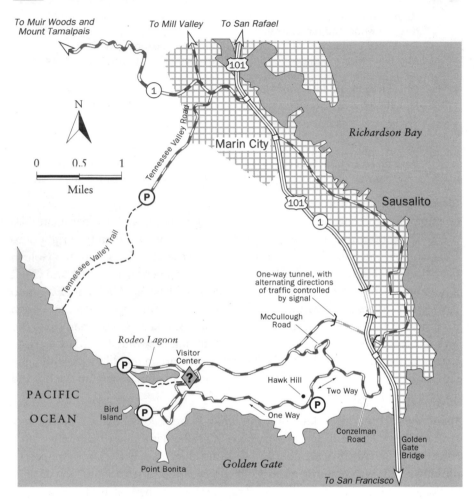

Since 1994, the Golden Gate Raptor Observatory has conducted an Accipiter Identification Study to see how well their watchers were doing on telling Sharp-shinned and Cooper's Hawks apart—a classic identification problem. Hawks netted for banding were carefully identified in hand, and then released. The results showed about 15 percent misidentifications, with male Cooper's Hawks being the ones most often identified incorrectly.

From Hawk Hill, take the one-way road about 2 miles to an intersection, turn sharply right, and go 0.4 mile to the **visitor center** (parking, restrooms, books). From the parking lot next to the restroom building, a trail (a fire road) goes down the hill and runs near Rodeo Lagoon to the beach. The habitat is mostly chaparral or coastal scrub, with some willow thickets and poison oak. Look for residents such as Black Phoebe, Western Scrub-Jay, Bewick's Wren, Wrentit, Song Sparrow, and migrant flycatchers, vireos, and warblers.

From the visitor center, go downhill to the main road, turn left, and drive to Rodeo Beach (parking, restrooms) next to **Rodeo Lagoon.** A bridge crosses a neck of the lagoon here, giving access to the beach and to the lower end of the lagoon. The lagoon can get summer visitors such as Brown Pelican and Caspian and Elegant Terns, and winter visitors such as Canvasback and Bufflehead. Red-necked Phalarope and various shorebirds appear in fall.

To get to **Tennessee Valley,** from the junction of US 101 and CA 1 north of Sausalito, go 0.4 mile west on CA 1 to Tennessee Valley Road, and turn left (south). It is 1.6 miles to the end of the road (parking, chemical toilet). This is a popular spot, and the parking lot can be overflowing on weekends. The "trail" is a paved road (barrier free), with a gate across it, used by hikers, bikers, and horseback riders. The habitats are willow thickets and eucalyptus groves along the creek bottom, with chaparral, coastal scrub, and grasslands on the slopes.

It's possible to get away from the mob a bit by following the horse trail whenever it departs the pavement. Also, about 0.2 mile from the parking lot, the **Fox Trail** (a dirt road) turns off to the right and runs next to some willows (lots of poison oak in the thickets). Birds to expect are residents California Quail; Western Scrub-Jay; Chestnut-backed Chickadee; Wrentit; Spotted and California Towhees; White-crowned Sparrow; and American Goldfinch, plus flycatchers, vireos, and warblers in migration, and Golden-crowned Sparrow in winter.

General information: Among units in the National Park system, Golden Gate National Recreation Area is exceeded only by the Blue Ridge Parkway in numbers of visitors per year (1990 figures: Blue Ridge, 17 million; Golden Gate, 15 million). The view of San Francisco and the Golden Gate Bridge from the Marin Headlands can only be described as sensational and has been featured in many movies.

Hawk Hill is the premier hawk-watching site in the western United States. As raptors drift southward in the fall, they tend to get funneled down the Marin peninsula to Hawk Hill, and then cross the Golden Gate. In 1995 hawk-watchers counted 20,543 raptors.

Fog is an almost automatic feature of the Golden Gate in summer and fall. Fog may be pouring through the Gate when other parts of the Bay Area are sparkling clear. If it's foggy overhead, the hawk-watching obviously will be a bust, but a day that starts out in dense fog may clear up into fine hawk-watching weather by midday.

ADDITIONAL HELP

NCA&G grid: Page 104, 1B.
Elevation: Sea level to 900 feet.
Hazards: Ticks, poison oak; rattlesnakes are possible.
Nearest food, gas, lodging: Mill Valley; Sausalito.
For more information: Golden Gate Raptor Observatory; Golden Gate National Recreation Area.

50 Presidio

Habitats: Sandy beach, forest consisting of introduced species, green lawns, ornamental plantings, small amount of riparian woodland.
Specialty birds: *Resident*—Hutton's Vireo, Chestnut-backed Chickadee, Pygmy Nuthatch. *Summer*—Heermann's Gull, Elegant Tern, Allen's Hummingbird, Hooded Oriole. *Winter*—Western Grebe, Black Turnstone, Surfbird, Mew Gull, Red-breasted Sapsucker, Varied Thrush, Townsend's Warbler.
Other key birds: *Resident*—Forster's Tern, Common Murre, Red-breasted Nuthatch, White-crowned Sparrow. *Summer*—Olive-sided Flycatcher; Swainson's Thrush; Orange-crowned and Wilson's Warblers. *Winter*—Golden-crowned Kinglet, Hermit Thrush, Red Crossbill.
Best times to bird: All year; March to July for breeding land birds.

Directions: When going south on U.S. Highway 101/California Highway 1 on the Golden Gate Bridge, get in right lane going through the toll booth, and exit on the right just beyond the toll booth. From US 101 from the south, turn west on Lombard Street (Lombard Street is US 101), get in the left lane as you approach the Presidio, and turn left off US 101, thus remaining on Lombard Street (US 101 angles off to the right at this point). Enter Presidio at Lombard Gate. If approaching on CA 1 from the south, turn east off CA 1 at California Street one block before coming to the Presidio, go 12 blocks, and turn north on Arguello Boulevard. Note: In general, no left turns from CA 1 are permitted.

The birding: Be alert for Hooded Orioles in the Presidio wherever there are fan palms. They usually build their nests in the palms.

El Polin Spring: In the eastern part of the Presidio, get on either Lincoln Boulevard or Lombard Street, and take Presidio Boulevard west. Turn on MacArthur Boulevard and follow it to the end, where there is a loop next to El Polin Spring (roadside parking, chemical toilet).

El Polin (po-LEEN) Spring is a tranquil spot with lawns, pines, cypress, eucalyptus trees, and willow thickets. Resident birds are Anna's Hummingbird; Black Phoebe; Hutton's Vireo; Western Scrub-Jay; Chestnut-backed Chickadee; Bushtit; Red-breasted (irregular) and Pygmy Nuthatches; Northern Mockingbird; California Towhee; White-crowned Sparrow; and Brown-headed Cowbird. Olive-sided Flycatcher; Swainson's Thrush; and Orange-crowned and Wilson's Warblers are summer visitors. In winter look for Red-breasted Sapsucker; Golden-crowned Kinglet; Hermit and Varied Thrushes; Townsend's Warbler; Golden-crowned Sparrow; and Red Crossbill (irregular).

To get to **Inspiration Point,** use Arguello Boulevard, either coming from the central part of the Presidio or entering the Presidio from the south. Inspiration Point is marked by a large parking area on the east side of Arguello Boulevard (no restrooms).

Inspiration Point offers fine views of San Francisco and gives access to the **Ecology Trail** via a set of stairs and a short connecting trail. The Ecology Trail

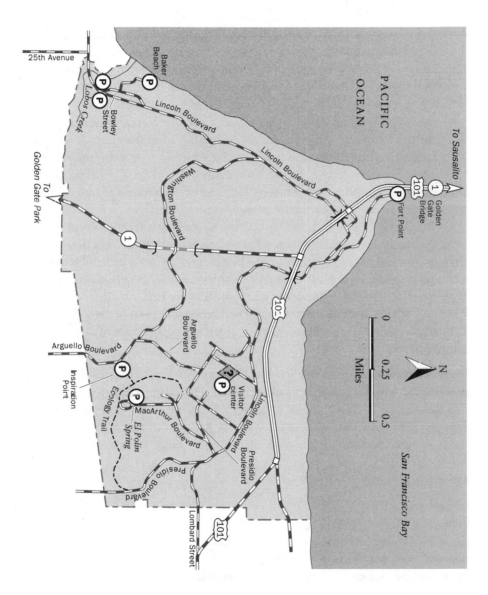

passes near outcroppings of serpentine, a type of rock that supports an unusual assembly of plant species, some of them classified as sensitive (the National Park Service asks that visitors stay on the trails). The area is wooded with pines, cypress, eucalyptus, and redwoods, all of them planted by the U.S. Army. Bird species are similar to those found at El Polin Spring. There is poison oak here and elsewhere in the Presidio.

Lobos Creek: Take Lincoln Boulevard going either north or south, and exit on Bowley Street, going south toward Baker Beach. Instead of taking the road into the Baker Beach parking lots, continue on Bowley Street to where it rejoins Lincoln Boulevard. The parking spaces here are adjacent to the trailhead for Lobos Creek (no restrooms, but there are restrooms near Baker Beach). If the spaces are full, there is a parking area on the opposite side of Lincoln Boulevard.

Lobos Creek is a delightful little spot, and one that has been called "the last free-flowing stream in San Francisco." Short trails lead to the creek. Birds at Lobos Creek are similar to those elsewhere in the Presidio, such as Chestnut-backed Chickadee, Pygmy Nuthatch, Brown Creeper, Bewick's Wren, California Towhee, Dark-eyed Junco, and House Finch. Allen's Hummingbirds occur during spring and summer. Eastern vagrants have shown up here in fall.

Baker Beach: The directions are the same as for Lobos Creek, except take the road leading to the parking lots for Baker Beach (restrooms). The lots may be crowded in summer or on weekends. The beach may have gulls such as Heermann's (summer and fall), Mew (fall and winter), California, and Western. Look for Black Turnstones and Surfbirds in winter on the nearby rocks. Offshore there may be Western Grebes, cormorants, scoters, and Common Murres. Forster's Terns occur throughout the year, and Elegant Terns are occasionally present during the late summer.

General information: The Presidio for many years was one of the major U.S. Army posts on the West Coast. In 1995 almost all of it was turned over to the National Park Service, to be administered as a part of Golden Gate National Recreation Area. **NOTE:** As is always the case in big city parks, you should be careful in the more isolated areas, where it is generally not a good idea to bird alone.

ADDITIONAL HELP

NCA&G grid: Page 104, 2B.
Elevation: Sea level to 400 feet.
Hazards: Automobile traffic, poison oak, ticks.
Nearest food, gas, lodging: San Francisco.
For more information: Golden Gate National Recreation Area.

51 Golden Gate Park

Habitats: Freshwater marsh, lake, riparian woodland, cultivated plantings.

Specialty birds: *Resident*—Band-tailed Pigeon, Chestnut-backed Chickadee, Pygmy Nuthatch. *Summer*—Cinnamon Teal, Allen's Hummingbird, Pacific-slope Flycatcher. *Winter*—Eurasian Wigeon, Mew Gull, Red-breasted Sapsucker, Varied Thrush, Townsend's Warbler.

Other key birds: *Resident*—Green Heron; Red-shouldered Hawk; Downy and Hairy Woodpeckers; White-crowned Sparrow. *Summer*—Yellow and Wilson's Warblers. *Winter*—Black-crowned Night-Heron, Green-winged Teal, Ring-necked Duck, Bufflehead, Ruddy Duck.

Best times to bird: All year

Directions: Golden Gate Park is in the western part of San Francisco, and is cut in two by California Highway 1. In general, no left turns from CA 1 are permitted. On weekends some of the roads in the congested eastern portion of the park are closed to auto traffic.

The birding: Strybing Arboretum: If you get here early enough in the day, parking can be found along Martin Luther King Jr. Drive near the entrance to the arboretum, which is closest to Stow Lake and called the Eugene Friend Gate. On weekends, however, both the traffic and the parking can only be described as impossible. To get around this problem, try parking near Stow Lake (see below).

Golden Gate, from Baker Beach.

51 Golden Gate Park

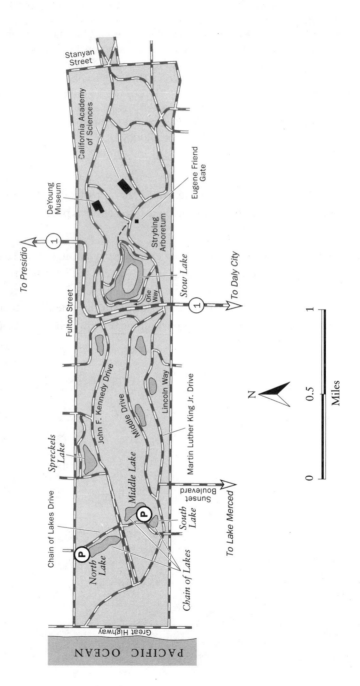

The pond near the Eugene Friend Gate can have large numbers of ducks and gulls. In winter there may be Mew and Herring Gulls, American Wigeon, Green-winged Teal, Bufflehead, and Ring-necked and Ruddy Ducks. The birds become so accustomed to people that you can actually get close enough to a Ring-necked Duck to be able to see the ring on the neck, which usually is invisible. In some winters a Eurasian Wigeon may show up with the American Wigeons.

Because of the large numbers of people who come to the arboretum, land birds may not be as much in evidence as at the Chain of Lakes, for example. A few California Quail are resident, although they are under pressure from the feral cats in the park. Look for Red-breasted Sapsucker, Varied Thrush (irregular), and Golden-crowned and White-crowned Sparrows. White-throated Sparrows occasionally turn up in the sparrow flocks in winter.

To get to **Stow Lake,** take the one-way road from Martin Luther King Jr. Drive (see arrow on map), and drive around the lake to the eastern end, where parking usually is available. If parking for Strybing Arboretum is difficult, it is usually possible to park here at the east end of the lake and walk down a path to the east about 300 yards, which will bring you to the Eugene Friend Gate of the arboretum.

Stow Lake has lots of ducks and gulls, as do other lakes in the park. American Wigeons (winter), Ruddy Ducks (winter), and Cinnamon Teal are among those to be found. Also, look for Black-crowned Night-Herons perched in the bushes. Red-shouldered Hawk, Band-tailed Pigeon (irregular), Pacific-slope Flycatcher, and Yellow Warbler occur, the last two in summer.

Chain of Lakes: Take Martin Luther King Jr. Drive west from CA 1 about 1.3 miles to Chain of Lakes Drive. Turn right (north) for South Lake, Middle Lake, and North Lake. Parking is available near Middle Lake and at the northern end of North Lake.

The three lakes composing the Chain of Lakes generally offer the best birding in Golden Gate Park, although Middle and North Lakes offer better birding habitat, particularly on the sides away from the road where it is quieter and there are brushy thickets. All three lakes have trails around them and all have marsh habitat, sometimes with Great Egrets and Green (rare) and Great Blue Herons.

Some resident birds are Downy Woodpecker, Chestnut-backed Chickadee, Bushtit, Pygmy Nuthatch, and California Towhee. In winter look for Hairy Woodpecker (rare), Varied Thrush (irregular), Townsend's Warbler, and Golden-crowned Sparrow. Allen's Hummingbird and Wilson's Warbler are summer breeders. This area is well known for rare vagrants from the east such as Tennessee and Prothonotary Warblers, Northern Parula, and American Redstart. It is worth checking with the Northern California Rare Bird Alert (Appendix D), for the latest reports, especially during migration.

General information: Golden Gate Park is one of the finest urban parks in the country, with grassy glades, lakes, mature trees, and many flowers. Strybing Arboretum, especially, is a delightful place for a stroll, and has good birds. **NOTE:** As is always the case in big city parks, you should be careful in the more isolated areas, where it is generally not a good idea to bird alone.

ADDITIONAL HELP

NCA&G grid: Page 104, 2B.
Elevation: Sea level to 300 feet.
Hazards: Automobile traffic, fast bicycles on the paths.
Nearest food, gas, lodging: San Francisco.
For more information: San Francisco Recreation and Parks.

52 Lake Merced

Habitats: Freshwater marsh, lake, limited riparian woodland.
Specialty birds: *Resident*—Chestnut-backed Chickadee. *Summer*—Allen's Hummingbird; Violet-green and Bank Swallows. *Winter*—Western and Clark's Grebes; Varied Thrush; Townsend's Warbler.
Other key birds: *Resident*—Green Heron; Virginia Rail; Marsh Wren; Common Yellowthroat; Song and White-crowned Sparrows; Purple Finch. *Summer*—Caspian Tern, Northern Rough-winged Swallow, Wilson's Warbler. *Winter*—Horned and Eared Grebes; Sora; Common Snipe; Hermit Thrush; Fox Sparrow. *Migrant*—Red-necked Phalarope, Warbling Vireo.
Best times to bird: October to May.

Directions: From the north, take Sunset Boulevard from Golden Gate Park directly to Lake Merced. When approaching the lake, bear left onto Lake Merced Boulevard, and turn right into the parking lot adjacent to North Lake (no restrooms). From California Highway 1, take Sloat Boulevard (California Highway 35) west to Sunset Boulevard, and then to the lake as above. From the south, from the junction of Interstate 280 and John Daly Boulevard, take John Daly Boulevard west to Lake Merced Boulevard, and turn north to the lake.

The birding: From the parking lot at **North Lake** both parts of the lake are visible, with a footbridge across the narrows between the two parts. A path leads to the footbridge, providing good views of the marshes and the willows below the path. The marsh has resident Marsh Wrens and Common Yellowthroats. Other possible residents are Green Heron and Virginia Rail, with Sora in winter (uncommon). The willows provide cover for residents such as Song Sparrow and Chestnut-backed Chickadee. In summer look for Allen's Hummingbird and Wilson's Warbler. On the lake, Western and Clark's Grebes are sometimes present in winter, as well as Double-crested Cormorant, Ruddy Duck, and Caspian Tern (the latter, primarily in summer).

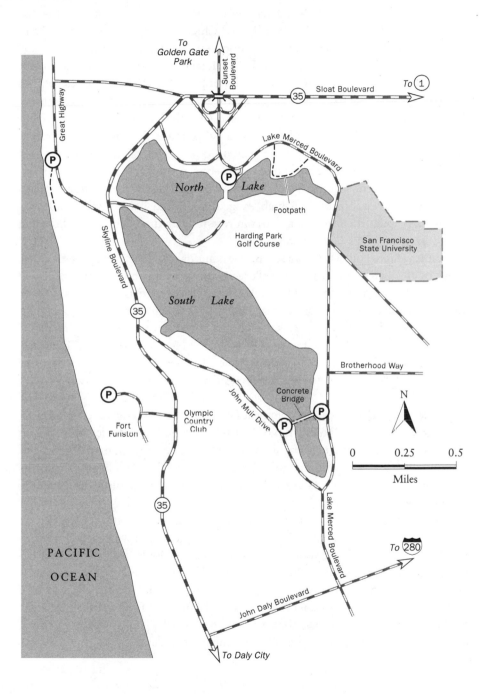

To
Golden Gate
Park

Sunset Boulevard

Sloat Boulevard

To 1

35

Great Highway

P

Lake Merced Boulevard

North Lake

P

Footpath

Harding Park
Golf Course

San Francisco
State University

Skyline Boulevard

35

South Lake

Brotherhood Way

N

P

Concrete
Bridge

P

P

John Muir Drive

Fort
Funston

Olympic
Country
Club

0   0.25   0.5

Miles

35

Lake Merced Boulevard

To 280

PACIFIC

OCEAN

John Daly Boulevard

To Daly City

217

From the parking lot, you can walk to the east on the bike path, to bird the large flat area shown with a footpath on the map. The footpath gets you away from the traffic noise on Lake Merced Boulevard, and into habitat with small resident land birds such as Chestnut-backed Chickadee, Bushtit, Bewick's Wren, and Purple and House Finches. In migration look for Warbling Vireo.

From North Lake, drive south on Lake Merced Boulevard to the parking lot near the **Concrete Bridge,** which spans the lower part of **South Lake** (no restrooms). Footpaths lead to the Concrete Bridge. Many gulls are often on the lake, plus the possibility of five kinds of grebes—Western, Clark's, Horned, Eared, and Pied-billed. Of these, Pied-billed is resident; the other four are most likely to be present in winter. During spring and fall migration, look closely on the water for Red (rare, irregular) and Red-necked Phalaropes—they are tiny and can easily be over-looked. Six different species of swallows may be over the lake in summer—Tree, Bank, Violet-green, Northern Rough-winged, Cliff, and Barn. Bank Swallow is classified as state-listed threatened, but in recent years there has been a breeding colony at nearby Fort Funston (see below).

At the western end of the Concrete Bridge is another parking area (no restrooms). Close by this end of the bridge a walk leads down to a fishing platform, which takes you directly among the willows. Any time of year there is likely to be a Black Phoebe around somewhere. In winter and in migration, look for Common Snipes along the muddy shores. (I once saw six of them in a row along the shore near here.) Also in winter, check the undergrowth for Hermit and Varied Thrushes, Townsend's Warbler, and Fox Sparrow. Note that in locations near the coast like Lake Merced, White-crowned Sparrow is resident, but in inland areas it is a winter visitor.

To get to the Bank Swallow colony at **Fort Funston,** from the junction of Sloat Boulevard and Sunset Boulevard, go west 0.7 mile on Sloat Boulevard to Great Highway. Go south on Great Highway 0.3 mile to a parking lot on the right, and walk about 0.2 mile south along the beach to where the cliffs begin. The holes made by the Bank Swallows are visible in the cliffs, and the birds are generally present from April through July.

The main part of Fort Funston (part of Golden Gate National Recreation Area) is reached by continuing 0.5 mile south on Great Highway to Skyline Boulevard, and then by going south 0.8 mile on Skyline Boulevard to the main entrance (accessible only by southbound traffic). The area consists of coastal bluffs and sand dunes, with groves of eucalyptus and cypress. In autumn this can be a good area for migrating flycatchers, vireos, and warblers. The park is popular on weekends, especially for hang gliders. There is an overlook platform near the parking lot from which you can view the cliffs and the hang gliders.

Bank Swallows can be seen at Fort Funston.

General information: Lake Merced is regarded by many birders as offering some of the best birding in the city of San Francisco. Much of the lake is surrounded by marsh and heavy willow growth, providing cover both for water birds and small passerines.

ADDITIONAL HELP

NCA&G grid: Page 104, 2C.
Elevation: Sea level.
Hazards: Auto traffic, rattlesnakes, poison oak, ticks.
Nearest food, gas, lodging: San Francisco.
For more information: San Francisco Recreation and Parks.

53 San Bruno Mountain &

Habitats: Limited riparian woodland, foothill woodland, chaparral.
Specialty birds: *Resident*—California Quail; Pygmy Nuthatch; Wrentit;
Spotted and California Towhees. *Summer*—Allen's Hummingbird,
Bullock's Oriole. *Winter*—Osprey, White-tailed Kite, Western
Meadowlark. *Migrant*—Western Tanager, Black-headed Grosbeak.
Other key birds: *Resident*—Bewick's and Winter Wrens; Northern
Mockingbird; Purple Finch. *Summer*—Swainson's Thrush, Wilson's
Warbler. *Migrant*—Warbling Vireo.
Best times to bird: October through May.

Directions: If going south on U.S. Highway 101, at 1.1 miles south of junction of US 101 and Interstate 280 take the exit for the Cow Palace. Follow signs for Brisbane, and get on Bayshore Boulevard. Turn west on Guadalupe Canyon Parkway, 1.9 miles after the exit. Go about 2.1 miles to the entrance gate on the north side of the road (fee, parking, restrooms). If going north on US 101, exit at the sign for Brisbane and Cow Palace, and go 2 miles on Bayshore Boulevard to Guadalupe Canyon Parkway. From Interstate 280 on the west, if going north, take the Mission Street exit, go left 1 block on Junipero Serra, then right on San Pedro Road to East Market Street. Turn right on East Market Street (East Market Street becomes Guadalupe Canyon Parkway) and follow it about 1.9 miles to the park entrance. If coming from the north on I-280, exit at John Daly Boulevard, turn left on John Daly Boulevard and go about 0.5 mile to Mission Street. Continue across Mission Street and angle right onto Hillside Boulevard. Go south on Hillside Boulevard about 1 mile to East Market Street, turn left (east), and go 1.9 miles to the park entrance.

The birding: The Bog Trail, coupled with a return on the Old Guadalupe Trail, has the best birding opportunities. Go to the northwest corner of the main parking area where there is a gate. The Old Guadalupe Trail is the paved road ahead of you; the **Bog Trail** branches off here. The main part of the Bog Trail is barrier free and leads to a junction with the **Old Guadalupe Trail.** From there it comes back to the parking lot, a round trip of about 0.7 mile. A narrow footpath branches from the Bog Trail that loops around and returns to the parking lot.

The first portion of the Bog Trail is on open, brushy slopes, but it soon curves back into a shallow valley with willow thickets and some cypresses. California Quail, California Towhees, and Wrentits live on the brushy slopes, and the thickets are good for Song Sparrows and warblers. The willows have harbored rarities such as White-throated Sparrow, American Redstart, and Rose-breasted Grosbeak. Wilson's Warblers nest here as well as Allen's Hummingbird, Pygmy Nuthatch, Winter Wren, Swainson's Thrush; Northern Mockingbird, Bullock's Oriole, and Purple Finch. Some spring migrants are Warbling Vireo, Western Tanager, and Black-headed Grosbeak. Look for Western Meadowlark in winter.

53 San Bruno Mountain

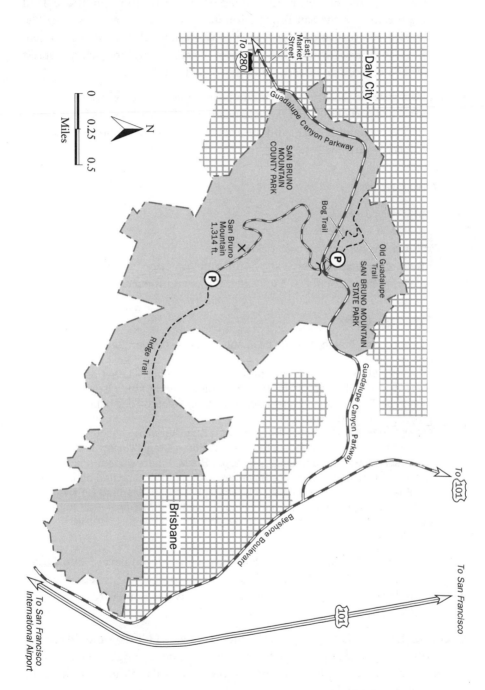

To get to the **Ridge Trail,** from the parking lot go under Guadalupe Canyon Parkway, and take the summit road to the parking lot on top. The Ridge Trail leads along the crest of the San Bruno Mountains, offering splendid views. The birds are typical of brushland habitat, such as Western Scrub-Jay, Bewick's Wren, Spotted and California Towhees, and sparrows. Watch for raptors such as Osprey, White-tailed Kite, Northern Harrier, and Red-tailed Hawk.

General information: San Bruno Mountain is an island of open space in the most densely populated part of the San Francisco peninsula. The area north of Guadalupe Canyon Parkway is a state park, and the area to the south is a county park. The two operate cooperatively.

ADDITIONAL HELP

NCA&G grid: Page 104, 2C.
Elevation: 400 to 1,300 feet.
Hazards: Rattlesnakes, poison oak, ticks.
Nearest food, gas, lodging: Daly City; South San Francisco.
For more information: County of San Mateo Parks and Recreation Division.

54 Foster City

Habitats: Salt marsh, coastal bays and lagoons, residential development.
Specialty birds: *Resident*—White-tailed Kite. *Summer*—Least and Elegant Terns; Hooded Oriole. *Winter*—Western and Clark's Grebes; Cinnamon Teal; Hooded Merganser; Peregrine Falcon; Long-billed Curlew; Short-eared Owl.
Other key birds: *Resident*—Black-necked Stilt, American Avocet, Forster's Tern. *Summer*—Caspian Tern. *Winter*—Green-winged Teal; Canvasback; Greater and Lesser Scaups; Black, White-winged, and Surf Scoters; Bufflehead; Barrow's Goldeneye; Merlin; Black-bellied and Semipalmated Plovers; Greater Yellowlegs; Whimbrel; Marbled Godwit; Sanderling; Long-billed and Short-billed Dowitchers. *Migrant*—Red Knot.
Best times to bird: October through March for most waterfowl and shorebirds.

Directions: From U.S. Highway 101, take East Hillsdale Boulevard into Foster City. Directions to each site described below are given from the junction of East Hillsdale Boulevard and Edgewater Boulevard. Edgewater Boulevard is about 0.8 mile east of US 101.

The birding: Leo J. Ryan Park: From the junction of East Hillsdale and Edgewater boulevards, go 0.5 mile northeast to Shell Boulevard and turn right, and then turn right again into a parking lot (restrooms about 200 yards to the west along the lakeshore, near the gazebo).

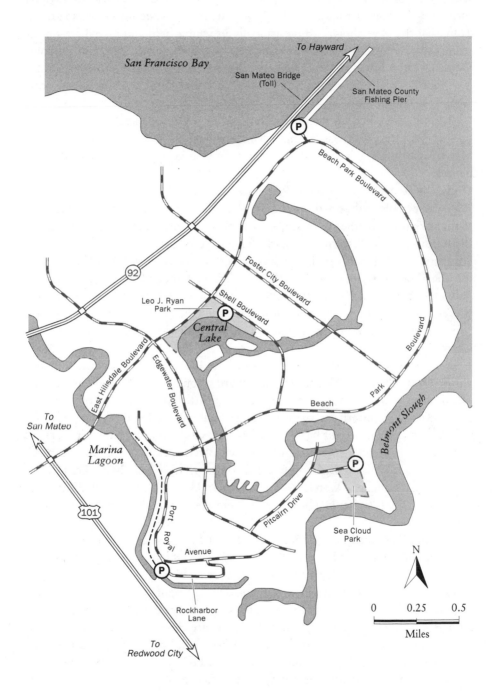

San Francisco Bay

To Hayward

San Mateo Bridge
(Toll)

San Mateo County
Fishing Pier

Beach Park Boulevard

Foster City Boulevard

92

Leo J. Ryan
Park

Shell Boulevard

Central
Lake

Boulevard

East Hillsdale Boulevard

Edgewater Boulevard

Park

Beach

Belmont Slough

To
San Mateo

Marina
Lagoon

101

Port Royal

Avenue

Pitcairn Drive

Sea Cloud
Park

N

Rockharbor
Lane

0   0.25   0.5

Miles

To
Redwood City

Leo J. Ryan Park is located adjacent to Central Lake, the largest single body of water in Foster City. The lake is popular with boaters and windsurfers. In winter there may be a considerable assemblage of water birds, including loons and grebes. Tufted Ducks have shown up occasionally in winter here and elsewhere on the waterways of Foster City, and a Smew was here two winters in a row. Barrow's Goldeneye and Hooded Merganser are rare but almost regular in winter. Watch for terns, especially Forster's and Caspian. Least and Elegant Terns appear occasionally in late summer.

Land birds should not be overlooked. Hooded Orioles have nested in the fan palms, and rarities such as Tropical Kingbird have been seen. I saw a Cooper's Hawk kill and carry off a Rock Dove, on the well-kept lawn of one of the residences.

San Mateo County Fishing Pier: From the junction of East Hillsdale and Edgewater boulevards, go about 1.5 miles northeast on East Hillsdale Boulevard to the parking lot on the left (restrooms). In winter many birds can be observed on the bay, including Western and Clark's Grebes; Canvasback; Greater and Lesser Scaups; Black, White-winged, and Surf Scoters; and Bufflehead. Depending upon the tide, shorebirds can be seen on the mudflats, including Black-bellied and Semi-palmated Plovers, Red Knot, and Sanderling. Wherever there are congregations of shorebirds, keep your eyes open for a Peregrine Falcon or a Merlin. In breeding season, check the tall transmission towers near the pier for nesting Double-crested Cormorants.

Sea Cloud Park: From the junction of East Hillsdale and Edgewater boulevards, go southeast on Edgewater Boulevard about 1.3 miles and turn left on Pitcairn Drive. It is 0.5 mile to the entrance to the parking area on the right (restrooms). The eastern end of the parking area is close to Belmont Slough, which may have a large variety of birds. I once saw about a thousand shorebirds resting here during high tide, consisting of Killdeer, Black-necked Stilts, American Avocets, Willets, Whimbrels, Long-billed Curlews, Marbled Godwits, Least Sandpipers, and dowitchers. Watch also for Northern Harriers. White-tailed Kites and Short-eared Owls (irregular) breed nearby and are sometimes seen flying over the marshes.

Marina Lagoon: From the junction of East Hillsdale and Edgewater boulevards, go southeast on Edgewater Boulevard about 0.8 mile and turn right on Port Royal Avenue. About 0.9 mile on Port Royal Avenue is the junction with Rockharbor Lane. Turn right, and immediately turn right again, into a small public parking lot (no restrooms). From the parking lot, a public path (paved) extends along the edge of Marina Lagoon. At first, you are close to US 101 and its noise, but you soon leave that behind. American Wigeon and Green-winged and Cinnamon Teal can be seen here, as well as Great Blue Heron, Great and Snowy Egrets, Black-necked Stilt, Greater Yellowlegs, and Forster's Tern.

General information: Foster City was created on the mudflats of San Francisco Bay. As a result, lagoons and sloughs are everywhere, resulting in abundant water-oriented bird life, even though this is a heavily built-up area. There are many No Trespassing signs. The descriptions given are for public sites.

ADDITIONAL HELP

NCA&G grid: Page 104, 3D.
Elevation: Sea level.
Hazards: Automobile traffic.
Nearest food, gas, lodging: Foster City.
For more information: Sequoia Audubon Society.

55 Pillar Point 🚻 ♿

Habitats: Sandy beach and mudflats, rocky headlands, coastal bays and lagoons, coastal scrub, planted trees and shrubs, freshwater marsh.
Specialty birds: *Resident*—Black Oystercatcher, Chestnut-backed Chickadee, Pygmy Nuthatch, Wrentit. *Summer*—Brown Pelican, Heermann's Gull, Elegant Tern, Pigeon Guillemot, Allen's Hummingbird. *Winter*—Western and Clark's Grebes; Wandering Tattler; Long-billed Curlew; Black Turnstone; Surfbird; Rock Sandpiper; Mew, Thayer's, and Glaucous-winged Gulls; Townsend's Warbler; Tricolored Blackbird.
Other key birds: *Resident*—Forster's Tern, Common Yellowthroat, Purple Finch. *Summer*—Caspian Tern, Wilson's Warbler. *Winter*—Red-breasted Merganser; Black, White-winged, and Surf Scoters; Black-bellied Plover; Whimbrel; Marbled Godwit; Sanderling.
Best times to bird: Fall and winter.

Directions: For Pillar Point, from the junction of California Highway 1 and California Highway 92 go about 3.8 miles north on CA 1 and go to the signal at Capistrano Road. Turn left and go west on Capistrano Road 0.4 mile to Prospect Way; turn left and go 1 block to Broadway, turn right, and immediately turn left onto Harvard Avenue. Go 3 blocks to a dead end at West Point Avenue, turn right, and go 0.3 mile to a small parking lot (chemical toilet). For **James V. Fitzgerald Marine Reserve,** from the junction of CA 1 and Capistrano Road (there are two junctions; this is the more southerly of the two), go 2.4 miles north on CA 1 to California Avenue in Moss Beach, and turn west at a sign that reads "Marine Life Refuge." Go about 0.2 mile to a dead end, and turn right into a parking lot (restrooms).

The birding: The walk along the edge of **Pillar Point Harbor** and out to **Pillar Point** (accessible at low tide), is mostly a broad, sandy road, and is barrier free as far as the base of the breakwater. A pond near the parking lot may have egrets and grebes, and sometimes has Tricolored Blackbirds in winter.

The harbor itself can have Western and Clark's Grebes; loons; Black, White-winged, and Surf Scoters; Red-breasted Merganser; Ruddy Duck; and Pigeon

55 Pillar Point

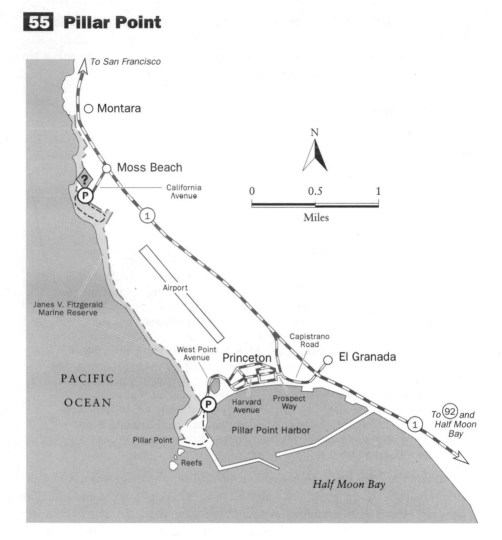

Guillemot. Check the gulls for Mew, California, Thayer's, and Glaucous-winged in fall and winter, for Heermann's in summer and fall, and Western (resident). Sometimes a Glaucous Gull shows up in winter. Caspian Terns should be present in summer, and Elegant Terns in late summer and fall; Forster's Terns may be here any time of year.

At low tide when the reefs beyond the base of the breakwater are exposed, they can have a wide variety of birds, often including flocks of Brown Pelicans (summer). On the beach and on the rocks (in winter) look for Black-bellied Plover, Willet, Whimbrel, Long-billed Curlew, Marbled Godwit, Wandering Tattler, Black Turnstone, Surfbird, and Sanderling. Black Oystercatcher is resident. This has been a traditional place to look for Rock Sandpiper (rare and irregular in winter), but in some years it is absent. **Be alert for unexpected large waves.**

At **James V. Fitzgerald Marine Reserve,** the crowds can often be avoided by walking toward the beach, turning to the left to cross the footbridge, and climbing onto the headlands. There is a network of trails here, but the best strategy is to stay close to the cliffs going out, circle about when you get into the area with plantings from an old garden, including some palm trees, and return along the opposite boundary fence of the reserve. Much of the area is planted with cypresses, but the old garden offers a mix of habitats.

Birds to be found in the cypresses, in the old garden, and in the marshy area near the footbridge are resident Anna's Hummingbird; Black Phoebe; Chestnut-backed Chickadee; Bushtit; Pygmy Nuthatch; Wrentit; Common Yellowthroat; Spotted and California Towhees; Song and White-crowned Sparrows; and Purple and House Finches. Allen's Hummingbird and Wilson's Warbler are summer visitors; and Townsend's and Yellow-rumped Warblers and Golden-crowned Sparrow are common in winter.

General information: The Fitzgerald Marine Reserve extends for about 3 miles, from Moss Beach to Pillar Point. The section reached by California Avenue is popular with classes of schoolchildren, especially at low tide when the reefs are exposed.

ADDITIONAL HELP

NCA&G grid: Page 104, 2D; page 114, 2A.
Elevation: Sea level to 100 feet.
Hazards: Abrupt cliff edges, unexpected big waves, poison oak, ticks.
Nearest food, gas, lodging: Half Moon Bay; El Granada.
Camping: Half Moon Bay State Park: 55 sites; in Half Moon Bay; turn west at Kelly Avenue (0.2 mile south of the junction of CA 1 and CA 92), and go 0.6 mile to the campground; RV dump station; some of the sites are essentially curbside parking.
For more information: James V. Fitzgerald Marine Reserve.

56 San Mateo Coast 🏠

Habitats: Sandy beach and mudflats, rocky headlands, coastal scrub, freshwater marsh, lake, riparian woodland, farm fields.

Specialty birds: *Resident*—Brandt's and Pelagic Cormorants; White-tailed Kite; Peregrine Falcon; Black Oystercatcher; Marbled Murrelet; Rhinoceros Auklet; Western Screech-Owl; Northern Pygmy-Owl; Chestnut-backed Chickadee; Wrentit. *Summer*—Brown Pelican, Cinnamon Teal, Heermann's Gull, Elegant Tern, Pigeon Guillemot, Black Swift, Allen's Hummingbird, Bank Swallow. *Winter*—Western Grebe; Wandering Tattler; Long-billed Curlew; Black Turnstone; Surfbird; Thayer's and Glaucous-winged Gulls; Say's Phoebe.

Other key birds: *Resident*—Black-crowned Night-Heron, Virginia Rail, Common Murre, Great Horned Owl, Winter Wren, Common Yellowthroat, Purple Finch, American Goldfinch. *Summer*—Caspian Tern, Grasshopper Sparrow. *Winter*—Red-throated Loon; Eared Grebe; Surf and White-winged Scoters; Bufflehead; Sora; Greater Yellowlegs; Marbled Godwit; Ruddy Turnstone; Sanderling; Loggerhead Shrike; Lincoln's Sparrow.

Best times to bird: Fall and winter; all year is good.

Directions: The San Mateo coast is most readily accessed from the Bay Area by going west from San Mateo on California Highway 92 to California Highway 1 at Half Moon Bay (allow 30 minutes). From the junction of CA 1 and CA 92, go 14.9 miles south on CA 1 to the parking lot (pit toilets) for **Pescadero State Beach** and **Pescadero Marsh Natural Preserve** (allow 20 minutes). There are two parking lots here: the north lot is opposite a large pond; the south lot is just after you cross the bridge for Pescadero Creek, and is recommended.

For **Phipps Country Store and Farm,** go 0.3 mile south from the "south lot" described above to Pescadero Road, and then east through the town of Pescadero 2.9 miles to the country store, on the right. Birders are welcome, but are asked to park along the road, outside the fence, because they often stay for a long time and the parking lot inside the fence is small.

To get to **Pigeon Point,** continue south 4.8 miles on CA 1 from its junction with Pescadero Road, to Pigeon Point Road, on the right. It is about 0.5 mile to the lighthouse. Park in one of the wide places next to the road, north of the lighthouse, which gives you direct access to the ocean. Chemical toilets are at the lighthouse (a state park). The junction of CA 1 and **Gazos Creek Road** is 2.2 miles south of Pigeon Point.

Año Nuevo State Reserve is 4.2 miles south of Gazos Creek Road, on CA 1. Coming from the south on CA 1, the reserve is about 21 miles north of Santa Cruz (allow 30 minutes).

The birding: Pescadero Marsh is a jewel. It is one of the larger wetlands along the coast, and is under the ownership of the state. From the south parking lot, descend the stairs to the walkway next to the highway, and go back across the bridge. From here, go down to the beach and back under the bridge. The trail leads along a lagoon, and then to a trail on top of an old levee, called the **Sequoia Audubon**

56 San Mateo Coast

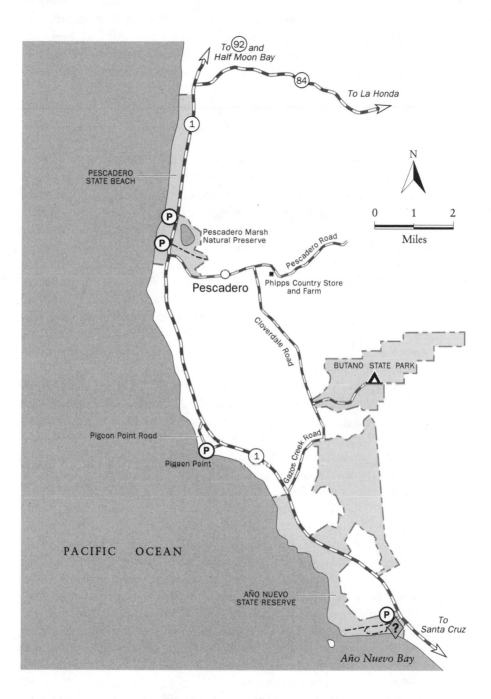

Trail. Near the beginning the trail divides into two parts, but they come together again. The distance to the end is about 1.2 miles.

Water birds dominate here, but about two-thirds of the way to the end the trail passes into groves of eucalyptus and willows, where land birds take over. The water birds are much less accustomed to people than at Charleston Slough (see Shoreline at Mountain View, page 238), and they tend to take flight as soon as you appear. A scope is essential.

Near the beach, look for Brown Pelican and Heermann's Gull, (summer and fall), and in fall and winter for Willet, Sanderling, and Thayer's Gull. Black Oystercatchers are resident on the rocky headlands.

In the lagoon and sloughs you may find Eared Grebe, Double-crested Cormorant, Cinnamon Teal, Northern Shoveler, Northern Pintail, Bufflehead, and Ruddy Duck. Surf and White-winged Scoters sometimes come into the lagoon close to the beach. Birds to look for in the marsh are egrets, Black-crowned Night-Heron, Greater Yellowlegs, Virginia Rail, Sora, Belted Kingfisher, Marsh Wren, Common Yellowthroat, and Song and Lincoln's Sparrows. Black Phoebes favor the wet areas, but even Say's Phoebes may be here (winter), in spite of their preference for dry locations. White-tailed Kite, Northern Harrier, and Red-tailed Hawk can be anywhere in the marsh. A Peregrine Falcon may show up, especially if there are shorebirds around. Another bird to look for here is Loggerhead Shrike (winter).

This is an excellent place for rare shorebirds during fall migration, provided there are exposed mudflats. Pacific Golden-Plover and Baird's and Pectoral Sandpipers are all rare but regular in fall, and Lesser Yellowlegs is uncommon.

Savannah Sparrows are resident and frequent the edges of the trail, as do Anna's Hummingbird (resident), and Allen's Hummingbird (spring and summer). In the wooded areas, expect resident California Quail, Chestnut-backed Chickadee, Bushtit, White-crowned Sparrow, and Purple Finch. Ruby-crowned Kinglet and Golden-crowned Sparrow are winter visitors. The distinctive song of the Wrentit becomes apparent as you approach the hills.

Phipps Country Store and Farm, 2.9 miles east of the coast on Pescadero Road, is a delightful spot. It has animals and birds on display (meaning that there are likely to be scads of school kids here), a nursery, and a gift shop. It also has pick-your-own berry fields in June, and an attractive garden toward the back. After walking through the Barnyard, continue toward the berry fields, and turn to the left when you get there. Cross a narrow bridge, and go to the right to the Wild Garden, which also brings you near the riparian growth of Pescadero Creek. Rarities have been found here, including Yellow-green Vireo and White-throated Sparrow, but it is more likely you will see Anna's and Allen's Hummingbirds; Chestnut-backed Chickadee; Steller's Jay; Song and White-crowned Sparrows; and American Goldfinch. Ruby-crowned Kinglet, Cedar Waxwing, and Golden-crowned Sparrow are winter visitors.

Pigeon Point is a classic location for spotting seabirds, especially those that are seldom seen from shore, such as shearwaters, storm-petrels, and jaegers. With a spotting scope, shearwaters are often visible on clear days, although if there are strong winds the birds are more likely to come close to shore. Most times, of course, the species are more conventional, such as Western Grebe, Brown Pelican, Surf Scoter, cormorants, and gulls, but Common Murre, Rhinoceros Auklet, and Marbled Murrelet are also often spotted. It is an enchanting spot, even if the shearwaters and jaegers don't show up.

Gazos Creek Road is worth a detour. The first 2 miles or so are through riparian habitat with scattered Douglas-firs, and there are several wide places next to the road where you can park. It is well known for producing rare migrants, but is attractive at any time of year. Some resident birds are Western Screech-Owl; Great Horned Owl; Northern Pygmy-Owl; Acorn, Downy, and Hairy Woodpeckers; Black Phoebe; Steller's Jay; and Winter and Bewick's Wrens. Along Cloverdale Road, which runs from Gazos Creek Road to Pescadero, watch for Grasshopper Sparrows, which are uncommon to fairly common in summer, but are inconspicuous.

Año Nuevo State Reserve is another jewel. It is best known for its elephant seals. Access to the outer portion of the reserve (beyond the so-called staging area) is by permit only. From April through November, permits are available on a first-come, first served basis. From December through March, reservations are recommended.

It is possible to take the first part of the trip and return along the beach without a permit (about 1.5 miles round trip). The trail heads west through coastal scrub and grasslands to the left of a small freshwater pond, and then down to Cove Beach. The route returns along Cove Beach to Año Nuevo Creek. A bit of rock-hopping might be required at the creek to get to the trail coming from the visitor center.

The pond will probably have coots and Mallards as well as Pied-billed and Eared Grebes; Black Phoebe; Virginia Rail; Sora; and Song Sparrow. The beach area should have cormorants and Western Gulls year-round, and in summer Brown Pelican, Heermann's Gull, Caspian and Elegant Terns, Pigeon Guillemot, and may have Common Murre, Marbled Murrelet, and Rhinoceros Auklet (check the ocean just beyond the surf). In fall and winter look for loons, Western Grebe, scoters, and gulls such as Thayer's and Glaucous-winged. In fall through early spring, the beach may have shorebirds such as Willet, Long-billed Curlew, Marbled Godwit, and Sanderling. In fall and winter, check the rocks for Wandering Tattler (uncommon), Ruddy Turnstone (uncommon), Black Turnstone, and Surfbird. Bank Swallows nest in the nearby cliffs in summer.

A much-sought bird at Año Nuevo is Black Swift (June and July). A few have nested here in recent years, although many birders come away disappointed. The recommendation is to go beyond the staging area (permit required) and look along the cliffs. The best chance is early in the morning (the reserve opens at 8 A.M.) or on overcast days.

231

General information: The San Mateo coast has spectacular vistas, rocky head-lands, and broad sandy beaches, surrounded by rural countryside. At rush hour, CA 92, the main access from San Mateo to Half Moon Bay, can be clogged with traffic, and on weekends it may seem as if everyone in the Bay Area is trying to get over to the coast. At other times, the coast can be so quiet it seems to belong to another world, giving little indication that 4 million people live just over the hill.

ADDITIONAL HELP

NCA&G grid: Page 114, 2B, 3D.
Elevation: Sea level to 100 feet.
Hazards: Poison oak, ticks.
Nearest food, gas, lodging: Half Moon Bay.
Camping: Butano State Park: 40 sites; from junction of CA 1 and Pescadero Road, go 2.5 miles east on Pescadero Road to Cloverdale Road, then south 4.2 miles to the entrance for the park.
For more information: San Mateo Coast District Office; Año Nuevo State Reserve.

57 Santa Cruz 🍴 ♿

Habitats: Rocky headlands, coastal scrub, freshwater marsh, lake, riparian woodland, eucalyptus groves.
Specialty birds: *Resident*—Wood Duck, Chestnut-backed Chickadee, Pygmy Nuthatch, Wrentit. *Summer*—Brown Pelican, Heermann's Gull, Elegant Tern, Allen's Hummingbird. *Winter*—Pacific Loon; Western and Clark's Grebes; Black Turnstone; Surfbird; Rock Sandpiper; Thayer's Gull.
Other key birds: *Resident*—Green Heron; Black-crowned Night-Heron; Virginia Rail; White-breasted Nuthatch; Song and White-crowned Sparrows. *Summer*—Caspian and Forster's Terns. *Winter*—Red-throated and Common Loons; Ring-necked Duck; Black, White-winged, and Surf Scoters; Sora; Ruddy Turnstone; Hermit Thrush.
Best times to bird: Fall, winter, spring.

Directions: Neary Lagoon: From the junction of California Highway 1 and California Highway 9 in the northern part of Santa Cruz, go 1.4 miles north on CA 1 (CA 1, generally speaking, is a north-south highway, but the direction here is actually southwest because of the east-west alignment of the coast) to Bay Street, and turn left. Drive 0.3 mile on Bay Street to California Street, turn left, and cross railroad tracks. The entrance to Neary Lagoon Park is on the right. Parking is along the curb on California Street. Do not go down the entrance road to the water pollution control facility. **West Cliff Drive:** From the junction of Bay and California streets (see above), go east on Bay Street 0.6 mile to West Cliff Drive and turn right, going south and then west. West Cliff Drive runs close to the cliffs for 2.5 miles to Natural Bridges State Beach, with many parking areas. **Natural Bridges State Beach:** From the junction of CA 1 and CA 9 in the northern part of

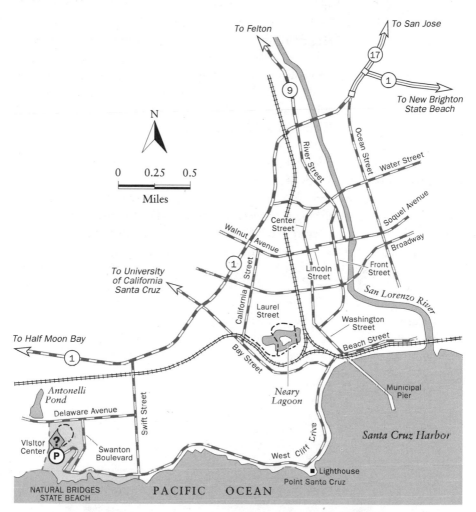

To Felton

To San Jose

17

1

To New Brighton
State Beach

N

0   0.25   0.5

Miles

River Street

Ocean Street

Water Street

Soquel Avenue

Walnut Avenue

Center Street

Broadway

Lincoln Street

Front Street

To University
of California
Santa Cruz

California Street

Laurel Street

San Lorenzo River

Washington Street

To Half Moon Bay

1

Bay Street

Beach Street

Antonelli Pond

Swift Street

Delaware Avenue

Neary Lagoon

Municipal Pier

Santa Cruz Harbor

Visitor Center

Swanton Boulevard

West Cliff Drive

NATURAL BRIDGES
STATE BEACH

PACIFIC   OCEAN

Lighthouse
Point Santa Cruz

Santa Cruz, go 1.9 miles north (actually southwest) to Swift Street, turn left, and go 0.4 mile. Turn right on Delaware Avenue and go 0.4 mile, and then left 0.4 mile on Swanton Boulevard to the park entrance (fee, parking, restrooms, visitor center). **Antonelli Pond:** Follow the directions for Natural Bridges, but do not turn at Swanton Boulevard. Continue on Delaware Avenue 0.2 mile to the pond, and park along the curb (no restrooms).

The birding: For **Neary Lagoon,** park along the curb on California Street. The trail begins here, and makes a loop of about 1 mile round trip, paved and barrier free. It passes between two chainlink fences before reaching the lagoon; much of it is on boardwalks. Look for Green Heron, Black-crowned Night-Heron, Wood Duck, Ring-necked Duck (winter), Virginia Rail, Sora, and Belted Kingfisher. The willows can have warblers, flycatchers, and sparrows. Rarities such as Lucy's Warbler and Dusky-capped Flycatcher have been seen here.

West Cliff Drive: The birds are typical of rocks and surf, such as Double-crested, Brandt's, and Pelagic Cormorants, and in winter Ruddy and Black Turnstones, Surfbird, and Rock Sandpiper (rare and irregular). Caspian and Forster's Terns are here in summer, Brown Pelicans, Heermann's Gulls, and Elegant Terns in late summer and early fall, Thayer's Gull (uncommon) in winter, and Western Gull all year. From late fall to early spring, look offshore for Western and Clark's Grebes; Red-throated, Pacific, and Common Loons; and Black, White-winged, and Surf Scoters.

Natural Bridges State Beach: Natural Bridges has a lovely beach and draws crowds of people. Thousands of monarch butterflies, which spend the winter here from mid-October to February, can be seen hanging in clusters from the eucalyptus trees in the grove near the visitor center, at the end of the barrier-free boardwalk. A nature trail departs from the boardwalk, climbs up out of the grove, and passes among pine trees. Resident birds are Anna's Hummingbird; Steller's Jay; Western Scrub-Jay; Chestnut-backed Chickadee; Pygmy and White-breasted Nuthatches; Bewick's Wren; California Towhee; and White-crowned Sparrow. Look for Allen's Hummingbird in spring and summer and Ruby-crowned Kinglet, Hermit Thrush, and Golden-crowned Sparrow in winter.

Antonelli Pond: The pond is surrounded by a heavy growth of willows and is lined in most places with cattails. Although there are trails on both sides of the

The coastline, surf, and a natural bridge at Santa Cruz.

pond, the one on the west side leads down into the willows and gets you close to the shore. The pond generally has Pied-billed Grebes, Great Blue and Green Herons, Mallards, and Ruddy Ducks. Black Phoebes and Song Sparrows are usually nearby. The willows have Chestnut-backed Chickadees, Bushtits, and, in winter have Ruby-crowned Kinglets and Yellow-rumped Warblers. In fall 1997, a Dusky Warbler, a vagrant from Asia, spent a few days here.

Pelagic trips: A few pelagic trips are scheduled each fall from Santa Cruz, operated by the same organization that conducts pelagic trips out of Monterey and Bodega Bay (see Shearwater Journeys in Appendix A). The species are generally the same as those seen at the other two locations, but there's a better chance for Black-footed Albatross, Black and Ashy Storm-Petrels, and Marbled Murrelet.

General information: Santa Cruz is a delightful place. So many people find it so that it is dreadfully crowded on weekends, especially in summer. Santa Cruz faces south on Monterey Bay, and there is often no fog here when it is foggy elsewhere. Many people live in Santa Cruz and commute to their jobs "over the hill" in the San Jose area, so California Highway 17, the main artery over the mountains, is choked at rush hours and on weekends.

ADDITIONAL HELP

Map grid: DeLorme Southern/Central California Atlas & Gazetteer, page 18, 2A.
Elevation: Sea level.
Hazards: Poison oak, ticks; rattlesnakes are possible.
Nearest food, gas, lodging: Santa Cruz.
Camping: New Brighton State Beach: 112 sites, 4 miles east of Santa Cruz on CA 1; RV dump station.
For more information: Natural Bridges State Beach.

58 Skyline Boulevard ⋔ ♿

> **Habitats:** Redwood forest, Douglas-fir forest, freshwater marsh, lake, chaparral.
> **Specialty birds:** *Resident*—Band-tailed Pigeon, Hutton's Vireo, Steller's Jay, Chestnut-backed Chickadee, Bushtit, Pygmy Nuthatch, Wrentit. *Summer*—Allen's Hummingbird; Western Wood-Pewee; Pacific-slope and Ash-throated Flycatchers; Cassin's Vireo; Violet-green Swallow; Hermit Warbler; Western Tanager; Black-headed Grosbeak; Lazuli Bunting. *Winter*—Townsend's Warbler.
> **Other key birds:** *Resident*—Winter Wren. *Summer*—Olive-sided Flycatcher; Warbling Vireo; Swainson's Thrush; Orange-crowned and Wilson's Warblers; Grasshopper Sparrow. *Winter*—Fox Sparrow.
> **Best times to bird:** Spring and summer are best, but all year is good.

58 Skyline Boulevard

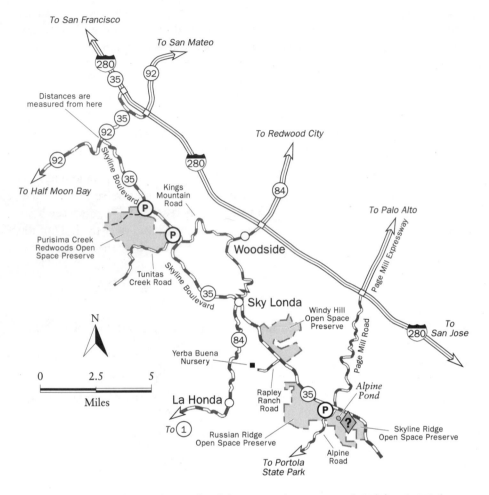

Directions: From the junction of California Highway 35 and California Highway 35/92, the distances to the various locations are as follows, going south on CA 35:

The north parking lot for **Purisima Creek Redwoods Open Space Preserve** is 4.4 miles (chemical toilet); the south lot is 6.4 miles.

It is 16.6 miles to Rapley Ranch Road, which is the access road for **Yerba Buena Nursery.** Go west on Rapley Ranch Road (good gravel road) 0.8 mile to Langley Hill Road, which angles to the right, then 1.2 miles to the Yerba Buena Nursery.

Alpine Road is 19.2 miles. Turn west on Alpine Road about 100 yards to the parking lot for **Russian Ridge Open Space Preserve** (chemical toilet), which has a barrier-free trail that goes through a tunnel and gives access to **Skyline Ridge Open Space Preserve.**

The birding: From the north parking lot of **Purisima Creek Redwoods**, a trail goes down the hill to the west that is heavily used by bicycles; however, birders can take a foot trail that begins shortly beyond the gate and zigzags down the hill through a forest of Douglas-fir, redwoods, madrone, and tan oak, with residents such as Steller's Jay, Chestnut-backed Chickadee, Bushtit, Pygmy Nuthatch, Brown Creeper, Winter Wren, and Spotted and California Towhees. The more open sections can have California Quail, Anna's Hummingbird, and Western Scrub-Jay. Swainson's Thrush and Hermit Warbler are summer visitors, whereas Ruby-crowned Kinglet, Yellow-rumped and Townsend's Warblers, and Fox and Golden-crowned Sparrows are winter visitors. Flocks of Band-tailed Pigeons may be spotted overhead. Wrentits sing from the hillsides nearby.

The **south parking lot** for Purisima Creek Redwoods gives access to a short barrier-free trail that goes down the hill through a grove of midsized redwoods. The species diversity is less here than at the north parking lot, but it is an attractive spot.

Yerba Buena Nursery is open 9 A.M. to 5 P.M. daily, and is a great place to visit, as well as a good place for birds. There is a garden shop, and casual beverage and pastry service is offered on weekends. (High teas are offered for groups, by reservation. See Appendix A. Also, the nursery grows native plants.) You are welcome to stroll the paths that wind through the nursery and native plant garden. Typical resident birds are California Quail, Anna's Hummingbird, Hutton's Vireo, Steller's Jay, Western Scrub-Jay, Chestnut-backed Chickadee, Wrentit, and Spotted and California Towhees. Summer visitors to look for are Allen's Hummingbird; Western Wood-Pewee; Olive-sided, Pacific-slope, and Ash-throated Flycatchers; Western Tanager; Orange-crowned and Wilson's Warblers; and Black-headed Grosbeak.

From the parking lot for **Russian Ridge Open Space Preserve,** the barrier-free trail goes through a pedestrian tunnel under Alpine Road, and to the David Daniels Nature Center (about 0.2 mile) above **Alpine Pond,** open in the afternoons on weekends from mid-March through November. The barrier-free trail extends entirely around Alpine Pond, providing a 0.5-mile round trip. Look here for residents such as Acorn Woodpecker and Western Meadowlark (the latter in grassy areas, such as at Russian Ridge). Common summer visitors are Warbling Vireo and Violet-green and Barn Swallows; Cassin's Vireo and Lazuli Bunting are also possible. Grasshopper Sparrows are uncommon summer visitors in open grassland.

General information: Skyline Boulevard (CA 35) runs down the backbone of the mountains that form the San Francisco peninsula. Much of the route is through redwoods and Douglas-fir forest, but there are also high grassy ridges, giving expansive views into the Bay Area and to the ocean to the west.

ADDITIONAL HELP

NCA&G grid: Page 114, 3A, 4B.

Elevation: 1,000 to 2,300 feet.

Hazards: Rattlesnakes, poison oak, ticks.

Nearest food, gas, lodging: San Mateo; Redwood City; Palo Alto.

Camping: Portola State Park: 52 sites, 6.5 miles west of CA 35 via Alpine Road and Portola State Park Road. The last few miles into the park are narrow and steep.

For more information: Midpeninsula Regional Open Space District

59 Palo Alto Baylands and Shoreline at Mountain View 🏕 ♿

Habitats: Mudflats, coastal bays and lagoons, coastal scrub, salt marsh, freshwater marsh.

Specialty birds: *Resident*—White-tailed Kite, Clapper Rail, Burrowing Owl, Western Meadowlark. *Summer*—Brown Pelican, Cinnamon Teal, Least Tern, Allen's Hummingbird. *Winter*—Black Rail, Long-billed Curlew, Thayer's Gull, Short-eared Owl, Tricolored Blackbird.

Other key birds: *Resident*—Black-crowned Night-Heron, Ruddy Duck, Cooper's Hawk, Virginia Rail, Black-necked Stilt, American Avocet, Black Skimmer, Common Yellowthroat. *Winter*—Horned and Eared Grebes; American White Pelican; Blue-winged and Green-winged Teal; Canvasback; Greater and Lesser Scaups; Common Goldeneye; Red-breasted Merganser; Sora; Black-bellied and Semipalmated Plovers; Greater Yellowlegs; Whimbrel; Marbled Godwit; Glaucous Gull; American Pipit. *Migrant*—Common Tern.

Best times to bird: August to March; shorebirds begin arriving in August; high tides in December and January are best for Black Rail.

Directions: Palo Alto Baylands: From the junction of U.S. Highway 101 and Embarcadero Road in Palo Alto, go east on Embarcadero Road about 1 mile to the Duck Pond (parking, chemical toilets), and 0.3 mile more to the Lucy Evans Baylands Nature Interpretive Center (parking, restrooms inside nature center, if open). **Shoreline at Mountain View:** From the junction of US 101 and San Antonio Road, take San Antonio Road north 0.2 mile to Terminal Boulevard (parking along the north side of the road; chemical toilets 0.2 mile out along the trail by Charleston Slough). For the main entrance of Shoreline at Mountain View, from the junction of US 101 and Shoreline Boulevard, go north on Shoreline Boulevard about 0.7 mile to the entrance. **Shoreline Lake** (parking, cafe, restrooms) is about 1 mile farther.

The birding: The first stop at Palo Alto Baylands is the **Lucy Evans Baylands Nature Interpretive Center.** If it's not open (the hours are erratic), walk around the building on the porch and take the boardwalk (barrier free) that goes out through

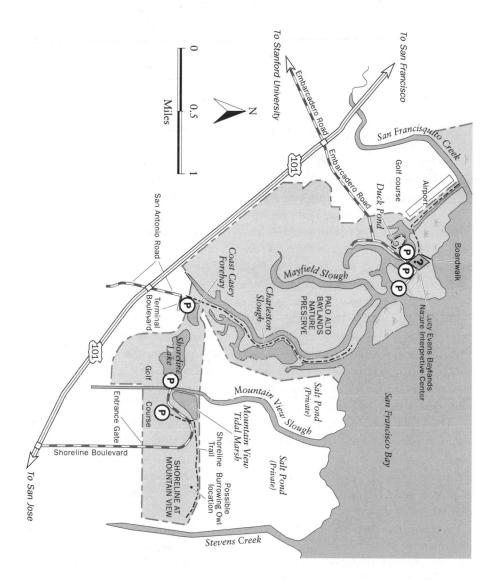

the marsh about 300 yards to the edge of the bay to look for Clapper Rails, which usually are seen when high tides force them into view. However, once on a *low* tide I saw three from the boardwalk, walking along the muddy channels. Marsh Wrens are also here. At low tide, look from the end of the boardwalk for shorebirds in winter: Willet, Long-billed Curlew, Marbled Godwit, dowitchers, and peeps are likely. Ducks on the bay may include scaups and Canvasback.

Black Rail is the premium bird at the Baylands, and birders consult the tide tables for the highest tides (usually in December). When it's high tide, line up at the edge of the marsh near the parking lot (you're not supposed to go beyond the big logs), and wait for a Black Rail to pop into view. When one does so, it generally won't stay in view for long because the marsh is also well populated by Snowy Egrets who are just waiting to have a Black Rail for dinner. While you are waiting, Song Sparrows and Common Yellowthroats flit about, perhaps pretending they are Black Rails.

If there have been recent heavy rains and there is a stiff wind blowing out of the east, almost any high tide may force Black Rails into view. The egrets and herons understand this combination well, and will show up to prey on rails and rodents that might be forced into the open.

A barrier-free trail runs to the west along the edge of the slough and then parallel to a channel next to the Palo Alto Airport. The channel contains a bit of freshwater marsh in which Virginia Rails and Soras are sometimes seen (more likely, heard). This is one of the places where birders come in winter to see if they can spot a rare Nelson's Sharp-tailed Sparrow or a Swamp Sparrow.

About 0.3 mile southeast of the interpretive center, another parking lot (chemical toilets) provides views of the mudflats and the grasslands to the south and east. The mudflats can have thousands of shorebirds on them during a low tide in winter, and the grasslands may have White-tailed Kite and even a Short-eared Owl (winter). Look also for American Pipit, and check blackbird flocks for the possibility of a Tricolored Blackbird.

The **Duck Pond** is worth a stop. Many of the ducks here have become so accustomed to humans that they will allow you to get close looks, and you can get good comparisons of Greater and Lesser Scaups here, to test yourself on telling these two apart. There also are likely to be Double-crested Cormorants, Black-crowned Night-Herons, Northern Shovelers (winter), Mallards, Ruddy Ducks, American Coots, and gulls galore, especially Western Gulls.

A trail leaves the Duck Pond and goes along the edge of the channel behind it, making a complete circuit of the Duck Pond area. Birds that might be seen in or near the channel in winter include Gadwall, Canvasback, Black-necked Stilt, and American Avocet. Blue-winged Teal (uncommon in California) can be seen here sometimes in winter. Land birds to look for along this trail are Anna's Hummingbird, Allen's Hummingbird (summer), Black Phoebe, and wintering sparrows.

The number one attraction at **Shoreline at Mountain View** is **Charleston Slough**. Park along Terminal Boulevard and walk out the trail next to the slough. It is about 2 miles along the top of the levee to the bay. The path is wide, smooth, and barrier free. It gets lots of pedestrians and bicycles, but is broad enough to accommodate the traffic. A benefit of all these people being present is that the birds become so accustomed to humans that they stay put and can be observed at fairly close range. Nevertheless, a scope is useful here.

American White Pelicans will probably be present beginning in August. In winter there are Gadwall; American Wigeon; Cinnamon and Green-winged Teal; Northern Shoveler; Northern Pintail; Canvasback; and Ruddy Duck. Black-necked Stilts and American Avocets can be here in large numbers, as well as Black-bellied and Semipalmated Plovers, Greater Yellowlegs, Willet, Whimbrel, Long-billed Curlew, Marbled Godwit, Dunlin, and peeps. Don't forget to look for Clapper Rail.

Look for Thayer's Gull among the Western and Herring Gulls, and there is always the possibility of a Glaucous Gull (rare) in winter. Least and Common Terns (both rare) may show up in late summer. The area managers have adopted a program to encourage Least Terns to nest in the slough, by spreading oyster shells and gravel over one of the islands. A rare possibility in summer here is Little Blue Heron (also possible near Alviso; see the section on Don Edwards Refuge). Another special bird to look for in recent years is Black Skimmer—as of 1998 there were 15 Black Skimmers here.

Early morning lends promise of Burrowing Owls at Shoreline at Mountain View.

Shoreline Lake gets lots of people, sailboats, and windsurfers, but it also gets Pied-billed, Horned, and Eared Grebes; Brown Pelican; Common Goldeneye; and Red-breasted Merganser, among others.

A bird of special interest in this area is Burrowing Owl. Park managers have gone to great lengths to provide habitat for them and have installed some artificial burrows. Park in the area near the golf course and walk back to the main entrance road; cross it and follow the paved **shoreline trail** to the east for about 0.5 mile. A large square post has been placed here that reads "Burrowing Owl Habitat. Please remain on path while observing owls." Early morning is best.

This same shoreline trail gives access to good marsh and pond habitat. Some birds to look for are grebes, egrets, Black-crowned Night-Heron, and American Avocet. I once counted about 2,000 Ruddy Ducks on a pond here. Along the grassy edges, look for American Pipit, Savannah Sparrow, and Western Meadowlark. Raptors include Northern Harrier and Cooper's and Red-tailed Hawks.

General information: Palo Alto Baylands is one of the best-known birding sites in the Bay Area. Its 1,500 acres include an extensive salt marsh where Clapper and Black Rails are both regularly seen. (The California Black Rail is classified as state-listed threatened, and the California Clapper Rail is classified as federally and state-listed endangered.) In addition to salt marsh, there are some freshwater marsh, extensive mudflats, and open grassy areas. Shoreline at Mountain View has much of the same kinds of habitats.

ADDITIONAL HELP

NCA&G grid: Page 115, 5A.
Elevation: Sea level.
Nearest food, gas, lodging: Palo Alto; Mountain View.
For more information: Palo Alto Baylands Nature Preserve; Shoreline at Mountain View.

60 Don Edwards San Francisco Bay National Wildlife Refuge ♔

Habitats: Sandy beach and mudflats, coastal bays and lagoons, coastal scrub, salt marsh, freshwater marsh.

Specialty birds: *Resident*—White-tailed Kite, Chestnut-backed Chickadee, Wrentit, Lesser Goldfinch. *Summer*—Cinnamon Teal. *Winter*—Long-billed Curlew; Mew and Thayer's Gulls; Tricolored Blackbird.

Other key birds: *Resident*—Black-crowned Night-Heron, Virginia Rail, Common Moorhen, Loggerhead Shrike, Common Yellowthroat. *Summer*—Caspian and Forster's Terns. *Winter*—Eared Grebe; American White Pelican; Green-winged Teal; Canvasback; Greater and Lesser Scaups; Sora; Black-bellied and Semipalmated Plovers; Black-necked Stilt; American Avocet; Greater Yellowlegs; Marbled Godwit; Long-billed and Short-billed Dowitchers; Bonaparte's Gull.

Best times to bird: October through March.

Directions: Refuge headquarters and visitor center: From California Highway 84 (going west toward Dumbarton Bridge), take Thornton Avenue south about 0.8 mile to the entrance to the refuge, and follow Marshlands Road to visitor center (parking, restrooms; main gate locked at 5 P.M.). Marshlands Road continues another 3 miles to Dumbarton Pier.

Ravenswood access: When going east toward Dumbarton Bridge on CA 84 from Palo Alto, exit at about 2 miles past U.S. Highway 101, just before getting on the bridge. When going west on Dumbarton Bridge, exit about 5.5 miles after going west on Dumbarton Bridge, exit about 5.5 miles after going through the toll plaza.

Coyote Hills Regional Park (fee): From CA 84 east of Dumbarton Bridge, take Paseo Padre Parkway north 1.1 miles to Patterson Ranch Road, turn west, and go 1.3 miles to the visitor center.

Environmental Education Center: From the junction of Interstate 880 and California Highway 237, take CA 237 west about 2.5 miles to North First Street. Turn north on North First Street and go 0.8 mile to Grand Boulevard and turn right. Go 1.5 miles to the parking lot for the center. (Where the road veers to the right, it becomes Los Esteros Road; Grand Boulevard continues straight.)

Alviso Marina: From the junction of I-880 and CA 237, take CA 237 west about 3.5 miles to the exit for Great America Parkway, Lafayette Street, and Gold Street. Follow the signs to Gold Street, and turn north. Go 0.7 mile to Elizabeth Street, turn left, go 0.2 mile to Hope Street, and turn right to the parking lot for the marina (chemical toilets). (Note: At this writing, the marina is scheduled for reconstruction, but this is also the parking lot to gain access to the trail to Alviso Slough.)

The birding: The refuge headquarters and visitor center is the natural starting point (restrooms, exhibits, books). Take the **Tidelands Interpretive Trail** (about 1.5 miles, round trip), which leads along the edge of some ponds, then climbs back up the

60 Don Edwards San Francisco Bay National Wildlife Refuge

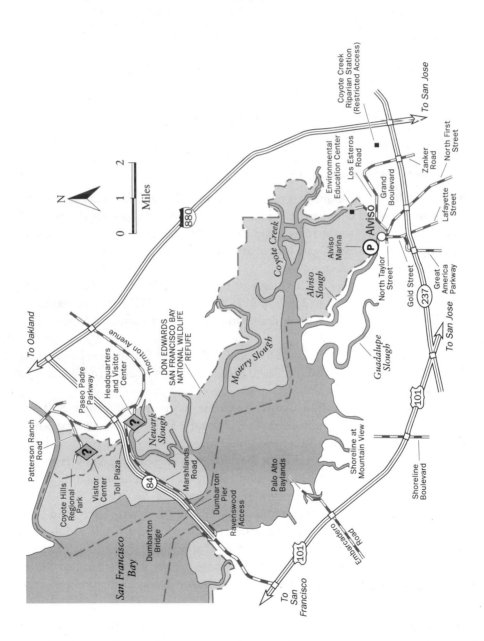

To San Jose

Coyote Creek Riparian Station (Restricted Access)

North First Street

Zanker Road

Lafayette Street

Environmental Education Center

Los Esteros Road

Grand Boulevard

880

N

Miles

0 1 2

Alviso

Coyote Creek

Alviso Marina

Alviso Slough

North Taylor Street

Gold Street

Great America Parkway

237

To San Jose

Guadalupe Slough

To Oakland

Thornton Avenue

Mowry Slough

Paseo Padre Parkway

Headquarters and Visitor Center

DON EDWARDS SAN FRANCISCO BAY NATIONAL WILDLIFE REFUFE

Patterson Ranch Road

Coyote Hills Regional Park

Visitor Center

Toll Plaza

Newark Slough

Marshlands Road

84

Dumbarton Pier

Ravenswood Access

Palo Alto Baylands

Shoreline at Mountain View

Shoreline Boulevard

101

Dumbarton Bridge

San Francisco Bay

Embarcadero Road

101

To San Francisco

hill and goes around behind the visitor center, to return over the crest. Typical birds are Pied-billed Grebe, Gadwall, Cinnamon Teal, Ruddy Duck, Black-necked Stilt, American Avocet, Greater Yellowlegs, Willet, Long-billed Curlew, and Marbled Godwit.

The marshes are likely to have Great Blue Heron, Great and Snowy Egrets, and an occasional Black-crowned Night-Heron (all residents). The open ponds can have American White Pelicans in the fall and Double-crested Cormorants any time of year. The land portions should have residents such as White-tailed Kite, Anna's Hummingbird, and Black Phoebe, and wintering Golden-crowned and White-crowned Sparrows. Northern Harriers might be anywhere. Check black-bird flocks for Tricolored Blackbird.

Ravenswood Access gets you out to the bayshore. At low tide, look for the shorebirds already mentioned, plus (in winter) Black-bellied and Semipalmated Plovers; Western and Least Sandpipers; Dunlin; and Long-billed and Short-billed Dowitchers. In winter open water anywhere could have Eared Grebe, American Wigeon, Northern Shoveler, Northern Pintail, Green-winged Teal, Canvasback, and Greater and Lesser Scaups. From spring through fall, look for Caspian and Forster's Terns. Access is possible going either way on the Dumbarton Bridge, and you can go from one side to the other by driving under the bridge.

Dumbarton Pier (chemical toilets on the pier) has birds similar to those at the Ravenswood Access.

Long-billed Curlew.

Coyote Hills Regional Park's habitats include coastal scrub, groves of trees, and some freshwater marsh. The areas with trees should have California Quail, Chestnut-backed Chickadee, California and Spotted Towhees, and Lesser Goldfinch, as well as wintering sparrows. Wrentits may be on the brushy hillsides. Look in the more open areas for Loggerhead Shrike and Western Meadowlark. There is a boardwalk across the freshwater marsh where Virginia Rail, Common Moorhen, Marsh Wren, and Common Yellowthroat are resident. Look for Sora in winter.

The **Environmental Education Center** is used by classes and organized groups, and is also open to the general public on a drop-in basis (the center is open 8:00 A.M. to 4:30 P.M. but is principally used for classes; the parking lot is open until 4:30 P.M.; chemical toilet). On weekends, the center offers slide shows and interpretive tours. Little Blue Herons have occasionally been seen on the nearby sloughs during summer.

A trail beginning at the **Alviso Marina** follows the levee that borders Alviso Slough and can be hiked for miles. This area seems to have more than the usual complement of gulls: Ring-billed, California, Herring, and Western are common, but you also may see Bonaparte's, Mew, and Thayer's in winter. Lesser Black-backed Gull (rare) has shown up here.

The **Coyote Creek Riparian Station** is a research and banding location, but is not open to the general public. (Contact the station concerning membership; see Appendix A.)

General information: Don Edwards San Francisco Bay NWR has been classified as a Globally Important Bird Area because of its California Clapper Rails, Western Snowy Plovers, Northern Shovelers (winter), Ruddy Ducks (winter), and Dunlin and Black-bellied Plovers (spring migration). Millions of birds are here in winter, with great rafts of ducks on the open water and thousands of shorebirds per mile along the edges at times. The winter counts of Black-necked Stilts and American Avocets are often the highest in the nation.

ADDITIONAL HELP

NCA&G grid: Page 105, 5D; page 115, 5A.
Elevation: Sea level to 200 feet.
Hazards: Ticks and poison oak are possible.
Nearest food, gas, lodging: Palo Alto; Mountain View; Fremont.
For more information: Don Edwards San Francisco Bay National Wildlife Refuge.

61 Alum Rock Park

Habitats: Stream, riparian woodland, foothill woodland, chaparral, cultivated park lawns.

Specialty birds: *Resident*—Golden Eagle; Acorn and Nuttall's Woodpeckers; Steller's Jay; Oak Titmouse; Canyon Wren; Wrentit; California Thrasher; Rufous-crowned Sparrow. *Summer*—Ash-throated Flycatcher; Western Kingbird; Cassin's Vireo; Black-headed Grosbeak; Bullock's and Hooded Orioles. *Winter*—American Dipper.

Other key birds: *Resident*—Bewick's Wren. *Summer*—Warbling Vireo, Northern Rough-winged Swallow, House Wren.

Best times to bird: October through May.

Directions: From the junction of Interstate 680 and Alum Rock Avenue (California Highway 130) east of San Jose, go northeast on Alum Rock Avenue 2.3 miles to the junction with Mount Hamilton Road, and then 1.1 miles farther on Alum Rock Avenue to the park entrance (fee, parking, restrooms).

The birding: Steller's Jays are everywhere. Birds typical of the Coast Ranges are easy to see, such as Anna's Hummingbird; Nuttall's and Acorn Woodpeckers; Western Scrub-Jay; Oak Titmouse; Bushtit; and Spotted and California Towhees. Wrentits sing from the surrounding hillsides. Summer visitors are Ash-throated Flycatcher; Warbling and Cassin's Vireos; Northern Rough-winged Swallow; Black-headed Grosbeak; and Bullock's and Hooded Orioles. In winter American Dipper can sometimes be seen along the stream. Golden-crowned Sparrows are winter visitors, and Black Phoebes are resident.

An easy trail goes upstream from the parking area near the Youth Science Institute to **Sycamore Grove Picnic Area,** passing near the mineral springs, most of which were enclosed with rockwork years ago. Canyon Wrens can sometimes be found upstream from the picnic areas.

At the lower parking area, near **Eagle Rock Picnic Area,** a trail along the stream passes near good riparian habitat. The birds here are similar to those already mentioned. Look also for House Wren and Bullock's Oriole in spring and summer, and Yellow-rumped Warbler in fall and winter.

The **North Rim Trail** begins near the Eagle Rock Picnic Area. It climbs the hillside and passes near areas of chaparral, which may produce California Quail, Bewick's Wren, California Thrasher, Wrentit, Spotted Towhee, and Rufous-crowned Sparrow, with Western Kingbird (summer) turning up in the more open areas. Golden Eagles sometimes soar overhead.

General information: Alum Rock Park was founded in 1872, and at one time had an indoor swimming pool, mineral baths, a tea garden, restaurant, and dance pavilion, all served by a railroad from San Jose. The dance pavilion is long gone, but the mineral springs are still here, and the railroad bed provides a footpath along the stream. There are picnic areas, lawns, and a visitor center. On weekends the park can be jammed, but during the week it is a pleasant, uncrowded place.

61 Alum Rock Park

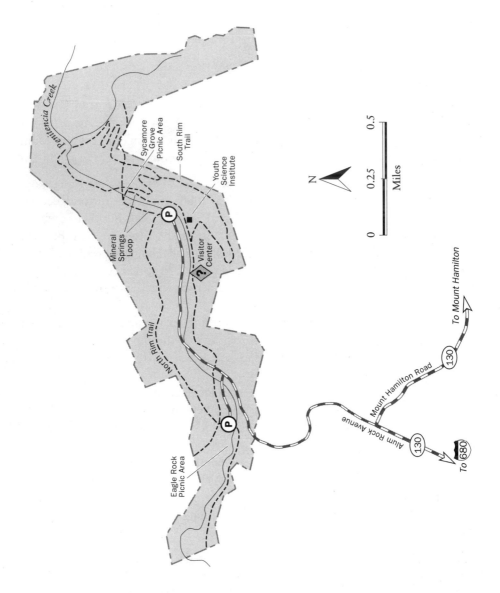

ADDITIONAL HELP

NCA&G grid: Page 115, 7A.

Elevation: 300 to 800 feet.

Hazards: Rattlesnakes, poison oak, ticks; the park staff reports that mountain lions have been seen in the park.

Nearest food, gas, lodging: San Jose.

Camping: None nearby.

For more information: Alum Rock Park.

62 Mines Road and Del Puerto Canyon

Habitats: Lake, riparian woodland, foothill woodland, oak savanna, chaparral.

Specialty birds: *Resident*—Wood Duck; Golden Eagle; Prairie Falcon; Greater Roadrunner; Western Screech-Owl; Northern Pygmy-Owl; White-throated Swift; Lewis's and Nuttall's Woodpeckers; Say's Phoebe; Hutton's Vireo; Steller's Jay; Yellow-billed Magpie; Rock and Canyon Wrens; Western Bluebird; California Thrasher; Phainopepla; Rufous-crowned and Sage Sparrows; Lesser Goldfinch. *Summer*—Lesser Nighthawk; Common Poorwill; Costa's Hummingbird; Western Wood-Pewee; Ash-throated Flycatcher; Cassin's and Western Kingbirds; Violet-green Swallow; Black-chinned Sparrow; Black-headed Grosbeak; Lazuli Bunting; Lawrence's Goldfinch. *Winter*—Bald Eagle.

Other key birds: *Resident*—Red-shouldered Hawk; Barn and Great Horned Owls; Loggerhead Shrike; White-breasted Nuthatch; Lark Sparrow. *Summer*—Blue-gray Gnatcatcher, Yellow-breasted Chat, Grasshopper Sparrow. *Winter*—Common Merganser, Hermit Thrush, Purple Finch.

Best times to bird: Mid-April to July.

Directions: From Interstate 580, exit at North Livermore Avenue, and go south 1.2 miles to the center of Livermore (flagpole). Continue straight, onto South Livermore Avenue. After 1.8 miles, South Livermore Avenue bends to the east and becomes Tesla Road. The junction with Mines Road is 2.3 miles from the flagpole.

The intersection of **Corral Hollow Road** with I-580 is marked "Corral Hollow Road"; however, the sign at the intersection of **Del Puerto Road** with Interstate 5 does not mention Del Puerto Road, but says "Patterson."

Mileposts (designated as MP 8.38 or MP 12.67, for example) for Mines Road **within Alameda County** are measured from Tesla Road, and increase going south. The mileages referenced in the text appear on small white signs along the roadside, and in Alameda County, large white figures are painted on the pavement for each mile.

Mileposts on Mines Road and San Antonio Valley Road **within Santa Clara County** are measured from where the road from Mount Hamilton enters San Antonio Valley; mileages increase going north. The mileages in Santa Clara County

62 Mines Road and Del Puerto Canyon

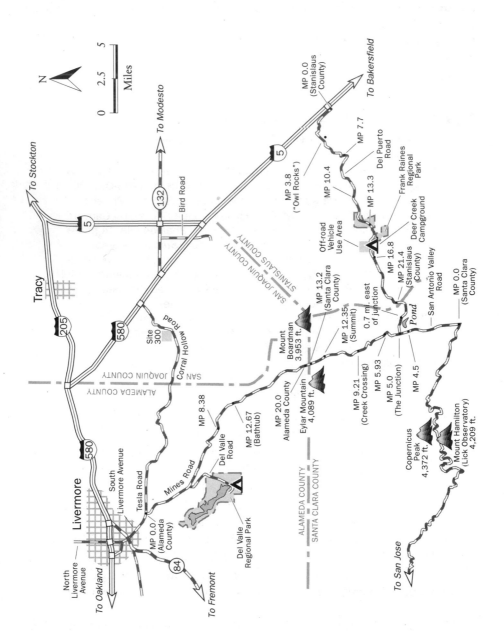

mentioned in the text generally appear on small roadside signs, although in some cases they have been estimated.

Mileposts on Del Puerto Road **within Stanislaus County** are measured from I-5, and mileages increase going west. Large white figures are painted on the pavement at each mile in Stanislaus County, and signs giving the mileage are installed at these points at the road edge. The "mileposts" given in the text (e.g., MP 10.4) are estimates of locations between mileage signs.

The birding: Records for Mines Road, Del Puerto Canyon, San Antonio Valley, and Corral Hollow covering 27 years have been kept by Art Edwards, of Livermore. Comments herein regarding abundance are primarily based on his records, as updated by Cliff Richer.

Almost all the property along the roads is private; therefore, birding must be done from the roadsides, with the exception of Del Valle Regional Park, Frank Raines Regional Park, and Minniear Day Use Area in Del Puerto Canyon. When stopping, avoid parking near houses, because some property owners reportedly have become upset with birders who stop near their houses. Also, it is important not to block any gates or roads. The milepost points described herein have been selected to provide adequate parking (in some cases, *barely* adequate), and to avoid disturbing property owners.

The principal birds looked for here by many birders are Greater Roadrunner, Lewis's Woodpecker, Phainopepla, and Lawrence's Goldfinch. All of them are uncommon to rare, and can be difficult to find. The most likely places for the Roadrunner are as follows: in Alameda County, around MP 6; in Santa Clara County, MP 10; in Stanislaus County, MP 10. For Lewis's Woodpecker, in Santa Clara County, MP 4.5; for Phainopepla, in Alameda County, at various places from about MP 5 to MP 13. For Lawrence's Goldfinch, "best" locations have varied from year to year, but in recent years a good place has been near "the Junction," where Mines Road, San Antonio Valley Road, and Del Puerto Road come together; another place is at Frank Raines Regional Park, but Lawrence's Goldfinches have been reported at one time or another from many points along Mines Road and San Antonio Valley Road.

Certain birds are common along the roads and in general will not be given special mention, such as California Quail, Acorn Woodpecker, Western Scrub-Jay, Oak Titmouse, and House Finch.

Del Valle Regional Park: About 3 miles from Tesla Road, Mines Road cuts sharply to the left, and the road straight ahead, Del Valle Road, leads to Del Valle Regional Park (fee, restrooms, campground). Where Del Valle Road crosses the lake, White-throated Swifts often are seen, at the west end of the bridge. A loop trail (about 1 mile round trip)—**Oak Hills Nature Trail**— begins at the far end of the day-use parking area, goes up over the hill, and returns to the parking area. Birds here are typical of foothill woodland habitat, such as Red-shouldered Hawk, Nuttall's Woodpecker, Yellow-billed Magpie, Oak Titmouse, Bushtit, Western

Bluebird, California and Spotted Towhees, and even a few Steller's Jays. In winter Ruby-crowned Kinglet, Hermit Thrush, Yellow-rumped Warbler, and Golden-crowned and White-crowned sparrows are common. The lake may have Double-crested Cormorants, Common Mergansers, gulls, and even a Bald Eagle.

MP 8.38 (Alameda County): There is sufficient room to park off the road, but be careful not to block the gate. This spot has Western Wood-Pewee, White-breasted Nuthatch, Western Bluebird, and Black-headed Grosbeak. Greater Roadrunners have been seen in the general area. Listen for their "lovesick" cooing call in the spring.

MP 12.67 (Alameda County). Park here and walk back along Mines Road to MP 12.62, where there is a bathtub just below the road, and a seasonal spring. Look for Ash-throated Flycatcher, House Wren, California Thrasher, California Towhee, Lesser Goldfinch, and various woodpeckers, warblers, and sparrows. Phainopepla and Lawrence's Goldfinch have been reported here. Also, Common Poorwill has been seen at dusk along the section of road from here to the county line at MP 20. 0 (Alameda County) and MP 13.2 (Santa Clara County).

MP 12.35 (Summit; Santa Clara County). Park on the south side, at the summit near extensive chaparral. Look for Ash-throated Flycatcher, Rock Wren, Black-headed Grosbeak (summer), and Sage Sparrow. Greater Roadrunner, Blue-gray Gnatcatcher, and Black-chinned Sparrow (the last two, rare summer visitors) are possibilities.

MP 9.21 (Creek Crossing; Santa Clara County). This is a pleasant spot when the creek has water. There is room to park, but don't block the gate. Look for Black Phoebe, Ash-throated Flycatcher, House Wren, and Killdeer, as well as swallows and woodpeckers. Lawrence's Goldfinch also has been seen.

MP 5.93 (Santa Clara County). The pond and marsh across from the entrance to the Digger Pine Ranch are good for Wood Duck, Nuttall's Woodpecker, Black Phoebe, Ash-throated Flycatcher (summer), Violet-green Swallow (summer), White-breasted Nuthatch, Lazuli Bunting (uncommon, summer), and Lesser and Lawrence's Goldfinches. Look for Purple Finch in winter.

The Junction at MP 5.0 (Santa Clara County). The cafe here is open every day except holidays from 10 A.M. to 7 P.M. for cold drinks and light meals. The owners put out hummingbird feeders, and visitors enjoy watching the Anna's Hummingbirds dispute over possession. It is a pleasant place to sit outdoors at a picnic table in the shade and look for Lawrence's Goldfinch, because this area has been one of the better places for them. Mostly, however, you will see and hear Acorn Woodpeckers. The area across the road around the fire station traditionally has been a good place for Lawrence's Goldfinch. Lewis's Woodpeckers have been seen along the road both north and south of the Junction. The road north from the Junction is called Mines Road; to the south, it is called San Antonio Valley Road.

MP 4.5 (Santa Clara County). This has been one of the better places for Lewis's Woodpecker. There is a ranch gate on the west side of the road with sufficient room to park without blocking access.

Approximately 0.7 mile east of the Junction on **Del Puerto Road** is an un-named pond. There is no good place to park near the pond, so go just beyond the cattle guard, to the east where there is room (barely) for a car to park off the road, and walk back to the pond. Wood Duck and Common Merganser have been seen here, as well as Belted Kingfisher, Western Wood-Pewee, Black Phoebe, and Cali-fornia Towhee.

MP 16.8 (Stanislaus County). The creek goes under the road through a cul-vert. Parking is available next to the road here. This stretch, both above and below the culvert, has regularly had Yellow-breasted Chat. In May they generally can be heard singing in the willow thickets along the creek. There are places along the edge of the road where you can look down into the creek and try to get a look, but watch out for cars. Hutton's Vireo and Spotted Towhee are residents. In migra-tion, watch for Warbling Vireo, Wilson's Warbler, and Western Tanager among others.

Deer Creek Campground (MP 16.2; Stanislaus County). This is a part of Frank Raines Regional Park. Access to the creek is possible here, although it is a popular place for off-road vehicles. Birding next to the creek can be good, provided the campground is not too crowded. Look for Lawrence's Goldfinch, as well as regu-lars such as Black Phoebe, Ash-throated Flycatcher, Lesser Goldfinch, woodpeck-ers, and warblers.

Frank Raines Park Day Use Area (MP 15.1; Stanislaus County). Picnicking and restrooms are available. Many of the birds previously mentioned will be here, too, provided there aren't too many people.

Minniear Day Use Area (MP 13.3; Stanislaus County). This is also a part of Frank Raines Regional Park. There is ample room next to the road to park, and there are pedestrian openings through the fences on both sides of the road. From the parking area on a quiet night in spring, Common Poorwills can be heard calling from the surrounding ridges. The nearby trees have had Western Screech-Owl (uncommon resident) and Northern Pygmy-Owl (rare resident).

MP 10.4 (Stanislaus County). At this point the creek makes a sharp double bend and passes beneath the road, with rocky cliffs nearby. Parking is available on a broad shoulder about 100 yards west of where the creek goes under the road. Rock and Canyon Wrens occur here, and there is a possibility of seeing a Say's Phoebe (uncommon resident). Look for Costa's Hummingbird (uncommon sum-mer visitor) here as well as elsewhere along this stretch of road, especially wher-ever there is tree tobacco growing.

MP 7.7 (Stanislaus County). Rocky outcroppings along road make parking impossible, so it is necessary to go beyond, and walk back. Cassin's Kingbird, which is at the northern limit of its range here, occurs on an irregular basis in summer. To distinguish Cassin's from the more common Western Kingbird, look for darker upperparts, a contrasting white chin, and brownish black tail with no white showing. In the Western Kingbird, look for light gray head and throat, and a blackish tail with white outer edges. Beware that, in the early fall, when the feathers are worn, a Western Kingbird may show little or no white in the tail. Other birds to look for are Say's Phoebe, Loggerhead Shrike, Rock Wren, and Lark and Rufous-crowned Sparrows. Grassy slopes may have Grasshopper Sparrow, which is rare in spring and summer. In this open country, don't forget to check the sky for a soaring Golden Eagle, Prairie Falcon, or Common Raven.

"Owl Rocks" MP 3.8 (Stanislaus County). The cliffs here abound with potholes, some of which have "whitewash" below them, showing they have been occupied. This spot is known for having had nesting Barn and Great Horned Owls, and has also had White-throated Swift, Say's Phoebe, and Phainopepla. In summer at dusk, look and listen for Common Poorwill.

Corral Hollow Road begins as Tesla Road in Alameda County, and becomes Corral Hollow Road as you pass into San Joaquin County. It is 18.7 miles from the junction of Tesla Road and Mines Road to I-580. The habitats are similar to those on Del Puerto Road, even including some "owl rocks" south of the road about 3.2 miles from I-580. However, these owl rocks are farther from the road than those along Del Puerto Road. About 4 miles from I-580 is Site 300 of the University of California's Lawrence Livermore National Laboratory. At dusk in late spring and summer, Lesser Nighthawks have sometimes been seen flying under the floodlights at Site 300. Unfortunately, both sides of the road along this section have "No Parking" and "No Loitering" signs, so viewing opportunities are limited. Just to the east of Site 300, and on the opposite side of the road, there is room to get off the road and park near a fire station. Lesser Nighthawks have been observed in the open fields to the south, and Barn Owls have roosted in the pine trees around the fire station.

Bird Road is a good place for Lesser Nighthawks. To get there, from the junction of I-5 and CA 132, go west 0.7 mile on CA 132 to Bird Road, and turn left (south). From the junction of I-580 and CA 132, go east about 2 miles on CA 132 to Bird Road, and turn right. Go about 2.5 miles south on Bird Road to the end. Arrange to be there a half hour or so before sunset. The nighthawks forage up and down the shallow canyon, generally fairly close to the ground, and sometimes over the small pond on the left side of the road about 100 yards before the end. May is the best month.

General information: Mines Road and Del Puerto Canyon are popular with birders because they provide access to the heart of the dry interior Coast Range mountains. The roads are paved and are reasonably good, although the section of Mines Road from MP 11.8 to MP 20 in Alameda County is narrow and lacks a white center line. Traffic is usually light, which is nice for birding, but it can lull you into a false sense of security. Watch for traffic—almost all birding is done from the roadside.

ADDITIONAL HELP

NCA&G grid: Page 106, 1C, 2D; page 116, 2A, 4A.

Elevation: 1,000 to 2,700 feet.

Hazards: Be alert for traffic, including bicycles, when standing on narrow road shoulders; poison oak, ticks, and rattlesnakes are present.

Nearest food, gas, lodging: Livermore.

Camping: Del Valle Regional Park: 150 sites, about 8.5 miles south of Livermore; go south on South Livermore Avenue, which becomes Tesla Road, and turn right (south) on Mines Avenue, then go 3 miles on Mines Road to the junction with Del Valle Road and then 3.1 miles on Del Valle Road to the park entrance; call for reservations. (See Appendix F.) Deer Creek Campground: 34 sites with full hook-ups, plus additional informal sites, at Frank Raines Regional Park; RV dump station. The campground is heavily used by off-road vehicle groups, especially on weekends from October through April. No reservations are taken, but if you plan to be there on a winter weekend, if would be wise to call the park in advance. (See Appendix A.)

For more information: Del Valle Regional Park; Frank Raines Regional Park.

63 Mount Diablo 🔭

Habitats: Riparian woodland, foothill woodland, oak savanna, chaparral.
Specialty birds: *Resident*—Golden Eagle; Prairie Falcon; Western Screech-Owl; White-throated Swift; Nuttall's Woodpecker; Hutton's Vireo; Oak Titmouse; Rock Wren; Western Bluebird; Wrentit; California Thrasher; Rufous-crowned and Sage Sparrows; Lesser Goldfinch. *Summer*—Common Poorwill; Pacific-slope and Ash-throated Flycatchers; Black-chinned Sparrow; Black-headed Grosbeak; Lawrence's Goldfinch. *Winter*—Varied Thrush. *Migrant*—Hammond's Flycatcher.
Other key birds: *Resident*—Cooper's Hawk, White-breasted Nuthatch, Purple Finch, American Goldfinch. *Summer*—Warbling Vireo, Blue-gray Gnatcatcher. *Winter*—Hermit Thrush, Fox Sparrow.
Best times to bird: All year; April through June for breeding birds.

Directions: Note: Park gates are open from 8 A.M. until sunset (fee required). **From the north:** From the junction of Interstate 680 and Treat Boulevard north of Walnut Creek, exit to Treat Boulevard and turn east. Go 1.1 miles to Bancroft Road and turn right. (Bancroft Road becomes Walnut Avenue.) Follow Bancroft/Walnut Avenue 3.6 miles to the North Gate of the park. **From the south:** From the junction of I-680 and Diablo Road in Danville, go east on Diablo Road. After 0.8 mile make a sharp right turn at a signal, go 2.1 miles, and turn left on Mount Diablo Scenic Boulevard. It is about 4.6 miles to **Rock City.** For **Mitchell Canyon:** From the junction of I-680 and Treat Boulevard north of Walnut Creek, exit to Treat Boulevard and turn east. Go 1.1 miles to Bancroft Road, turn right, drive 0.6 mile to Ygnacio Valley Road, and turn left. Travel 5.1 miles to Clayton Road

63 Mount Diablo

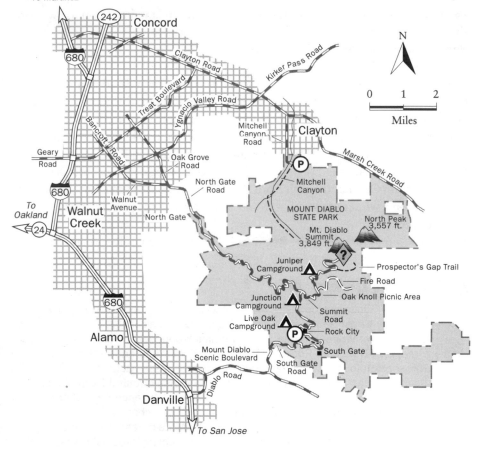

and turn right, then 1 mile on Clayton Road and turn right on Mitchell Canyon Road to a parking lot (fee, restrooms).

The birding: The natural beginning point is **Rock City,** named because of many rounded rock outcroppings. Park by the sign that reads "Rock City, Live Oak." From this small parking lot, take the fire road directly to the south, past the locked gate, which leads along a ridge among groves of live oaks. Typical birds here are California Quail; Acorn and Nuttall's Woodpeckers; Western Scrub-Jay; Bewick's Wren; Western Bluebird; and Lesser Goldfinch (all residents). Some winter visitors are Ruby-crowned Kinglet; Varied Thrush (irregular); Golden-crowned and White-crowned Sparrows; and Dark-eyed Junco.

From this same small parking lot, if you walk directly west across a grassy swale on a fairly well-trod informal trail, you will come out on a ridge looking

On Mount Diablo, near Rock City.

straight down on chaparral slopes. Wrentits and Spotted Towhees (residents) live in the chaparral, and Rufous-crowned Sparrows (uncommon resident) may be present. Ash-throated Flycatcher (summer visitor), Black-chinned Sparrow (rare summer visitor), and Sage Sparrow (resident) should be looked for. An occasional look at the sky is advisable. Mostly, you will see lots of Turkey Vultures, but Red-tailed Hawks, White-throated Swifts, and Common Ravens also occur, and there might even be a Golden Eagle or Prairie Falcon (both rare residents).

Fire road: From Rock City, drive 2.2 miles toward the summit to the "Junction," turn right on Summit Road, and go 1.6 miles, just beyond Oak Knoll Picnic Area to a dirt parking area on the right, and a fire road with a locked gate. The fire road is surrounded by chaparral, and a walk here should produce California Quail, Anna's Hummingbird, Bewick's Wren, Wrentit, California Thrasher, Spotted Towhee, and Sage Sparrow. Look also for Blue-gray Gnatcatcher (uncommon in summer, rare in winter). Observant birders will note that the dominant shrub in the chaparral is chamise, not sagebrush. The coastal race of the Sage Sparrow most commonly is found in association with chamise, in spite of its name.

The **Prospector's Gap Trail** is about 1.9 miles up the road from the fire road. There is a fairly large dirt parking area on the right, and a trail that goes near rocky formations. Look for Rock Wren, Wrentit, and Black-chinned Sparrow, which is a rare summer visitor.

Other locations along Summit Road, such as the picnic areas, can offer good birding. Acorn Woodpecker; Oak Titmouse; California Thrasher; Spotted and California Towhees; and Lesser Goldfinch are possibilities, and there's always a chance (rare, summer) for a Lawrence's Goldfinch. If you are camping overnight, you may be able to find a Western Screech-Owl in the wooded areas or a Common Poorwill at dusk in the chaparral.

The summit is worth a visit for the view and for looking for soaring raptors, but it can have a lot of people.

Mitchell Canyon, on the north slope of the mountain, may be the best birding site of all. The Mitchell Canyon Trail for a couple of miles is a fairly gentle grade next to a seasonal stream. Oak Titmice abound. Look also for Cooper's Hawk; Acorn and Nuttall's Woodpeckers; Hutton's Vireo; Bushtit; White-breasted Nuthatch; Wrentit; California Thrasher; Spotted and California Towhees; Purple Finch; and American Goldfinch (all resident). In late spring and summer look for Pacific-slope and Ash-throated Flycatchers; Warbling Vireo; Orange-crowned Warbler; and Black-headed Grosbeak, and in winter for Ruby-crowned Kinglet; Hermit Thrush; and Fox, Golden-crowned, and White-crowned Sparrows. Hammond's Flycatchers are migrants.

General information: Mount Diablo, at 3,849 feet, dominates the San Francisco Bay Area. Because of its isolated position, it provides sensational views of the surrounding territory—provided it isn't foggy or smoggy. On a clear day in winter or early spring it is possible to see Mount Lassen, 165 miles to the north. The mountain has extensive recreational developments, including three campgrounds, numerous picnic areas, and miles of trails. The park is at its best in spring, when things are green, the birds are singing, and the wildflowers are blooming, although the winters are also very pleasant.

ADDITIONAL HELP

NCA&G grid: Page 105, 6A, 6B.
Elevation: 600 to 3,849 feet.
Hazards: Watch out for bicycles. They go very slow uphill, and you often cannot pass for long intervals because of the narrow winding road. Coming down, most of them go very fast. Other hazards are poison oak, rattlesnakes, and ticks.
Nearest food, gas, lodging: Concord; Walnut Creek; Danville.
Camping: Juniper: 34 sites, 2.3 miles from the Junction, on Summit Road. Junction: 6 sites, at the Junction. Live Oak: 18 sites, near Rock City; closed in winter.
For more information: Mount Diablo State Park.

64 Point Pinole Regional Shoreline 🏃

Habitats: Sandy beach and mudflats, coastal bays and lagoons, salt marsh, valley grassland, eucalyptus groves.
Speciality birds: *Resident*—White-tailed Kite, Anna's Hummingbird, Western Meadowlark. *Summer*—Cinnamon Teal; Elegant and Least Terns. *Winter*—Pacific Loon; Western and Clark's Grebes; Black Turnstone.
Other key birds: *Resident*—Black-necked Stilt, American Avocet, Forster's Tern, Loggerhead Shrike. *Summer*—Caspian Tern. *Winter*—Common Loon; Horned and Eared Grebes; Green-winged Teal; Canvasback; Greater and Lesser Scaups; Surf and White-winged Scoters; Bufflehead; Common Goldeneye; Greater Yellowlegs; Marbled Godwit; Spotted Sandpiper; Ruddy Turnstone; Long-billed and Short-billed Dowitchers. *Migrant*—Wilson's and Red-necked Phalaropes.
Best times to bird: October through June.

Directions: From Interstate 80 north of Richmond, exit at Richmond Parkway and go west. At about 2.0 miles turn right and exit onto Giant Highway. The entrance to Point Pinole Regional Shoreline is on Giant Highway, about 0.8 mile north of Richmond Parkway. Turn west into a parking lot (fee, chemical toilets).

The birding: Point Pinole offers a mixture of shoreline and woods birding. The **Bay View Trail,** for example, runs along the shore, but also borders a eucalyptus forest. The bay may have thousands of ducks on it in winter, some of them so far out that a scope is necessary. Typical birds (mostly in winter) are Gadwall; American Wigeon; Cinnamon and Green-winged Teal; Northern Shoveler; Northern Pintail; Canvasback; Greater and Lesser Scaups; Surf and White-winged Scoters; Common Goldeneye; Bufflehead; and Ruddy Duck. Common and Pacific Loons may be present, as well as Pied-billed, Horned, Eared, Western, and Clark's Grebes. Forster's Terns are resident, whereas Caspian and Least Terns may be present in summer, and Elegant Terns in late summer and fall. Wilson's and Red-necked Phalaropes also may show up in fall.

Along the shore, look for Black-necked Stilt and American Avocet year-round, and Greater Yellowlegs, Marbled Godwit, Red Knot, Dunlin, and Long-billed and Short-billed Dowitchers in fall and winter. Along the rocky shores in fall and winter, there may be Ruddy and Black Turnstones and Spotted Sandpiper, the latter two uncommon.

Typical resident land birds are White-tailed Kite (uncommon); Red-tailed Hawk; Anna's Hummingbird; Loggerhead Shrike; Bushtit; Spotted and California Towhees; Western Meadowlark; and House Finch.

General information: Point Pinole Regional Shoreline is a delight. It was once the location of a huge dynamite factory, sited remotely for fear of explosions. The views across the bay to the Marin shore are tranquil, and the eucalyptus groves scattered across the hilly terrain give little sign of the area's industrial past. There

64 Point Pinole Regional Shoreline

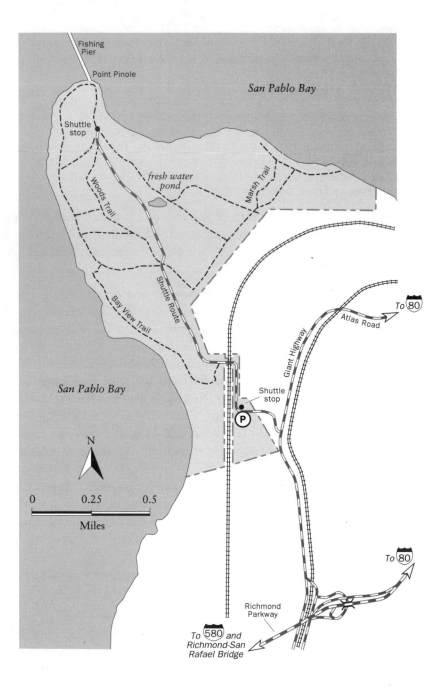

are 12 miles of trails in the park, plus a shuttle that runs hourly every day from the parking lot to the point, except Tuesday and Wednesday (fee).

ADDITIONAL HELP

NCA&G grid: Page 94, 3D.
Elevation: Sea level.
Hazards: Rattlesnakes, poison oak; ticks are possible.
Nearest food, gas, lodging: Richmond.
For more information: East Bay Regional Parks District.

65 Lake Merritt

Habitats: Lake, cultivated parklands.
Specialty birds: *Resident*—Anna's Hummingbird, Nuttall's Woodpecker, Black Phoebe, Chestnut-backed Chickadee, Oak Titmouse, Bushtit. *Summer*—Least Tern, Allen's Hummingbird. *Winter*—Greater White-fronted Goose, Wood Duck, Hooded Merganser.
Other key birds: *Resident*—Black-crowned Night-Heron, Ruddy Duck. *Summer*—Forster's Tern. *Winter*—Horned Grebe; Double-crested Cormorant; American Wigeon; Canvasback; Redhead; Ring-necked Duck; Greater and Lesser Scaups; Bufflehead; Common and Barrow's Goldeneyes.
Best times to bird: All year, but November to March is best for waterfowl.

Directions: From Interstate 580 take the exit for Grand Avenue and go west on Grand Avenue. Look for Bellevue Avenue, which is one way. You cannot turn onto Bellevue Avenue the first time you come to it; turn left the second time, and enter Lakeside Park (fee). Continue on Bellevue Avenue and park near the waterfowl ponds and Rotary Nature Center (streetside parking, difficult on weekends). Restrooms are in the nature center building.

The birding: Lakeside Park: Besides the expected collection of Pied-billed Grebes, Canada Geese, Mallards, American Coots, and Herring Gulls, there may be Horned Grebes; Greater White-fronted Geese; Wood Ducks (uncommon); American Wigeons; Canvasbacks; Redheads (uncommon); Ring-necked Ducks; Greater and Lesser Scaups; Buffleheads; Common Goldeneyes; and Ruddy Ducks. This is a good place to get close comparative looks at gulls, including Mew, California, Herring, Thayer's, Western, and Glaucous-winged. Forster's and Least Terns are possible in summer.

Barrow's Goldeneye and Hooded Merganser occur here also, but are rare. Even rarer have been Tufted Duck and Oldsquaw. Snowy and Great Egrets may be on the islands, as well as Double-crested Cormorants and Black-crowned Night-Herons. The plantings near the lake may have land birds such as Anna's and Allen's Hummingbirds (the latter, in summer), Nuttall's Woodpecker, Black Phoebe,

65 Lake Merritt

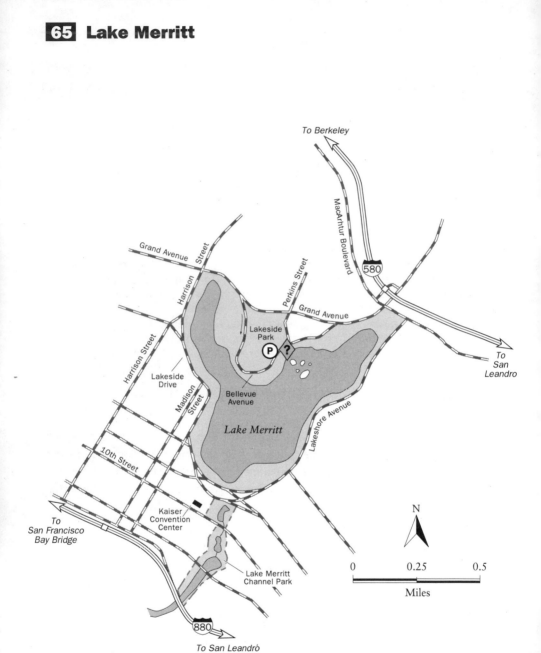

To Berkeley

MacArthur Boulevard

580

Grand Avenue

Harrison Street

Perkins Street

Grand Avenue

To San Leandro

Harrison Street

Lakeside Park

P ?

Lakeside Drive

Madison Street

Bellevue Avenue

Lake Merritt

Lakeshore Avenue

10th Street

To San Francisco Bay Bridge

Kaiser Convention Center

Lake Merritt Channel Park

N

0   0.25   0.5
Miles

880

To San Leandro

Chestnut-backed Chickadee, Oak Titmouse, and Bushtit.

To get to **Lake Merritt Channel Park,** leave Lakeside Park via Perkins Street, and turn left at Grand Avenue. Go 0.4 mile and turn left onto Harrison Street, then bear left on Lakeside Drive until you come to Madison Street; turn right, go 0.5 mile, and turn left on Tenth Street. After about 0.4 mile, start looking for a parking place along the curb, near the Henry J. Kaiser Convention Center. Parking often is difficult. The **Muckelroy Nature Trail** begins just beyond the bridge and leads downstream into Lake Merritt Channel Park.

The birds will be similar to those at Lake Merritt proper, although this often is a good place for Barrow's Goldeneye. A bridge over the estuary can allow good looks at the birds.

General information: Lake Merritt is a lake in a park in a big city; nevertheless, it gets large amounts of waterfowl, and sometimes gets rarities. The birds get so accustomed to people that you often can see them at close range. Lake Merritt was the nation's very first wildlife refuge, created in 1870.

ADDITIONAL HELP

NCA&G grid: Page104, 3B.
Elevation: Sea level.
Hazards: As in any big city park, it is probably not best to bird alone.
Nearest food, gas, lodging: Oakland.
For more information: City of Oakland, Rotary Nature Center.

66 Martin Luther King Jr. Regional Shoreline &

Habitats: Mudflats, coastal bays and lagoons, coastal scrub, cultivated plantings.
Specialty birds: *Resident*—Clapper Rail, Burrowing Owl. *Summer*—Least Tern. *Winter*—Western and Clark's Grebes; Eurasian Wigeon; Long-billed Curlew.
Other key birds: *Resident*—Ruddy Duck, Black-necked Stilt, American Avocet, Marsh Wren. *Winter*—Horned and Red-necked Grebes; American Wigeon; Blue-winged Teal; Greater and Lesser Scaups; Surf and White-winged Scoters; Bufflehead; Common Goldeneye; Greater Yellowlegs; Willet; Marbled Godwit. *Migrant*—Red Knot.
Best times to bird: November through June.

Directions: Directions to **Arrowhead Marsh** are given here; directions to other locations are given below. From Interstate 880 south of Oakland, exit west on Hegenberger Road. After about 1 mile, turn right onto Doolittle Drive (California Highway 61) and then right again on Swan Way, and almost immediately turn left onto a gravel entrance road. A parking lot is on the left, and about 0.5 mile farther, at the end of the road, is another parking lot with a barrier-free viewing platform (restrooms).

66 Martin Luther King Jr. Regional Shoreline

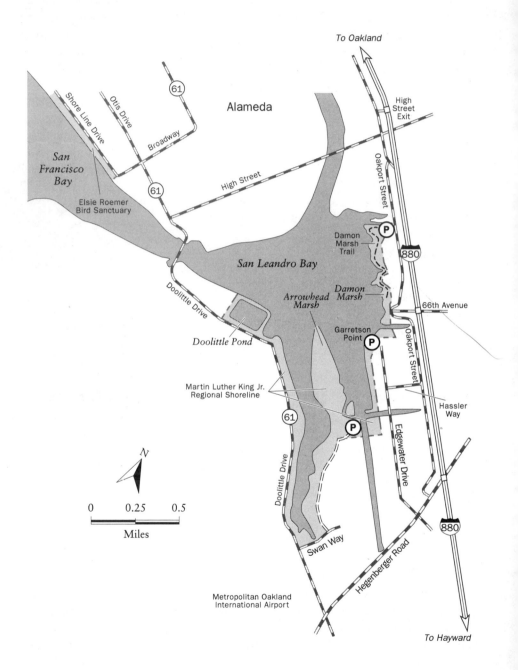

To Oakland

Alameda

High Street Exit

61

Shore Line Drive

Otis Drive

Broadway

Oakport Street

San Francisco Bay

High Street

61

880

Elsie Roemer Bird Sanctuary

Damon Marsh Trail

P

San Leandro Bay

Damon Marsh

Doolittle Drive

Arrowhead Marsh

66th Avenue

Doolittle Pond

Garretson Point

P

Oakport Street

Martin Luther King Jr. Regional Shoreline

Hassler Way

61

P

Edgewater Drive

N

0   0.25   0.5

Miles

Doolittle Drive

880

Swan Way

Hegenberger Road

Metropolitan Oakland International Airport

To Hayward

The birding: **Arrowhead Marsh:** In addition to a viewing platform there is a boardwalk extending partway into the marsh. Some of the ducks here (primarily in winter) are American Wigeon; Greater and Lesser Scaups; Surf and White-winged Scoters; Bufflehead; Common Goldeneye; and Ruddy Duck. Blue-winged Teal and Eurasian Wigeon are rare in winter. This is also a good place for Western, Clark's, Red-necked (rare), and Horned Grebes. Shorebirds may be in or next to the marsh, especially Black-necked Stilts, American Avocets, Greater Yellowlegs, Willets, Long-billed Curlews, and Marbled Godwits. At high tide, Clapper Rails may be visible. The fields nearby are full of ground squirrel burrows, so keep an eye open for Burrowing Owls.

In the large rectangular pond, known as **Doolittle Pond,** directly west of the tip of Arrowhead Marsh and adjacent to Doolittle Drive, I once saw 2,000 scaups crowded into the pond. To get there, go about 1 mile north on Doolittle Drive from Swan Way, and park on a wide dirt shoulder. Be careful: The traffic is heavy and fast.

Damon Marsh: From I-880 take the High Street exit. Turn south on Oakport Street, which closely parallels I-880. Go about 0.6 mile south on Oakport Street, being careful to avoid the on-ramp, which would take you back on the freeway, to a very small parking lot on the right. This lot comes up just after crossing a short bridge and just before you come to the big plant of the East Bay Municipal Utility District. From here there is a good paved trail along the slough, connecting to the **Damon Marsh Trail** (no restrooms).

Good views may be had from the Damon Marsh Trail into the bay, although in late afternoon you will be looking directly into the sun. The birds are similar to those at Arrowhead Marsh. The habitat next to the trail has shrubs and weeds. Look for California Towhee, House Finch, and Ruby-crowned Kinglet and various sparrows in winter.

Garretson Point: From the junction of Oakport Street and Sixty-sixth Avenue, go about 0.6 mile south on Oakport Street, turn right on Hassler Way, and then right again onto Edgewater Drive. It is about 0.3 mile north on Edgewater Drive to a parking lot on the left (restrooms). This may be the single most delightful spot along the shore, with a paved trail, picnic tables, and attractive views across the bay to Arrowhead Marsh. There may be many birds clustered on the bay at one time, including all of the species mentioned above. Morning light is best.

Elsie Roemer Bird Sanctuary: From I-880, take the High Street exit and go west on High Street about 1.3 miles to Otis Drive (which is also CA 61), and turn right (north). Go about 0.3 mile on Otis Drive to Broadway, turn left and then right when you come to the bayfront at Shore Line Drive; park along Shore Line Drive. Elsie Roemer Sanctuary is adjacent to the road (no restrooms), along the shoreline of San Francisco Bay, and is a part of Robert S. Crown Memorial State Beach. The birds at the sanctuary are much the same as those mentioned above. A short boardwalk extends partway into the marsh, giving good views. The marsh is fenced off, which discourages dogs and people from entering. Marsh Wrens and Song Sparrows are plentiful, and there may be Black-necked Stilts, American Avocets, Willets, Long-billed Curlews, and Marbled Godwits in the marsh. Red Knots are sometimes seen during migration, and Least Terns may show up in late summer.

General information: The sheltered waters of San Leandro Bay are appealing to thousands of ducks in winter, plus other birds such as grebes, shorebirds, and gulls. Most of the shoreline of the bay is contained within Martin Luther King Jr. Regional Shoreline.

ADDITIONAL HELP

NCA&G grid: Page 104, 4C.
Elevation: Sea level.
Hazards: Watch for automobile traffic, especially along Doolittle Drive.
Nearest food, gas, lodging: Oakland; San Leandro.
For more information: East Bay Regional Parks District.

Black-necked Stilt.

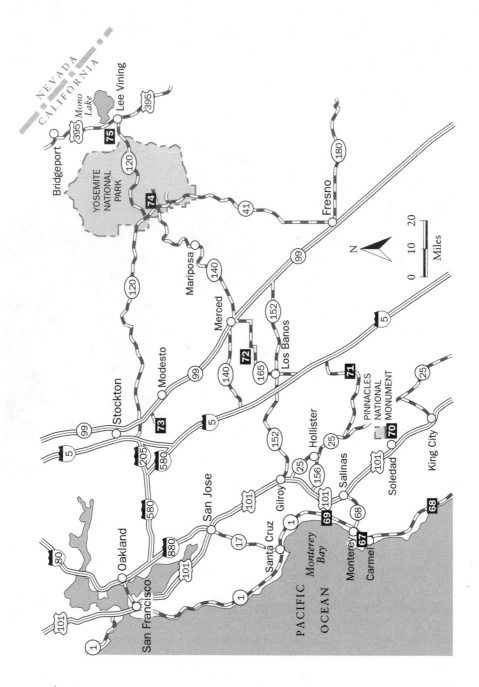

Monterey to Yosemite

The birding trail that connects these sites includes some of the most dramatic spots in America—Monterey, Big Sur, Yosemite, and Mono Lake. Every one of them is a Class-A destination, but other outstanding birding places, such as Elkhorn Slough, Pinnacles, and the San Luis Refuges, should not be overlooked.

In the view of many, Monterey is the number one birding location in the state, perhaps in the country. The beauty of its coastline is fabled, as are its marvelous pelagic boat trips. Its extensive pine forests have Pygmy Nuthatches and Townsend's Warblers, and the neighboring Elkhorn Slough region is noted for its shorebirds. Farther south, the magnificent Big Sur coast is a place where California Condors have been released back into the wild.

Pinnacles National Monument, in the remote South Coast Range, offers a chance to see the elusive Lawrence's Goldfinch. Even more remote is Panoche Valley, with Chukar, Greater Roadrunner, and Mountain Plover. Beyond, in the Central Valley, lies a great complex of refuges—a good place to see White-faced Ibis, Sandhill Crane, Yellow-billed Magpie, and Tricolored Blackbird.

In the minds of many birders, Yosemite is linked with the Great Gray Owl, although other highly sought birds, such as Black-backed Woodpecker, Williamson's Sapsucker, Pine Grosbeak, and Cassin's Finch are also found here.

Mono Lake is famous for its breeding California Gulls, but it also gets thousands of Phalaropes and Eared Grebes. Here is the place to find such species as Sage Thrasher, Gray Flycatcher, Sage Sparrow, Brewer's Sparrow, and Green-tailed Towhee. The nearby ghost town of Bodie attracts birders searching for Mountain Bluebird, and who then sometimes discover Sage Grouse right in the streets of town.

67 Monterey Peninsula 🚻 ♿

Habitats: Pelagic, sandy beach and mudflats, rocky headlands, coastal bays and lagoons, coastal scrub, closed-cone pine forest, freshwater marsh, riparian woodland.

Specialty birds: *Resident*—Brandt's and Pelagic Cormorants; Black Oystercatcher; Band-tailed Pigeon; Hutton's Vireo; Steller's Jay; Chestnut-backed Chickadee; Pygmy Nuthatch; Wrentit; Tricolored Blackbird. *Summer*—Black-footed Albatross, Brown Pelican, Heermann's Gull, Elegant Tern, Pigeon Guillemot, Allen's Hummingbird, Violet-green Swallow. *Winter*—Pacific Loon; Western and Clark's Grebes; Laysan Albatross; Short-tailed and Black-vented Shearwaters; Fork-tailed Storm-Petrel; Harlequin Duck; Wandering Tattler; Black Turnstone; Surfbird; Mew and Glaucous-winged Gulls; Ancient Murrelet; Rhinoceros Auklet; Townsend's Warbler. *Migrant or postbreeding visitor*—Pink-footed, Flesh-footed, and Buller's Shearwaters; Ashy, Black, and Least Storm-Petrels; Sabine's Gull; Xantus's and Craveri's Murrelets; Cassin's Auklet.

Other key birds: *Resident*—Black-crowned Night-Heron, Red-shouldered Hawk, Common Murre, Hairy Woodpecker, Brown Creeper, Common Yellowthroat, White-crowned Sparrow, Purple Finch, Pine Siskin. *Summer*—Sooty Shearwater, Leach's Storm-Petrel, Forster's Tern. *Winter*—Red-throated and Common Loons; Horned and Red-necked Grebes; Northern Fulmar; Surf and White-winged Scoters; Virginia Rail; Sora; Black-bellied Plover; Greater Yellowlegs; Willet; Whimbrel; Ruddy Turnstone; Sanderling; Bonaparte's Gull; Black-legged Kittiwake. *Migrant*—Red-necked and Red Phalaropes; South Polar Skua; Pomarine, Parasitic, and Long-tailed Jaegers; Common and Arctic Terns.

Best times to bird: August through November for most pelagic birds; October through April for most wintering water birds, shorebirds, warblers, and sparrows. Late summer for Brown Pelican, Heermann's Gull, and Elegant Tern.

Directions: For **pelagic trips:** If you are approaching Monterey from the north on California Highway 1, exit for Del Monte Avenue, go 1.8 miles to Washington Street, and turn right into the parking lot. Fisherman's Wharf is a short walk to the northwest. If you are taking a pelagic trip, be sure to get your parking ticket validated. Note that the parking lots here are rather confusing, so give yourself ample time if you haven't been here before. Above all, don't get Fisherman's Wharf confused with the Municipal Wharf. The Municipal Wharf is accessed by turning right off Del Monte Avenue at Figueroa Street, which is 1 block to the east of Washington Street.

The birding: Pelagic trips: The pelagic birding off the coast of Monterey may be the best on the North American continent. Sometimes there are tens of thousands of birds in view, often quite close to shore. One of the reasons for the abundance is because deep submarine canyons occur just offshore in this region.

About 50 pelagic trips per year are scheduled out of Monterey by Shearwater Journeys, most of them during the prime months of August, September, and October. Sooty Shearwater (May through October) is often abundant. Black-footed

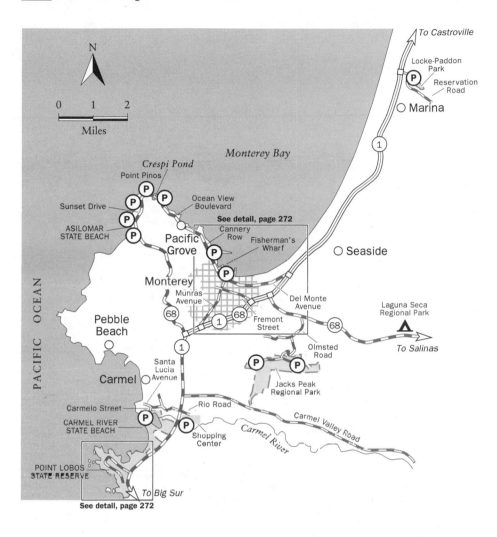

N

0   1   2
Miles

To Castroville

Locke-Paddon Park

Reservation Road

○ Marina

Monterey Bay

Crespi Pond

Point Pinos

Sunset Drive

Ocean View Boulevard

See detail, page 272

ASILOMAR STATE BEACH

Pacific Grove

Cannery Row

Fisherman's Wharf

○ Seaside

Monterey

Munras Avenue

Del Monte Avenue

Laguna Seca Regional Park

68

68

Fremont Street

68

To Salinas

Pebble Beach

Olmsted Road

Santa Lucia Avenue

Jacks Peak Regional Park

Carmel

Carmelo Street

Rio Road

Carmel Valley Road

CARMEL RIVER STATE BEACH

Shopping Center

Carmel River

POINT LOBOS STATE RESERVE

To Big Sur

See detail, page 272

PACIFIC OCEAN

Albatross is fairly common from May to August, Leach's Storm-Petrel is uncommon well offshore in the same period, and Laysan Albatross (uncommon) is most likely in winter but is sometimes seen in June and July. From August to October, the following are fairly common: Pink-footed Shearwater; Ashy and Black Storm-Petrels; Red-necked and Red Phalaropes; Pomarine and Parasitic Jaegers; Sabine's Gull; and Common and Arctic Terns. Uncommon from August to October are Buller's Shearwater and Xantus's and Craveri's Murrelets, and Flesh-footed Shearwater, Least Storm-Petrel, South Polar Skua, and Long-tailed Jaeger are rare. Cassin's and Rhinoceros Auklets are most common in winter, and Fork-tailed Storm-Petrel is rare. Northern Fulmar, Short-tailed and Black-vented Shearwaters, Black-legged Kittiwake, and Ancient Murrelet all are irregular winter visitors.

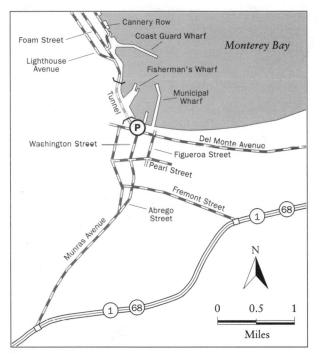

Central Monterey detail.

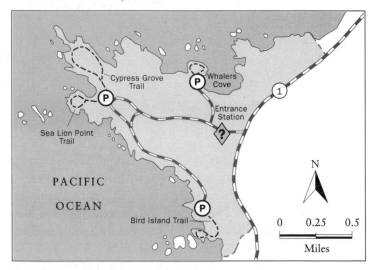

Point Lobos State Reserve detail.

For more information on pelagic trips, contact Shearwater Journeys (see Appendix A for the address), an organization that has been conducting pelagic trips for many years.

To get to the parking near the **Municipal Wharf,** exit from Del Monte Avenue at Figueroa Street, and turn toward the water. A large parking area extends from here toward Fisherman's Wharf, but metered parking is also available on Municipal Wharf itself, which is not the case at Fisherman's Wharf. (Restrooms are at the foot of Municipal Wharf, and at the outer end of Fisherman's Wharf.) The crowds of tourists at Fisherman's Wharf reduce the appeal of that location for birders, but Municipal Wharf can offer some good opportunities, similar to those at the Coast Guard Wharf (see next paragraph). In winter look for Pacific, Red-throated, and Common Loons; Horned, Red-necked (rare), Western, and Clark's (rare) Grebes; Surf and White-winged Scoters; Red-breasted Merganser; and from April through September, for Pigeon Guillemot. In winter Harlequin Duck and Marbled Murrelet (both rare at this location) have been seen.

The **Coast Guard Wharf** can be reached by walking on the paved bike path that runs along the waterfront. You can reach the wharf by car by turning west onto Del Monte Avenue and entering the tunnel that leads to Pacific Grove. Exit onto Foam Street as you leave the tunnel, turn right where it says "Cannery Row," and go to the large parking lot on the right with parking meters (restrooms). It is a walk of about 0.2 mile to the end of the wharf. The rock jetty at the end has sea lions and cormorants, and Brown Pelicans and Heermann's Gulls during summer.

Buller's Shearwater.

Ruddy and Black Turnstones may show up on the jetty in winter. From the wharf you can look directly out into Monterey Bay, where there may be Red-necked Grebes (rare, winter), Red-necked Phalaropes (fall), Pigeon Guillemots (summer), and Common Murres (resident). In winter look for Red-throated, Pacific, and Common Loons and Red Phalarope (rare). In late winter or early spring, following strong northwest winds that last for more than a day, look for Fork-tailed Storm-Petrels near the wharfs or in the harbor.

To reach **Point Pinos** and **Asilomar State Beach,** return to Foam Street, go 0.7 mile toward the west until it deadends at David Avenue, turn right one block, and then turn left onto what becomes Ocean View Boulevard. Continue on Ocean View Boulevard, making sure you don't miss the abrupt right turn that comes about 1 mile after David Avenue, and follow it along the shoreline to Point Pinos, which is about 3 miles from the Coast Guard Wharf parking lot. There are numerous dirt parking lots along the road that provide excellent views of the rocky coastline. This is a good place for Heermann's Gull in summer, and for Mew, Glaucous-winged, and California Gulls in winter. The area is especially good for shorebirds such as Black-bellied Plover, Black Oystercatcher, Willet, Whimbrel, Ruddy Turnstone, and Surfbird. During storms with strong winds, pelagic species are sometimes seen from the point.

Almost directly across the road from Point Pinos is **Crespi Pond,** which generally has American Coots and Mallards, but also is a well-known place for Virginia Rail and Sora in winter. Check for Black-crowned Night-Herons (common in winter) lurking in the cattails, and for Tropical Kingbird (rare, September through October) perched on the wires. The cypress trees near the pond may have migrant warblers in fall; however, because the pond and adjacent area are part of the golf course, you must be careful not to create problems for the golfers (golfers have the right of way).

After you round the bend at Point Pinos and head south, the road becomes Sunset Drive. About 0.5 mile after leaving the point, you will come to **Asilomar State Beach,** which has a trail running along the coastline for the next mile or so, with several short barrier-free boardwalks leading to the edge of the rocky shoreline. This is a good place for Black Oystercatcher (resident), and winter visitors such as Willet, Wandering Tattler, and Surfbird. I once saw about 500 Willets roosting here in a tightly packed flock.

For **Jacks Peak Regional Park,** from the junction of CA 1 and California Highway 68, go 1.5 miles east on CA 68 to Olmsted Road, turn right, go 0.9 mile, and turn left on the road to Jacks Peak Park. It is 1.3 miles to the entrance gate (fee). Turn left to go 0.4 mile to East Picnic Area, or turn right to go 0.7 mile to Jacks Peak parking lot. The park has many hiking trails, but a particularly attractive one is the **Skyline Nature Trail,** which starts at the Jacks Peak parking lot and leads along the side of Jacks Peak. You can return over the top of Jacks Pack for a total hike of about 0.7 mile, without much climbing. The forest is almost entirely made up of Monterey pines, with some coast live oak and much poison oak. Some resident birds are Band-tailed Pigeon (irregular), Steller's Jay, Pygmy Nuthatch, Brown Creeper, Spotted Towhee, and Purple Finch. In winter look for Townsend's Warbler.

To get to the **Carmel River,** go south from Monterey about 4.5 miles on CA 1, past Carmel Valley Road, to Rio Road. Turn left, and then turn right almost immediately, into the large parking lot belonging to the shopping center. Go all the way to the end of the parking lot and park close to where the bridge on CA 1 crosses the Carmel River. Walk up over the embankment and down into the sandy riverbed, which is usually dry in summer and fall. (Note: This area is somewhat isolated, so it is probably best to bird with a companion.) Turn to the right, under the bridge, and walk down the riverbed. Both banks are heavily foliaged. Look for resident Downy Woodpecker, Black Phoebe, Hutton's Vireo, Chestnut-backed Chickadee, Bushtit, Bewick's Wren, Wrentit, and Song Sparrow. In summer are Warbling Vireo and Yellow and Wilson's Warblers. Fall vagrants have been found here, including Red-eyed Vireo; Lucy's, Magnolia, Prairie, Blackpoll, and Black-and-white Warblers; and Northern Waterthrush. About 0.5 mile downstream is the famous **"Green Pipe."** This pipe once carried sewage across the river to the nearby treatment plant, but is slated to be replaced by a pedestrian bridge. If the water is backed up from the lagoon downstream, this may be as far as you can go. You might even be stopped sooner.

To get to the lagoon, which lies at the mouth of the Carmel River, go to **Carmel River State Beach.** From the junction of CA 1 and Rio Road, drive 0.4 mile west on Rio Road to Santa Lucia Avenue, which is served by a special left-hand turn lane. Turn left on Santa Lucia Avenue, go 0.4 mile to Carmelo Street, and turn left again. Carmelo Street leads (0.4 mile) directly into the paved parking lot for Carmel River State Beach. The **Carmel River Lagoon and Wetlands Natural Reserve** is to your left. The marsh around the lagoon can hold egrets, Great Blue Heron, Virginia Rail, Sora, and Common Yellowthroat. Other birds are Brown Pelican; Greater Yellowlegs; Bonaparte's, Heermann's, Ring-billed, California, and Western Gulls; and Elegant and Forster's Terns. On the beach side, look for Sanderlings. If you walk past the mouth of the lagoon down the beach, you can climb up on the low hill that has the cross and look directly down into the lagoon. The hill is part of the park and has a trail leading up it.

South of the junction of CA 1 and Rio Road 2.2 miles, is **Point Lobos State Reserve** (fee, open 9 A.M. to 5:30 P.M., no trailers, small motor homes okay except on weekends). Point Lobos is almost certain to be crowded on weekends, so it is best to go during the week if you can. The main attraction is the **Cypress Grove Trail,** which gives many looks at gorgeous seascapes. Along the trail leading to the grove are heavy masses of bushes (and lots of poison oak), containing Anna's and Allen's Hummingbirds (the latter in spring and early summer); Western Scrub-Jay; Chestnut-backed Chickadee; Bewick's Wren; Ruby-crowned Kinglet (winter); Spotted and California Towhees; Song, White-crowned, and Golden-crowned (winter) Sparrows; and Dark-eyed Junco. Note that in most places in California,

White-crowned Sparrow is a winter visitor, but in a narrow strip along the coast it is a year-round resident. In the cypress trees, look for Townsend's Warbler in winter. Watch for Violet-green Swallow in summer.

Take the **Sea Lion Point Trail** for close views of the rocky shoreline. White-crowned Sparrows are much in evidence, and the songs of Wrentits are common. Sea otters are often seen in the coves.

It is worthwhile to hike the **Bird Island Trail,** which provides additional spectacular views. There generally are fewer people here than on some of the other trails. The trail runs next to a grove of Monterey pines, along the edge of the cliffs. Birds that should be here are Red-shouldered Hawk, Hairy Woodpecker, Steller's Jay, Pygmy Nuthatch, and Pine Siskin. The trail takes you to a promontory, where you can look directly down on the ocean. Brandt's Cormorants nest on Bird Island. You might spot some Snowy or Great Egrets below, riding on floating masses of seaweed, waiting for something edible to turn up.

The pond at **Locke-Paddon Park** is worth a visit. It is in Marina, about 8 miles north of Monterey on CA 1. Take the exit for Reservation Road, and turn east. At the first stop, 0.2 mile from the exit, Reservation Road turns sharply to the right, and 0.2 mile after that you will come to the park. Turn left into the parking lot (restrooms). Trails are next to the pond, and a boardwalk crosses it about halfway down. The birds are mostly Pied-billed Grebes, American Coots, and Mallards, but there are patches of willows that can hold warblers and sparrows. Tricolored Blackbirds have nested in the cattails here, but Tricoloreds often shift their nesting sites.

General information: In a state that abounds with superb scenic attractions, the Monterey Peninsula stands at the head of the list, along with Yosemite, Lake Tahoe, and Mount Shasta. The beauty of Point Lobos has been called "the greatest meeting of land and water in the world," by landscape artist Francis McComas. Because of its attractiveness, the area often abounds with tourists, and if there is a festival or golf tournament under way it may be impossible to get a motel reservation or campsite. It is wise to check ahead and to make reservations as far in advance as possible.

ADDITIONAL HELP

Map grid: DeLorme Southern/Central California Atlas, page 18, 3D.
Elevation: Sea level to 500 feet.
Hazards: Abrupt cliff edges, rattlesnakes, poison oak, ticks.
Nearest food, gas, lodging: Monterey; Carmel; Pacific Grove; Seaside.
Camping: Laguna Seca Regional Park: 183 sites, about 7 miles east of Monterey, on CA 68; RV disposal station. Reservations are recommended because the campground is immediately adjacent to the Laguna Seca Raceway, and the park is jammed on race days. (See Appendix F.)
For more information: Point Lobos State Reserve; Shearwater Journeys.

68 Big Sur 🍴 ♿

Habitats: Rocky headlands, coastal scrub, redwood forest, stream, riparian woodland, foothill woodland, chaparral.
Specialty birds: *Resident*—Peregrine Falcon, Band-tailed Pigeon, Northern Pygmy-Owl, Spotted Owl, White-throated Swift, Nuttall's Woodpecker, Hutton's Vireo, Steller's Jay, Chestnut-backed Chickadee, American Dipper, Wrentit, California Thrasher. *Summer*—Black and Vaux's Swifts; Allen's Hummingbird; Pacific-slope and Ash-throated Flycatchers; Cassin's Vireo; Violet-green Swallow; Black-throated Gray Warbler; Black-chinned Sparrow; Black-headed Grosbeak. *Winter*—Townsend's Warbler; Golden-crowned Sparrow.
Other key birds: *Resident*—Red-shouldered Hawk, Northern Saw-whet Owl, Hairy Woodpecker, Winter Wren, Hermit Thrush, Purple Finch. *Summer*—Warbling Vireo; Purple Martin; Swainson's Thrush; Orange-crowned and Wilson's Warblers. *Migrant*—Yellow-breasted Chat.
Best times to bird: All year. Andrew Molera State Park is an outstanding area for vagrants in spring and fall.

Directions: The area known as the Big Sur Coast begins just south of Carmel and extends to San Simeon, a distance of more than 80 miles. In a narrower sense, Big Sur begins at **Andrew Molera State Park** and extends more or less to Julia Pfeiffer Burns State Park. Andrew Molera State Park is about 22 miles south of Carmel on California Highway 1 (allow 45 minutes), **Pfeiffer Big Sur State Park** is 4.3 miles south of Andrew Molera State Park, and **Julia Pfeiffer Burns State Park** is 10.7 miles south of Pfeiffer Big Sur State Park. The Big Sur post office is 1.5 miles south of Pfeiffer Big Sur State Park.

The birding: Andrew Molera State Park (no trailers, fee, parking, restrooms) is generally regarded as one of the best birding sites in Monterey County. The **Big Sur Ornithology Lab** (open to the public, with drop-in hours from 8 A.M. to noon daily) is located here. Among the vagrants the lab has banded are Yellow-green Vireo; Gray Catbird; Prothonotary, Mourning, and Worm-eating Warblers; Northern Waterthrush; and Rose-breasted Grosbeak.

Take the trail that leads to the trail camp, along the north side of the river. If you go all the way to the end of the trail at Point Molera, it will be a round trip of about 2.5 miles. This takes you to the mouth of the Big Sur River. In fact, the terms "Big Sur River mouth" and "Andrew Molera State Park" are interchangeable terms with many birders. The trail leads through sycamores, coast live oaks, bay laurels, alders, and willows. Chestnut-backed Chickadees and Bushtits are common, and warblers often move with the chickadee flocks. Orange-crowned and Wilson's Warblers are summer visitors, and Townsend's Warbler visits in winter. Some resident species are Red-shouldered Hawk; Anna's Hummingbird; Acorn, Nuttall's, and Downy Woodpeckers; Hutton's Vireo; Steller's Jay; Bewick's Wren; Wrentit; Spotted and California Towhees; Song and White-crowned Sparrows; and Purple Finch.

68 Big Sur

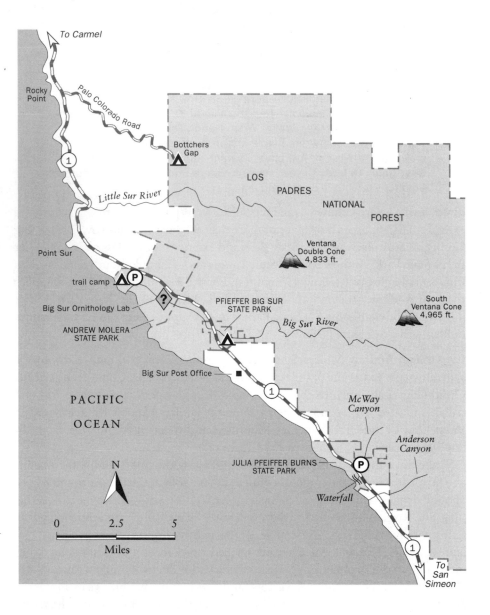

To Carmel

Rocky
Point

Palo Colorado Road

1

Bottchers
Gap

Little Sur River

LOS

PADRES

NATIONAL

FOREST

Point Sur

Ventana
Double Cone
4,833 ft.

trail camp · P

Big Sur Ornithology Lab

?

PFEIFFER BIG SUR
STATE PARK

South
Ventana Cone
4,965 ft.

ANDREW MOLERA
STATE PARK

Big Sur River

Big Sur Post Office ·

1

McWay
Canyon

Anderson
Canyon

PACIFIC

OCEAN

JULIA PFEIFFER BURNS
STATE PARK

P

N

Waterfall

0   2.5   5

Miles

1

To
San
Simeon

Regular summer visitors are Allen's Hummingbird (February through June), Pacific-slope Flycatcher, Purple Martin (uncommon; look for them near the Big Sur Ornithology Lab), Violet-green Swallow, House Wren, and Black-headed Grosbeak. Ruby-crowned Kinglet and Golden-crowned Sparrow are common winter residents. Be alert for Vaux's Swift, which is an uncommon summer visitor. Yellow-breasted Chat is a rare spring migrant.

Pfeiffer Big Sur State Park is heavily used, but it is a lovely place with wonderful redwood groves along the Big Sur River. After the summer season it quiets down, except on weekends. Some woodland birds to expect are Hairy Woodpecker, Steller's Jay, Brown Creeper, and Winter Wren, all of which are common residents. Swainson's Thrush is a summer visitor, and Hermit Thrush is common in winter and uncommon in summer. American Dipper is a rare resident, but you might see one if you are willing to spend enough time along the river.

Julia Pfeiffer Burns State Park (fee, parking, restrooms) is often overlooked, but it contains a wonderful surprise—a small waterfall that plunges onto the beach, or directly into the ocean if the tide is up. A paved barrier-free trail (about 0.5 mile round trip) goes from the parking lot down McWay Canyon to an overlook above the cove containing the waterfall (no beach access). There is a lot of good habitat en route (and lots of poison oak), with resident birds such as Steller's Jay, Bushtit, Wrentit, Bewick's Wren, and Song Sparrow. Townsend's Warbler is common in winter.

The waterfall at Julia Pfeiffer Burns State Park.

Black Swifts (rare summer visitors) have nested on the cliffs near the waterfall, although they are not present every year. **Anderson Canyon,** 0.4 mile to the south on CA 1 has also had Black Swifts. Yet another place is **Rocky Point,** about 8.7 miles south of Point Lobos. At any of the viewpoints along the highway, watch for Peregrine Falcon (rare); a few pairs have nested on the sea cliffs in this region. Also, be alert for White-throated Swift (uncommon).

Palo Colorado Road, 8.7 miles south of Point Lobos, takes you into country that is quite different from most of Big Sur. The road is narrow and twisty, but is paved all the way to the top at **Bottchers Gap,** 7.5 miles from the beginning, where there is a small USDA Forest Service campground. The road mostly leads through redwood groves, but climbs into foothill woodland and chaparral toward the end. There is a terrific view from an overlook just a few feet from the campground, but be careful, because there is an abrupt cliff here with no guardrail. From here you can look into the rugged heart of the Ventana Wilderness. A dirt road, blocked by a gate, continues over the top and down to the Pico Blanco Boy Scout Camp.

Some of the residents include Wrentit and California Thrasher, and summer visitors such as Ash-throated Flycatcher, Cassin's and Warbling Vireos, and Black-throated Gray Warbler. This is a good place to look for Band-tailed Pigeon (irregular). Black-chinned Sparrow (rare summer visitor) has been found on the dry rocky chaparral slopes above the campground. Northern Pygmy-Owl and Northern Saw-whet Owls are uncommon residents. The dirt road to the Pico Blanco Boy Scout Camp leads down into redwoods, and both Spotted Owl and Northern Saw-whet Owl have been reported about a mile or two down the dirt road, where the redwoods begin. Also, people have reported seeing "small" owls at dusk on the gate blocking the road leading to the Scout camp.

California Condors are occasionally seen along the Big Sur coast. These are released captive birds, part of the California Condor Recovery Program. As of late 1998, there were five free-flying immature condors in the region, with several more scheduled for release in 1999. There also are released condors in Southern California and Arizona. It is hoped by the program's sponsors that these birds will eventually establish self-perpetuating wild populations. Condors don't reach breeding age until they are five to seven years old.

General information: The Big Sur Coast virtually stands on end, and the highway is precariously hacked into the cliffs. The road is narrow and winding in places, permitting an average speed of only 25 miles per hour or so. However, it is one of the outstanding scenic locations in the United States, and there are many viewpoints where you can stop. California gray whales can often be seen heading south in December and January, and back north in March and April.

Andrew Molera State Park has been classified as a Globally Important Bird Area because of its numbers of seabirds, and also because released California Condors sometimes forage over the area.

ADDITIONAL HELP

Map grid: DeLorme Southern/Central California Atlas, page 30, 3A; page 31, 5C.
Elevation: Sea level to 2,100 feet.
Hazards: Abrupt cliff dropoffs, poison oak, rattlesnakes, ticks. Signs are posted concerning dangerous "sleeper waves" that may appear without warning.
Nearest food, gas, lodging: Big Sur.
Camping: Pfeiffer Big Sur State Park: 218 sites, 26 miles south of Carmel on CA 1; RV dump station. Big Sur Lodge (see Appendix A) is located inside the state park. Andrew Molera State Park: walk-in campsites 0.3 mile from the parking lot; 22 miles south of Carmel on CA 1. Bottchers Gap (USDA Forest Service): 8 sites, 3 of which are accessible by auto; the rest are walk-in sites; not suitable for RVs; about 11 miles south of Carmel on CA 1 to Palo Colorado Road, and then 7.5 miles east on Palo Colorado Road (narrow, winding).
For more information: Pfeiffer Big Sur State Park.

69 Elkhorn Slough and Moss Landing 🚹 ♿

Habitats: Sandy beach and mudflats, coastal bays and lagoons, coastal scrub, salt marsh.
Specialty birds: *Resident*—White-tailed Kite, Peregrine Falcon, Snowy Plover, Tricolored Blackbird. *Summer*—Brown Pelican, Cinnamon Teal, Heermann's Gull, Elegant Tern, Allen's Hummingbird. *Winter*—Western and Clark's Grebes; Eurasian Wigeon; Long-billed Curlew; Thayer's and Glaucous-winged Gulls; Say's Phoebe.
Other key birds: *Resident*—Black-necked Stilt, American Avocet, Common Yellowthroat, Purple Finch. *Summer*—Caspian and Forster's Terns; Orange-crowned Warbler. *Winter*—Green-winged Teal; Greater and Lesser Scaups; Black-bellied Plover; Greater Yellowlegs; Willet; Marbled Godwit; Ruddy Turnstone; Sanderling; Long-billed Dowitcher; Bonaparte's Gull; Lincoln's Sparrow. *Migrant*—Blue-winged Teal, Semipalmated Plover, Lesser Yellowlegs, Whimbrel, Short-billed Dowitcher.
Best times to bird: August through April for most shorebirds; October through March for most waterfowl.

Directions: For **Elkhorn Slough National Estuarine Research Reserve,** from California Highway 1, turn east on Dolan Road in Moss Landing, at the southern edge of the huge power plant. Go 3.6 miles east on Dolan Road and turn left at Elkhorn Road (Dolan Road merges with Castroville Boulevard). Go 2 miles north on Elkhorn Road to the reserve entrance on the left (open 9 A.M. to 5 P.M., except Mondays and Tuesdays; fee, visitor center, restrooms).

For **Kirby Park,** go 2.5 miles north of the visitor center (see above) on Elkhorn Road. Turn left at Kirby Road and go 0.2 mile to the paved parking lot next to the slough (chemical toilet).

For **Moss Landing Wildlife Area** (entrance 1), go about 0.5 mile north from junction of CA 1 and Dolan Road to the inconspicuous entrance on the east side

69 Elkhorn Slough and Moss Landing

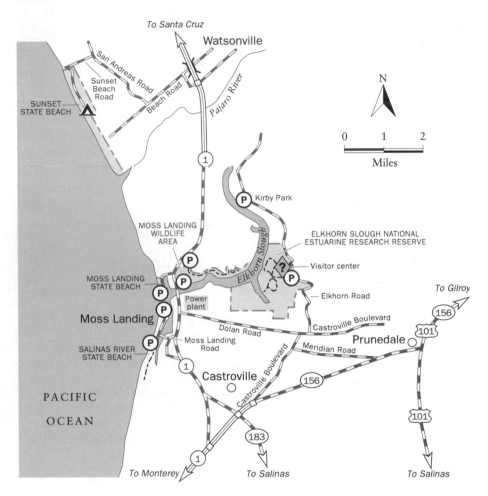

of the road, which appears just after you cross the bridge. Turn in on the gravel road and follow signs around the buildings 0.1 mile to the gravel parking lot (no restrooms). For entrance 2, go 1.4 mile farther north on CA 1, turn right on an obscure gravel road at the edge of a farm field, and go 0.1 mile to the parking lot (no restrooms).

For **Moss Landing State Beach,** go about 0.7 mile north from the junction of CA 1 and Dolan Road to the entrance on the west side of the road (fee, parking, chemical toilets).

To get to the small town of **Moss Landing,** go 0.3 mile south from CA 1 and Dolan Road on CA 1 to Moss Landing Road and turn right. Turn right after 0.1 mile on Sandholdt Road and go across a one-lane bridge. On the other side of the bridge, it is 0.1 mile on the left to a parking area belonging to Salinas River State

Beach (restrooms). To the right, it is 0.4 mile to the end of the road near the jetty and harbor channel, with parking for about four cars.

The birding: Several trails originate from the visitor center at **Elkhorn Slough National Estuarine Research Reserve.** The South Marsh Loop Trail (2.2 miles round trip) takes you first to an overlook (the trail to the overlook, about 0.2 mile long, is paved and is barrier free) and then down to the marshes. To the north of the trail is a group of trees used as a rookery by Great Egrets and Great Blue Herons. Look for wintering waterfowl such as Gadwall, Northern Shoveler, Northern Pintail, Green-winged Teal, and Greater and lesser Scaups, plus others. Cinnamon Teal is a summer resident, and Blue-winged Teal is an uncommon migrant, especially in March and April. Eurasian Wigeon in rare in winter.

Black-necked Stilt and American Avocet are residents, and Black-bellied Plover; Greater Yellowlegs; Willet; Long-billed Curlew; Marbled Godwit; Ruddy Turnstone; Western and Least Sandpipers; Dunlin; and Long-billed Dowitcher are winter visitors. Look for Semipalmated Plover, Lesser Yellowlegs (uncommon), Whimbrel, and Short-billed Dowitcher in fall migration. Black Phoebe, Marsh Wren, Common Yellowthroat, and Song Sparrow should be in or near the marshes. Tricolored Blackbird is resident, but becomes more common in fall and winter. Lincoln's Sparrow is uncommon in winter.

Western Grebe and Clark's Grebe (rare) are winter visitors. So are Bonaparte's, California, Herring, Thayer's (rare), and Glaucous-winged Gulls. Heermann's Gull is common in summer and fall, and Caspian, Elegant, and Forster's Terns are fairly common then. Western Gull is the most common gull and is resident year-round.

The reserve has much varied habitat, including coastal scrub and woodlands, so don't overlook resident land birds such as White-tailed Kite; Anna's Hummingbird; Bushtit; Wrentit; Spotted and California Towhees; White-crowned Sparrow; Western Meadowlark; and Purple Finch. Orange-crowned and Wilson's Warblers are summer visitors, whereas Say's Phoebe (uncommon), Yellow-rumped Warbler, and Golden-crowned Sparrow are winter visitors.

Watch for Peregrine Falcon (rare) throughout the area, especially when shorebirds are present.

Kirby Park is next to the slough, providing access to the **Upper Slough Trail** (about 0.5 mile one way), a barrier-free trail that runs along the slough and terminates in a boardwalk. The birds here are similar to those previously mentioned. A somewhat surprising sight here can be of a sea otter floating on its back in the middle of the estuary.

A short trail leaves the parking area at **Moss Landing Wildlife Area** entrance 1, and goes about 0.2 mile to a viewing platform. Shorebirds should be in the muddy branch sloughs, and gulls and terns work the general area. The large ponds, dry much of the year, are nesting areas for Snowy Plover. A short distance up the slough is a major roosting area for Brown Pelicans. From entrance 2, a rather poorly maintained trail leads to the slough, past salt- and freshwater ponds, mudflats, and marsh. Depending upon water conditions, the resident birds that might be here are Great Blue Heron, Black-necked Stilt, American Avocet, and Cinnamon Teal. Typical winter visitors are Great and Snowy Egrets, Greater Yellowlegs, Willet, and Marbled Godwit. Forster's Tern is a summer visitor.

Moss Landing State Beach (fee, chemical toilets) is a favorite for California birders, partly because of the rarities that show up here, such as Harlequin Duck, Oldsquaw, and King Eider. But there are also lots of other good birds, and this is one of the better places in the state to watch shorebirds at fairly close range. Some of the shorebirds will be on the flats inside the harbor, whereas others such as Sanderling and Snowy Plover are more likely to be on the beach side. In 1992, both Mongolian Plover and Wilson's Plover were on the beach here simultaneously.

In **Moss Landing,** a good trail leads south from the parking area (see directions above) belonging to Salinas River State Beach, between the dunes and the slough to the east. However, the trail soon becomes distant from the slough. The birds are similar to those mentioned above for other areas. A boardwalk leads over the dunes to the beach. At the small parking lot at the end of the road near the jetty and harbor channel (see above), it is only a few yards to the base of the jetty, with a view directly into the channel.

General information: Elkhorn Slough is a relatively undisturbed coastal wetland. It winds 7 miles into the interior and includes 2,500 acres of marsh and tidal flats. The centerpiece of the area, the National Estuarine Research Reserve, is managed by the California Department of Fish and Game and the National Oceanic and Atmospheric Administration.

ADDITIONAL HELP

Map grid: DeLorme Southern/Central California Atlas, page 19, 4B.
Elevation: Sea level.
Hazards: Poison oak, ticks.
Nearest food, gas, lodging: Watsonville.
Camping: Sunset State Beach: 90 sites; from CA 1 near Watsonville, exit for Beach Road, go west on Beach Road 1.5 miles to San Andreas Road, and go north 2 miles to Sunset Beach Road.
For more information: Elkhorn Slough National Estuarine Research Reserve.

70 Pinnacles National Monument

Habitats: Riparian woodland, foothill woodland, oak savanna, chaparral, cliffs.

Specialty birds: *Resident*—Golden Eagle; Prairie Falcon; California Quail; Greater Roadrunner; Northern Pygmy-Owl; White-throated Swift; Acorn and Nuttall's Woodpeckers; Say's Phoebe; Hutton's Vireo; Steller's Jay; Yellow-billed Magpie; Oak Titmouse; Bushtit; Rock and Canyon Wrens; Western Bluebird; Wrentit; California Thrasher; Phainopepla; California Towhee; Rufous-crowned and Sage Sparrows; Western Meadowlark; Lesser Goldfinch. *Summer*—Western Wood-Pewee; Pacific-slope and Ash-throated Flycatchers; Black-headed Grosbeak; Lazuli Bunting; Lawrence's Goldfinch. *Winter*—Golden-crowned Sparrow.

Other key birds: *Resident*—Wild Turkey; Great Horned and Long-eared Owls; Common Raven; White-breasted Nuthatch; Bewick's Wren. *Summer*—Warbling Vireo, Blue-gray Gnatcatcher, Orange-crowned Warbler, Yellow-breasted Chat. *Winter*—Fox Sparrow.

Best times to bird: Spring, fall, and winter.

Directions: To arrive at the west side: from the center of Soledad, follow California Highway 146 east for 12.2 miles to the Chaparral Ranger Station (fee, parking). To get to the east side: from the junction of California Highway 25 and Fourth Street in the center of Hollister, follow CA 25 south for 29 miles to CA 146, then take CA 146 west for 3.2 miles to the entrance station (fee). The visitor center is 1.7 miles farther.

Note: The two sections of CA 146, one from the west and the other from the east, do not meet. To get from one side of the monument to the other by car requires a trip of approximately 60 miles, via King City. To hike from one side to the other is only 3.3 miles.

The birding: The west side is less visited than the east, but it has the best views of the high peaks. The Balconies Trail is recommended because of its varied habitats and scenery (2.4 miles round trip if you combine the Balconies Cliffs Trail with a trip through the caves). If you go through the Balconies Caves, you'll need a flashlight, but the caves can be bypassed by using the Balconies Cliffs Trail. Several pairs of Prairie Falcons nest regularly at the monument, especially in the Balconies Cliffs area. They are most active in the late afternoon. White-throated Swifts are also near the cliffs, common in summer and uncommon in winter.

Look for California Quail; Anna's Hummingbird; Western Scrub-Jay; Oak Titmouse; Bushtit; White-breasted Nuthatch; Spotted and California Towhees; Lesser Goldfinch; and in winter, Golden-crowned Sparrow.

In the open country on the road leading to the west side, look for Greater Roadrunner, Say's Phoebe, Western Bluebird, Phainopepla, and Western Meadowlark. In the chaparral are resident Wrentit and Sage Sparrow, and Blue-Gray Gnatcatcher in summer. Wherever there are oaks and nearby water, look for Lawrence's Goldfinch (summer). In this foothill country, check the skies regularly

70 **Pinnacles National Monument**

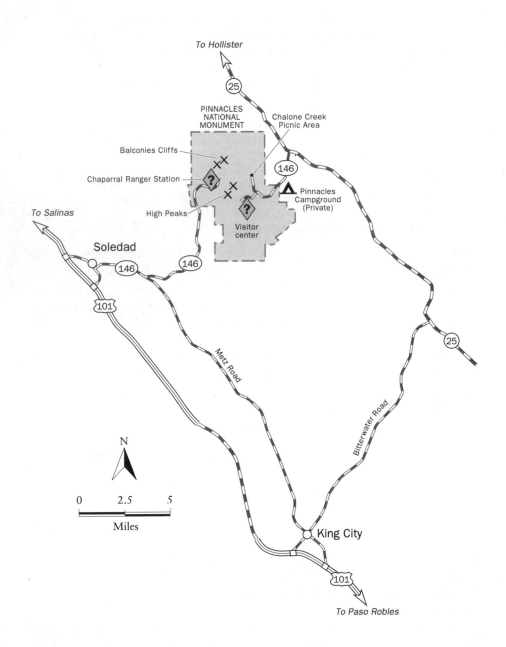

for Golden Eagle (uncommon), Red-tailed Hawk, Prairie Falcon, and Common Raven.

The east side is also dramatic but does not have quite the views as does the west side. The most popular trail is the **Moses Spring Trail** to Bear Gulch Caves (round trip of about 2 miles; flashlight required in the caves). Acorn and Nuttall's Woodpeckers; Hutton's Vireo; Steller's Jay; Western Scrub-Jay; California Thrasher; and Dark-eyed Junco all are resident. Other residents to look for are Rock Wren, Canyon Wren (uncommon), and Rufous-crowned Sparrow, all of which favor dry rocky slopes. Ruby-crowned Kinglet, Yellow-rumped Warbler, and Fox Sparrow are winter visitors. Summer visitors are Western Wood-Pewee; Pacific-slope and Ash-throated Flycatchers; Warbling Vireo; Orange-crowned Warbler; Black-headed Grosbeak; and Lazuli Bunting.

If you don't want to go through the caves, the Moses Spring Trail bypasses them and leads you along a spectacular path among the gigantic fallen rocks that form the roof of the caves. The cave route and the bypass lead to the same place—Bear Gulch Reservoir, constructed in the 1930s by the Civilian Conservation Corps. Black Phoebes and Canyon Wrens favor this location, and Wrentits abound in the surrounding chaparral. Lawrence's Goldfinches (summer) have been seen near the reservoir. An attractive alternate route for the return is the Rim Trail, which rejoins the Moses Spring Trail near the parking area.

About 1.4 miles back down the road from the visitor center is a T junction. The road to the right leads back to the entrance, and the one to the left goes to the

Wrentit.

Chalone Creek Picnic Area. A trail leads along the creek through a riparian area that has most of the birds mentioned above. Yellow-breasted Chat and Lawrence's Goldfinch have been seen here. In the more open country along the park access road, look for Yellow-billed Magpie and Greater Roadrunner. Keep your eyes open for Wild Turkeys, and don't be surprised if you see a bobcat or a coyote. Lewis's Woodpeckers have been seen along CA 25, north of the road leading into the park.

Great Horned Owls occur in the canyon near the visitor center, and Long-eared Owls have nested irregularly near the Chalone Creek Picnic Area. Northern Pygmy-Owl is a rare resident in riparian areas.

General Information: Pinnacles National Monument is a unit of the National Park system. It is often referred to as the "unknown" park, because it is in a little-visited part of California—unknown that is, except for rock climbers and wildflower enthusiasts who jam the park on weekends and holidays, especially in spring. The best-known features of the park are its two cave systems, formed when massive boulders fell off the surrounding cliffs and jammed the narrow gorges below, creating intricate passageways. If there is much water in the streams, the caves are impassable.

ADDITIONAL HELP

Map grid: DeLorme Southern/Central California Atlas, page 32, 2A.
Elevation: 1,000 to 1,700 feet.
Hazards: Rattlesnakes, poison oak, ticks; many of the trails are on the edges of abrupt cliffs and require sure footing.
Nearest food, gas, lodging: Hollister (east side); Soledad (west side).
Camping: There is no camping within the monument. The only nearby camping is at a privately owned campground: Pinnacles Campground, which has 78 sites, plus 36 electric hook-up sites on the east side just outside the park (on CA 146), and an RV dump station.
For more information: Pinnacles National Monument.

71 Panoche Valley

Habitats: Valley grassland, foothill woodland, oak savanna, chaparral.
Specialty birds: *Resident*—Golden Eagle; Prairie Falcon; Chukar; Greater Roadrunner; Lewis's and Acorn Woodpeckers; Say's Phoebe; Yellow-billed Magpie; Oak Titmouse; Rock Wren; Western Bluebird; Phainopepla; Rufous-crowned Sparrow; Western Meadowlark. *Winter*—Ferruginous Hawk, Mountain Plover, Mountain Bluebird.
Other key birds: *Resident*—Red-tailed Hawk, American Kestrel, Common Raven, Horned Lark, Lark Sparrow. *Winter*—Loggerhead Shrike; Savannah and Vesper Sparrows .
Best times to bird: November through March.

71 Panoche Valley

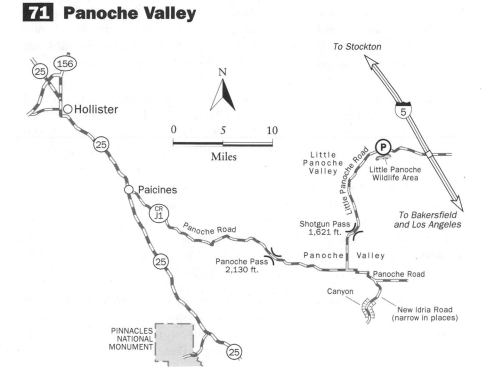

Directions: From the junction of California Highway 25 and Fourth Street in the center of Hollister, go 11.8 miles south on CA 25 to Paicines (no services) and turn east on Panoche Road (County Road J1). Go east on Panoche Road 27.5 miles to the T junction of Panoche Road and Little Panoche Road in the center of Panoche Valley. If coming from Interstate 5, turn west at the interchange with Little Panoche Road, and go 20.3 miles west, then south on Little Panoche Road to the T junction with Panoche Road. Be sure to have a full gas tank.

The birding: The route from Paicines to Panoche Valley is primarily through foothill woodland and oak savanna, with resident birds such as Golden Eagle; California Quail; Greater Roadrunner; Lewis's and Acorn Woodpeckers; Western Scrub-Jay; Yellow-billed Magpie; Oak Titmouse; Western Bluebird; Phainopepla; California Towhee; and Rufous-crowned Sparrow. In the valley itself, in winter large flocks of birds such as Horned Lark; Savannah, Lark, and White-crowned Sparrows; Western Meadowlark; Brewer's Blackbird; and House Finch are common. Vesper Sparrows, though rare, are generally found in the valley in winter.

Say's Phoebe, Loggerhead Shrike, and Mountain Bluebird (winter) are in the open country. Wherever there are trees adjacent to open country, look for Yellow-billed Magpie.

Many birders come to Panoche Valley to find a Chukar, but it is by no means a sure thing. There are two places to look. One is in the rocky hills of Shotgun

Pass, about 5 miles north of the T junction, on Little Panoche Road; the other is along New Idria Road as it passes through a rocky canyon about 3 to 4 miles south of Panoche Valley. Look here also for Greater Roadrunner and Rock Wren. Also, roadrunners are sometimes seen at the eastern end of the road through Little Panoche Valley.

Many birders come to Panoche Valley in winter to find Mountain Plover. Look for them in the short grass fields along Little Panoche Road as it heads from the T junction to Shotgun Pass and along Panoche Road to the east of its junction with Little Panoche Road. They are hard to spot, partly because they are about the same color as the brown grass, and because they may be some distance away from the road. Ploverlike, they often run a short distance and then stop, run, and stop. A bit of advice from veteran plover watchers is to listen for them calling, which may guide you where to look.

Panoche Valley is prized by birders for its raptors, especially in winter. It seems as if Red-tailed Hawks and American Kestrels are everywhere. Be sure to look for a soaring Ferruginous Hawk (winter), Prairie Falcon, or Common Raven.

General information: Panoche Valley is a remote part of California that gets little visitation except by birders. The flat basin of Panoche Valley is grazed by cattle, and traffic is just about nil. Most of the land is private property, so you must bird from the roadside, usually with a spotting scope. During winters of heavy rain, some of the roads may become impassable.

ADDITIONAL HELP

Map grid: DeLorme Southern/Central California Atlas, page 21, 5C.
Elevation: 1,500 to 2,100 feet.
Hazards: Rattlesnakes, ticks.
Nearest food, gas, lodging: Hollister.
Camping: See Pinnacles National Monument, east side.
For more information: Bureau of Land Management (Hollister).

72 San Luis Refuge Complex

Habitats: Freshwater marsh, lake, stream, riparian woodland, farm fields, valley grassland.

Specialty birds: *Resident*—White-faced Ibis, Wood Duck, Cinnamon Teal, White-tailed Kite, Yellow-billed Magpie, Tricolored Blackbird, Western Meadowlark. *Summer*—Ash-throated Flycatcher, Western Kingbird, Yellow-headed Blackbird. *Winter*—Greater White-fronted and Ross's Geese; Sandhill Crane; Long-billed Curlew.

Other key birds: *Resident*—American Bittern, Virginia Rail, Sora, Common Moorhen, Black-necked Stilt, American Avocet, Loggerhead Shrike, Horned Lark, Marsh Wren. *Summer*—Blue Grosbeak. *Winter*—American White Pelican; Snow Goose; Gadwall; American Wigeon; Blue-winged and Green-winged Teal; Northern Shoveler; Northern Pintail; Ring-necked Duck; Black-bellied Plover; Greater Yellowlegs; Common Snipe; American Pipit; Savannah, Lincoln, and White-crowned Sparrows.

Best times to bird: November through February for most waterfowl and Sandhill Cranes; January and February for geese.

Directions: All directions are given from the junction of California Highway 33/152 and California Highway 165, in the center of Los Banos. For the San Luis Unit of the **San Luis National Wildlife Refuge,** go 6.2 miles north on CA 165, turn east on Wolfsen Road, then 2.3 miles to the entrance of the San Luis Unit (parking, restrooms). For **Merced National Wildlife Refuge** (NWR), go 3 miles north of Los Banos on CA 165 and turn east on Henry Miller Road. Drive 6.9 miles to Turner Island Road, and turn north. Follow the right-angle turns, keeping to the main road each time, as the road names progressively become Sand Slough Road, Nickel Road, and Sandy Mush Road. The entrance to Merced NWR is on Sandy Mush Road, 10.5 miles from the junction of Henry Miller and Turner Island roads (parking, restrooms).

The birding: Most birders come to the San Luis Refuge Complex for the abundant waterfowl in the winter. Greater White-fronted Geese and Snow Geese are everywhere. Look for the smaller Ross's Geese along with the Snow Geese as well as the rare "blue morph" form of the Snow Goose, once classified as a separate species. Virtually all of the usual wintering ducks will be found here. Mallards and Green-winged Teal are especially abundant in the winter. Common breeders are Wood Duck, Gadwall, Mallard, and Cinnamon Teal. Blue-winged Teal, Northern Shoveler, Northern Pintail, and Ruddy Duck are uncommon breeders.

As you drive from Los Banos to the San Luis Unit, scan the fields for egrets, ducks, and shorebirds in the wet areas, and Western Kingbird, Horned Lark, American Pipit, and Savannah Sparrow in the drier areas. Be especially alert for Sandhill Crane and White-faced Ibis, both of which often feed in the fields by the hundreds. Also watch for Tricolored Blackbirds, which could be with mixed blackbird flocks anywhere in pasturelands, especially in flooded fields. One good possibility for Tricoloreds is in cattle feedlots, such as the one near the intersection of Edminster Road and California Highway 140. They may be in with the cattle,

72 San Luis Refuge Complex

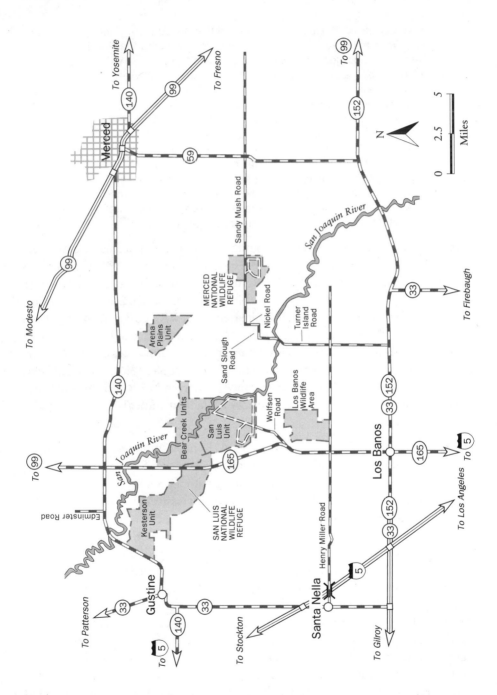

Wood Ducks breed at the San Luis Refuge Complex.

along with Red-winged and Yellow-headed Blackbirds, Brown-headed Cowbirds, and House Sparrows.

At the **San Luis Unit,** take the **Waterfowl Tour Route,** a gravel road that gives a sampling of the refuge. After 1 mile, the route splits, with the Tule Elk Tour Route going to the left and the Waterfowl Tour Route to the right. The **Chester Marsh Trail** is 3.2 miles from the entrance on the Waterfowl Tour Route and offers a walk around an attractive marsh (1 mile round trip). Look for marsh birds such as American Bittern, Sora, and Virginia Rail. Western Meadowlarks and Black Phoebes may be anywhere, and White-tailed Kites are fairly common. In summer look for Blue Grosbeak, and in winter for Golden-crowned, White-crowned, and Lincoln's (uncommon) Sparrows. The Central Valley of California, of which the San Luis Complex is a part, gets a major winter concentration of White-crowned Sparrows. Also, where there are trees and bushes, look for Ash-throated Flycatcher (summer), and Spotted and California Towhees (residents).

About 7.7 miles along the Waterfowl Tour Route from the entrance is the **Winton Marsh Trail,** with birds similar to those at Chester Marsh, except that Winton Marsh has a viewing platform. There can be large numbers of American Coots here, and the buzzing and chattering of the Marsh Wrens often fills the air. Song Sparrows are common, and so are Common Moorhens.

Returning to the **Tule Elk Tour Route** at the split in the routes 1 mile from the entrance, go to the left for a tour of about 3.5 miles around the elk enclosure. There is a barrier-free observation platform about halfway around the loop, and the elk herd, numbering 40 to 50, can usually be seen somewhere. Keep your eyes open for land birds such as Northern Harrier, Loggerhead Shrike, and Yellow-billed Magpie.

The **Merced Refuge** is one of the best places to see Snow and Ross's Geese, Sandhill Cranes, and shorebirds (parking, restrooms, barrier-free observation platform). Here, the auto tour route (about 5 miles round trip) takes you next to the ponds, where there may be thousands of Snow Geese in addition to the hundreds of Sandhill Cranes feeding in the fields. American White Pelicans and Double-crested Cormorants might be seen in fall and winter. The observation platform is near some mudflats, giving views of wintering shorebirds such as Black-bellied Plover, Greater Yellowlegs, Long-billed Curlew, Dunlin, Long-billed Dowitcher, and lots of peeps. Common Snipe is uncommon in the fall and winter, and American Avocet and Black-necked Stilts are residents.

General information: The San Luis National Wildlife Refuge Complex consists of San Luis and Merced national wildlife refuges, and Grasslands Ecological Area. In addition, the area contains the Los Banos and Volta wildlife areas (state of California), plus tens of thousands of acres in the surrounding territory managed by Grasslands State Park, Grassland Resource Conservation District, and Grassland Water District. The refuges have thousands of geese, ducks, and Sandhill Cranes in the winter. During the spring, the grassland wetlands support the largest concentration of shorebirds in interior California.

ADDITIONAL HELP

Map grid: Page 118, 1C, 2C.
Elevation: 100 feet.
Hazards: Mosquitoes, ticks.
Nearest food, gas, lodging: Merced; Los Banos.
Camping: Basalt Campground, San Luis Reservoir State Recreation Area: 79 sites, 12 miles west of Los Banos on CA 152.
For more information: San Luis National Wildlife Refuge Complex.

73 Caswell Memorial State Park ⋔

Habitats: Stream, riparian woodland.
Specialty birds: *Resident*—Wood Duck; Acorn and Nuttall's Woodpeckers; Yellow-billed Magpie; Oak Titmouse; Bushtit; Wrentit; Spotted Towhee. *Summer*—Swainson's Hawk, Ash-throated Flycatcher, Black-headed Grosbeak. *Winter*—Golden-crowned Sparrow.
Other key birds: *Resident*—Cooper's Hawk, Red-shouldered Hawk, Great Horned Owl, Downy Woodpecker, Loggerhead Shrike, White-breasted Nuthatch, Bewick's Wren. *Summer*—House Wren, Orange-crowned Warbler. *Winter*—Ruby-crowned Kinglet, Hermit Thrush, Cedar Waxwing, Yellow-rumped Warbler, Fox Sparrow.
Best times to bird: Spring and fall.

73 Caswell Memorial State Park

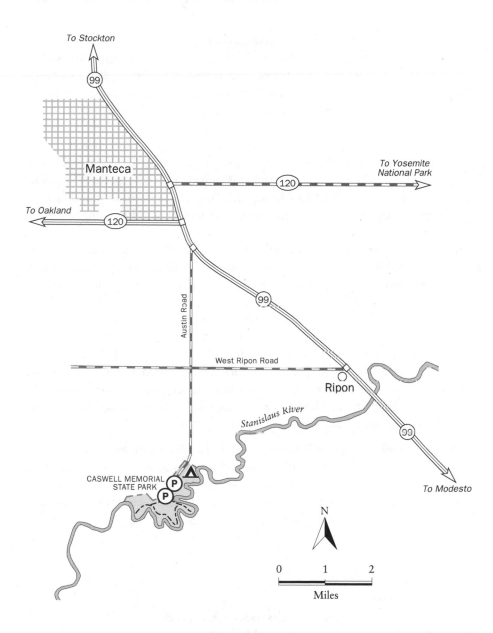

To Stockton

99

Manteca

To Yosemite
National Park

120

To Oakland

120

99

Austin Road

West Ripon Road

Ripon

99

Stanislaus River

CASWELL MEMORIAL
STATE PARK

To Modesto

N

0   1   2

Miles

Directions: From the junction of California Highway 99 and Austin Road (1.6 miles south of Manteca) go about 5 miles south on Austin Road to the park entrance (fee, parking). From CA 99 at Ripon, go about 3.5 miles west on West Ripon Road to Austin Road, and south on Austin Road about 2 miles to the park entrance.

The birding: Two large parking lots give access to picnic areas. Nature trails begin at both lots. The trail from the first lot leads north to the camping area, and the other trail connects to an elaborate system of trails running through thick riparian forest. Poison oak is present in isolated patches, and mosquitoes can be a problem.

The forest is full of birds in spring and in late fall after the first rains, the most obvious of which are Western Scrub-Jays, Acorn Woodpeckers with their loud *"YA-cob! YA-cob! YA-cob!,"* and Nuttall's Woodpeckers with their soft *"prrrrt! prrrrrt!"* An occasional Yellow-billed Magpie may show up in the forest, but they are more likely to be found in the orchards outside the park. A Red-shouldered Hawk may give its *"KEER! KEER! KEER!,"* and the prehistoric-sounding rattle of Sandhill Cranes may come from overhead in winter. Wrentits' songs are heard frequently.

Some other residents are California Quail, Red-tailed Hawk, Downy Woodpecker, White-breasted Nuthatch, Oak Titmouse, Bushtit, Bewick's Wren, American Robin, Spotted Towhee, Song Sparrow, and House Finch. Great Blue Herons and Wood Ducks (uncommon) may be along the river. Great Horned Owls and Cooper's Hawks are present, but not often seen. Loggerhead Shrikes are sometimes spotted along the road approaching the park.

In summer Swainson's Hawks return from Mexico and South America to nest in the tall trees. Some other summer visitors are Ash-throated Flycatcher, House Wren, Orange-crowned Warbler, and Black-headed Grosbeak. Winter brings Ruby-crowned Kinglet, Hermit Thrush, Cedar Waxwing, Yellow-rumped Warbler, and Fox, Golden-crowned, and White-crowned Sparrows.

General information: Caswell Memorial State Park is a genuine riparian jungle. The overstory consists of huge valley oaks and cottonwoods, festooned with grapevines. The understory is a thicket of brambles, wild rose, and poison oak. Summer can be hot, but spring and fall are delightful; so is winter except after heavy rains, when the Stanislaus River might flood.

ADDITIONAL HELP

NCA&G grid: Page 107, 5C.
Elevation: 50 feet.
Hazards: Poison oak, stinging nettles, ticks, mosquitoes.
Nearest food, gas, lodging: Manteca; Modesto.
Camping: Campground at the park, 65 sites.
For more information: Caswell Memorial State Park.

74 Yosemite National Park

Habitats: Riparian woodland, mixed conifer forest, lodgepole–red fir forest, meadow, cliffs.

Specialty birds: *Resident*—Northern Goshawk; Blue Grouse; Great Gray Owl; Williamson's Sapsucker; White-headed and Black-backed Woodpeckers; Steller's Jay; Mountain Chickadee; Canyon Wren; American Dipper; Townsend's Solitaire; Cassin's Finch. *Summer*—Black and White-throated Swifts; Calliope Hummingbird; Western Wood-Pewee; Hammond's and Dusky Flycatchers; Cassin's Vireo; Black-throated Gray, Hermit, and MacGillivray's Warblers; Western Tanager; Black-headed Grosbeak. *Migrant*—Rufous Hummingbird.

Other key birds: *Resident*—Hairy and Pileated Woodpeckers; Red-breasted Nuthatch; Brown Creeper; Winter Wren; Golden-crowned Kinglet; Pine and Evening Grosbeaks; Purple Finch; Red Crossbill; Pine Siskin. *Summer*—Warbling Vireo; Nashville and Yellow-rumped Warblers; Lincoln's Sparrow.

Best times to bird: May through October.

Directions: From Manteca, on California Highway 99, take California Highway 120 east about 105 miles (allow 2.5 hours) to Crane Flat, and then about 16 miles (allow 45 minutes) more on Big Oak Flat Road to Yosemite Valley. From Merced, on CA 99, take California Highway 140 east about 80 miles (allow 2 hours) to Yosemite Valley. From Fresno, on CA 99, take California Highway 41 north about 90 miles (allow 2 hours) to Yosemite Valley. From Lee Vining, on U.S. Highway 395, take CA 120 west over Tioga Pass about 55 miles (allow 1.5 hours, closed in winter) to Crane Flat, and then about 16 miles (allow 45 minutes) east on Big Oak Flat Road to Yosemite Valley. Gasoline is available at Crane Flat, but not in Yosemite Valley. There is an entrance fee of $20.

The birding: Many birders avoid Yosemite Valley because of the crowds; nevertheless, there are lots of good birds here. White-throated and Black Swifts are sometimes seen near the cliffs and waterfalls, American Dippers are in the whitewater of the Merced River, Canyon Wrens sing from the rocks, and Winter Wrens sing from the thickets. Steller's Jays; American Robins; Nashville, Black-throated Gray, and MacGillivray's Warblers; and Black-headed Grosbeaks are breeders, and sometimes nest in the campgrounds. The lower end of the valley, near El Capitan, may often be relatively uncrowded. Birding along the river and around the meadows can be good. Check for Purple Finch in the riparian zone.

South Rim: From Yosemite Valley, take the Fresno Road (CA 41) about 14 miles to the turnoff for the Glacier Point Road. Go 7.7 miles to Bridalveil Creek Campground. **Peregoy Meadow** is visible from Glacier Point Road, and lies adjacent to the campground. Great Gray Owls have been seen here, usually at dawn or dusk; walk the meadow edges at dusk. About 0.1 mile west of the campground entrance road is the trail that leads north to **McGurk Meadow,** another favored place for Great Gray Owls. There are a few places next to the road where you can park, about 100 yards east of the beginning of the trail. It is a 0.7-mile hike to the

74 Yosemite National Park

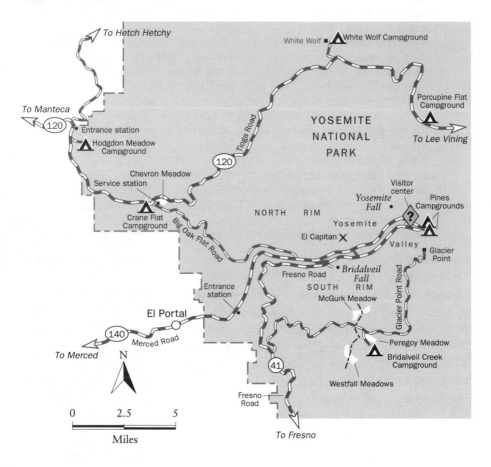

meadow, and then another mile or so along the edge of the meadow— about 3 miles round trip. You have less than a 50 percent chance of finding the owl because there are only a few pairs in the entire park. Most often, they are perched near the edge of a meadow, or sometimes can be spotted flying low. During the day they usually roost in dense foliage and can be easy to miss.

On the opposite side of the road from where the trail to McGurk Meadow begins, a trail runs south to Bridalveil Creek Campground (about 1 mile), and to **Westfall Meadows** (about 1 more mile). McGurk, Peregoy, and Westfall meadows belong to a general meadow system, and the owls use them all.

The park rangers urge that birders not approach Great Gray Owls closely or otherwise disturb them. They say that research has shown the owls may not resume foraging for an hour after being disturbed, which can adversely affect their welfare.

Other specialty birds in this area are Black-backed Woodpecker and Pine Grosbeak. In addition to the owl, these two are at about the southern limit of their

Female Blue Grouse.

ranges in the United States here. Other birds are resident Blue Grouse, Williamson's Sapsucker, and Brown Creeper; summer visitors such as Calliope Hummingbird, Dusky Flycatcher, Western Tanager, and Hermit, Yellow-rumped, and MacGillivray's Warblers; and migrants such as Rufous Hummingbird, which migrate south so early in the summer that they were once thought to be breeders.

In addition to birding, go another 10 miles beyond Bridalveil to the end of the road at Glacier Point, where the views of Half Dome, the Sierra, and of Yosemite, Vernal, and Nevada falls are superb.

North Rim: From Yosemite Valley, take the Big Oak Flat Road about 16 miles to **Crane Flat,** at the junction with the Tioga Road (gas station, restrooms). Directly behind the service station is **Chevron Meadow,** a classic place for Great Gray Owl, but again, less than half of those who seek the owl actually succeed. It is possible to get around the bottom part of the meadow without getting your feet wet, and to walk up the north edge of the meadow. Dawn or dusk is best.

Other birds to be expected at Chevron Meadow are Hairy, White-headed, and Pileated Woodpeckers; Western Wood-Pewee; Hammond's Flycatcher; Cassin's and Warbling Vireos; Mountain Chickadee; Red-breasted Nuthatch; Golden-crowned Kinglet; Townsend's Solitaire; Hermit and MacGillivray's Warblers; Lincoln's Sparrow; and Pine Siskin. Northern Goshawk (rare) is a possibility.

White Wolf (lodgings, restaurant, campground) is 14 miles from Crane Flat on the Tioga Road. Many people come to White Wolf for Pine Grosbeak (irregular); look behind the lodge at the old horse corral. Other birds are Western Wood-Pewee, Mountain Chickadee, Yellow-rumped Warbler, Dark-eyed Junco, Cassin's

Finch, Red Crossbill, Pine Siskin, and Evening Grosbeak (irregular). Great Gray Owls have shown up here in September, after the campground is closed.

General information: In the minds of many, Yosemite is the nation's number one park. If you plan to stay anywhere in or near the park, whether in lodges or in the more popular campgrounds, you will need reservations. Even for day-users, the rangers sometimes turn people away after a certain number of cars have passed through the gates. At this writing, there is talk of reservations being required for day-users. Unless this reservation system comes into being, the way to avoid being turned away is to get there early in the morning. But if you have overnight reservations, you will be able to get in.

Elevations range from 2,000 feet to 13,114 feet (Mount Lyell). Yosemite Valley lies at 4,000 feet, and temperatures can reach 95 or 100 degrees F in August. Tuolumne Meadows, however, is at 8,600 feet, and is cooler. Tioga Pass (the eastern entrance to the park) is at 9,945 feet, and lies in superb subalpine country. Mosquitoes can be a nuisance in the high country, but are seldom a problem in Yosemite Valley.

ADDITIONAL HELP

NCA&G grid: Page 110, 3B, 4C.
Elevation: 4,000 to 8,000 feet.
Hazards: High-elevation sun exposure, fast water (people drown almost every year), rattlesnakes and ticks are possible. Also, people die each year in the park from falls off rocks or cliffs. Black bears are present, and should not be approached; they have learned that people leave food in cars and often break in to get the food, so the park service urges that absolutely no food be left in cars. In 1997 bears caused property damage valued at $580,000, and four of them had to be killed after they became aggressive from eating food stolen from cars.
Nearest food, gas, lodging: Yosemite Valley has food service, but no gas. The only gas in the park is at Crane Flat. Lodging requires reservations that may have to be made months in advance. El Portal (Merced Road) and Fish Camp (Fresno Road) have motels, but getting accommodations may be difficult there, also. You might have to go as far as Mariposa (about 25 miles), Groveland (about 25 miles), or Oakhurst (about 15 miles), to get a place to stay in high season.
Camping: (campgrounds in the park are often full in the summer, and hard to get into; reservations are essential): Upper, Lower, and North Pines: 475 sites, in Yosemite Valley; RV dump stations. Crane Flat: 165 sites, near the junction of Big Oak Flat Road and Tioga Road, about 17 miles from Yosemite Valley. Hodgdon Meadow: 110 sites, near the entrance station on CA 120, about 25 miles from Yosemite Valley. Bridalveil Creek: 110 sites, on Glacier Point Road, about 22 miles from Yosemite Valley. White Wolf: 88 sites, 14 miles from Crane Flat, on Tioga Road. Porcupine Flat: 52 sites, about 24 miles from Crane Flat, on Tioga Road.
For more information: Yosemite National Park.

75 Mono Lake Region

Habitats: Lake, stream, riparian woodland, yellow pine forest, pinyon-juniper woodland, sagebrush scrub, subalpine zone.

Specialty birds: *Resident*—Sage Grouse; White-tailed Ptarmigan; Steller's and Pinyon Jays; Clark's Nutcracker; Black-billed Magpie; Mountain Chickadee; Pygmy Nuthatch; Rock Wren; Gray-crowned Rosy-Finch; Cassin's Finch. *Summer*—Snowy Plover; California Gull; Common Poorwill; Calliope Hummingbird; Lewis's Woodpecker; Red-naped and Red-breasted Sapsuckers; Western Wood-Pewee; Dusky and Gray Flycatchers; Say's Phoebe; Violet-green Swallow; Mountain Bluebird; Sage Thrasher; MacGillivray's Warbler; Western Tanager; Green-tailed Towhee; Brewer's and Sage Sparrows; Lazuli Bunting.

Other key birds: *Resident*—Long-eared Owl, Common Raven, Horned Lark. *Summer*—American Avocet; Common Snipe; Wilson's Phalarope; Common Nighthawk; Warbling Vireo; Northern Rough-winged Swallow; Hermit Thrush; Yellow and Yellow-rumped Warblers; Vesper Sparrow. *Winter*—Northern Shrike. *Migrant*—Eared Grebe, Red-necked Phalarope.

Best times to bird: April through July for most birds; October for peak numbers of Eared Grebes; July and August for phalaropes; late July for White-tailed Ptarmigan and other high-elevation birds.

Directions: Lee Vining, the "headquarters" for the area, is about 140 miles (2.5 hours) south of Reno, Nevada, via U.S. Highway 395. From Yosemite Valley, Lee Vining is about 75 miles (2 hours) east via the Tioga Road and California Highway 120, closed in winter. See directions to specific sites below.

The birding: Go about 6 miles north of Lee Vining on U.S. Highway 395, and turn east 0.4 mile to **Mono Lake County Park** (fee, parking, restrooms). The Mono Lake Visitor Center is on the way, about 0.6 mile north of town. At the county park, take the trail to the lake, which leads through willows and marshy habitat to some tufa formations. Around the county park and along the trail, look for Violet-green and Northern Rough-winged Swallows; Mountain Chickadee; House Wren; Yellow and MacGillivray's Warblers; and Lazuli Bunting. In summer there should be California Gulls on the lake scooping up brine shrimp, and Eared Grebes, whose numbers may swell to as many as 750,000 in October. In July and August, watch for Wilson's and Red-necked Phalaropes. At the park in late spring, listen for Common Snipe "winnowing" overhead, and for Common Nighthawks making their *"peent!"* call at dusk. Long-eared Owls have been known to roost here in the willows. Also, in summer after it's dark, you might see a Common Poorwill sitting in the road, provided there isn't too much traffic.

On the opposite side of the road from the park is an area owned by Los Angeles Water and Power. Birds likely to be found here include many of the above, plus Western Wood-Pewee, Warbling Vireo, Black-billed Magpie, and Common Raven.

South Tufa Area: This is probably the most heavily visited area around the lake. Go about 5 miles south of Lee Vining on US 395/CA 120, and turn east on CA 120. Go 4.7 miles to the turnoff for South Tufa Beach (fee, parking, restrooms),

75 Mono Lake Region

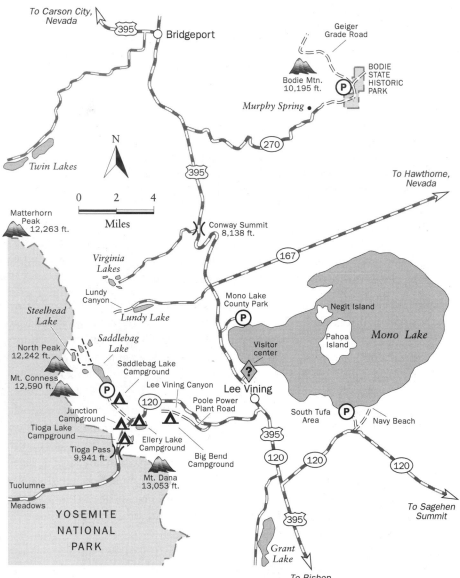

To Carson City, Nevada

395

Bridgeport

Geiger Grade Road

BODIE STATE HISTORIC PARK

Bodie Mtn. 10,195 ft.

P

Murphy Spring

270

N

Twin Lakes

395

0 2 4
Miles

To Hawthorne, Nevada

Matterhorn Peak 12,263 ft.

Conway Summit 8,138 ft.

Virginia Lakes

167

Lundy Canyon

Mono Lake County Park

Negit Island

Steelhead Lake

Lundy Lake

P

Mono Lake

North Peak 12,242 ft.

Saddlebag Lake

Pahoa Island

Visitor center

Saddlebag Lake Campground

Mt. Conness 12,590 ft.

?

Lee Vining

P

Lee Vining Canyon

120

Poole Power Plant Road

South Tufa Area

P

Navy Beach

Junction Campground

Tioga Lake Campground

Ellery Lake Campground

Big Bend Campground

395

Tioga Pass 9,941 ft.

120

120

120

Tuolumne Meadows

Mt. Dana 13,053 ft.

YOSEMITE NATIONAL PARK

395

To Sagehen Summit

Grant Lake

To Bishop

where a trail leads to some of the best tufa formations to be found around the lake. Tufa towers are formed under water by the precipitation of calcium carbonate. When the water levels fall the towers become visible.

Birds to look for at the South Tufa area, in addition to many of those already mentioned, are Killdeer, American Avocet, Horned Lark, Green-tailed Towhee, and Brewer's Sparrow. Snowy Plovers are possible, because they nest on the flats on the east side of the lake. Gray Flycatchers, Sage Thrashers, and Sage Sparrows are more likely to be found in the sagebrush scrub along the road leading to the lake than near the lake itself.

If you don't find Gray Flycatcher or Sage Sparrow at South Tufa, try going east 10 miles or so beyond South Tufa on CA 120 to **Sagehen Summit** (8,137 feet). (Believe it or not, you should be prepared for mosquitoes.) David Gaines, an authority on Mono birds, wrote that Sage Sparrows are more common at Sagehen Summit than around the lake. Note that the subspecies of Sage Sparrow *(Amphispiza belli nevadensis)* found here is quite different from that found on the California coast *(A. b. belli)*. The coastal subspecies *(belli)* is resident there and inhabits chaparral dominated by chamise; the interior subspecies at Mono Lake *(nevadensis)* is migratory and inhabits chaparral dominated by sagebrush. The two subspecies are candidates for a split into full-fledged species.

On the way to Sagehen Summit, you pass through some dry, open forests of Jeffrey pine. Lewis's Woodpeckers have nested here, and Pinyon Jays are sometimes seen in these open parklike forests, but are irregular. Watch for Vesper Sparrow (uncommon in summer) in grassy open places.

Bodie State Historic Park is most famous as a well-preserved ghost town, but it is probably one of the best places in California to see Sage Grouse. Go about 19 miles north from Lee Vining on US 395, and then east about 13 miles on California Highway 270 to Bodie. The road is mostly paved, but the last 3 miles are gravel; the road is closed in winter. Sage Grouse are sometimes seen along CA 270 at dawn, perhaps coming to Murphy Spring, which is about 0.2 mile west of the end of the pavement. Park rangers report that the grouse often are in the streets of Bodie in July and August when the park opens at 8:00 A.M. (possibly drawn by the fresh grass and forbs), but soon retire to the nearby sagebrush plots as the crowds thicken. Bodie is also known for its Mountain Bluebirds, which nest here; look also for Say's Phoebe. In this wide-open country, watch for Golden Eagle and Prairie Falcon, both uncommon residents. Rock Wren, Sage Thrasher, and Green-tailed Towhee all occur in the rocky, brushy terrain along the road into Bodie.

Lee Vining Canyon: From Lee Vining, go west about 4 miles on CA 120 to the Poole Power Plant Road. This road runs more or less parallel to CA 120, but follows the creek along the bottom of the canyon. It ends about 3.5 miles from its beginning and is paved except for the last mile or so. The habitat is a mixture of sagebrush scrub, meadows, and riparian forest. At places there are groves of Jeffrey pines, and even some pinyon pines and junipers. There are many attractive pullouts for birding, but an especially nice one is about 0.9 mile after leaving

CA 120, where there is a fairly large gravel parking lot on the left, below the road. An old bridge, barred by a gate, goes across the stream, leading to prime birding habitat. The USDA Forest Service asks that people be careful if they use this bridge because it has holes and rotting planks. Long-range plans call for replacement of the bridge.

Look in Lee Vining Canyon for Calliope Hummingbird, Red-breasted Sapsucker, Western Wood-Pewee, Dusky Flycatcher, Warbling Vireo, Steller's Jay, Tree and Violet-green Swallows, Pygmy Nuthatch, House Wren, Yellow and Yellow-rumped Warblers, Western Tanager, Song Sparrow, and Cassin's Finch. Red-naped Sapsucker occurs here (rare). Here and elsewhere in the region, look for Northern Shrike in winter (rare).

To get to **Saddlebag Lake,** go about 10 miles west on CA 120 from Lee Vining, turn north, and then travel about 2.5 miles on a gravel road to the lake. The main reason birders go to Saddlebag Lake is to look for White-tailed Ptarmigan. Ptarmigans are not native to the Sierra, but were introduced by the California Department of Fish and Game in the early 1970s. They have now established a wild population along the eastern boundary of Yosemite National Park. They nest in alpine meadows and are heavily dependent on the low-growing willows on which they feed. To get to the ptarmigans at the opposite end of Saddlebag Lake from where the road ends, birders generally purchase a trip on a water taxi, operated by the Saddlebag Lake Resort. This cuts out a 2-mile hike along the shore. You must wait until most of the snow has melted—usually in late July—in order to get around in this high subalpine terrain.

Saddlebag Lake is rather bleak, but the country beyond it is spectacular, with great peaks rising above the alpine meadows. Ptarmigans have been reported at various places beyond the upper end of Saddlebag Lake, to the head of Lundy Canyon, at 10,000 to 11,000 feet. One of two trails goes due north to Lundy Canyon, and the other goes northwest to Steelhead Lake. One place the birds have been found is on the alpine benches (11,000 feet) lying west of Steelhead Lake, so cross-country scrambling will probably be necessary, involving a round-trip hike of 6 miles or more plus the boat trip. Most people fail in their search, because ptarmigans can camouflage themselves very well. It is said that to find a ptarmigan, watch for a rock that moves.

Some other birds to watch for in this high country are Clark's Nutcracker, Gray-crowned Rosy-Finch, and Cassin's Finch. In summer you need to go to the highest passes and slopes to find Gray-crowned Rosy-Finch, but early in the season they occur somewhat lower, such as at Tioga Lake.

General information: Mono Lake is well known because of the legal battles that were fought over water diversions by the city of Los Angeles. The most publicized part of the issue was the threat to the breeding colonies of California Gulls on Negit Island. As more and more water was diverted from the lake, a land bridge appeared between the island and the mainland, permitting predators to gain access to the gull colonies. Furthermore, it was suspected that a continued lowering of the water would jeopardize the food resources of the lake, consisting of billions of tiny brine shrimp and alkali flies. California Gulls depend upon these, and so do tens of thousands of migrating Wilson's and Red-necked Phalaropes, and hundreds of thousands of Eared Grebes. The outcome of the legal battle was that the city of Los Angeles agreed to limit its diversions, so the lake could be maintained at a healthy level.

The region covered here includes not only the lake itself but also some of the watershed to the west, extending to 10,000 feet at Saddlebag Lake. It also covers some of the sagebrush country to the east, and north to Bodie. In the fall, the slopes of the Sierra Nevada in many places turn to spectacular yellow and gold colors because of the extensive aspen groves.

ADDITIONAL HELP

NCA&G grid: Page 101, 6C; page 102, 1C; page 111, 6A; page 112, 2A.
Elevation: 6,400 to 11,000 feet.
Hazards: Sun exposure and lightning are probably the greatest hazards, although there are also rattlesnakes, ticks, mosquitoes, and biting gnats. Also, going from low elevation to high elevation and engaging immediately in strenuous exercise is not a good idea. Be careful on nonpaved roads around Mono Lake; many people have gotten stuck in the sand. Snowstorms have been known to occur as late as early June.
Nearest food, gas, lodging: Lee Vining; Bridgeport.
Camping: Saddlebag Lake: 20 sites, about 10 miles west of Lee Vining on CA 120, turn north, and go 2.5 miles (gravel) to Saddlebag Lake and Campground. Junction: 13 sites, at junction of CA 120 and road to Saddlebag Lake, about 10 miles west of Lee Vining. Tioga Lake: 12 sites, 11 miles west of Lee Vining on CA 120. Ellery Lake: 12 sites, 9.5 miles west of Lee Vining on CA 120. Big Bend: 17 sites; go west of Lee Vining about 4 miles on CA 120 to Poole Power Plant Road, and then about 3 miles to the campground; part of the road is gravel.
For more information: Mono Lake Ranger District; Bodie State Historic Park.

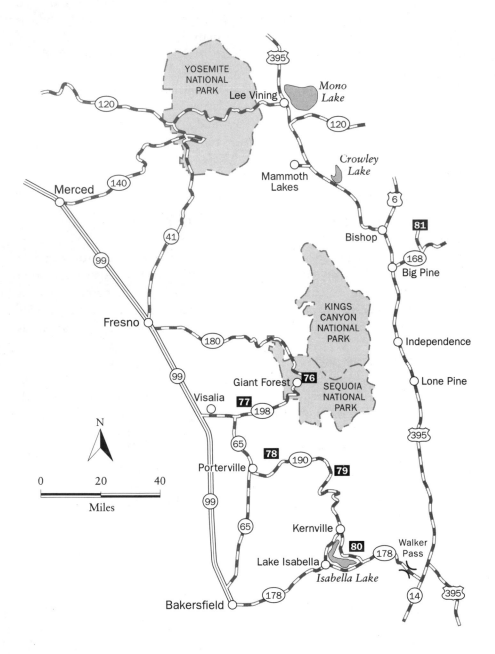

YOSEMITE
NATIONAL
PARK

Lee Vining

Mono Lake

120

120

Crowley Lake

Mammoth
Lakes

Merced

140

6

Bishop

81

41

168

Big Pine

99

KINGS
CANYON
NATIONAL
PARK

Fresno

180

Independence

Giant Forest **76**

99

Lone Pine

Visalia **77**

SEQUOIA
NATIONAL
PARK

198

395

N

65

0   20   40

78

190

79

Miles

Porterville

99

65

Kernville

Walker
Pass

Lake Isabella **80**

178

Isabella Lake

14

395

Bakersfield

178

Southern Sierra

The Southern Sierra Nevada and the White Mountains, which dominate this part of the state, contain the highest peak in the lower 48 states, the largest trees in the world (the sequoias), and the oldest trees in the world (the bristlecone pines). The Sierra Nevada is rugged and craggy, with twelve mountains higher than 14,000 feet. The White Mountains are almost as high, and have an alpine moonscape along their crest.

The birding trail linking the sites in the Southern Sierra is 350 miles long, and consists entirely of good paved roads. Of the various sites, Sequoia National Park is popular and attracts lots of visitors, but most of the areas along the trail are relatively uncrowded.

Sequoia, and its lookalike, the Western Divide Highway, are good for birds like White-headed Woodpecker, Red-breasted Sapsucker, Townsend's Solitaire, and Western Tanager. The foothill regions have Western Kingbird, Ash-throated Flycatcher, Bullock's Oriole, and Spotted and California Towhees.

Kern River Valley is special, because it is the meeting place for several different bioregions. As a result, it has birds typical of the mountains to the north and west, but also has species from the desert regions to the south, like Ladder-backed Woodpecker, Cactus Wren, Summer Tanager, and Scott's Oriole. It is one of the best places to see Western Yellow-billed Cuckoo, Willow Flycatcher, Black-chinned Sparrow, and Lawrence's Goldfinch.

The White Mountains bring together species from the Sierra Nevada and from the Great Basin. Here you can find Chukar, Pinyon Jay, and Mountain Bluebird, and it is one of the few places in California where you can see Broad-tailed Hummingbird, Juniper Titmouse and Plumbeous Vireo.

76 Sequoia National Park

77 Kaweah Oaks and Yokohl Valley

78 Bartlett Park and Success Lake

79 Western Divide Highway

80 Kern River Valley

81 White Mountains

76 Sequoia National Park 🚹 ♿

Habitats: Stream, foothill woodland, chaparral, mixed conifer forest, lodgepole–red fir forest, meadow, cliffs.

Specialty birds: *Resident*—Northern Goshawk, Golden Eagle; Peregrine Falcon; Blue Grouse, Mountain Quail, Western Screech-Owl; Northern Pygmy-Owl; White-throated Swift; Red-breasted Sapsucker; Acorn, Nuttall's, and White-headed Woodpeckers; Steller's Jay; Clark's Nutcracker; Mountain Chickadee; Canyon Wren; American Dipper; Western Bluebird; Townsend's Solitaire; Wrentit; California Thrasher; Spotted and California Towhees; Rufous-crowned Sparrow; Lesser Goldfinch. *Summer*—Flammulated Owl; Common Poorwill; Calliope Hummingbird; Western Wood-Pewee; Hammond's and Ash-throated Flycatchers; Hermit and MacGillivray's Warblers; Western Tanager; Green-tailed Towhee; Black-headed Grosbeak; Bullock's Oriole; Lawrence's Goldfinch.

Other key birds: *Resident*—Great Horned and Northern Saw-whet Owls; Hairy and Pileated Woodpeckers; Common Raven; Red-breasted and White-breasted Nuthatches; Winter Wren; Dark-eyed Junco; Pine Siskin; Evening Grosbeak. *Summer*—Orange-crowned, Yellow-rumped, and Wilson's Warblers; Chipping, Fox, and Lincoln's Sparrows.

Best times to bird: June through August for higher elevations (Giant Forest); winter and spring for lower elevations (Hospital Rock).

Directions: From Fresno, it is about 82 miles via California Highway 180 and the Generals Highway to Giant Forest (allow 2.5 hours). From Visalia, it is about 51 miles via California Highway 198 to Giant Forest (allow 2 hours). The road from Visalia is narrow, steep, and winding for the last 13 miles, and is not recommended for vehicles longer than 22 feet. The road leading from Grant Grove to Giant Forest is known as the Generals Highway.

The birding: The natural beginning point is at **Giant Forest.** At one time this was the center of visitor concentration, with four campgrounds, a lodge, and housekeeping cabins, but the campgrounds and lodgings have been removed. **Round Meadow** is 0.3 mile north of the junction of the main road with the road that goes to Crescent Meadow and Moro Rock. This junction is at the location once known as Giant Forest Village. It will be referred to herein as Crescent Meadow Junction.

A barrier-free paved trail at Round Meadow, called the **Trail for All People** (about 0.6 mile round trip), goes around the meadow. Some of the brushy patches adjacent to the meadow can contain birds such as MacGillivray's and Wilson's Warblers, Green-tailed Towhee (uncommon), and Lincoln's and Fox Sparrows. Look in the conifers for Pileated and White-headed Woodpeckers, Hammond's Flycatcher, Mountain Chickadee, Red-breasted Nuthatch, Chipping Sparrow, and Pine Siskin. Probably the most characteristic sound of these forests is the nasal *"anhk! anhk! anhk!"* call of the Red-breasted Nuthatch, sounding for all the world like someone blowing on a little toy horn.

76 Sequoia National Park

To Fresno

Azalea Campground

Grant Grove

Crystal Springs Campground

180

Sunset Campground

Entrance station

Generals Highway

Grant Grove Section of Kings Canyon National Park

N

0   2.5   5
Miles

Stony Creek Campground (U.S. Forest Service)

KINGS CANYON NATIONAL PARK

Dorst Campground

Halstead Meadow

SEQUOIA NATIONAL PARK

Round Meadow

Giant Forest (Crescent Meadow Junction)

Marble Fork Kaweah River

Tokopah Valley

Tokopah Falls

Lodgepole Campground

Wolverton

General Sherman Tree

Crescent Meadow

Moro Rock

Buckeye Flat Campground

Potwisha Campground

North Fork Kaweah River

Hospital Rock

Entrance station

Ash Mountain

East Fork Kaweah River

Three Rivers

198

To Visalia

On the opposite side of the main road from Round Meadow, and up the road about 50 yards, is the parking lot for the **Hazelwood Nature Trail** (about 1 mile round trip). It leads through a delightful sequoia grove and has essentially the same birds as Round Meadow.

Before the dust settled

When I scouted this area in 1997, I paused by a fallen sequoia tree about 15 feet in diameter lying near the upper end of the nature trail. This was the tree that almost killed me in 1947.

It happened this way: I was working as a seasonal park ranger and was driving over a narrow road that passed above Hazelwood, which was then a picnic area. I came around a bend and discovered a giant sequoia tree lying across the road. The dust was still billowing up from its impact, and small branches that had been knocked loose were falling from neighboring trees. It had apparently fallen just a few seconds before I got there, and I would have been squashed like a bug if I had arrived a little sooner. My wife heard the tree fall from a half-mile away at the tent cabin where we lived, and didn't realize that she had almost been turned into a widow, at age 17.

The only consequence of my fallen tree is that the National Park Service closed the narrow road I had been on, and abandoned it. But a few years later a tree fell on a picnic table in the Hazelwood Picnic Area, killing a woman. The picnic area was promptly closed and turned into the Hazelwood Nature Trail. In the early 1990s two more giant trees fell near Round Meadow, near a lodge. No one was killed, but one of the trees fell close to a parking lot. This, plus the fact that the Park Service had long wanted to move all visitor facilities out of the Giant Forest, made them decide to move everything out as soon as possible.

About 4 miles northeast of Round Meadow is **Lodgepole** (visitor center, campground, parking) and the trailhead for **Tokopah Valley.** Parking for this trailhead is at the far end of the huge parking lot, about 100 yards before coming to the bridge across the Marble Fork. The trail begins on the other side of the bridge, and it is about 1.7 miles to the end at Tokopah Falls. If you get on the trail early in the morning, you will have it mostly to yourself.

Steller's Jays, Mountain Chickadees, and Dark-eyed Juncos are abundant, plus other common birds such as Red-breasted Nuthatch, Brown Creeper, and MacGillivray's and Wilson's Warblers. An American Dipper or a Belted Kingfisher may be working the river, and Common Raven and Clark's Nutcracker are likely to be overhead. Other birds to watch for are Blue Grouse; Calliope Hummingbird;

Red-breasted Sapsucker; Hairy and White-headed Woodpeckers; Western Wood-Pewee; Winter Wren; Townsend's Solitaire; Orange-crowned, Hermit, and Yellow-rumped Warblers; Western Tanager; Fox Sparrow; and Evening Grosbeak (irregular). In the rocky talus slopes near the falls, listen for Canyon Wrens, singing their songs, a descending series of clear, sweet whistles. Many people consider this to be the most beautiful bird song of all.

A spot to consider is **Halstead Meadow** if you find the other places too crowded. The parking place for the meadow (pit toilet) is about 3.7 miles from Lodgepole on the south side of the road, on the way to Grant Grove. If it is crowded, go west from the restrooms parallel to the road for 200 yards or so, through an old control burn, and into an open forest with grassy understory. This area seems to be favored by birds, essentially the same species already described. Northern Goshawk has been seen in this region.

If you would like to get to a spot where you are likely to see even fewer people, try **Wolverton,** and the **Long Meadow Loop.** When I hiked this loop in midsummer 1997, I encountered no one. The Wolverton road leaves the main highway about 1.6 miles south of Lodgepole, and ends in a gigantic parking lot that was constructed for an alpine skiing center. Long Meadow is the big meadow that is visible as you drive in, and your trail completely encircles the meadow.

The trailhead for the Lakes Trail is located to the left of your entry point, but go past that all the way to the east end of the lot. Walk east, to the water treatment plant. Directly across from the plant is Wolverton Creek. Walk to the creek edge and you will find the Long Meadow Trail, which crosses the creek at this point (no bridge) and heads south. The complete loop makes about a 2-mile round trip. The east side is generally better birding than the west side, probably because there is more cover. Northern Saw-whet Owl has been reported from Long Meadow. Otherwise, the bird species are generally the same as at Tokopah Valley. If you choose to make the entire loop, then you will eventually get back to the Wolverton road, next to Wolverton Creek. When you get to the road, turn right and use the road to get to the other side of the creek, where there is a trail that leads you back to the parking lot.

To get to **Moro Rock,** from Crescent Meadow Junction go 1.6 miles on the Crescent Meadow/Moro Rock road, following signs to the parking area (restrooms). The climb to the top of the rock is only about 0.2 mile, but it consists almost entirely of concrete steps. The reasons for climbing the rock are that the view of the Great Western Divide is sensational, and there is a remote possibility of sighting a Peregrine Falcon. In recent years a pair of falcons has nested on the face of the rock. You might also see a Golden Eagle or a White-throated Swift.

When you leave Giant Forest and head down into the foothills toward Visalia, you enter a different realm. The foothills can be hot in summer but in winter can be delightful. The road is narrow and steep; consequently, it is advisable to use second gear, or even first gear, when coming down, in order to avoid brake failure. At the bottom of the steep part is **Hospital Rock** (parking, exhibits, restrooms).

Farther down the road, about 2.3 miles, is **Potwisha Campground.** The birds at both locations are similar.

Hospital Rock and Potwisha abound in Acorn Woodpeckers, Western Scrub-Jays, Oak Titmice, and California Towhees. Other resident birds are California Quail; Great Horned Owl; Northern Pygmy-Owl; Anna's Hummingbird; Downy and Nuttall's Woodpeckers; Northern Flicker; Black Phoebe; Common Raven; Bushtit; White-breasted Nuthatch; Canyon and Bewick's Wrens; American Dipper; Western Bluebird; Wrentit; California Thrasher; Spotted Towhee; Rufous-crowned Sparrow; and Lesser Goldfinch. Mountain Quail spend the winter and spring at this altitude, but then move upslope in summer. Typical summer visitors are Ash-throated Flycatcher, House Wren, Black-headed Grosbeak, and Bullock's Oriole.

At Hospital Rock, after checking around the parking lot (nice and quiet early in the morning, turning into a zoo later in the day), walk across the road next to the entry road for Buckeye Flat Campground to see the pictographs on the left side of the Buckeye Flat road. Then, cross to the other side of the road to a short, steep trail leading down to the Middle Fork Kaweah River.

At the upper end of Potwisha Campground, next to campsite number 16, is a short dirt road that leads to a small parking area, and the Marble Fork Trail. The first part of the trail is a dirt road that goes to a diversion dam in about 0.2 mile. Or you can cross the main road opposite the campground entrance, and go to the end of the short paved road, past the RV dump station. A rough trail here leads to the Middle Fork of the Kaweah River, and to a swinging bridge. The trail climbs the hill beside a huge iron pipe to join the Middle Fork Trail, which leads back to the RV dump station.

If you are staying overnight in Potwisha Campground in summer, look for Flammulated Owl, Western Screech-Owl, and Common Poorwill, all of which have been seen in the vicinity. Check for Lawrence's Goldfinch in summer around the visitor center near the entrance station at **Ash Mountain.**

General information: Sequoia National Park ranges from the hot, dry foothills at Ash Mountain (1,700 feet), to Mount Whitney (14,494 feet), the highest peak in the lower 48 states. The largest trees in the world grow here—the giant sequoias. The park is popular and can be crowded on holidays and weekends. Campgrounds and lodgings fill up every night during the summer; however, the crowding is not as bad as publicity releases would have you believe, and you can find places where the birding is good and where you will see practically no one else.

ADDITIONAL HELP

Map grid: DeLorme Southern /Central California Atlas, page 25, 6C, 7D; page 37, 7A.
Elevation: 1,700 to 7,300 feet.
Hazards: Poison oak below 5,000 feet; danger of lightning strike on Moro Rock;

overexposure to high-elevation sun; rattlesnakes and ticks, especially at lower elevations; the National Park Service says the principal cause of death in the national parks is drowning.

Nearest food, lodging: No gasoline is available in the parks. Limited supplies are available at Lodgepole and Grant Grove. Lodging is available at Grant Grove and Stony Creek. Full services are available at Three Rivers.

Camping: At Grant Grove (RV dump station nearby): Azalea: 114 sites; year-round; Crystal Springs: 66 sites; Sunset: 119 sites. Stony Creek (USDA Forest Service): 49 sites, on Generals Highway about 17 miles north of Giant Forest. Dorst: 218 sites, on Generals Highway about 12.5 miles north of Giant Forest; RV dump station. Lodgepole: 150 sites, on Generals Highway 4 miles north of Giant Forest; RV dump station. Buckeye Flat: 28 sites, on Ash Mountain Road 10.2 miles south of Giant Forest, then 0.6 mile on paved side road; no RVs or trailers. Potwisha: 44 sites, on Ash Mountain Road about 12.5 miles south of Giant Forest; RV dump station; open year-round.

For more information: Sequoia and Kings Canyon national parks.

77 Kaweah Oaks and Yokohl Valley

Habitats: Lake, riparian woodland, valley grassland, foothill woodland, oak savanna.

Specialty birds: *Resident*—Wood Duck; Golden Eagle, Anna's Hummingbird; Acorn and Nuttall's Woodpeckers; Black Phoebe; Oak Titmouse; Western Bluebird; Spotted and California Towhees; Western Meadowlark; Lesser Goldfinch. *Summer*—Black-chinned Hummingbird, Western Wood-Pewee, Ash-throated Flycatcher, Western Kingbird, Black-headed Grosbeak, Lazuli Bunting, Bullock's Oriole.

Other key birds: *Resident*—Sharp-shinned, Cooper's, Red-tailed, and Red-shouldered Hawks; Downy Woodpecker; Loggerhead Shrike; Bewick's and House Wrens.

Best times to bird: All year; April through July for breeding birds.

Directions: For **Kaweah Oaks:** From the junction of California Highway 99 and California Highway 198 west of Visalia, go 13.4 miles east on CA 198 through Visalia to Road 182. Turn north on Road 182 and go 0.5 mile to a gravel parking lot on the left side of the road. For **Yokohl Valley,** from the junction of California Highway 65 and CA 198 east of Visalia, go about 3.3 miles east on CA 198 to Yokohl Drive (called Yokohl Valley Road on some maps), where a sign reads "Balch Park, 42 miles." Turn south on Yokohl Drive.

The birding: From the **Kaweah Oaks** parking lot, walk about 0.2 mile across the open field to a location with picnic tables and a chemical toilet, and then 0.2 mile more to a footbridge on the left. When you pass through a gate with a snap fastener, be sure to close the gate behind you because there may be cattle in the field. After you cross the footbridge and a dam that holds back a pond, you will come to a nature trail loop, then another footbridge, and another trail loop. Each loop is

77 Kaweah Oaks and Yokohl Valley

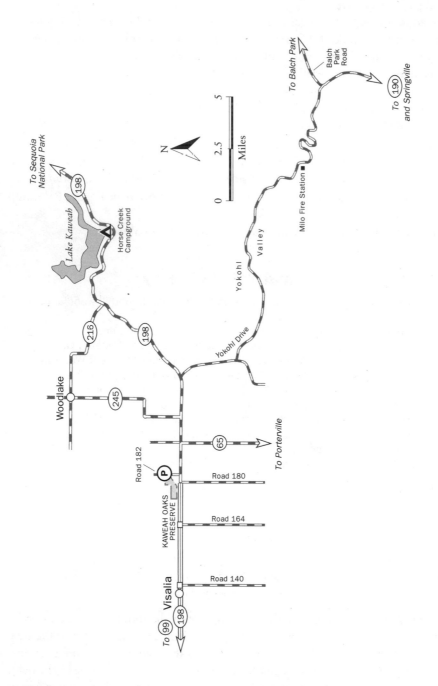

about 0.2 mile long. The round trip from the parking lot, including both trail loops, is about 1.5 miles

In the woods you will probably find resident Red-shouldered Hawk; Anna's Hummingbird; Acorn, Nuttall's, and Downy Woodpeckers; Western Scrub-Jay; Bushtit; Bewick's Wren; Spotted Towhee; and House Finch. Wood Ducks could be on the pond. In the more open areas, especially near water, look for Great Blue Heron, Great Egret, Belted Kingfisher, and Black Phoebe. Red-tailed Hawks, Killdeer, and Loggerhead Shrikes might be anywhere.

Typical summer visitors are Black-chinned Hummingbird (uncommon), Western Wood-Pewee, Ash-throated Flycatcher, Tree Swallow (a few stay around during the winter), House Wren, Black-headed Grosbeak, Lazuli Bunting, and Bullock's Oriole. Golden-crowned and White-crowned Sparrows and Dark-eyed Juncos are common winter visitors. Look also, especially in winter, for Sharp-shinned and Cooper's Hawks.

The first part of the trip on **Yokohl Drive** is through open grasslands in a broad valley, and then through oak savanna and foothill woodland. The total route is 28 miles from CA 198 to California Highway 190 near Springville, and is on good paved road. Houses are few, and the traffic in general is light. Look for raptors such as Golden Eagle (uncommon), Red-tailed Hawk, and American Kestrel, and in winter, for Rough-legged Hawk. Western Meadowlark (resident) and Western Kingbird (summer) are common.

As you enter foothill woodland, look for resident Acorn Woodpecker, House Wren, and Western Bluebird, and for summer visitors such as Ash-throated Flycatcher and Bullock's Oriole. The Milo Fire Station is about 16.5 miles from CA 198, and offers a good place to park. Most of the birds mentioned above are here, plus Red-shouldered Hawk, California Quail, Oak Titmouse, California Towhee, and Lesser Goldfinch, all resident. At 19 miles from CA 198 you will cross over a divide at about 2,700 feet of elevation, meet Balch Park Road at 22 miles from CA 198, and descend to CA 190 just outside Springville. On this side, especially after Balch Park Road, the houses are more frequent and the traffic is heavier. At CA 190 you can turn east to go to Quaking Aspen and the Western Divide Highway, or turn west to Success Lake and Porterville.

Spotted Dove, an introduced species that has become established in Los Angeles, has also been reported from Porterville, Bakersfield, and Fresno. Bakersfield is outside the region covered by this guide, and the species has not been seen in recent years in Porterville. However, there have been recent sightings in **Fresno** (about 28 miles north of Visalia), in the old Fig Garden area. To get there, exit from CA 99 north of downtown Fresno at Ashlan Avenue, go west about 3.5 miles to North Maroa Avenue. Check the residential streets in the area surrounding North Maroa, bounded by East Ashlan Avenue, North College Avenue, East Lansing Way, and North Van Ness Boulevard. Portions of this area have luxuriant plantings, with many large trees. There is no guarantee that you will see a Spotted Dove, but this is where they are regularly found.

General information: Kaweah Oaks consists of about 300 acres owned by The Nature Conservancy. It is essentially a riparian jungle, with valley oak, sycamore, cottonwood, willow, elderberry, blackberry, and wild rose, with huge grapevines in the oaks. The route through Yokohl Valley offers a fine example of southern Sierra foothill country and provides a shortcut from CA 198, the Sequoia National Park entrance highway, over to CA 190, the route leading up the Tule River to Quaking Aspen and Redwood Meadow.

ADDITIONAL HELP

Map grid: DeLorme Southern/Central California Atlas, page 37, 4B, 7C.
Elevation: 350 to 2,700 feet.
Hazards: Rattlesnakes, ticks, poison oak.
Nearest food, gas, lodging: Visalia.
Camping: Horse Creek: 87 sites, reduced to 37 sites when lake level is high; about 14 miles east of junction of CA 65 and CA 198, on CA 198, at Lake Kaweah (U.S. Army Corps of Engineers); RV dump station.
For more information: For Kaweah Oaks—Four Creeks Land Trust; Lake Kaweah (Corps of Engineers).

78 Bartlett Park and Success Lake

Habitats: Lake, stream, riparian woodland, foothill woodland, valley grassland.
Specialty birds: *Resident*—Western Grebe, Wood Duck, Anna's Hummingbird, Nuttall's Woodpecker, Oak Titmouse, Western Bluebird, Rufous-crowned Sparrow, Lesser Goldfinch. *Summer*—Black Swift, Western Kingbird. *Migrant*—Rufous Hummingbird.
Other key birds: *Resident*—Mourning Dove, Belted Kingfisher, Bewick's Wren, House Finch. *Summer*—House Wren.
Best times to bird: April through August for summer breeders; Success Lake has wintering waterfowl November through March.

Directions: For **Bartlett Park:** From the junction of California Highway 65 and California Highway 190 in Porterville, go about 5.7 miles east on CA 190, turn left on Road 284 and follow signs about 1 mile to the park entrance. For the headquarters area of **Success Lake** and **Big Sycamore Nature Trail,** go about 7.4 miles from the junction of CA 65 and CA 190 on CA 190, and turn left to the headquarters.

The birding: The best birding is at **Bartlett Park** except on weekends, when it is crowded. After entering the park (fee), drive to the opposite side of the park and park near the levee along the Tule River. Walk north along the levee toward the dam, which gives you excellent views into the river, and may have Wood Ducks and other waterfowl. Belted Kingfishers, Black Phoebes, and Song Sparrows are likely to be near the water, and birds such as Mourning Dove, Nuttall's Woodpecker,

78 Bartlett Park and Success Lake

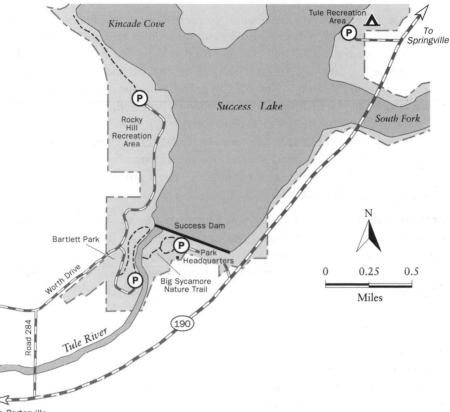

Bewick's and House Wrens, House Finch, Lesser Goldfinch, and, of course, Western Scrub-Jay should be in the trees.

When you get close to the dam, take the gravel road that begins just behind the water treatment plant, and return to the main part of Bartlett Park. This leads you back through drier habitat with lots of tree tobacco, so keep your eye open for Anna's Hummingbird and perhaps a migrating Rufous Hummingbird. This is a good place to look for California Quail, Oak Titmouse, and California Towhee. In the well-groomed part of the park, don't overlook the opportunity to spot a Western Kingbird or Western Bluebird. In June and early July it is possible to see Black Swifts in the late afternoon (6 to 8 P.M.) returning to their nest sites in the mountains after foraging over the San Joaquin Valley.

The **Big Sycamore Nature Trail,** on the opposite side of Tule River, begins and ends near the Success Lake headquarters building. The trail has birds similar to those already listed for this site, but leads through somewhat denser riparian habitat, with many large California sycamore trees. It is possible to get to the Big

Sycamore Nature Trail from Bartlett Park by walking all the way up the levee to the base of the dam, crossing over, and coming back down the levee on the opposite side.

On the approach to Bartlett Park, if you continue straight instead of turning into the park, you will come to the **Rocky Hill Recreation Area** and **Kincade Cove.** The paved road extends 2.7 miles beyond Bartlett Park, and it is even possible to drive a bit farther on a dirt road if it isn't too muddy. Beyond that, you can walk the dirt road to get views into Kincade Cove. The area is primarily grassland, and characteristic birds are Mourning Dove, Western Kingbird, and Western Meadowlark. Check also for Rufous-crowned Sparrow. In summer a Western Grebe or two may be on the lake, and herons and egrets often congregate along the shores of Kincade Cove. This is a good place to look for waterfowl in late fall and winter, although the area is also managed for hunting. Great-tailed Grackles have occasionally been seen around the lake.

General information: Success Lake was constructed by the U.S. Army Corps of Engineers and has extensive recreational development. The main focus is on fishing and waterfowl hunting, but the riparian area just below the dam has excellent bird habitat. Bartlett Park is owned by the Corps of Engineers but is operated by Tulare County.

ADDITIONAL HELP

Map grid: DeLorme Southern/Central California Atlas, page 37, 6D.
Elevation: 1,000 feet.
Hazards: Poison oak, rattlesnakes, ticks.
Nearest food, gas, lodging: Porterville.
Camping: Tule Recreation Area: 104 sites, on CA 190 about 9 miles east from Porterville, on Success Lake; RV dump station.
For more information: U.S. Army Corps of Engineers, Success Lake.

79 Western Divide Highway ♿

Habitats: Mixed conifer forest, meadow, chaparral.

Specialty birds: *Resident*—Northern Goshawk; Mountain Quail; Red-breasted Sapsucker; White-headed Woodpecker; Steller's Jay; Townsend's Solitaire; Wrentit; Cassin's Finch. *Summer*—Black Swift; Calliope Hummingbird; Western Wood-Pewee; Hammond's Flycatcher; Black-throated Gray, MacGillivray's, and Hermit Warblers; Green-tailed Towhee; Black-chinned Sparrow; Lazuli Bunting; Bullock's Oriole.

Other key birds: *Resident*—Hairy Woodpecker; Red-breasted and White-breasted Nuthatches; Red Crossbill; Evening Grosbeak. *Summer*—Olive-sided Flycatcher; Warbling Vireo; Blue-gray Gnatcatcher; Orange-crowned, Nashville, Yellow-rumped, and Wilson's Warblers; Chipping Sparrow.

Best times to bird: April through June for lower elevations such as at Milepost 3; May to August for Quaking Aspen and Redwood Meadow.

Directions: From Porterville, go east on California Highway 190 about 41 miles (allow 1.75 hours) to Quaking Aspen Campground. Redwood Meadow is about 13.5 miles farther. Before heading into the mountains, make sure your gas tank is full. The road may not be cleared of snow until May.

The birding: The beginning point is at **Quaking Aspen Campground**, where there is a lovely meadow with lots of birdy habitat and usually not many people. The group campground, if not occupied, can be attractive. (Note: a sign reads, "No Picnicking Please.") The bushes here may harbor Red-breasted Sapsucker, Green-tailed Towhee, and MacGillivray's and Orange-crowned Warblers. Birds of the forested areas are Hairy and White-headed Woodpeckers; Western Wood-Pewee; Steller's Jay; Common Raven; Mountain Chickadee; Red-breasted and White-breasted Nuthatches; Brown Creeper; Townsend's Solitaire (uncommon); and Hermit and Yellow-rumped Warblers. Red Crossbills and Evening Grosbeaks occur, but are irregular.

After birding Quaking Aspen, go back down the main road toward Camp Nelson 0.2 mile to Forest Road 21S50 (paved), and take it toward the northeast (the sign says the road goes to Golden Trout Pack Station). After 0.4 mile, turn right on a dirt road and then almost immediately turn left, at the sign for **Freeman Creek Trailhead**. The trailhead is about 0.3 mile down the road (dirt, but passable for ordinary cars unless muddy). Park when you get to a gate. The trail goes downhill to the Freeman Creek Grove of giant sequoias (about 6 miles round trip). The first part of the trail passes near meadows and a small stream, with birds similar to those at Quaking Aspen. Watch for Calliope Hummingbird.

On the way to Redwood Meadow, you might want to stop briefly at **Dome Rock**. The dirt road (passable for ordinary cars unless muddy) turns toward the east about 3.5 miles south of Quaking Aspen, and goes 0.6 mile to a parking area. Walk about 200 yards past a gate up an old rocky road to the summit. Dome Rock does not offer anything special of birding interest, except for the possibility of

79 Western Divide Highway

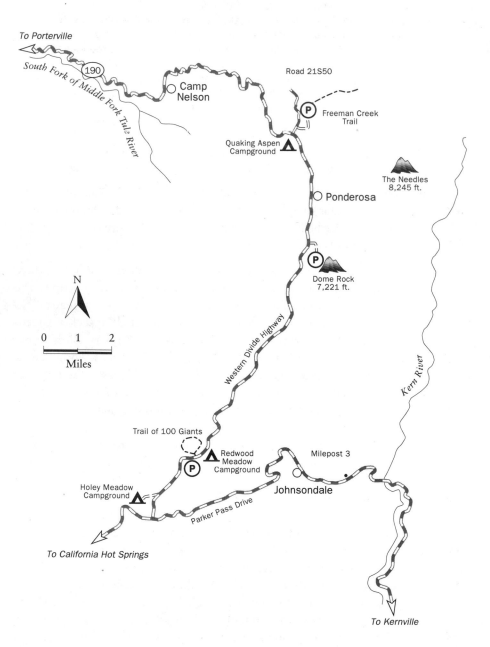

To Porterville

South Fork of Middle Fork Tule River

190

Road 21S50

Camp Nelson

P Freeman Creek Trail

Quaking Aspen Campground

The Needles 8,245 ft.

Ponderosa

Dome Rock 7,221 ft.

P

N

0   1   2
Miles

Western Divide Highway

Kern River

Trail of 100 Giants

Redwood Meadow Campground

P

Milepost 3

Holey Meadow Campground

Johnsondale

Parker Pass Drive

To California Hot Springs

To Kernville

spotting a soaring Golden Eagle, but gives great views of the Kern River below, the Needles to the north, and the Kern Plateau to the east.

Redwood Meadow, about 13.5 miles south of Quaking Aspen, is a delightful place, with a campground, meadow, and lovely grove of giant sequoias. A large parking area (fee, restrooms) just south of the campground gives access to the barrier-free **Trail of 100 Giants,** which circles through the sequoia grove. Look for Olive-sided and Hammond's Flycatchers, Warbling Vireo, and Chipping Sparrow, as well as the birds listed previously for Quaking Aspen. Cassin's Finch is resident. A pair of Northern Goshawks has nested near the trail in some years.

Holey Meadow is about 2.3 miles south of Redwood Meadow. The birds are similar to those already listed, but some quiet moments can be experienced here by birding along the campground access road (dirt, about 0.5 mile long) and along the meadow edges.

Less than 0.5 mile beyond Holey Meadow, the Western Divide Highway intersects Parker Pass Drive, which goes to California Hot Springs on the right, and to Johnsondale and Kernville on the left. The road is paved all the way to Kernville, a distance of 30 miles, and is steep enough in spots so that the use of lower gears is advisable. About 10 miles after turning toward Kernville, pause near **Milepost 3** (look for a small sign next to the road marking the mileage from Johnsondale, on the uphill side), park directly across the road in a wide pullout, and walk uphill about 100 yards to where you can stand safely off the road and look over the canyon slopes below. Birds to look for here are summer visitors such as Black Swift (uncommon in June); Blue-gray Gnatcatcher; Nashville and Black-throated Gray Warblers; Black-chinned Sparrow; Lazuli Bunting; and Bullock's Oriole, and resident birds such as Mountain Quail; Wrentit; and Spotted and California Towhees.

General information: The Western Divide Highway has many of the qualities of Sequoia National Park, but with only a fraction of the crowds. The road up from the foothills is steep, narrow, and twisty. When you get to about the 6,000-foot level, the road turns into an excellent high-standard highway through a wonderful forest next to emerald meadows, much like the Generals Highway from Giant Forest to Grant Grove. There is even a grove of giant sequoia trees. The campgrounds are generally peaceful, except on weekends, when they fill up.

ADDITIONAL HELP

Map grid: DeLorme Southern/Central California Atlas, page 38, 2C, 2D; page 50, 2A, 3A.
Elevation: 4,500 to 7,000 feet.
Hazards: Exposure to high-elevation sun; rattlesnakes; ticks.
Nearest food, gas, lodging: Porterville; Kernville.
Camping: Quaking Aspen: 32 sites, on CA 190 41 miles from Porterville. Redwood Meadow: 15 sites, on Western Divide Highway about 13.5 miles from Quaking

Aspen. Holey Meadow: 10 sites, 0.5 mile off the Western Divide Highway on a dirt side road, about 16 miles from Quaking Aspen.

For more information: For Quaking Aspen, Tule River Ranger District; for Redwood Meadow, Hot Springs Ranger District.

80 Kern River Valley

Habitats: Riparian woodland, lake, stream, valley grassland, chaparral, Joshua tree woodland, pinyon-juniper woodland, sagebrush scrub.

Specialty birds: *Resident*—Western and Clark's Grebes; Wood Duck; Golden Eagle; Prairie Falcon; Chukar; Mountain Quail; Greater Roadrunner; Nuttall's and Ladder-backed Woodpeckers; Say's Phoebe; Pinyon Jay; Rock, Canyon, and Cactus Wrens; Western Bluebird; California Thrasher; Phainopepla; Black-throated and Sage Sparrows; Tricolored Blackbird; Lesser Goldfinch. *Summer*—Cinnamon Teal; Osprey; Yellow-billed Cuckoo; Lesser Nighthawk; Common Poorwill; Black-chinned and Costa's Hummingbirds; Western Wood-Pewee; Willow, Vermilion, Ash-throated, and Brown-crested Flycatchers; Western Kingbird; Brewer's and Black-chinned Sparrows; Black-headed Grosbeak; Lazuli Bunting; Yellow-headed Blackbird; Bullock's, Hooded, and Scott's Orioles; Lawrence's Goldfinch. *Winter*—Ferruginous Hawk. *Migrant*—Hammond's, Dusky, Gray, and Pacific-slope Flycatchers; MacGillivray's Warbler; Western Tanager.

Other key birds: *Resident*—Hairy Woodpecker. *Summer*—Turkey Vulture, Yellow Warbler, Common Yellowthroat, Yellow-breasted Chat, Summer Tanager, Blue Grosbeak, Indigo Bunting. *Winter*—Bonaparte's Gull. *Migrant*—Solitary Sandpiper, Wilson's Warbler.

Best times to bird: Late April through July.

Directions: From Bakersfield, go about 43 miles east on California Highway 178 (about 1 hour) to the community of Lake Isabella which lies next to the dam that holds back Isabella Lake. The **Kern River Preserve** is 12 miles beyond Lake Isabella to the east, on CA 178. Kernville is 13 miles to the north from the junction of CA 178 and California Highway 155. Directions to the various sites given below are all referenced to a starting point at the junction of CA 178 and Sierra Way, which is 1.1 miles west of the entrance to the Kern River Preserve.

The birding: Every April, the Kern River Preserve and Kernville host the **Kern Valley Bioregions Festival,** which features field trips, workshops, and exhibits. For more information, contact Kern Valley Bioregions Festival at the address in Appendix A.

Kern River Preserve is open dawn to dusk, 7 days a week (fee, parking, restrooms, visitor center). The preserve has many unusual nesting species for California, but the Yellow-billed Cuckoo (state-listed threatened) is probably the most famous. Cuckoos, never easy to see, are best found in the riparian areas from late June through July. Another species for which the preserve is well known is the "Southwestern" Willow Flycatcher, which is federally listed endangered. More

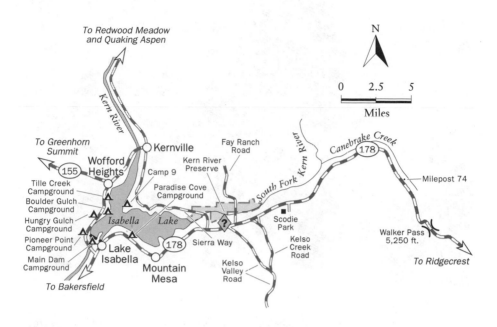

than one-third of California's known "Southwestern" Willow Flycatchers nest in the valley, and they are sometimes seen next to the preserve headquarters. In addition, the preserve has nesting Brown-crested Flycatchers (rare), Summer Tanagers (fairly common), and Indigo Buntings (rare). Even Red-eyed Vireo (extremely rare) and Vermilion Flycatcher (rare) have nested in the valley. Birders who have been searching for a place where they can see Tricolored Blackbird or Lawrence's Goldfinch have a good chance of finding both species in the valley, sometimes at the preserve headquarters. The preserve personnel maintain a "Birders' Board" at the headquarters, which gives the locations of recent sightings of key species.

The River Trail, a self-guided nature trail 1.5 miles round trip, is highly recommended. The trail passes through some restoration areas, and then makes a loop along the South Fork of the Kern River through mature riparian forest.

Some resident birds are Anna's Hummingbird; Nuttall's and Hairy Woodpeckers; Western Bluebird; and Lesser Goldfinch. Some fairly common summer visitors are Black-chinned Hummingbird, Western Wood-Pewee, Ash-throated Flycatcher, Western Kingbird, Yellow Warbler, Common Yellowthroat, Lazuli Bunting, and Black-headed and Blue Grosbeaks. Phainopepla is an uncommon resident, and Yellow-breasted Chat, Yellow-headed Blackbird, and Bullock's Oriole are uncommon summer visitors. Some fairly common migrants are Pacific-slope Flycatcher, Wilson's and MacGillivray's Warblers, and Western Tanager. Some uncommon ones are Hammond's, Dusky, and Gray Flycatchers.

Birders at Kern River Preserve.

On Isabella Lake, look for Western and Clark's Grebes, Osprey, and Bonaparte's, Ring-billed, California, and Herring Gulls.

Fay Ranch Road: From the junction of CA 178 and Sierra Way, go 1.9 miles east on CA 178 to Fay Ranch Road, and turn north. In 0.4 mile you will come to the South Fork of the Kern River. Park here and bird the road edges. Portions of the road adjoin private property, so it is important to stay on the road.

The birds along the river are similar to those at the Kern River Preserve; however, there are some quiet water stretches visible from the road where Wood Duck and Cinnamon Teal are sometimes seen. Also look for Solitary Sandpiper (rare) in wet areas west of the bridge in late April and early May. At dusk in summer, watch for Lesser Nighthawks foraging over the road just north of the bridge.

Continue 1.4 miles farther north, to where the paved road makes an abrupt right-angle turn to the left, and there are dry brushy slopes. Cactus Wren can be seen here (more often, heard), as well as Black-throated Sparrow. Both are uncommon residents. Common Poorwills can sometimes be heard at dusk.

Kelso Creek Road: From the junction of California Highway 178 and Sierra Way, go 3.2 miles east on CA 178 to Kelso Creek Road, on the south. Turn on Kelso Creek Road, drive 4.4 miles to Kelso Valley Road, and turn right (north) to return to CA 178, a loop trip of about 9.5 miles. Note that the valley traversed by this loop is *not* Kelso Valley, which lies beyond the divide, but more properly might be called Kelso Creek Valley. This route gives access to an unusual mixture of landscapes, combining rocky desert slopes, green agricultural fields, Joshua tree woodland, and pastureland. Birds to look for are Golden Eagle, Ferruginous Hawk (winter), Prairie Falcon, and Common Raven. The presence of extensive stands of Joshua trees is evidence of the diversity for which the region is famous. Ladder-backed Woodpecker, Cactus Wren, Black-throated Sparrow, and Scott's Oriole (summer) can be found here. This is good country for Say's Phoebes (resident), and Western Kingbirds abound in spring and summer.

A Chukar might be spotted in the rockier sections, and Bendire's Thrasher (exceedingly rare in this location) has been found nesting. LeConte's Thrasher (exceedingly rare) has also been found here, but you should be careful to not confuse it with California Thrasher. California Thrasher is dark all over, whereas LeConte's tends to be lighter colored on the body, and the body contrasts with a dark tail.

Every September this is the site of the Turkey Vulture count, which is a feature of the annual **Turkey Vulture Festival.** In 1996 almost 33,000 Turkey Vultures passed over the Kern River valley, in addition to hundreds of hawks and eagles. For more information, contact Vulture Festival (see Appendix A).

Scodie Park: From the junction of CA 178 and Sierra Way, travel 6.5 miles east on CA 178 and turn right (south) to Scodie Park, which lies 0.3 mile from CA 178 (parking, restrooms). If you missed Lawrence's Goldfinch at the Kern River Preserve, this is a good place to look for it; listen for its tinkling song. Hooded Orioles nest nearby in summer along the upper edge of the park near Cypress Street. They have nested in a couple of small fan palms here, located on private property.

Milepost 74 and **Walker Pass:** From the junction of CA 178 and Sierra Way, go 17.9 miles east on CA 178, watching for the mileages on the white paddle-shaped markers at the road edge. Near Milepost 74 is a short dirt loop on the left side of the road that offers ample parking. Take care when walking on the road shoulders because the traffic moves fast. There are a few cottonwoods here that may shelter Nuttall's and Ladder-backed Woodpeckers, because the Kern River valley is where the two species overlap. The white barring on the back of the Ladder-backed is more pronounced than on the Nuttall's, and extends higher up onto the nape. Also, there is more white on the face of the Ladder-backed than on the Nuttall's, and the black lines are narrower and more crisply outlined. You might even see a hybrid, which will show intermediate characteristics of the two.

Milepost 74 is good for Mountain Quail, Ash-throated Flycatcher, Cactus Wren, Canyon and Rock Wrens, California Thrasher, and Scott's Oriole. Mountain Quail can be hard to see, but is often heard in the spring because of its loud *"quee-ark"* call, which can be heard a mile away. This is a good spot, also, for the hard-to-find Black-chinned Sparrow (spring). Listen for its song on the steep hillsides, which starts with a slow *"sweet sweet sweet,"* and then speeds up into a rapid trill. Watch for Costa's Hummingbird (rare summer visitor).

About 1.3 miles back down the hill from Milepost 74 is a pleasant little oasis with ample parking on the north side of the road, adjacent to willow habitat. There is a bit of marsh, with tules and cattails, and resident birds such as Nuttall's Woodpecker, Bushtit, Bewick's Wren, Song Sparrow, and winter visitors such as Yellow-rumped Warbler.

There is a great deal of pinyon pine between here and the top of Walker Pass (5,250 feet), and it is a good idea to keep your eyes open for Pinyon Jays, which favor this particular habitat. They tend to travel in flocks, and you often hear them before you see them. Also, be alert for the possibility of Brewer's and Sage Sparrows.

General information: Kern River Valley must be counted as one of the best birding sites in California because of its diversity. The South Fork of the Kern River supports the largest remaining stand of Great Valley cottonwood-willow riparian forest in California, and has been designated a Globally Important Bird Area, because it is a major migration path for Turkey Vultures (28,000 per year), because of its breeding southwestern Willow Flycatchers (federally endangered species), and because almost the entire world population of Kern Red-winged Blackbird (a subspecies of Red-winged) is located in the valley. A total of 318 species of birds have been recorded in the valley, with 2,000 species of plants (almost a third of the flora of California) and 115 mammals (the highest diversity in the United States) in the immediate area. In 1997 National Audubon Society—California took over the management of the Kern River Preserve from The Nature Conservancy.

ADDITIONAL HELP

Map grid: DeLorme Southern/Central California Atlas, page 50, 3C; page 51, 6C.
Elevation: 2,600 to 5,250 feet
Hazards: Fast automobile traffic, rattlesnakes, ticks.
Nearest food, gas, lodging: Kernville; Wofford Heights; Mountain Mesa.
Campgrounds: Main Dam: 82 sites, at the southern end of Isabella Lake on CA 155; RV dump station. Pioneer Point: 78 sites, on the west side of Isabella Lake on CA 155. Hungry Gulch: 78 sites, on the west side of Isabella Lake on CA 155. Boulder Gulch: 78 sites, on the west side of Isabella Lake on CA 155. Tillie Creek: 159 sites, south of Wofford Heights on CA 155; RV dump station. Paradise Cove: 138 sites, on the south shore of Isabella Lake on CA 178; RV dump station. Camp 9: 109 sites, on the east side of Isabella Lake, off Sierra Way; RV dump station.
For more information: Kern River Preserve.

81 White Mountains 🏚

Habitats: Pinyon-juniper woodland, sagebrush scrub, bristlecone-limber pine woodland, subalpine zone.
Specialty birds: *Resident*—Chukar, Pinyon Jay, Clark's Nutcracker, Juniper Titmouse, Pygmy Nuthatch, Rock Wren, Cassin's Finch. *Summer*—Broad-tailed Hummingbird; Dusky and Gray Flycatchers; Plumbeous Vireo; Violet-green Swallow; Mountain Bluebird; Black-throated Gray Warbler; Green-tailed Towhee; Brewer's Sparrow; Black-headed Grosbeak; Lazuli Bunting
Other key birds: *Resident*—Great Horned and Long-eared Owls; White-breasted Nuthatch. *Summer*—Olive-sided Flycatcher, Blue-gray Gnatcatcher, Hermit Thrush, Yellow-rumped Warbler, Chipping Sparrow, "Gray-headed" Dark-eyed Junco.
Best times to bird: Late spring through summer; the Ancient Bristlecone Pine Forest is generally open from June to October (roads closed by snow in winter).

Directions: From the junction of U.S. Highway 395 and California Highway 168 on the north edge of Big Pine, it is about 7.9 miles on CA 168 to **Tollhouse Spring,** and about 5 miles farther to **Cedar Flat,** which is at the junction with White Mountain Road. **Westgard Pass** lies about 0.8 mile beyond the junction, on CA 168. It is 5.3 miles to **Grandview Campground** along White Mountain Road, and another 5 miles to **Schulman Grove.** The road to Schulman Grove is paved, although winding and steep in places (use lower gears on return). Be sure you have a full tank of gas before you start out because there are no services after leaving Big Pine.

The birding: When you're on your way to the higher mountains, a stop at **Tollhouse Spring** (6,000 feet) is worthwhile. There is a small dirt parking area here, and two springs—one is piped into an old concrete watering trough, and the other is on the hillside above a small grove of cottonwoods. A rough trail climbs the hillside for about 100 yards to a point above the latter spring. Here you can sit and watch the birds from above and admire the view of the Sierra Nevada to the west. This is a good place for migrants because most of the countryside in the nearby region is desertlike. Look for Spotted Towhee (resident), and Lazuli Bunting and House Finch in summer. Pinyon Jays have been spotted coming for water, and Chukars have been seen on the nearby hillsides.

About 2 miles above Tollhouse Spring, the road enters a narrow canyon with a one-way stretch (The Narrows), where it is essential to watch for opposing traffic. Also, if it is raining anywhere nearby, be alert for flash floods. The general rule is, if a dip in the road has water in it, don't proceed, but wait for the water to go down.

From the Narrows to **Westgard Pass** and **Cedar Flat** and beyond, you are in pinyon-juniper woodland. As you emerge from the Narrows, look for Plumbeous Vireo on the slopes in summer, and also for Rock Wren (resident), Blue-gray Gnatcatcher, and Mountain Bluebird (the last two, summer visitors). Other species in the pinyons and junipers are Broad-tailed Hummingbird, Gray Flycatcher, Pinyon

81 White Mountains

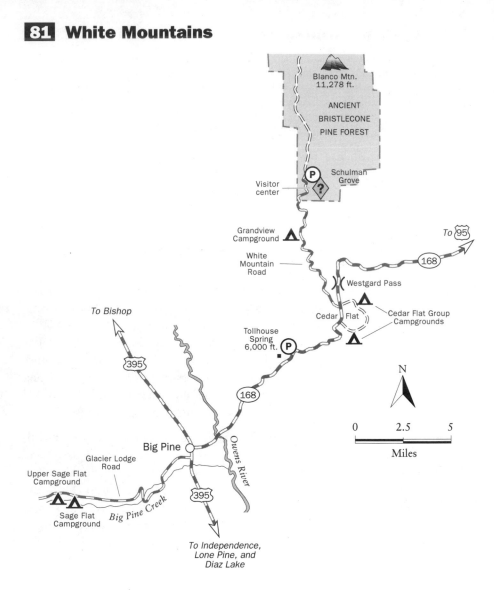

Jay, Violet-green Swallow, Juniper Titmouse, Bushtit, White-breasted Nuthatch, Black-throated Gray Warbler, Chipping and Brewer's Sparrows, and Black-headed Grosbeak. Great Horned Owl is fairly common, and Long-eared Owl (uncommon) may be in the dense pinyons. Dark-eyed Juncos are summer visitors—both the "Oregon" and the "Gray-headed" (uncommon). A drive around the dirt road that makes the circuit of the group campgrounds at Cedar Flat takes you through good pinyon-juniper habitat (may be impassable in wet weather).

The region has developed a special interest for birders since 1997, when the Plain Titmouse was split into Oak Titmouse and Juniper Titmouse, and the Solitary

Vireo was split into Cassin's, Plumbeous, and Blue-headed Vireos. Juniper Titmouse is paler and grayer than the one along the coast, now called Oak Titmouse. Also, the two species have different songs. The Oak Titmouse sings a ringing *"pee-two pee-two pee-two,"* whereas the Juniper Titmouse makes a sound more like a rattle, with a series of rapid syllables at a steady frequency. However, just to make things tough for birders, Juniper Titmice sometimes produce a loud *"pee-two pee-two pee-two"* that resembles the song of the Oak Titmouse. Both species give a *"tsicka dee dee"* call. Juniper Titmice are more patchily distributed than are Oak Titmice, so it may take some searching to find one. It is helpful to listen for the "rattle" call.

The Plumbeous Vireo, which is in California only in this restricted area east of the Sierra Nevada, is a relatively large vireo, mostly gray and white. The Cassin's Vireo (primarily on the coast) has more of an olive green back and rump, with yellowish flanks. Plumbeous Vireos have sometimes been mistaken for Gray Vireos. (The third member of the former "Solitary" Vireo complex, the eastern Blue-headed Vireo, does not occur in California except as a vagrant.) Ned Johnson and Carla Cicero, authorities on the birds of the White Mountains, state that pairs of Plumbeous Vireos are generally so widely spaced that only four or five may be encountered in a hike of several miles through appropriate habitat.

The **Grandview Campground** is situated in a shallow bowl, and if it is not too crowded, it can offer attractive birding on the surrounding slopes. Pinyon Jays are regular, and Black-throated Gray Warblers are common. If a male Broad-tailed Hummingbird is in the area, you are more likely to hear it (a loud cricketlike trill produced by the wings) than to see it.

It is inconceivable that one would come this far without going on to **Schulman Grove** (10,000 feet), site of the oldest living bristlecone pine, the Methuselah tree (4,600-plus years). The oldest trees are generally the most weathered-looking ones, squat and gnarled with lots of dead wood, usually with only a narrow strip of living tissue. Schulman Grove has a visitor center and two nature trails; the Discovery Trail, is about 0.8 mile round trip, and the Methuselah Trail, is a 4.5 mile round trip.

The bristlecone pines are generally mixed with limber pines. Some of the birds are the same as those at lower elevations, but in this habitat look for Olive-sided and Dusky Flycatchers; Clark's Nutcracker; Mountain Chickadee; Pygmy Nuthatch; Ruby-crowned Kinglet; Mountain Bluebird; Hermit Thrush; Yellow-rumped Warbler; Chipping Sparrow; and Cassin's Finch. In the sagebrush slopes nearby, Green-tailed Towhees (uncommon, at this elevation) can be found.

The road goes beyond the Schulman Grove another 16 miles or so, but it is a rough road, best traveled in a four-wheel drive vehicle. It takes you well above tree line, to 11,000 feet, and into an alpine landscape unlike anything else in California. The road over Tioga Pass in Yosemite comes the closest to it, but Tioga Pass, though dramatic and beautiful, seems almost pastoral in comparison with the moonscape on the top of the White Mountains.

The following two locations are not part of the White Mountains, but offer some good nearby birding opportunities. When you're traveling through Owens Valley on US 395, stop at **Diaz Lake**, about 3 miles south of Lone Pine, a delightful little oasis. Much of the lake is bordered by picnic grounds and campsites, but there are marshes along the edges with Yellow-headed Blackbirds. Great-tailed Grackles breed here, and at the southern end of the lake is a riparian patch with Bewick's Wren and Song Sparrow.

Directly opposite the White Mountains, and tucked up in the High Sierra against Middle Palisade Peak (14,040 feet) is Glacier Lodge, on **Big Pine Creek**. Glacier Lodge Road, a high-standard paved road, goes west from the center of Big Pine and ends 10.2 miles later at 7,700 feet, at Glacier Lodge. Look for Golden Eagle, Common Nighthawk, Red-breasted Sapsucker, Hairy Woodpecker, Western Wood-Pewee, Ash-throated Flycatcher, Warbling Vireo, Violet-green Swallow, Western Tanager, and Lazuli Bunting.

General information: The White Mountains lie parallel to the Sierra Nevada only 30 miles away, and are almost as high (White Mountain Peak is 14,246 feet; Mount Whitney is 14,494 feet). The White Mountains are more rounded than the Sierra, less glaciated, and have a vast alpine area reachable by auto. The range has great groves of bristlecone pines, the oldest living things on earth.

ADDITIONAL HELP

NCA&G grid: Page 123, 6C, 7C; page 124, 1A, 1C.
Elevation: 6,000 to 10,000 feet.
Hazards: Flash flooding, exposure to high-elevation sun, lightning, ticks, rattle-snakes.
Nearest food, gas, lodging: Big Pine, Bishop.
Camping: Grandview: 36 sites, 5.3 miles north from the junction of CA 168 and White Mountain Road, on White Mountain Road; dirt interior roads, no water. Sage Flat: 28 sites, 8.8 miles west of Big Pine, on Glacier Lodge Road. Upper Sage Flat: 21 sites, 9.4 miles west of Big Pine, on Glacier Lodge Road.
For more information: White Mountain Ranger District.

7. Specialty birds

In this chapter, 173 "specialty birds" are listed together with maps of Northern California showing their approximate distributions in summer and winter. The category "specialty birds" includes the "western specialties," (defined below) that occur regularly in Northern California, plus those classified as "endangered" or "threatened," and a few others of special interest. In general, this category consists of birds that people from other parts of the country might be especially interested in coming to California to see, and also includes those that could be of special interest to California birders.

A "western specialty" is a species that occurs primarily in the western part of the country (meaning mostly west of the Mississippi River), is found in Northern California at least at the "rare" level, and is considered "regular." It excludes those that occur on a "casual" or "accidental" basis. "Summer," in general, means April through August, and "winter" means October through February. However, note that these seasons may vary with respect to certain species, and they are discussed in more detail in Chapter 1.

Range maps of birds necessarily represent compromises. Small numbers of birds can almost always be found in places where they are not supposed to be, or at seasons when they are not supposed to be there. Other reasons for compromise are that sources of information are not always in agreement, and birds do not stop sharply at the boundaries of their regions; they may even be in the process of expanding their ranges. Hence, the range maps must be considered as general guides, not as absolutes. By their nature they cannot include indications of abundance. Abundance information is given in the next chapter, on bar graphs.

The principal sources for the maps are David Zeiner, et al., *California's Wildlife, Volume II: Birds,* California Department of Fish and Game (1990), and Joseph Grinnell and Alden Miller, *The Distribution of the Birds of California,* Cooper Ornithological Society (1944). These sources have been modified, where appropriate, by information from local checklists and especially by information from the following references: Edward Beedy and Stephen Granholm, *Discovering Sierra Birds,* Yosemite and Sequoia National History Associations (1985); David Gaines, *Birds of Yosemite and the East Slope,* Artemisia Press (1988); Stanley Harris, *Northwestern California Birds,* 2nd ed., Humboldt State University Press (1996); Don Roberson, *Monterey Birds,* Monterey Peninsula Audubon Society (1985); and Arnold Small, *California Birds: Their Status and Distribution,* Ibis Publishing Company (1994).

For each specialty bird, some helpful comments are provided, and some key sites are listed where the species might be found.

Pacific Loon

Comments: In winter, common along coast and in bays in Central California. In spring and fall, large numbers migrate northward along the coast. A few remain on coast in summer.

Key Sites: Point Reyes (Fish Docks), Bodega Harbor, Pillar Point Harbor, Monterey, and along coast generally.

Western Grebe

Comments: In winter, congregates along coast and in bays. In summer, breeds on large lakes in the interior, especially NE.

Key Sites: Lake Earl, Point Reyes (Fish Docks), Richardson Bay, Bodega Harbor, Klamath Basin, Clear Lake, Eagle Lake, Honey Lake, Lake Almanor.

Clark's Grebe

Comments: Often found with Western Grebes, but is not nearly as common.

Key Sites: Lake Earl, Point Reyes (Fish Docks), Richardson Bay, Bodega Harbor, Klamath Basin, Clear Lake, Eagle Lake, Honey Lake, Lake Almanor.

Laysan Albatross

Comments: Uncommon in winter, generally over deep water, with small numbers in May and June. Rarely seen from shore, although one bird regularly came into the Point Arena harbor on the Mendocino Coast in the winters of 1994 through 1998 to spend the nights near the pier.

Key Sites: Pelagic trips from Bodega Bay or Monterey Bay.

Black-footed Albatross

Comments: Fairly common well offshore, with small numbers occurring throughout the year. Best time is May to August. Occasionally seen from shore, especially after strong onshore winds, at places such as Point Pinos and Pigeon Point.

Key Sites: Pelagic trips from Monterey Bay or Bodega Bay.

Pink-footed Shearwater

Comments: Relatively common offshore in summer and fall, rare in winter. Occasionally seen from shore.

Key Sites: Pelagic trips from Monterey Bay or Bodega Bay.

Shaded areas indicate bird species distribution ■ Summer range ■ Winter range ▤ Permanent resident

▨ Special (e.g., post breeding, or seen only in migration)

Flesh-footed Shearwater

Comments: Rare offshore. Usually with other shearwaters. Numbers increase somewhat in late summer and early fall, although generally no more than one or two are seen per trip, if any.
Key Sites: Pelagic trips from Monterey Bay or Bodega Bay.

Buller's Shearwater

Comments: Uncommon well offshore in fall. Usually found with other shearwaters. May be more common in warm-water years.
Key Sites: Pelagic trips from Monterey Bay or Bodega Bay.

Short-tailed Shearwater

Comments: Uncommon winter visitor in open ocean. Requires excellent views for identification.
Key Sites: Pelagic trips from Monterey Bay or Bodega Bay.

Black-vented Shearwater

Comments: Often seen in coastal waters. Sometimes common, sometimes virtually absent, depending upon warm-water events such as El Niño. Individuals may start arriving in late August, and reach peak numbers in winter.
Key Sites: Pelagic trips from Monterey Bay. Often seen from shore, as at Point Pinos or Pigeon Point.

Fork-tailed Storm-Petrel

Comments: Uncommon. Breeds in Aleutian Islands, with a small breeding population in California on islands off north coast. Has been recorded throughout the year, but mostly in winter months.
Key Sites: Pelagic trips from Bodega Bay or Monterey Bay.

Ashy Storm-Petrel

Comments: Fairly common summer and early fall visitor, sometimes abundant. In September, thousands may congregate in Monterey Bay in great "rafts." Breeds on Farallon Islands.
Key Sites: Monterey Bay pelagic trips, in late summer and fall.

Shaded areas indicate bird species distribution   ■ Summer range   ■ Winter range   ▦ Permanent resident
▨ Special (e.g., post breeding, or seen only in migration)

Black Storm-Petrel
Comments: Common late summer and fall visitor, sometimes abundant. In September, thousands congregate with Ashy Storm-Petrels in huge "rafts" in Monterey Bay.
Key Sites: Monterey Bay pelagic trips in late summer and fall.

Least Storm-Petrel
Comments: Rare and irregular visitor in late summer and early fall. More common in Southern California than in the north, but small numbers may be seen in Northern California in El Niño years.
Key Sites: Annually, small numbers are found with large mixed flocks of storm-petrels on Monterey Bay.

Brown Pelican
Comments: Common in late summer and fall along the coast, in nearshore waters, and coastal bays. ("California" subspecies is classified as endangered by both the federal and state governments.)
Key Sites: Virtually any coastal site in late summer and fall. Elkhorn Slough has a large nighttime roost.

Brandt's Cormorant
Comments: Common resident along central coast, and common summer visitor on northern coast, on rocky cliffs and offshore islands.
Key Sites: Monterey Peninsula, Bodega Bay, Sonoma Coast. Almost never found away from ocean.

Pelagic Cormorant
Comments: Fairly common resident along coastline, on rocky cliffs and offshore islands. Contrary to its name, it is not a strongly pelagic species.
Key Sites: Virtually any rocky coastal site. Almost never found away from ocean.

White-faced Ibis
Comments: Uncommon, but status in state is complex and subject to change, because White-faced Ibises may move their nesting colonies from year to year. Wintering populations in Central Valley are increasing, but breeding locations are variable. Often feeds in flocks in agricultural fields.
Key Sites: Klamath Basin, Ash Creek Wildlife Area, Sierra Valley, San Luis Refuge Complex.

Shaded areas indicate bird species distribution   ■ Summer range   ■ Winter range   ▤ Permanent resident
                                    ▨ Special (e.g., post breeding, or seen only in migration)

Greater White-fronted Goose

Comments: Common winter visitor, sometimes in flocks numbering in the thousands, most arriving in November. Frequents freshwater lakes and marshes, and agricultural fields.

Key Sites: Sacramento National Wildlife Refuge, Gray Lodge, Yolo Bypass.

Ross's Goose

Comments: Common winter visitor, usually mixing with its larger relative, the Snow Goose. Frequents freshwater lakes and marshes.

Key Sites: Sacramento National Wildlife Refuge, Gray Lodge, Yolo Bypass, Merced National Wildlife Refuge.

"Aleutian" Canada Goose

Comments: Virtually the entire world population winters in the northern San Joaquin Valley. (This small subspecies of the Canada Goose is classified as threatened by the federal government.)

Key Sites: In fall, at Sacramento National Wildlife Refuge. In March and April, thousands gather at Castle Rock for migration.

Wood Duck

Comments: Uncommon. However, the Wood Duck population in California is on the increase because of a major nesting box program. They are very wary, and are often seen only when they flush, but flocks of hundreds have sometimes been seen in the fall.

Key Sites: Sacramento National Wildlife Refuge, Colusa National Wildlife Refuge, Gray Lodge.

Eurasian Wigeon

Comments: Rare winter visitor, but apparently on the increase. Usually found with American Wigeons.

Key Sites: Arcata Bottoms, Sacramento National Wildlife Refuge, Gray Lodge, Bolinas Lagoon.

Cinnamon Teal

Comments: Status is complex, but breeds in most of state, in ponds, marshes, and tidal estuaries. Appreciable numbers remain in parts of breeding range during winter.

Key Sites: Klamath Basin, Sacramento National Wildlife Refuge, Gray Lodge, Grizzly Island Wildlife Area, Yolo Bypass.

Shaded areas indicate bird species distribution ■ Summer range ■ Winter range ☰ Permanent resident
░ Special (e.g., post breeding, or seen only in migration)

Harlequin Duck

Comments: Rare in winter along rocky coastlines. Sometimes found in harbors. Breeds in rushing mountain streams from Oregon to Alaska. Occasionally reported in summer in Sierra, but breeding there has not been confirmed for many years.

Key Sites: Point St. George, Crescent City Harbor, Chimney Rock (Point Reyes).

Hooded Merganser

Comments: Uncommon winter visitor to ponds and quiet backwaters, usually those with vegetated margins. A small number breed in Northern California.

Key Sites: Tule Lake National Wildlife Refuge, Lake Almanor, Sacramento National Wildlife Refuge, Lake Solano/Putah Creek, Foster City.

Osprey

Comments: Uncommon breeder on coast, along rivers, and at mountain lakes. Builds conspicuous nests at the tops of tall trees.

Key Sites: Lake Almanor, Eagle Lake, Lake Hennessey.

White-tailed Kite

Comments: Formerly called Black-shouldered Kite. In some years, the highest "Christmas Counts" in the nation for this species have come from Benicia or Cosumnes River. Often forms large nighttime roosts in winter in cities in the Sacramento Valley, such as Yuba City and Davis.

Key Sites: Sacramento National Wildlife Refuge, Benicia, Grizzly Island, Yolo Farmlands, Cosumnes River, American River, San Luis Refuge Complex.

Bald Eagle

Comments: Uncommon to rare in most of area, but locally common in winter in Klamath Basin. Scattered breeding locations in northern part of state. (Classified as threatened by the federal government.)

Key Sites: Klamath Basin, Butte Valley, Eagle Lake, Sacramento National Wildlife Refuge, District 10.

Northern Goshawk

Comments: Uncommon to rare resident in coniferous forest in mountain areas. Your sighting may be only a glimpse of a hawk flying fast among the trees.

Key Sites: Hard to find anywhere in its range, but try Warner Mountains, Gerle Creek, and Giant Forest.

Shaded areas indicate bird species distribution ▮ Summer range ▮ Winter range ▤ Permanent resident
▨ Special (e.g., post breeding, or seen only in migration)

Swainson's Hawk

Comments: Uncommon to fairly common in northeast, and in lower Sacramento and Upper San Joaquin valleys from April to September. Migrates to Mexico and South America in winter, but small numbers have remained during recent winters in Delta Region near Stockton. (Classified as threatened by state government.)

Key Sites: Butte Valley, Sacramento, Yolo, and San Joaquin counties.

Ferruginous Hawk

Comments: Rare to common in open areas from October to March.

Key Sites: Butte Valley, Surprise Valley, Honey Lake, Sierra Valley, Sacramento Valley, Panoche Valley.

Golden Eagle

Comments: Uncommon resident in mountain areas, rolling foothills, desert edges, and oak savanna. Rare on immediate coast and in flat agricultural lands. Avoids dense forests.

Key Sites: Butte Valley, Modoc National Wildlife Refuge, Clear Lake, Mount Diablo, Del Puerto Canyon, Panoche Valley, Pinnacles, Kern River Valley.

Peregrine Falcon

Comments: Rare breeder, with numbers increasing in migration and in winter, but still rare at those times. A few pairs nest on rocky cliffs at the coast. Look for them during migration and winter seasons in locations where large numbers of shorebirds are present. (Classified as endangered by federal government.)

Key Sites: Arcata Marsh, Mendocino Coast, Point Reyes, Elkhorn Slough.

Prairie Falcon

Comments: Uncommon breeder in dry, open, and broken terrain with cliffs. Rare to uncommon winter visitor in other parts of state. A few usually spend the winter on the Northwest coastal plains, but they are generally absent otherwise in the Northwest.

Key Sites: Klamath Basin, Butte Valley, Modoc National Wildlife Refuge, Sierra Valley, Pinnacles, Panoche Valley, Mono Lake, Kern River Valley.

Chukar

Comments: Introduced species, originally from Middle East. Birds continue to be released into the wild for hunting purposes. Generally uncommon, although can be fairly common in some localities.

Key Sites: Panoche Valley, Tollhouse Spring (White Mountains).

Shaded areas indicate bird species distribution   ■ Summer range   ■ Winter range   ▤ Permanent resident

▨ Special (e.g., post breeding, or seen only in migration)

Sage Grouse

Comments: Uncommon resident of rolling hills and flats with sagebrush. In spring, (mostly, late March and early April), males strut and display early in the mornings at mating grounds called leks.

Key Sites: Shaffer Lek, north of Honey Lake, Bodie. (Note: some of the accessible leks described in the past have either become less accessible or inactive.)

White-tailed Ptarmigan

Comments: Introduced from Rocky Mountains circa 1971. A small population has established itself in alpine habitat along the east boundary of Yosemite National Park, centered around Tioga Pass.

Key Sites: Basin north of Saddlebag Lake, at about 11,000 feet.

Blue Grouse

Comments: Uncommon resident of coniferous forests to as high as 11,000 feet. Not very easy to find, but often tame when discovered, causing some people to call them "fool hens." Male makes vibrant, deep hooting call in spring.

Key Sites: Titlow Mountain Road, Yuba Pass, Carson Pass, Yosemite National Park, Sequoia National Park.

Mountain Quail

Comments: Fairly common in chaparral and montane forests, but difficult to see. Easy to hear in April and May, when male's loud *"quee-ark!"* call can be heard over long distances.

Key Sites: Titlow Mountain Road, Yuba Pass, Mix Canyon, Crystal Basin.

California Quail

Comments: Widespread common resident in chaparral, brushlands, oak savanna, and riparian habitats, but generally not in heavily forested zones. Male makes characteristic call which sounds like *"chi-CA-go!"*

Key Sites: One of the easiest birds to see. Some representative locations are Klamath Basin, Clear Lake, Skyline Wilderness Park, Mount Diablo, and Bartlett Park.

Black Rail

Comments: Rare to uncommon resident, difficult to see. In some years, the highest "Christmas Counts" in the nation have come from Benicia, where these birds are primarily detected by their vocalizations at night. ("California" subspecies is classified as threatened by state.)

Key Sites: Best chance for seeing Black Rail is during extremely high December tides at Palo Alto Baylands.

Shaded areas indicate bird species distribution █ Summer range ■ Winter range ▤ Permanent resident
▒ Special (e.g., post breeding, or seen only in migration)

Clapper Rail

Comments: Populations are currently found only in the Suisun and San Francisco bays. ("California" subspecies is classified as endangered by both the federal and state governments.)

Key Sites: Palo Alto Baylands, at high December tides. They are also sometimes seen feeding in tidal channels at low tides.

Sandhill Crane

Comments: "Lesser" and "Greater" Sandhill Cranes both winter in the state, and the winter range is shown for the combined species. The summer range shown is for "Greaters" only. "Lessers" do not breed in California. ("Greater" subspecies is classified as threatened by state government.)

Key Sites: Consumnes Preserve, Woodbridge Road, Merced National Wildlife Refuge.

Pacific Golden-Plover

Comments: Very rare to rare winter visitor along coast at estuaries and in short-grass fields. Occasionally occurs inland during fall migration.

Key Sites: Arcata Bottoms, Loleta Bottoms, Point Reyes outer peninsula.

Snowy Plover

Comments: Fairly common summer visitor at Mono Lake; uncommon resident on scattered sections of coast. (Populations within 50 miles of coast are classified as threatened by federal government.)

Key Sites: Point Reyes, San Mateo County beaches, Moss Landing.

Mountain Plover

Comments: Uncommon winter visitor in short-grass plains and freshly plowed fields. Often hard to spot against the background. The usual recommendation is to "watch for a dirt clod that moves."

Key Sites: Yolo Farmlands, Panoche Valley.

Black Oystercatcher

Comments: Fairly common resident on rocky ocean shores and breakwaters. All-black body sometimes makes it difficult to spot against the black rocks. Often heard before it is seen. Listen for loud, high *"yeep! yeep! yeep!"*

Key Sites: Point St. George, Bodega Head, Chimney Rock (Point Reyes), San Mateo Coast, Asilomar State Beach.

Shaded areas indicate bird species distribution | ■ Summer range | ■ Winter range | ▤ Permanent resident

▨ Special (e.g., post breeding, or seen only in migration)

Wandering Tattler

Comments: Uncommon spring and fall transient along entire coast, and uncommon winter visitor on coast south of Sonoma County. Seen on rocky coasts, usually singly. Often teeters and bobs as it walks.
Key Sites: Bodega Head, Point Reyes, Asilomar State Beach.

Long-billed Curlew

Comments: Uncommon breeder in northeast. Uncommon winter visitor on north coast. Fairly common winter visitor on central coast and in Central Valley. Favors mudflats, grasslands, and agricultural fields. Sometimes seen in flocks of hundreds of birds in winter.
Key Sites: Yolo Bypass, Elkhorn Slough, San Luis Refuges.

Black Turnstone

Comments: Fairly common winter resident on rocky coastlines and breakwaters. Often difficult to see against dark background.
Key Sites: Point St. George, Mendocino Coast, Bodega Head, Point Reyes, San Mateo Coast, Asilomar State Beach.

Surfbird

Comments: Fairly common winter resident on rocky coastlines and breakwaters, often in association with Black Turnstones.
Key Sites: Point St. George, Mendocino Coast, Bodega Head, Point Reyes, San Mateo Coast, Asilomar State Beach.

Rock Sandpiper

Comments: Rare winter visitor on rocky coastlines and jetties on northwest coast. Very rare south of there. Sometimes found in company with Black Turnstones and Surfbirds.
Key Sites: Point St. George, jetty at Crescent City, irregularly at Bodega Head and Pillar Point.

Heermann's Gull

Comments: Common post-breeding visitor to entire coastline, generally appearing in early summer, and gone back to the breeding grounds in Baja California by December. A few may remain on the coast year round. Exceedingly rare inland.
Key Sites: Bodega Bay, Point Reyes, San Mateo Coast, Monterey Peninsula, Big Sur.

Shaded areas indicate bird species distribution ■ Summer range ■ Winter range ▤ Permanent resident
▤ Special (e.g., post breeding, or seen only in migration)

Mew Gull

Comments: Fairly common winter visitor along coast, more numerous in north than in south. Frequents beaches, estuaries, harbors, and agricultural fields near coast. Small numbers appear regularly at some inland locations.
Key Sites: Crescent City, Arcata, Bodega Bay, Monterey.

California Gull

Comments: Largest breeding colony in state is at Mono Lake. There are smaller breeding colonies at such locations as Klamath Basin, Butte Valley, and Honey Lake. Some remain all year on coast and in Central Valley.
Key Sites: Klamath Basin, Mono Lake, from April to October. American River, and almost anywhere on coast, in winter.

Thayer's Gull

Comments: Rare to uncommon winter visitor along coast. Small numbers appear at Central Valley locations in winter. Some authorities feel that Thayer's Gull should be classified as a subspecies of Iceland Gull.
Key Sites: Bodega Bay, Point Reyes, Lake Merced, American River, Elkhorn Slough.

Western Gull

Comments: Common to abundant resident on entire coastline. Rarely seen inland. Hybridization with Glaucous-winged Gull takes place.
Key Sites: One of the easiest birds to see. Seen at virtually all coastline sites.

Glaucous-winged Gull

Comments: Common winter visitor on coast, more common in north than south. Uncommon in Central Valley in winter. Hybridization with Western Gull takes place.
Key Sites: Crescent City, Arcata, Bodega Bay, Point Reyes.

Sabine's Gull

Comments: Uncommon, highly pelagic spring and fall transient. Rarely seen at coastline or inland. (Named for Edward Sabine, who pronounced his name SAB-in.)
Key Sites: Pelagic trips from Monterey Bay or Bodega Bay.

Shaded areas indicate bird species distribution   ■ Summer range   ■ Winter range   ▤ Permanent resident
Special (e.g., post breeding, or seen only in migration)

Elegant Tern
Comments: Fairly common post-breeding visitor along entire coast, less numerous in north, but increases in El Niño years.
Key Sites: Point Reyes (Limantour Lagoon), Bolinas Lagoon, Carmel River Lagoon, Elkhorn Slough.

Least Tern
Comments: In Northern California, limited to a breeding colony (April to September) in San Francisco Bay area ("California" subspecies classified as endangered by both federal and state governments.)
Key Sites: Occasionally seen in post-breeding period at Foster City, Palo Alto Baylands, and Shoreline at Mountain View.

Black Tern
Comments: Fairly common breeder at lakes and marshes in northeast. Breeding also occurs in Central Valley, especially in rice fields. Distribution is patchy. Seen in migration throughout central part of state.
Key Sites: Some breeding areas are Grass Lake (Siskiyou County), Modoc National Wildlife Refuge, Eagle Lake, and Honey Lake.

Pigeon Guillemot
Comments: Locally common summer visitor along coastline, nesting on cliffs and offshore islands. Becomes rare after September when birds move out to sea, and wintering areas are not well known.
Key Sites: Present at most rocky shores in summer, as at Point St. George, Mendocino Coast, Bodega Bay and Point Reyes. Usually seen as boats are leaving the harbor on pelagic trips out of Monterey Bay.

Marbled Murrelet
Comments: Uncommon during breeding season on northwest coast, and on coast of San Mateo and Santa Cruz counties. Usually detected making dawn or dusk flights to nesting locations in old-growth forests. Sparsely distributed on coast in winter. (Classified as threatened by the federal government, and endangered by the state.)
Key Sites: For breeding: Año Nuevo, Prairie Creek Redwoods State Park.

Xantus's Murrelet
Comments: Uncommon post-breeding visitor to Northern California. Breeding colonies are on Channel Islands, in Southern California. Usually seen a few miles out to sea. Rare north of Monterey Bay except in El Niño years. Subspecies *hypoleucus* is occasionally seen.
Key Sites: Pelagic trips out of Monterey Bay, and out of Bodega Bay in El Niño years.

Shaded areas indicate bird species distribution ■ Summer range ■ Winter range ▤ Permanent resident
▨ Special (e.g., post breeding, or seen only in migration)

Craveri's Murrelet

Comments: Rare post-breeding visitor along coast as far north as Monterey Bay. May be seen as far north as Cordell Bank in El Niño years. Usually seen well out to sea.

Key Sites: Pelagic trips out of Monterey Bay, and out of Bodega Bay in El Niño years.

Ancient Murrelet

Comments: Rare to uncommon winter visitor along entire coast, often at sea, but sometimes seen from shore.

Key Sites: Pelagic trips from Monterey Bay and Bodega Bay, also Point St. George, Bodega Head, Point Reyes, Point Pinos.

Cassin's Auklet

Comments: Uncommon to fairly common resident, with winter populations probably increased by birds from the north. Often seen well out to sea, but rarely seen from shore. Major breeding location is Farallon Islands.

Key Sites: Pelagic trips from Monterey Bay and Bodega Bay, also Point St. George, Bodega Head, Point Reyes, Pillar Point.

Rhinoceros Auklet

Comments: Fairly common resident on north coast and winter visitor further south. Often seen at sea, but also seen frequently from shore. Some major breeding colonies are at Castle Rock and Farallon Islands.

Key Sites: Pelagic trips from Monterey Bay and Bodega Bay, also Castle Rock, Bodega Head, Point Reyes, Año Nuevo, Point Pinos.

Tufted Puffin

Comments: Rare breeder on north coast, and rare winter resident well offshore.

Key Sites: Castle Rock; in some years at Green Rock (Trinidad State Beach). Occasionally seen on pelagic trips.

Band-tailed Pigeon

Comments: Fairly common but somewhat irregular resident. Rare in winter in northwest. May wander, based upon availability of acorns. Generally does not occur in forests without oak trees. Once was more abundant, but was almost exterminated by overhunting early in this century.

Key Sites: Lake Earl, Titlow Mountain Road, Clear Lake, Mount Tamalpais, Skyline Boulevard.

Shaded areas indicate bird species distribution   ■ Summer range   ■ Winter range   ▤ Permanent resident

░ Special (e.g., post breeding, or seen only in migration)

Yellow-billed Cuckoo
Comments: Rare summer visitor, with limited breeding along the Sacramento River and in the Kern River Valley. ("Western" subspecies is classified as endangered by state.)
Key Sites: Bidwell-Sacramento River State Park, Kern River Preserve (late June through July).

Greater Roadrunner
Comments: Rare resident in arid, brushy habitats of interior, but not including cultivated and inhabited areas of Central Valley floor.
Key Sites: Mines Road, Pinnacles, Panoche Valley, Kern River Valley.

Flammulated Owl
Comments: Rare to uncommon summer visitor in mountainous areas with ponderosa pine and black oaks. More likely to be heard than seen, in May and June. Range incompletely known, because of difficulty in making observations.
Key Sites: Mosquito Ridge. Known to be of widespread occurrence, but hard to find.

Western Screech-Owl
Comments: Uncommon to fairly common resident in oaks, mixed hardwoods and conifers, riparian woodland, and in towns.
Key Sites: Widespread. Some places to try are Lake Solano/Putah Creek, Mount Diablo, Skyline Boulevard, Del Puerto Canyon.

Northern Pygmy-Owl
Comments: Uncommon resident in foothill woodlands, riparian canyons, and montane mixed oak-conifer woodlands. Often active in the daytime.
Key Sites: Yuba Pass, Bothe-Napa Valley State Park, Putah Creek, Bottchers Gap, Del Puerto Canyon.

Burrowing Owl
Comments: Uncommon and declining resident on grasslands and open bare ground. Spottily distributed. The Burrowing Owls in Northern California mostly are located around the lower San Francisco Bay, or around the Delta Region from Yolo County south to Stanislaus County. Rare on coast and in Great Basin.
Key Sites: Yolo Grasslands Regional Park, Shoreline at Mountain View, Martin Luther King Jr. Regional Shoreline.

Shaded areas indicate bird species distribution   ■ Summer range   ■ Winter range   ▤ Permanent resident
▒ Special (e.g., post breeding, or seen only in migration)

Spotted Owl

Comments: Uncommon resident. "Northern" subspecies prefers old-growth conifers on the coast. The "California" subspecies in the Cascades and Sierra uses mixed conifer forest, often with an understory of oaks. ("Northern" subspecies is classified as threatened by federal government.)
Key Sites: Prairie Creek, Tomales Bay State Park, Bothe-Napa Valley State Park.

Great Gray Owl

Comments: As a breeding species, it principally occurs in the middle elevations of the Sierra near Yosemite National Park. Occasionally reported in Warner Mountains. Prefers red fir-lodgepole forests bordering meadows. (Classified as endangered by state.)
Key Sites: Yosemite National Park (Chevron Meadow, Peregoy Meadow, McGurk Meadow).

Short-eared Owl

Comments: Uncommon resident in Great Basin. Sparse and irregular breeder in lower Sacramento Valley, and at Grizzly Island Wildlife Area. Prefers marshes (both saltwater and fresh), and grasslands. Needs tall grass or bushes for daytime roosting. Often hunts just at dusk.
Key Sites: Klamath Basin, Yolo Farmlands, Grizzly Island Wildlife Area.

Lesser Nighthawk

Comments: Uncommon summer visitor to open, dry valleys. Nests in gravelly areas. Active at dawn and dusk.
Key Sites: Corral Hollow Road, Bird Road, Kern River Valley.

Common Poorwill

Comments: Widespread and fairly common summer visitor to brushy slopes, chaparral, and pinyon-juniper woodland. Song is a loud whistled "poor-WILL!" often heard at dusk in spring. Sometimes seen at night, along lightly traveled roads, sitting on road, with eyes showing as bright spots reflected in headlights.
Key Sites: Mix Canyon Road, Mount Diablo, Mines Road, Del Puerto Canyon, Kern River Valley.

Black Swift

Comments: Rare summer visitor to rocky cliffs at seacoast and in mountains. Often constructs nests close to or behind waterfalls. Large, flocks sometimes seen in migration.
Key Sites: Largest known breeding colony in state is at McArthur-Burney Falls State Park. Also, Yosemite Valley, Año Nuevo, Big Sur coast (Rocky Point, Julia Pfeiffer Burns State Park).

Shaded areas indicate bird species distribution   ■ Summer range   ■ Winter range   ☰ Permanent resident
░ Special (e.g., post breeding, or seen only in migration)

Vaux's Swift

Comments: Fairly common summer visitor to forests of the northern and central coasts, and to some degree in the Sierra. Rare in Great Basin. Nests in hollow trees. Sometimes seen in large flocks during migration. (Named for an American, William Vaux, who pronounced his name VAWKS.)

Key Sites: Lake Earl, Prairie Creek, Arcata area.

White-throated Swift

Comments: Fairly common resident in central Coast Range, and uncommon summer visitor in the Sierra. Uncommon east of the Sierra. Needs areas with cliffs for breeding and roosting.

Key Sites: Monticello Dam (Putah Creek), Del Valle Regional Park, Big Sur Coast, Pinnacles, Yosemite Valley.

Black-chinned Hummingbird

Comments: Common summer visitor to lowlands and foothills, in brushy canyons, riparian woodlands, orchards, and residential gardens.

Key Sites: Kaweah Oaks Preserve, Kern River Preserve.

Anna's Hummingbird

Comments: Widespread common resident in chaparral, riparian woodlands, and residential gardens. This is the most common hummingbird in California.

Key Sites: An easy bird to see. Representative locations are Arcata area, Clear Lake, Skyline Wilderness Park, Palo Alto Baylands, Mines Road, and Kaweah Oaks Preserve.

Costa's Hummingbird

Comments: Rare summer visitor in dry chaparral, gravelly alluvial fans, and washes. Costa's is generally considered a desert species, and in Northern California it's at the edge of its normal range.

Key Sites: Del Puerto Canyon.

Calliope Hummingbird

Comments: Fairly common summer visitor in mountain meadows and streamside thickets, mostly from ponderosa pine to red fir zone. It is the smallest hummingbird that regularly appears in the U.S.

Key Sites: Warner Mountains, Lassen Volcanic National Park, Yuba River, Sequoia National Park.

Shaded areas indicate bird species distribution   ■ Summer range   ■ Winter range   ▤ Permanent resident

▨ Special (e.g., post breeding, or seen only in migration)

Broad-tailed Hummingbird

Comments: Fairly common summer visitor in White Mountains to pinyon-juniper woodlands and riparian thickets along wet or dry watercourses, at elevations of 6,000 feet to 9,000 feet. Occasionally has been seen at locations on east side of Sierra. Male's wings make characteristic trilling noise in flight.

Key Sites: Westgard Pass, Grandview Campground.

Rufous Hummingbird

Comments: Fairly common transient, primarily up the coast in spring, and down the Sierra in fall, although they may appear widely in the state in both migrations. Peak of spring migration is mid-March to mid-April; in fall, July through August, with males migrating first.

Key Sites: Arcata area, Yosemite National Park, Bartlett Park.

Allen's Hummingbird

Comments: Common summer visitor to coastal lowlands, from February to July, in coastal scrub, open woodlands, and riparian woodlands.

Key Sites: Arcata area, Mendocino Coast, Point Reyes, Mount Tamalpais, Lake Merced, Monterey Peninsula, Andrew Molera State Park.

Lewis's Woodpecker

Comments: Rare to fairly common resident in pinyon-juniper woodlands and open ponderosa pine forest. Irregular and unpredictable. May be absent for several years in breeding locations and suddenly reappear. Wanders widely in winter, sometimes becoming common.

Key Sites: Janesville. Can sometimes be found at Mines Road, Spenceville, and east of Mono Lake.

Acorn Woodpecker

Comments: Widespread common resident in oak woodlands and riparian woodlands containing oaks. Lives in family groups centered around "granary trees" containing holes stuffed with acorns. Its distinctive call, often heard, sounds like raucous laughter: *"ya-caw! ya-caw! ya-caw!"*

Key Sites: Easy to find. Representative locations are Battle Creek, Clear Lake, Effie Yeaw Nature Center, Mines Road.

Williamson's Sapsucker

Comments: Uncommon resident in higher coniferous forests from 7,000 feet to 8,500 feet. Prefers subalpine forests dominated by lodgepole pines. Males and females differ strikingly in appearance.

Key Sites: Lake Almanor, Summit Lake (Lassen), Yuba Pass, Carson Pass, Bridalveil Creek Campground (Yosemite).

Shaded areas indicate bird species distribution   ■ Summer range   ■ Winter range   ▦ Permanent resident
■ Special (e.g., post breeding, or seen only in migration)

Red-naped Sapsucker

Comments: Rare summer visitor to canyons with riparian growth, especially aspens and willows. Breeds in Warner Mountains, and perhaps along east slope of the Sierra. More numerous in White Mountains, where it breeds in canyons on the eastern side.

Key Sites: Warner Mountains. In White Mountains, occasionally found in bristlecone pines.

Red-breasted Sapsucker

Comments: Uncommon resident in northwest, fairly common summer visitor in the Sierra, and widespread but irregular winter visitor throughout most of remainder of state. Prefers mixed conifer forests that are close to riparian woodlands. Formerly was considered same species as Red-naped and Yellow-breasted Sapsuckers.

Key Sites: Lassen Volcanic National Park, Yuba Pass, Sequoia National Park.

Ladder-backed Woodpecker

Comments: Uncommon resident in Kern River Valley in open pinyon-juniper woodland and adjacent riparian woodlands. Similar to Nuttall's Woodpecker, but black lines on face are more crisply outlined, and white barring on back is more pronounced. Hybridization occurs between the two species.

Key Sites: Walker Pass.

Nuttall's Woodpecker

Comments: Widespread common resident in oak woodlands and riparian woodlands. Often found in residential neighborhoods. Is almost a California endemic (range extends into Baja California). Call is a low *pr-r-r-rt*.

Key Sites: Widespread; Annadel State Park, Lake Solano, American River, Cosumnes Preserve, Mount Diablo, Andrew Molera State Park.

White-headed Woodpecker

Comments: Fairly common resident of pine forests, especially those with large trees. In some years, the highest "Christmas Counts" in the nation for this species have come from Lake Almanor.

Key Sites: Lassen Volcanic National Park, Lake Almanor, Yuba Pass, Crystal Basin, Lake Tahoe, Yosemite National Park, Sequoia National Park.

Black-backed Woodpecker

Comments: Rare resident of subalpine forests, especially those with lodgepole pines. Much sought by birders, but often without success.

Key Sites: Warner Mountains, Lassen Volcanic National Park, Yuba Pass, Bridalveil Creek Campground (Yosemite).

Shaded areas indicate bird species distribution   ■ Summer range   ■ Winter range   ▤ Permanent resident

▨ Special (e.g., post breeding, or seen only in migration)

Western Wood-Pewee

Comments: Common summer visitor in wide variety of habitats: oak woodland, riparian woodland, and coniferous forests up to subalpine zone. Sits on exposed perches. Call is a down-slurred *"pee-e-er."*

Key Sites: McCloud River Loop, Warner Mountains, Lassen Volcanic National Park, Yuba Pass, Crystal Basin, Yosemite National Park, Sequoia National Park.

Willow Flycatcher

Comments: Uncommon summer visitor in riparian woodlands with dense willows adjacent to meadows. Most likely to be found in the region from north of Lake Tahoe to the McCloud River, and at Kern River Valley, with scattered numbers in between. (Classified as endangered by the state.)

Key Sites: McCloud River Loop, Kern River Valley.

Hammond's Flycatcher

Comments: Fairly common summer visitor in mixed conifer and red fir forests, generally preferring habitat that is shadier and more moist than does its look-alike, the Dusky Flycatcher.

Key Sites: Lassen National Park, Yuba Pass, Crystal Basin, Yosemite National Park.

Gray Flycatcher

Comments: Fairly common summer visitor in dry open terrain with sagebrush, pinyon pine, juniper, and ponderosa pine. It wags its tail downward rather than up as do other members of the genus.

Key Sites: Devils Garden, Warner Mountains, Mono Lake, White Mountains.

Dusky Flycatcher

Comments: Fairly common summer visitor from ponderosa pine belt to subalpine terrain. Generally prefers more open, sunny, habitat than Hammond's. Is widespread on east slope in breeding season, unlike Hammond's.

Key Sites: Carson Pass, Yosemite National Park, Lee Vining Canyon, White Mountains.

Pacific-slope Flycatcher

Comments: Fairly common summer visitor in low-level coniferous forests, mixed oak woodlands, and riparian woodland. In migration, common throughout state. Call is a sharp, up-slurred *"suwheet!"*

Key Sites: Prairie Creek, Point Reyes, Annadel State Park, Napa Valley.

Shaded areas indicate bird species distribution ■ Summer range ■ Winter range ▤ Permanent resident

▢ Special (e.g., post breeding, or seen only in migration)

Cordilleran Flycatcher

Comments: Uncommon summer resident in cool, dense, mixed conifers, up to subalpine zone. Cordilleran and Pacific-slope Flycatchers once were regarded as a single species, Western Flycatcher. Distinguished from Pacific-slope Flycatcher by the two syllables of its call: *"su-WHEET!"*
Key Sites: Warner Mountains.

Black Phoebe

Comments: Common resident of a variety of habitats, usually in association with water. (Say's Phoebe, by contrast, prefers dry habitats.) Often utters a sharp *"tsip!"*
Key Sites: Widespread. Some representative sites are Lake Earl, Battle Creek, Clear Lake, Putah Creek, Point Reyes.

Say's Phoebe

Comments: Uncommon summer visitor in northeast, uncommon resident in southern Coast Range, and uncommon winter visitor to Coast Range and Central Valley, utilizing open, sunny, arid terrain. Perches on bush-tops, rocks, and fence posts.
Key Sites: Klamath Basin, Del Puerto Canyon, Panoche Valley, Kern River Valley.

Vermilion Flycatcher

Comments: This is a desert species that barely penetrates the southern boundary of the area covered by this book. Is a very rare summer visitor at Kern River Preserve.
Key Sites: Kern River Preserve.

Ash-throated Flycatcher

Comments: Uncommon to fairly common summer visitor in riparian woodland, oak woodland, chaparral, dry washes, open mixed conifer forest, and pinyon-juniper woodland.
Key Sites: Battle Creek, Bobelaine Sanctuary, Annadel State Park, Cosumnes Preserve, Mount Tamalpais, Mount Diablo, Mines Road.

Brown-crested Flycatcher

Comments: This is a species that barely penetrates the southern boundary of the area covered by this book. It is a rare summer visitor (three to five breeding pairs) at Kern River Preserve.
Key Sites: Kern River Preserve.

Shaded areas indicate bird species distribution   ■ Summer range   ■ Winter range   ▦ Permanent resident
            Special (e.g., post breeding, or seen only in migration)

Cassin's Kingbird

Comments: Rare and irregular summer visitor to dry, inner Coast Range, as far north as southern Alameda County, utilizing open grassy foothills with scattered trees. A few birds may over-winter.
Key Sites: Del Puerto Canyon.

Western Kingbird

Comments: Widespread common summer visitor in open grasslands with scattered trees, farmlands, and oak savanna. Often perches on roadside fences.
Key Sites: Ash Creek Wildlife Area, Battle Creek, Clear Lake, Sacramento National Wildlife Refuge, Bidwell Park, Yolo Bypass, Mines Road, San Luis Refuges.

Plumbeous Vireo

Comments: Uncommon summer visitor, mostly in pinyon-juniper woodland. Fairly large vireo, with a clean gray-and-white form. Can be mistaken for Gray Vireo.
Key Sites: Westgard Pass.

Cassin's Vireo

Comments: Fairly common summer visitor in oak woodland, oak-coniferous woodland, and riparian woodland. Cassin's, Plumbeous, and Blue-headed Vireos were split from Solitary Vireo in 1997.
Key Sites: Trinity River, Lewiston Lake, Tower House Historical District, McCloud River Loop, McArthur-Burney Falls State Park, Annadel State Park, Mitchell Canyon, Bottcher's Gap.

Hutton's Vireo

Comments: Uncommon to fairly common resident in evergreen oak forests, mixed oak-coniferous woodland, and riparian woodland.
Key Sites: Bidwell Park, Annadel State Park, Bothe-Napa Valley State Park, Point Reyes, Mount Tamalpais, Mount Diablo, Andrew Molera State Park.

Steller's Jay

Comments: Widespread common resident, mostly in coniferous forests. Calls include a rapid *"shack shack shack,"* occasionally soft "whisper" notes, and imitations of Red-tailed Hawk.
Key Sites: Prairie Creek, McCloud River Loop, Warner Mountains, Lake Almanor, Russian Gulch State Park, Yuba Pass, Donner Country, Annadel State Park, Point Reyes, Crystal Basin, Lake Tahoe, Big Sur, Yosemite National Park, Sequoia National Park, Western Divide Highway.

Shaded areas indicate bird species distribution   ■ Summer range   ■ Winter range   ▤ Permanent resident
▨ Special (e.g., post breeding, or seen only in migration)

Western Scrub-Jay

Comments: Widespread common resident, utilizing chaparral, oak woodlands, riparian woodlands, and mixed hardwood-conifer forests, mostly at lower elevations. Sometimes, on the east side of the Sierra, wanders to as high as 10,000 feet after breeding.

Key Sites: Almost impossible to miss. Typical locations: Battle Creek, Clear Lake, Bidwell Park, Skyline Wilderness Park, Putah Creek, Point Reyes, Monterey Peninsula, Kaweah Oaks.

Pinyon Jay

Comments: Uncommon resident of pinyon-juniper forests, but may forage into ponderosa pines, chaparral, or sagebrush flats. Roves in noisy flocks, in unpredictable manner.

Key Sites: Westgard Pass, Grandview Campground, Tollhouse Spring, Modoc Plateau, east of Mono Lake, Walker Pass.

Clark's Nutcracker

Comments: Fairly common resident of subalpine areas, generally above 8,000 feet. Call is a grating, loud *"kra-a-a,"* usually heard before the bird is seen.

Key Sites: Warner Mountains, Lassen Volcanic National Park, Carson Pass, Saddlebag Lake, Tokopah Valley.

Black-billed Magpie

Comments: Fairly common resident in riparian woodlands, edges of sagebrush flats, and agricultural lands. Range does not overlap that of Yellow-billed, although extralimital birds, possible escapees, have been observed in Central Valley.

Key Sites: Butte Valley, Klamath Basin, Modoc Plateau, Ash Creek Wildlife Area, Eagle Lake, Sierra Valley, Mono Lake.

Yellow-billed Magpie

Comments: Common resident in flat valleys, edges of riparian woodlands, oak savanna, agricultural fields, and residential areas. Often seen in small flocks. Not found outside Central California. Range does not overlap that of Black-billed.

Key Sites: Most numerous in lower Sacramento Valley. Try Sacramento National Wildlife Refuge, Putah Creek, Yolo Farmlands, Chico, Cosumnes River Preserve, Pinnacles, San Luis Refuges.

Violet-green Swallow

Comments: Fairly common to common summer visitor. Breeds from near sea level to 6,000 feet. Small numbers remain in central part of state in winter. Nests in crevices and holes in trees, and, at Mono Lake, in cavities in tufa towers.

Key Sites: Prairie Creek, Arcata area, Butte Valley, Point Reyes, Mount Tamalpais, Lake Merced, Monterey Peninsula, Mono Lake.

Shaded areas indicate bird species distribution ■ Summer range ■ Winter range ▦ Permanent resident
▨ Special (e.g., post breeding, or seen only in migration)

Bank Swallow

Comments: Some colonies still exist along Sacramento River and in northeast, with scattered colonies at Fort Funston, Año Nuevo, and in Siskiyou and Mono counties. Nests in colonies. (Classified as threatened by state.)

Key Sites: Tulelake town disposal site, Fall River Mills, Lake Merced, Año Nuevo.

Mountain Chickadee

Comments: Common resident in montane forests, from ponderosa pines to the highest subalpine forests. Isolated population in high mountains in center of Monterey County.

Key Sites: McCloud River Loop, Modoc Plateau, Warner Mountains, Lassen Volcanic National Park, Lake Almanor, Yuba Pass, Crystal Basin, Lake Tahoe, Carson Pass, Yosemite National Park, Mono Lake, Sequoia National Park, Western Divide Highway, White Mountains.

Chestnut-backed Chickadee

Comments: Fairly common to common resident in riparian woodlands (often in willows), coastal redwood and pine forests. In recent decades, has spread southward along western flank of Sierra to about Yosemite National Park.

Key Sites: Lake Earl, Prairie Creek, Arcata area, Mendocino Coast, Annadel State Park, Bothe-Napa Valley State Park, Point Reyes, Mount Tamalpais, Richardson Bay Sanctuary, Monterey Peninsula.

Oak Titmouse

Comments: Common resident in mixed oak woodlands, and riparian areas with oaks. Split in 1997 (along with Juniper Titmouse) from Plain Titmouse. Browner than Juniper Titmouse. Spring song is a ringing *"pee-two pee-two pee-two."*

Key Sites: Battle Creek, Clear Lake, Bobclaine Sanctuary, Bidwell Park, Annadel State Park, Skyline Wilderness Park, Putah Creek, American River, Cosumnes Preserve, Mount Tamalpais, Alum Rock Park, Mines Road, Mount Diablo, Hospital Rock.

Juniper Titmouse

Comments: Rare resident in northeast, uncommon resident in White Mountains. Sparsely and unevenly distributed in pinyon-juniper woodland. Juniper Titmouse is paler and grayer than Oak Titmouse. Call is something like a rattle, with a series of syllables at a steady frequency, but sometimes gives song similar to that of Oak Titmouse.

Key Sites: Westgard Pass.

Bushtit

Comments: Common resident of oak woodland, riparian woodland, chaparral, and pinyon-juniper woodland. Usually found at low and middle elevations, but may drift upslope after breeding. Moves about in flocks in non-breeding season.

Key Sites: Battle Creek, Mendocino Coast, Clear Lake, Bidwell Park, Annadel State Park, Putah Creek, American River, Cosumnes Preserve, Mount Tamalpais, Mount Diablo, Andrew Molera State Park, Kaweah Oaks.

Shaded areas indicate bird species distribution　■ Summer range　■ Winter range　▤ Permanent resident
　　　　　　　▨ Special (e.g., post breeding, or seen only in migration)

Pygmy Nuthatch
Comments: Uncommon to fairly common resident in coniferous forests with pines. In White Mountains, almost exclusively tied to bristlecone pine forests. Irregular and discontinuous on west side of the Sierra; more common on east side. Often detected by their high, rapid *"peep-peep-peep"* calls.
Key Sites: Donner Camp, Lake Tahoe, Point Reyes, Presidio, Point Lobos, Lee Vining Canyon.

Cactus Wren
Comments: Primarily a desert species. Rare resident in Kern River Valley, usually in desert scrub or Joshua tree woodland.
Key Sites: Kern River Valley.

Rock Wren
Comments: Fairly common resident of Coast Range and the Sierra, and uncommon in the northeast, in rocky terrain with crevices for foraging and nesting, extending from the foothills to the alpine zone.
Key Sites: Tule Lake National Wildlife Refuge, Warner Mountains, Eagle Lake, Del Puerto Canyon, Mount Diablo, Kern River Valley.

Canyon Wren
Comments: Uncommon resident of cliff faces, rocky slopes, and canyons, but generally not at the higher elevations of the Cascades or Sierra. Song is a beautiful series of silvery notes, cascading downward. When seen, the white breast (sometimes described as "mirrorlike") stands out.
Key Sites: Tule Lake National Wildlife Refuge, Warner Mountains, Putah Creek, Del Puerto Canyon, Tokopah Valley, Hospital Rock.

American Dipper
Comments: Rare to uncommon resident, widely dispersed. Favors clear, swift, cold streams with waterfalls and rocky cliffs. Often builds nests near or even behind waterfalls.
Key Sites: Trinity River, McCloud River Loop, McArthur-Burney Falls State Park, Yuba River, Sly Park, Big Sur, Yosemite Valley, Tokopah Valley, Hospital Rock.

Western Bluebird
Comments: Fairly common resident in oak savanna, open mixed forests, riparian woodlands, and orchards.
Key Sites: Modoc Plateau, Clear Lake, Bobelaine Sanctuary, Annadel State Park, Putah Creek, Cosumnes Preserve, Mount Tamalpais, Mines Road, Mount Diablo, Bartlett Park, Kern River Valley.

Shaded areas indicate bird species distribution | ■ Summer range ■ Winter range ▤ Permanent resident
▨ Special (e.g., post breeding, or seen only in migration)

Mountain Bluebird

Comments: Fairly common summer visitor in higher mountains and Great Basin, utilizing open subalpine forests, alpine tundra, meadows, and open sagebrush flats. Sometimes seen in agricultural fields in winter. Often hovers in stationary position as it forages.

Key Sites: Butte Valley, Modoc Plateau, Warner Mountains, Eagle Lake, Sierra Valley, Carson Pass, Little Panoche Valley, Bodie.

Townsend's Solitaire

Comments: Uncommon resident in mountains, mostly in the mixed conifer and red fir zones. Sings lengthy song from tops of trees, but generally silent. Most retreat to the lowlands in winter. Fond of junipers and other berries.

Key Sites: Warner Mountains, Lassen Volcanic National Park, Eagle Lake, Carson Pass, Western Divide Highway.

Varied Thrush

Comments: Uncommon resident in humid forests in the northwest. Irregular winter visitor in region shown. Song is an unusual series of slow buzzy whistles, each at a different pitch.

Key Sites: Lake Earl, Prairie Creek (especially), Trinidad State Beach, Russian Gulch State Park (winter), Tomales Bay State Park (winter).

Wrentit

Comments: Common resident in chaparral and tangled riparian habitat, mostly in the mountains and foothills, but also in some parts of the Central Valley. Almost a California endemic (occurs in Oregon and Baja California).

Key Sites: Lake Earl, Trinidad State Beach, Mendocino Headlands, Skyline Wilderness Park, Point Reyes, Mount Diablo, Carmel River, Bottcher's Gap, Hospital Rock.

Sage Thrasher

Comments: Uncommon to fairly common on sagebrush flats. Once was called the "mountain mockingbird," even though it is generally not found in the mountains.

Key Sites: Modoc Plateau, Sierra Valley, Mono Lake.

California Thrasher

Comments: Uncommon to fairly common resident in chaparral and thick brush in riparian woodlands. Generally absent from floor of Central Valley except in a few scattered locations. Almost a California endemic (occurs in Baja California).

Key Sites: Clear Lake, Skyline Wilderness Park, Stebbins Cold Canyon Reserve, Mines Road, Mount Diablo, Bottcher's Gap, Hospital Rock.

Shaded areas indicate bird species distribution ■ Summer range ■ Winter range ▤ Permanent resident
Special (e.g., post breeding, or seen only in migration)

Bohemian Waxwing

Comments: Rare and irregular winter visitor in northeast, in areas where ripe fruit may be found, such as apples, elderberries, juniper, and *Pyracantha*. Nomadic. Occasionally, individuals may appear farther south in the state.

Key Sites: Klamath Basin, Surprise Valley, sometimes in Susanville.

Phainopepla

Comments: Rare, uncommon, and discontinuously distributed resident in foothill riparian woodlands. The small numbers that spend the winter in the areas shown are joined by summer visitors from the south.

Key Sites: Feather River (Oroville), Lake Solano, American River, Mines Road; check trees with mistletoe.

Black-throated Gray Warbler

Comments: Fairly common summer visitor in mixed oak-conifer woodland, oak woodland interspersed with chaparral, and pinyon-juniper woodland.

Key Sites: Trinity River, Tower House Historical District, McArthur-Burney Falls State Park, Annadel State Park, Sly Park, Bottcher's Gap.

Townsend's Warbler

Comments: Uncommon winter visitor on north coast, fairly common on central coast found in mixed oak-coniferous forests, and coniferous forests. Monterey Peninsula usually leads the nation for this species during Audubon Christmas Counts. Seen widely in migration.

Key Sites: Prairie Creek, Russian Gulch State Park, Point Reyes, Monterey Peninsula, Point Lobos, Andrew Molera State Park.

Hermit Warbler

Comments: Fairly common summer visitor in coastal forests and in mixed conifer forests inland. Its buzzy song is easily confused with that of Black-throated Gray Warbler.

Key Sites: Prairie Creek, McCloud River Loop, Lassen Volcanic National Park, Lake Almanor, Yuba Pass, Donner Country, Placer County Big Trees, Crystal Basin, Yosemite National Park, Sequoia National Park, Western Divide Highway.

MacGillivray's Warbler

Comments: Fairly common summer visitor in dense shrubbery, mostly near wet areas, but sometimes in dry huckleberry oak or manzanita. Orange-crowned Warblers with grayish heads can sometimes be confused with MacGillivray's Warblers.

Key Sites: McCloud River Loop, Warner Mountains, McArthur-Burney Falls State Park, Lassen Volcanic National Park, Lake Almanor, Crystal Basin, Carson Pass, Yosemite National Park, Sequoia National Park.

Shaded areas indicate bird species distribution ■ Summer range ■ Winter range ▤ Permanent resident
Special (e.g., post breeding, or seen only in migration)

Western Tanager

Comments: Fairly common summer visitor in mixed conifer zone and into subalpine zone.

Key Sites: Titlow Mountain Road, McCloud River Loop, Warner Mountains, McArthur-Burney Falls State Park, Lake Almanor, Yuba Pass, Placer County Big Trees, Crystal Basin, Lake Tahoe, Yosemite National Park, Lee Vining Canyon, Sequoia National Park, Kern River Valley.

Green-tailed Towhee

Comments: Uncommon to fairly common summer visitor in dense shrubs and sagebrush, in the mixed conifer and red fir zones. Song is easily confused with that of the Fox Sparrow.

Key Sites: Warner Mountains, Donner Camp, Crystal Basin, Carson Pass, Mono Lake.

Spotted Towhee

Comments: Widespread and common resident in brushy habitats and chaparral up to the ponderosa pine zone. Formerly called Rufous-sided Towhee.

Key Sites: Arcata area, Trinity River, McArthur-Burney Falls State Park, Clear Lake, Bobelaine Sanctuary, Bidwell Park, Annadel State Park, American River, Cosumnes Preserve, Mount Tamalpais, Mount Diablo, Mines Road, Andrew Molera State Park.

California Towhee

Comments: Common resident in thickets, brush tangles, and chaparral. Uncommon in Klamath Basin. Occurs in Baja California and to a small extent in Oregon; otherwise, is confined to California.

Key Sites: Clear Lake, Bobelaine Sanctuary, Bidwell Park, Annadel State Park, Skyline Wilderness Park, Putah Creek, American River, Point Reyes, Richardson Bay Sanctuary, Hospital Rock.

Rufous-crowned Sparrow

Comments: Uncommon resident in foothill areas, on dry rocky hillsides with grass and scattered shrubs.

Key Sites: Spenceville Wildlife Area, Lake Hennessey, Mount Tamalpais, Alum Rock Park, Del Puerto Canyon, Mount Diablo.

Brewer's Sparrow

Comments: Common summer visitor in high plains, slopes, and valleys with sagebrush. Sings a complex song that generally continues so long that one wonders why the bird doesn't run out of breath.

Key Sites: Butte Valley, Modoc Plateau, Warner Mountains, Sierra Valley, Mono Lake.

Shaded areas indicate bird species distribution ■ Summer range ■ Winter range ▤ Permanent resident

Special (e.g., post breeding, or seen only in migration)

Black-chinned Sparrow

Comments: Rare to uncommon summer visitor on dry, rocky, brushy slopes with moderately dense vegetation. Best found by listening for song in April and May. Begins with *"sweet sweet sweet"* and ends in a rapid trill.
Key Sites: Mines Road, Mount Diablo, Bottchers Gap, Western Divide Highway, Walker Pass.

Black-throated Sparrow

Comments: Uncommon to rare in Northern California. This is a bird most often associated with hot, dry deserts. There are scattered irregular breeding locations in Siskiyou, Butte, and El Dorado counties west of the Cascade-Sierra axis.
Key Sites: Kern River Valley.

Sage Sparrow

Comments: The coastal subspecies *(Amphispiza belli belli)* is resident. The subspecies in the northeast and near Mono Lake *(A. b. nevadensis)* is a summer visitor. Another subspecies *(A. b. canescens)* is an uncommon resident in the San Joaquin Valley and a summer visitor in the southern half of Mono County.
Key Sites: Mix Canyon Road, Mines Road, Mount Diablo, Sagehen Summit.

Golden-crowned Sparrow

Comments: Fairly common and widespread winter visitor to lowlands, in dense thickets, riparian tangles, and brush piles. Often associates with White-crowned Sparrows.
Key Sites: Crescent City Area, Arcata Area, Battle Creek, Mendocino Coast, Clear Lake, Bidwell Park, Benicia State Recreation Area, Putah Creek, Cosumnes Preserve, Point Reyes, Mount Tamalpais, Mount Diablo, Monterey Peninsula.

Black-headed Grosbeak

Comments: Widespread common summer visitor in riparian woodland, foothill woodlands, and up to the mixed conifer zone. Has beautiful song, resembling that of the American Robin, but more complex.
Key Sites: Trinity River, Tower House Historical District, McCloud River Loop, Warner Mountains, McArthur-Burney Falls State Park, Bobelaine Sanctuary, Mount Diablo, Yosemite National Park, Sequoia National Park.

Lazuli Bunting

Comments: Fairly common summer visitor in riparian areas, chaparral, second-growth forests, and in old burns. (Pronunciation of Lazuli is LAZZ-you-lye.)
Key Sites: Annadel State Park, Skyline Wilderness Park, Cosumnes Preserve, Crystal Basin (Cleveland Burn), Mines Road, Mono Lake.

Shaded areas indicate bird species distribution   ■ Summer range   ■ Winter range   ▤ Permanent resident
▨ Special (e.g., post breeding, or seen only in migration)

Tricolored Blackbird

Comments: Fairly common but declining resident (summer visitor, in northern locations). Nests in dense colonies in freshwater marshes, and sometimes in thistles or blackberry tangles.

Key Sites: Klamath Basin, Sacramento National Wildlife Refuge, Point Reyes, Monterey Peninsula, San Luis Refuge Complex, Kern River Preserve.

Western Meadowlark

Comments: Widespread resident common in meadows, pastures, and grasslands. Generally withdraws from snowy regions in winter. Often forms large flocks in lowlands in winter. Has beautiful flutelike song, more complex than that of Eastern Meadowlark.

Key Sites: Butte Valley, Sacramento National Wildlife Refuge, Gray Lodge, Grizzly Island, Yolo Farmlands, Point Reyes, San Luis Refuges.

Yellow-headed Blackbird

Comments: Fairly common resident in Central Valley near freshwater marshes. Common summer visitor in Great Basin.

Key Sites: Butte Valley, Klamath Basin, Modoc Plateau, Ash Creek Wildlife Area, Eagle Lake, Sierra Valley, Mono Lake, San Luis Refuges, Kern River Valley.

Great-tailed Grackle

Comments: First detected in California near Colorado River in 1964. Breeding is increasingly being seen at scattered locations in Northern California, and it is expected to become common with time.

Key Sites: No particular site in Northern California could presently be called "key" but the species is present in Kern River Valley, and at Success Lake.

Hooded Oriole

Comments: Uncommon to rare summer visitor in Northern California, favoring locations where there are fan palms. Scattered breeding locations exist outside mapped region, as in the Arcata area. Visits hummingbird feeders.

Key Sites: Presidio, Foster City, Alum Rock Park, Monterey Peninsula, Kern River Valley.

Bullock's Oriole

Comments: Fairly common summer visitor in riparian woodlands with large trees, up to the ponderosa pine zone. Comes to hummingbird feeders.

Key Sites: Sacramento National Wildlife Refuge, Bobelaine Sanctuary, Bidwell Park, Annadel State Park, American River, Cosumnes Preserve, Point Reyes, Mount Tamalpais, Richardson Bay Sanctuary, Alum Rock Park, Kaweah Oaks, Kern River Valley.

Shaded areas indicate bird species distribution　　■ Summer range　■ Winter range　▤ Permanent resident
▨ Special (e.g., post breeding, or seen only in migration)

Scott's Oriole
Comments: This is a bird of the desert regions. Rare to uncommon summer visitor in Kern River Valley, especially in Joshua trees.
Key Sites: Kern River Valley.

Gray-crowned Rosy-Finch
Comments: Fairly common to uncommon resident of alpine habitat, ranging to the tops of the highest peaks, but in disjunct populations. Isolated populations on Mount Shasta and Mount Lassen. Descends to nearby valleys in winter when snows are heavy, and may come in large flocks to feeders.
Key Sites: Tioga Pass, Saddlebag Lake, Lassen Peak.

Cassin's Finch
Comments: Uncommon to fairly common resident of higher altitude forests in mixed conifers and lodgepole-red fir forest, to timberline. In winter, descends the slopes to middle and lower elevations.
Key Sites: Warner Mountains, Lassen Volcanic National Park, Lake Almanor, Yuba Pass, Lake Tahoe, Carson Pass, Yosemite National Park, White Mountains.

Lesser Goldfinch
Comments: Uncommon to fairly common in oak woodland, mixed oak-conifer forest woodland, riparian woodland, and pinyon-juniper woodland, mostly in the foothills.
Key Sites: Tower House Historical District, Battle Creek, Clear Lake, Bidwell Park, Annadel State Park, Bothe-Napa Valley State Park, Putah Creek, American River, Mount Tamalpais, Richardson Bay Sanctuary, Mines Road, Mount Diablo, Hospital Rock.

Lawrence's Goldfinch
Comments: Rare to uncommon irregular summer visitor in arid interior valleys and foothills with water nearby, in oak woodlands, or mixed oak-conifer woodlands. A few remain behind in winter.
Key Sites: Mix Canyon Road, Mines Road, Mount Diablo, Pinnacles, Kern River Valley.

Shaded areas indicate bird species distribution   ■ Summer range   ■ Winter range   ▦ Permanent resident
▨ Special (e.g., post breeding, or seen only in migration)

Red-shouldered Hawks in the western U.S. are almost entirely confined to California, with a small overlap into southern Oregon.

8. Status and Distribution Chart

The bar graphs attempt to show where birds are most likely to be found in the various regions. Northern California is very diverse, with a great deal of diversity within the regions themselves. In addition, the boundaries between regions can only be considered as approximate, so the bar graphs cannot be interpreted with exactness. Nevertheless, they can be of great use in giving an indication of the regions and seasons in which certain species are likely to be found. The information for the bar graphs is drawn from the sources listed in Appendix B.

Abundances are indicated by the line widths shown at the bottom of the chart pages and have been divided into three categories: common to abundant, uncommon to fairly common, and rare, as defined in Chapter 1. Species found in Northern California only on a casual or accidental basis, meaning that they do not appear every year or have shown up only a few times, are not shown on the bar graphs. They are included in a list at the end of this chapter.

The graphs are to be interpreted as giving the likelihood of seeing a member of the species in question, rather than as an indication of actual abundance. For example, it is said that Flammulated Owl is locally common in appropriate habitat, but it such a difficult species to locate that it seems more informative to indicate it as rare, in terms of its likelihood of being observed.

If a species is found in a region at the common or uncommon level, and only at the rare level in other regions, the regions of rarity are omitted. Species that are found *only* at the rare level in Northern California, but that meet the following conditions, are included in the bar graphs: resident breeders, such as Great Gray Owl and Black Rail; breeding summer visitors that are reasonably regular, such as Cassin's Kingbird; species at the southern end of their normal wintering ranges, such as Rock Sandpiper and Bohemian Waxwing; regular migrants, such as Baird's and Pectoral Sandpipers.

Eastern vagrants are treated in a special way. Many Eastern birds have shown up in Northern California at one time or another, usually along the coast. Some of them show up often enough that their appearances might represent genuine extensions of their wintering range, such as with White-throated and Swamp Sparrows. I arbitrarily set a limit that if the recent records show an average of 25 appearances per year in Northern California, based on Hampton (1997), I include it. Using this criterion, the following were included: Blackpoll Warbler (41 per year); Black-and-white Warbler (25 per year); and Clay-colored Sparrow (41 per year). The following borderline cases were excluded: Tennessee Warbler (23 per year) and Chestnut-sided Warbler (21 per year).

The regions (see page 363) are to be interpreted as given below. Note that the regions roughly correspond to many of the landforms described in Chapter 2. However, some of these landforms are combined, where appropriate. For

Status and Distribution Regions

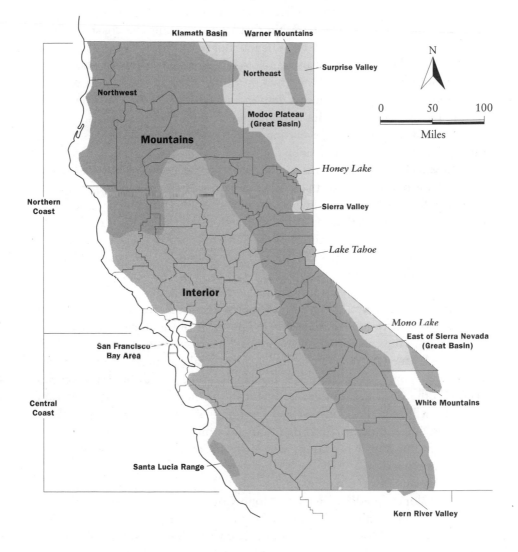

example, the Cascade, Sierra Nevada, and Klamath mountains have been lumped into "Mountains," along with some of the higher portions of the Coast Ranges.

Pelagic. Species in this region generally are observed from boats well out to sea, although occasionally they may be observed from shore.

Coast. This applies to sightings made directly at the shore, either in near-shore waters, on the beach or rocky headlands, or in harbors and bays. It also includes land and marsh areas adjacent to the coast or bays, and the nearby lowlands and foothills. The term **Northern Coast** means the coast north of Point Reyes, more or less, to the Oregon Border. **Central Coast** means the coast from and including the San Francisco Bay Area to the southern border of Monterey County. Note that the usual meaning of the Central Coast extends to regions farther south than this, and includes San Luis Obispo County. In fact, in the eyes of many, Santa Barbara and Ventura counties are also part of the Central Coast; however, everything south of Monterey County is outside the region of coverage in this book.

Interior. This imprecise term is intended to include the Central Valley, the lower elevation portions of the Coast Ranges, and the foothills of the Cascades and Sierra Nevada up to where the pines begin to outnumber the oaks. It is worth remembering that the Delta, although technically part of the interior, shares many of the characteristics of the San Francisco Bay Area.

Mountains. This includes the Sierra Nevada, the Cascades, the Klamath Mountains, the higher mountains of the North Coast Ranges, and the Santa Lucia Range in Monterey County. In the Sierra Nevada, this generally includes elevations higher than 3,000 feet in the north and 5,000 feet in the south. On the east slope of the Sierra, the timbered portions of the upper slopes are included within the category of "Mountains." Many mountain species also occur in the Warner and White mountains, but special notations for these ranges will be made only for those species principally to be found there. If a species occurs in the Cascades, but generally not in the Sierra Nevada, the notation **Cascades** will be made. Conversely, the notation **Sierra Nevada** may occasionally be used. It should be recognized that many mountain species that are normally found at higher elevations will move to lower elevations when snow covers the ground.

Great Basin. This is generally understood to include the Modoc Plateau and the lower slopes, predominantly in Mono County, of the eastern Sierra Nevada. The upper timbered portions of the eastern Sierra are included within the category of "Mountains." Where necessary, **Modoc Plateau, Northeast,** and **East of Sierra** will be used if there is a difference between the occurrence of a species in these areas. Northeast applies generally to the northern part of the Modoc Plateau (including the Klamath Basin, but not the Warner Mountains) and east of Sierra mainly refers to that portion of the Great Basin lying in Mono County.

Notations for certain locations (examples are given below) are made when it seems necessary to draw attention to the occurrence of various species in those particular areas.

Northwest: Includes Del Norte and Humboldt counties and the northern half of Mendocino County.

Klamath Basin: Refers to the area surrounding and including Lower Klamath and Tule Lake national wildlife refuges.

Warner Mountains

S F Bay: Meaning, San Francisco Bay Area.

Sacramento River: Includes the riparian strips along the river, as well as the river itself.

Central Valley Floor: The flat part of the Central Valley, usually consisting of pastures, irrigated farm fields, and flooded rice fields.

Foothills: Consists of the ring of foothills surrounding the flat floor of the Central Valley, extending up to the pine belt.

Inner Coast Ranges: The variably wooded slopes, often with chaparral or oak savanna, of the eastern portion of the Coast Ranges, generally south of Glenn County to the border between Monterey and San Luis Obispo counties.

South Coast Ranges: Refers to that part of the Coast Ranges extending from Alameda County south through San Benito and Monterey counties.

White Mountains

Kern River Valley

In a few cases, other specific localities are mentioned, such as Tioga Pass, Yosemite, and Yuba County.

If a common species is generally resident in most parts of Northern California, the notation *Widespread* is used. If a species is found in scattered locations in a region, the term *local* is used. If a bird is not native to California, but has been introduced from elsewhere, *Intro* (meaning introduced) is shown.

The names and sequence of species are consistent with the *Seventh Edition of the Check-list of North American Birds* (1998), published by the American Ornithologists' Union. Possessive forms of birds' names, as in **Lewis's Woodpecker,** are rendered in accordance with that checklist.

ABBREVIATIONS

C Coast	Central Coast	Modoc Pl	Modoc Plateau
C V Floor	Central Valley Floor	Mtns	Mountains
E of Sierra	East of Sierra	NE	Northeast
G Basin	Great Basin	N Coast	Northern Coast
Inner Coast R	Inner Coast Ranges	NW	Northwest
Int	Interior	Sac R	Sacramento River
Intro	Introduced	Sac Valley	Sacramento Valley
Kern R	Kern River Valley	S F Bay	San Francisco Bay Area
Kl Basin	Klamath Basin	S Coast R	South Coast Ranges

Status and distribution

Bird Species	Region	Month of Occurrence (J F M A M J J A S O N D)
LOONS		
☐ Red-throated Loon	Coast	
☐ Pacific Loon	N Coast	
	C Coast	
☐ Common Loon	Coast	
GREBES		
☐ Pied-billed Grebe	* Coast; Int	
	* Modoc Pl	
☐ Horned Grebe	Coast	
☐ Red-necked Grebe	Coast	
☐ Eared Grebe	Coast; Int	
	* G Basin	
☐ Western Grebe	Coast	
	* Int (local)	
	* G Basin	
☐ Clark's Grebe	Coast	
	* Int (local)	
	* G Basin	
ALBATROSSES		
☐ Laysan Albatross	Pelagic	
☐ Black-footed Albatross	Pelagic	
SHEARWATERS and PETRELS		
☐ Northern Fulmar	Pelagic	
☐ Pink-footed Shearwater	Pelagic	
☐ Flesh-footed Shearwater	Pelagic	
☐ Buller's Shearwater	Pelagic	
☐ Sooty Shearwater	Pelagic	
☐ Short-tailed Shearwater	Pelagic	
☐ Black-vented Shearwater	Pelagic	
☐ Fork-tailed Storm-Petrel	Pelagic	
☐ Leach's Storm-Petrel	* Pelagic	
☐ Ashy Storm-Petrel	* Pelagic	
☐ Black Storm-Petrel	Pelagic	
☐ Least Storm-Petrel	Pelagic	
PELICANS		
☐ American White Pelican	SF Bay; Int	
	* G Basin	

See abbreviations on page 365

* = Breeds in region
? = Breeding uncertain

Bird Species	Region	Month of Occurrence (J F M A M J J A S O N D)
☐ Brown Pelican	Coast	
CORMORANTS		
☐ Brandt's Cormorant	* N Coast	
	* C Coast	
☐ Double-crested Cormorant	* Coast	
	* Int	
	* G Basin	
☐ Pelagic Cormorant	* Coast	
HERONS *and* BITTERNS		
☐ American Bittern	* N Coast; Int	
	* Modoc Pl	
☐ Least Bittern	* Int	
	* Kl Basin	
☐ Great Blue Heron	* Widespread	
☐ Great Egret	* Coast; Int; Kl Basin	
☐ Snowy Egret	* Coast; Int	
	* Modoc Pl	
☐ Little Blue Heron	? SF Bay	
☐ Cattle Egret	Coast	
	* Int	
☐ Green Heron	* Coast; Int	
☐ Black-crowned Night-Heron	* Coast; Int; Kl Basin	
	* Modoc Pl	
IBISES		
☐ White-faced Ibis	* Int	
	* Modoc Pl	
NEW WORLD VULTURES		
☐ Turkey Vulture	* N Coast; G Basin	
	* Int	
DUCKS, GEESE, *and* SWANS		
☐ Greater White-fronted Goose	Int; NE	
☐ Snow Goose	Int; NE	
☐ Ross's Goose	Int; NE	
☐ Canada Goose	Coast	
	* Int	
	* G Basin	
☐ Brant	Coast	
☐ Tundra Swan	N Coast; Int; Modoc Pl	
☐ Wood Duck	* Coast; Int	

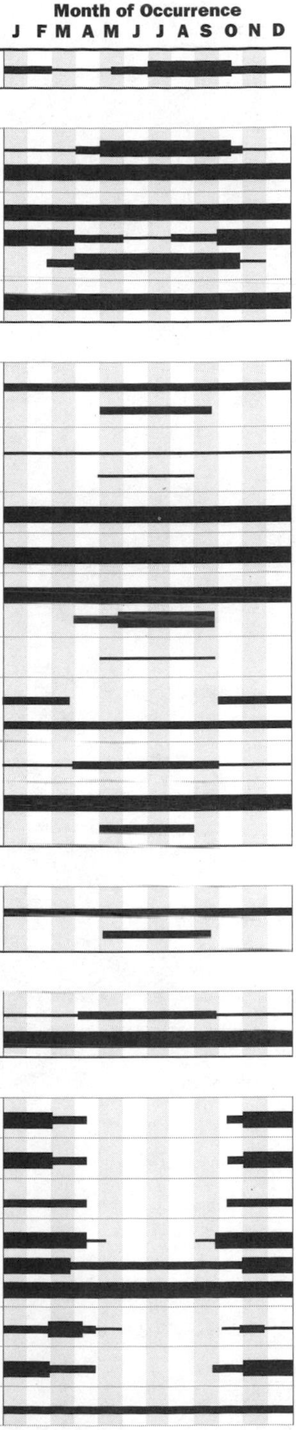

Legend:
- Common to abundant
- Uncommon to fairly common
- Rare
- Irregular; common
- Irregular; uncommon if present

Bird Species	Region	Month of Occurrence J F M A M J J A S O N D
☐ Gadwall	* N Coast	
	* C Coast; Int	
	* G Basin	
☐ Eurasian Wigeon	Coast; Int; Kl Basin	
☐ American Wigeon	Coast; Int; E of Sierra	
	* Modoc Pl	
☐ Mallard	* Widespread	
☐ Blue-winged Teal	* Coast; Int	
	* NE	
☐ Cinnamon Teal	* N Coast; G Basin	
	* Int	
☐ Northern Shoveler	* Coast; Int	
	* Modoc Pl	
	E of Sierra	
☐ Northern Pintail	* Coast; Int	
	* Modoc Pl	
	* E of Sierra	
☐ Green-winged Teal	Coast; Int	
	* Modoc Pl	
	E of Sierra	
☐ Canvasback	Coast	
	Int	
	* NE	
☐ Redhead	* Int	
	* G Basin	
☐ Ring-necked Duck	Coast; Int	
	* Modoc Pl	
☐ Greater Scaup	Coast	
☐ Lesser Scaup	Coast	
	Int	
	* NE	
☐ Harlequin Duck	N Coast	
☐ Surf Scoter	Coast	
☐ White-winged Scoter	Coast	
☐ Black Scoter	Coast	
☐ Oldsquaw	Coast	
☐ Bufflehead	Coast	
	Int; Mtns; E of Sierra	
	* Modoc Pl	
☐ Common Goldeneye	Coast; Int	
	Modoc Pl	
☐ Barrow's Goldeneye	Coast; Int; NE	
☐ Hooded Merganser	Int; NE	

See abbreviations on page 365

* = Breeds in region
? = Breeding uncertain

368

Bird Species	Region	Month of Occurrence J F M A M J J A S O N D
☐ Common Merganser	* Coast; Mtns * Modoc Pl Int; E of Sierra	
☐ Red-breasted Merganser	Coast	
☐ Ruddy Duck	* Coast; Int; G Basin	

HAWKS, KITES, *and* EAGLES

Bird Species	Region	Month of Occurrence J F M A M J J A S O N D
☐ Osprey	* N Coast; Mtns C Coast; Int * NE	
☐ White-tailed Kite	* Coast; Int	
☐ Bald Eagle	N Coast; Int; E of Sierrra * Modoc Pl; Mtns	
☐ Northern Harrier	* N Coast; Int; G Basin	
☐ Sharp-shinned Hawk	* Coast; Mtns; NE Int	
☐ Cooper's Hawk	* Coast; Mtns; G Basin * Int	
☐ Northern Goshawk	* Mtns	
☐ Red-shouldered Hawk	* Coast; NW; Int	
☐ Broad-winged Hawk	Marin Headlands	
☐ Swainson's Hawk	* CV Floor; Modoc Pl	
☐ Red-tailed Hawk	* Widespread	
☐ Ferruginous Hawk	Coast; Int; G Basin	
☐ Rough-legged Hawk	Coast; Int; G Basin	
☐ Golden Eagle	* Mtns; Foothills; G Basin	

FALCONS

Bird Species	Region	Month of Occurrence J F M A M J J A S O N D
☐ American Kestrel	* Widespread	
☐ Merlin	Coast; Int; Modoc Pl	
☐ Peregrine Falcon	* Coast; Mtns Int; G Basin	
☐ Prairie Falcon	Int * Foothills; G Basin	

PARTRIDGES, GROUSE, *and* TURKEYS

Bird Species	Region	Month of Occurrence J F M A M J J A S O N D
☐ Chukar (**Intro**)	* G Basin; S Coast R	
☐ Ring-necked Pheasant (**Intro**)	* Int; G Basin	
☐ Ruffed Grouse	* NW	
☐ Sage Grouse	* G Basin	
☐ White-tailed Ptarmigan (**Intro**)	* Tioga Pass	

Common to abundant   Rare   Irregular; uncommon if present
Uncommon to fairly common   Irregular; common

Bird Species	Region	Month of Occurrence J F M A M J J A S O N D
☐ Blue Grouse	* Mtns	
☐ Wild Turkey (**Intro**)	* Foothills	

NEW WORLD QUAILS

Bird Species	Region	
☐ Mountain Quail	* Mtns	
☐ California Quail	* Widespread	

RAILS, GALLINULES, *and* COOTS

Bird Species	Region	
☐ Black Rail	* Coast; SF Bay; Yuba Co	
☐ Clapper Rail	* SF Bay	
☐ Virginia Rail	Coast * Int * G Basin	
☐ Sora	Coast * Int * G Basin	
☐ Common Moorhen	* Int	
☐ American Coot	* Coast * Int; G Basin	

CRANES

Bird Species	Region	
☐ Sandhill Crane	Int * Modoc Pl	

PLOVERS

Bird Species	Region	
☐ Black-bellied Plover	Coast Int Kl Basin	
☐ American Golden-Plover	Coast; Int	
☐ Pacific Golden-Plover	Coast; Int	
☐ Snowy Plover	* Coast * G Basin (local)	
☐ Semipalmated Plover	Coast Int; G Basin	
☐ Killdeer	* Coast; Int * G Basin	
☐ Mountain Plover	Int	

OYSTERCATCHERS

Bird Species	Region	
☐ Black Oystercatcher	* Coast	

STILTS *and* AVOCETS

Bird Species	Region	
☐ Black-necked Stilt	* SF Bay; C Coast * Int; Modoc Pl	

* = Breeds in region
? = Breeding uncertain

Bird Species	Region	Month of Occurrence J F M A M J J A S O N D
☐ American Avocet	* SF Bay; C Coast * N Coast * Int; G Basin	

SANDPIPERS *and* PHALAROPES

Bird Species	Region	Month of Occurrence J F M A M J J A S O N D
☐ Greater Yellowlegs	Coast; Int G Basin	
☐ Lesser Yellowlegs	Coast; Int; NE	
☐ Solitary Sandpiper	Coast; Int; NE	
☐ Willet	Coast; SF Bay * Modoc Pl	
☐ Wandering Tattler	N Coast C Coast	
☐ Spotted Sandpiper	* Coast Int * Mtns; G Basin	
☐ Whimbrel	Coast Int	
☐ Long-billed Curlew	Coast; Int * Modoc Pl	
☐ Marbled Godwit	Coast; SF Bay	
☐ Ruddy Turnstone	Coast	
☐ Black Turnstone	Coast; SF Bay	
☐ Surfbird	Coast	
☐ Red Knot	Coast (local); SF Bay	
☐ Sanderling	Coast	
☐ Semipalmated Sandpiper	Coast	
☐ Western Sandpiper	Coast Int; G Basin	
☐ Least Sandpiper	Coast; Int G Basin	
☐ Baird's Sandpiper	Coast	
☐ Pectoral Sandpiper	Coast	
☐ Rock Sandpiper	Coast (local)	
☐ Dunlin	Coast; Int Kl Basin	
☐ Short-billed Dowitcher	Coast	
☐ Long-billed Dowitcher	Coast; Int G Basin	
☐ Common Snipe	Coast; Int * G Basin	

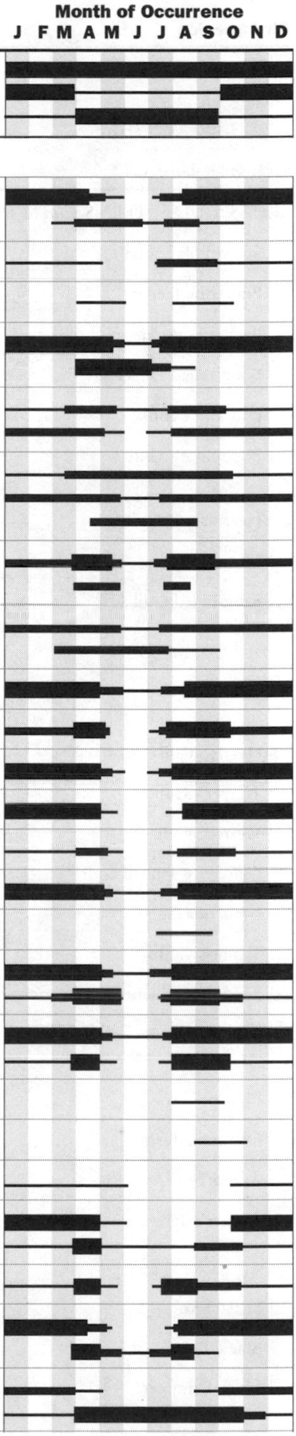

Legend:
- ▬ Common to abundant
- ▬ Uncommon to fairly common
- — Rare
- ▓ Irregular; common
- ▓ Irregular; uncommon if present

Bird Species	Region	Month of Occurrence J F M A M J J A S O N D
☐ Wilson's Phalarope	Coast; Int	
	* G Basin	
☐ Red-necked Phalarope	Coast; Int; G Basin	
☐ Red Phalarope	Coast	

SKUAS, GULLS, TERNS, and SKIMMERS

Bird Species	Region	Month of Occurrence J F M A M J J A S O N D
☐ South Polar Skua	Pelagic	
☐ Pomarine Jaeger	Pelagic	
☐ Parasitic Jaeger	Pelagic	
☐ Long-tailed Jaeger	Pelagic	
☐ Franklin's Gull	G Basin	
☐ Bonaparte's Gull	Coast; Int	
	Kl Basin	
☐ Heermann's Gull	Coast	
☐ Mew Gull	Coast	
☐ Ring-billed Gull	Coast; Int	
	* Modoc Pl	
	E of Sierra	
☐ California Gull	Coast; Int	
	* G Basin	
☐ Herring Gull	Coast; Int	
☐ Thayer's Gull	Coast; Int	
☐ Western Gull	* Coast	
☐ Glaucous-winged Gull	Coast	
☐ Glaucous Gull	Coast	
☐ Sabine's Gull	Pelagic	
☐ Black-legged Kittiwake	Usually pelagic	
☐ Caspian Tern	* Coast; G Basin	
	Int	
☐ Elegant Tern	Coast	
☐ Common Tern	Coast	
☐ Arctic Tern	Usually pelagic	
☐ Forster's Tern	* C Coast	
	N Coast; Int	
	* G Basin	
☐ Least Tern	* SF Bay	
☐ Black Tern	* Modoc Pl; CV Floor	
☐ Black Skimmer	* SF Bay	

See abbreviations on page 365

* = Breeds in region
? = Breeding uncertain

Bird Species	Region	Month of Occurrence J F M A M J J A S O N D
AUKS, MURRES, *and* PUFFINS		
☐ Common Murre	* Coast	
☐ Pigeon Guillemot	* Coast	
☐ Marbled Murrelet	* Coast	
☐ Xantus's Murrelet	Pelagic	
☐ Craveri's Murrelet	Pelagic	
☐ Ancient Murrelet	Usually pelagic	
☐ Cassin's Auklet	* Usually pelagic	
☐ Rhinoceros Auklet	* Usually pelagic	
☐ Tufted Puffin	* N Coast	
PIGEONS *and* DOVES		
☐ Rock Dove (**Intro**)	* Widespread	
☐ Band-tailed Pigeon	* Coast; Mtns	
☐ Spotted Dove (**Intro**)	* Fresno	
☐ Mourning Dove	* Coast; Int * G Basin	
CUCKOOS *and* ROADRUNNERS		
☐ Yellow-billed Cuckoo	* Sac R; Kern R	
☐ Greater Roadrunner	* Int	
BARN OWLS		
☐ Barn Owl	* Widespread	
TYPICAL OWLS		
☐ Flammulated Owl	* Mtns	
☐ Western Screech-Owl	* Widespread	
☐ Great Horned Owl	* Widespread	
☐ Northern Pygmy-Owl	* Coast; Mtns	
☐ Burrowing Owl	* SF Bay; Int	
☐ Spotted Owl	* Coast; Mtns	
☐ Barred Owl	* NW	
☐ Great Gray Owl	* Yosemite	
☐ Long-eared Owl	* C Coast; G Basin Int	
☐ Short-eared Owl	* Coast; Int * G Basin	
☐ Northern Saw-whet Owl	* Coast; Mtns	

Common to abundant   Rare   Irregular; uncommon if present
Uncommon to fairly common   Irregular; common

Bird Species	Region	Month of Occurrence J F M A M J J A S O N D

GOATSUCKERS

☐ Lesser Nighthawk — * Int; Kern R

☐ Common Nighthawk — * Mtns; G Basin

☐ Common Poorwill — * Foothills, G Basin

SWIFTS

☐ Black Swift — * C Coast; Mtns

☐ Vaux's Swift — * N Coast; Mtns

☐ White-throated Swift — * C Coast; S Coast R / * Sierra Nevada

HUMMINGBIRDS

☐ Black-chinned Hummingbird — * Int; Modoc Pl

☐ Anna's Hummingbird — * Coast; Int / * Mtns

☐ Costa's Hummingbird — * S Coast R; Kern R

☐ Calliope Hummingbird — * Mtns; E of Sierra

☐ Broad-tailed Hummingbird — * White Mtns

☐ Rufous Hummingbird — Coast; Int; Mtns

☐ Allen's Hummingbird — * Coast

KINGFISHERS

☐ Belted Kingfisher — * Coast; Int / * Mtns; G Basin

WOODPECKERS

☐ Lewis's Woodpecker — Int / * G Basin; Inner Coast R

☐ Acorn Woodpecker — * C Coast; Int; Mtns

☐ Williamson's Sapsucker — * Mtns

☐ Red-naped Sapsucker — * Warner & White Mtns

☐ Red-breasted Sapsucker — C Coast; Int / * N Coast; Mtns

☐ Ladder-backed Woodpecker — * Kern R

☐ Nuttall's Woodpecker — * C Coast; Int

☐ Downy Woodpecker — * Widespread

☐ Hairy Woodpecker — * Coast; Mtns

☐ White-headed Woodpecker — * Mtns

☐ Black-backed Woodpecker — * Mtns

☐ Northern Flicker — * Widespread

☐ Pileated Woodpecker — * N Coast; Mtns

See abbreviations on page 365

* = Breeds in region
? = Breeding uncertain

374

Bird Species	Region	Month of Occurrence (J F M A M J J A S O N D)
TYRANT FLYCATCHERS		
☐ Olive-sided Flycatcher	* Coast; Mtns	
	Int	
☐ Western Wood-Pewee	* Widespread	
☐ Willow Flycatcher	Int	
	* Mtns; Kern R	
☐ Hammond's Flycatcher	Int	
	* Mtns	
☐ Gray Flycatcher	* G Basin	
☐ Dusky Flycatcher	Int	
	* Mtns	
☐ Pacific-slope Flycatcher	* Coast; Mtns	
	Int	
☐ Cordilleran Flycatcher	* Warner Mtns	
☐ Black Phoebe	* Coast; Int	
☐ Say's Phoebe	Coast; Int	
	* G Basin	
	* S Coast R; Kern R	
☐ Vermilion Flycatcher	* Kern R	
☐ Ash-throated Flycatcher	* Int; Modoc Pl; Kern R	
☐ Brown-crested Flycatcher	* Kern R	
☐ Cassin's Kingbird	* S Coast R	
☐ Western Kingbird	* Int; G Basin	
SHRIKES		
☐ Loggerhead Shrike	* Int	
	* G Basin	
☐ Northern Shrike	G Basin	
VIREOS		
☐ Plumbeous Vireo	* White Mtns	
☐ Cassin's Vireo	* Mtns	
	Int; G Basin	
☐ Hutton's Vireo	* Coast; Foothills; Mtns	
☐ Warbling Vireo	* Coast; Mtns; E of Sierra	
	Int; Modoc Pl	
CROWS *and* JAYS		
☐ Gray Jay	* NW; Cascades	
☐ Steller's Jay	* Coast; Mtns	
☐ Western Scrub-Jay	* Coast; Int	
	* G Basin	

Legend:
- ▇ Common to abundant
- ▬ Uncommon to fairly common
- — Rare
- ▒ Irregular; common
- ░ Irregular; uncommon if present

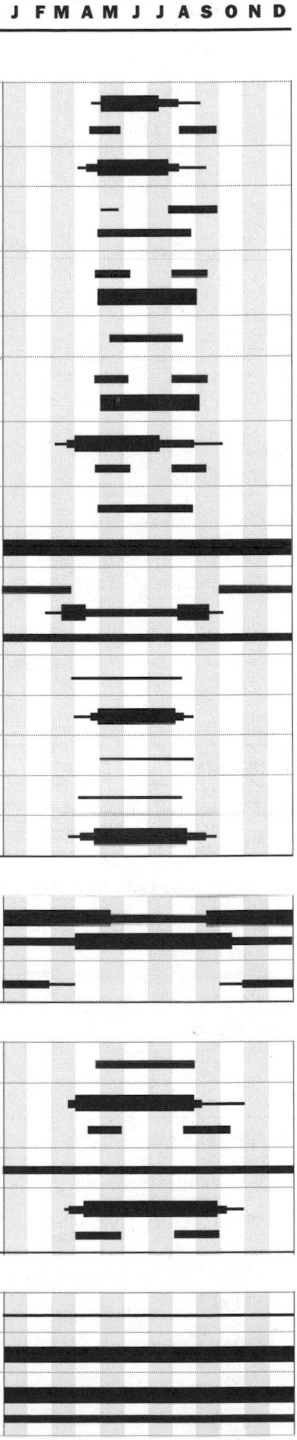

Bird Species	Region	Month of Occurrence J F M A M J J A S O N D
☐ Pinyon Jay	* G Basin	
☐ Clark's Nutcracker	* Mtns	
☐ Black-billed Magpie	* G Basin	
☐ Yellow-billed Magpie	* Int	
☐ American Crow	* Widespread	
☐ Common Raven	* Int * N Coast; Mtns; G Basin	

LARKS

☐ Horned Lark	* Widespread	

SWALLOWS

☐ Purple Martin	* Local: Coast; Int; NE	
☐ Tree Swallow	* Widespread	
☐ Violet-green Swallow	* N Coast; Mtns; G Basin * C Coast; Int	
☐ Northern Rough-winged Swallow	* Widespread	
☐ Bank Swallow	* C Coast; Sac Valley * Modoc Pl	
☐ Cliff Swallow	* Widespread	
☐ Barn Swallow	* Widespread	

CHICKADEES *and* TITMICE

☐ Black-capped Chickadee	* NW	
☐ Mountain Chickadee	* Mtns	
☐ Chestnut-backed Chickadee	* Coast; NW * N Sierra (local)	
☐ Oak Titmouse	* C Coast; Int	
☐ Juniper Titmouse	* G Basin	

BUSHTITS

☐ Bushtit	* Coast; NW; Int * G Basin	

NUTHATCHES

☐ Red-breasted Nuthatch	* Mtns	
☐ White-breasted Nuthatch	* Widespread	
☐ Pygmy Nuthatch	* Coast; Mtns; E of Sierra	

CREEPERS

☐ Brown Creeper	* Coast; Mtns	

WRENS

☐ Cactus Wren	* Kern R	

See abbreviations on page 365

* = Breeds in region
? = Breeding uncertain

Bird Species	Region	Month of Occurrence J F M A M J J A S O N D
☐ Rock Wren	* Int; Mtns * G Basin	
☐ Canyon Wren	* Int (local); Mtns; G Basin	
☐ Bewick's Wren	* Coast; Int; Mtns; Modoc Pl * E of Sierra	
☐ House Wren	* Widespread	
☐ Winter Wren	* Coast * Mtns	
☐ Marsh Wren	* Coast; Int * Modoc Pl	

DIPPERS

☐ American Dipper	* Coast; Mtns	

KINGLETS

☐ Golden-crowned Kinglet	* N Coast; Mtns * G Basin	
☐ Ruby-crowned Kinglet	Coast; Int * Mtns G Basin	

GNATCATCHERS

☐ Blue-gray Gnatcatcher	* Int; G Basin	

THRUSHES

☐ Western Bluebird	* Int; Mtns; Modoc Pl	
☐ Mountain Bluebird	* Mtns * G Basin	
☐ Townsend's Solitare	* Mtns; G Basin	
☐ Swainson's Thrush	* Coast	
☐ Hermit Thrush	* Coast Int * Mtns	
☐ American Robin	* Widespread	
☐ Varied Thrush	* N Coast C Coast; Int; Mtns	

BABBLERS

☐ Wrentit	* Coast; NW; Int	

MOCKINGBIRDS and THRASHERS

☐ Northern Mockingbird	* C Coast; Int	
☐ Sage Thrasher	* G Basin	
☐ California Thrasher	* Coast; Int	

Common to abundant   Rare   Irregular; uncommon if present
Uncommon to fairly common   Irregular; common

Bird Species	Region	Month of Occurrence J F M A M J J A S O N D

STARLINGS

☐ European Starling (**Intro**) — * Widespread

PIPITS

☐ American Pipit — Coast; Int; G Basin / * Alpine Sierra Nevada

WAXWINGS

☐ Bohemian Waxwing — NE; Surprise Valley

☐ Cedar Waxwing — C Coast; Int / * N Coast

SILKY-FLYCATCHERS

☐ Phainopepla — * Foothills

WOOD-WARBLERS

☐ Orange-crowned Warbler — * Coast / * Int / Mtns; E of Sierra / Modoc Pl

☐ Nashville Warbler — Int / * Mtns

☐ Yellow Warbler — * Coast; Mtns; G Basin / ? Int

☐ Yellow-rumped Warbler — Coast; Int / * Mtns / G Basin

☐ Black-throated Gray Warbler — * Mtns; Foothills / CV Floor

☐ Townsend's Warbler — Coast / Int; Mtns; E of Sierra

☐ Hermit Warbler — * N Coast; Mtns / * C Coast

☐ Palm Warbler — Coast

☐ Blackpoll Warbler — Coast

☐ Black-and-white Warbler — Coast

☐ American Redstart — C Coast / * N Coast

☐ MacGillivray's Warbler — Coast; Int; G Basin / * Mtns

☐ Common Yellowthroat — * N Coast; G Basin / * C Coast; Int

☐ Wilson's Warbler — * Coast; Mtns / Int; G Basin

☐ Yellow-breasted Chat — * NW; Int (local)

See abbreviations on page 365

* = Breeds in region
? = Breeding uncertain

Bird Species	Region	Month of Occurrence (J F M A M J J A S O N D)
TANAGERS		
☐ Summer Tanager	* Kern R	
☐ Western Tanager	* N Coast; Mtns	
	C Coast; Int; NE	
EMBERIZIDS		
☐ Green-tailed Towhee	* Mtns; G Basin	
☐ Spotted Towhee	* Coast; Int; G Basin	
☐ California Towhee	* C Coast; Int	
☐ Rufous-crowned Sparrow	* Foothills	
☐ Chipping Sparrow	* Coast; Mtns	
☐ Clay-colored Sparrow	Coast	
☐ Brewer's Sparrow	* G Basin	
☐ Black-chinned Sparrow	* Foothills	
☐ Vesper Sparrow	* G Basin	
☐ Lark Sparrow	* Int	
	* G Basin	
☐ Black-throated Sparrow	* G Basin; Kern R	
☐ Sage Sparrow	* Foothills	
	* G Basin	
☐ Savannah Sparrow	* Coast	
	Int	
	* G Basin	
☐ Grasshopper Sparrow	* C Coast; Foothills	
☐ Fox Sparrow	Coast; Int	
	* Mtns	
☐ Song Sparrow	* Widespread	
☐ Lincoln's Sparrow	Coast; Int	
	* Mtns	
	G Basin	
☐ Swamp Sparrow	Coast	
☐ White-throated Sparrow	Coast; Int	
☐ White-crowned Sparrow	* Coast	
	Int	
	* Mtns	
	G Basin	
☐ Golden-crowned Sparrow	Coast; Int	
	G Basin	
☐ Dark-eyed Junco ("Oregon")	* Coast; Mtns	
	Int; G Basin	
☐ Lapland Longspur	N Coast; G Basin	

Legend:

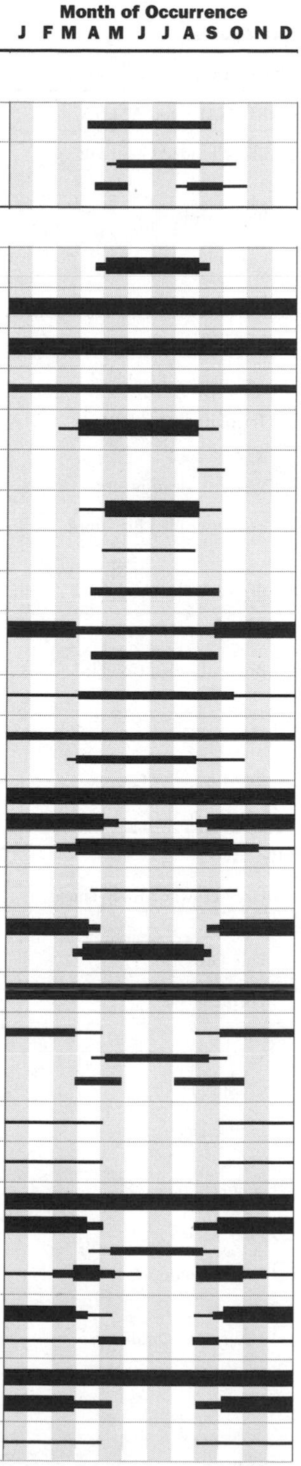

■ Common to abundant
▬ Uncommon to fairly common
— Rare
▨ Irregular; common
▦ Irregular; uncommon if present

Bird Species	Region	Month of Occurrence J F M A M J J A S O N D

| Chestnut-collared Longspur | G Basin | |

CARDINALS *and* ALLIES

Black-headed Grosbeak	* Coast; Int; Mtns * G Basin	
Blue Grosbeak	* Int	
Lazuli Bunting	* Int; Mtns; G Basin	
Indigo Bunting	* Kern R	

BLACKBIRDS

Red-winged Blackbird	* Widespread	
Tricolored Blackbird	* C Coast; Int; Kern R * NE	
Western Meadowlark	* Widespread	
Yellow-headed Blackbird	* Int * G Basin	
Brewer's Blackbird	* Widespread	
Great-tailed Grackle	* Int; Kern R	
Brown-headed Cowbird	* Coast; Int * Mtns; G Basin	
Hooded Oriole	* Coast; CV Floor; Kern R	
Bullock's Oriole	* Coast; NW; Int; G Basin	
Scott's Oriole	* Kern R	

FINCHES

Gray-crowned Rosy-Finch	* Mtns G Basin	
Pine Grosbeak	* Sierra Nevada	
Purple Finch	* Coast * Mtns Foothills	
Cassin's Finch	* Mtns	
House Finch	* Coast; Int; Modoc Pl * E of Sierra	
Red Crossbill	* N Coast; Mtns	
Pine Siskin	* Coast; Mtns	
Lesser Goldfinch	* Coast; Int * G Basin	
Lawrence's Goldfinch	* Foothills; Kern R	
American Goldfinch	* C Coast; Int * N Coast * Modoc Pl E of Sierra	

See abbreviations on page 365

* = Breeds in region
? = Breeding uncertain

380

Bird Species	Region	Month of Occurrence J F M A M J J A S O N D
☐ Evening Grosbeak	* Mtns	

OLD WORLD SPARROWS

☐ House Sparrow (**Intro**)	* Widespread	

Common to abundant   Rare   Irregular; uncommon if present
Uncommon to fairly common   Irregular; common

Unexpected birds

Species that are very rare in Northern California, are accidental vagrants, or are extirpated (shown by an "E")

Arctic Loon
Yellow-billed Loon
Light-mantled Albatross
Wandering Albatross
Short-tailed Albatross
Murphy's Petrel
Mottled Petrel
Dark-rumped Petrel
Cook's Petrel
Stejneger's Petrel
Streaked Shearwater
Greater Shearwater
Wedge-tailed Shearwater
Manx Shearwater
Wilson's Storm-Petrel
Wedge-rumped Storm-Petrel
Red-billed Tropicbird
Red-tailed Tropicbird
Masked Booby
Blue-footed Booby
Brown Booby
Red-footed Booby
Anhinga
Magnificent Frigatebird
Great Frigatebird
Tricolored Heron
Reddish Egret
Yellow-crowned Night-Heron
Roseate Spoonbill
Wood Stork
Black Vulture
California Condor
Fulvous Whistling-Duck (E)
Emperor Goose
Trumpeter Swan
Whooper Swan
American Black Duck
Garganey
Baikal Teal

Tufted Duck
Steller's Eider
King Eider
Smew
Mississippi Kite
Gyrfalcon
Sharp-tailed Grouse (E)
Yellow Rail
Purple Gallinule
Mongolian Plover
Wilson's Plover
Eurasian Dotterel
Spotted Redshank
Terek Sandpiper
Upland Sandpiper
Little Curlew
Bristle-thighed Curlew
Hudsonian Godwit
Bar-tailed Godwit
Red-necked Stint
Little Stint
Long-toed Stint
White-rumped Sandpiper
Sharp-tailed Sandpiper
Curlew Sandpiper
Stilt Sandpiper
Buff-breasted Sandpiper
Ruff
Jack Snipe
Laughing Gull
Little Gull
Black-headed Gull
Lesser Black-backed Gull
Yellow-footed Gull
Royal Tern
White-winged Tern
Thick-billed Murre
Long-billed Murrelet
Parakeet Auklet
Least Auklet
Crested Auklet

Horned Puffin
White-winged Dove
Common Ground-Dove
Black-billed Cuckoo
Snowy Owl
Chuck-will's-widow
Whip-poor-will
White-collared Swift
Chimney Swift
Broad-billed Hummingbird
Violet-crowned Hummingbird
Blue-throated Hummingbird
Ruby-throated Hummingbird
Red-headed Woodpecker
Yellow-bellied Sapsucker
Three-toed Woodpecker
Greater Pewee
Eastern Wood-Pewee
Yellow-bellied Flycatcher
Least Flycatcher
Eastern Phoebe
Dusky-capped Flycatcher
Great Crested Flycatcher
Sulphur-bellied Flycatcher
Tropical Kingbird
Thick-billed Kingbird
Eastern Kingbird
Scissor-tailed Flycatcher
Fork-tailed Flycatcher
Brown Shrike
White-eyed Vireo
Bell's Vireo
Gray Vireo
Yellow-throated Vireo
Blue-headed Vireo
Philadelphia Vireo
Red-eyed Vireo
Yellow-green Vireo

Blue Jay
Sky Lark
Sedge Wren
Lanceolated Warbler
Dusky Warbler
Arctic Warbler
Red-flanked Bluetail
Northern Wheatear
Veery
Gray-cheeked Thrush
Wood Thrush
Gray Catbird
Brown Thrasher
Bendire's Thrasher
LeConte's Thrasher
Yellow Wagtail
Gray Wagtail
White Wagtail
Black-backed Wagtail
Red-throated Pipit
Sprague's Pipit
Blue-winged Warbler
Golden-winged Warbler
Tennessee Warbler
Virginia's Warbler
Lucy's Warbler
Northern Parula

Chestnut-sided Warbler
Magnolia Warbler
Cape May Warbler
Black-throated Blue
    Warbler
Golden-cheeked Warbler
Black-throated Green
    Warbler
Blackburnian Warbler
Yellow-throated Warbler
Grace's Warbler
Pine Warbler
Prairie Warbler
Bay-breasted Warbler
Cerulean Warbler
Prothonotary Warbler
Worm-eating Warbler
Ovenbird
Northern Waterthrush
Louisiana Waterthrush
Kentucky Warbler
Connecticut Warbler
Mourning Warbler
Hooded Warbler
Canada Warbler
Red-faced Warbler
Painted Redstart

Hepatic Tanager
Scarlet Tanager
Cassin's Sparrow
American Tree Sparrow
Field Sparrow
Lark Bunting
Baird's Sparrow
LeConte's Sparrow
Nelson's Sharp-tailed
    Sparrow
Harris's Sparrow
McCown's Longspur
Smith's Longspur
Rustic Bunting
Snow Bunting
Rose-breasted Grosbeak
Painted Bunting
Dickcissel
Bobolink
Rusty Blackbird
Common Grackle
Orchard Oriole
Baltimore Oriole
Brambling
Black Rosy Finch
White-winged Crossbill
Common Redpoll

Appendix A: Addresses and Phone Numbers

Almanor Ranger District, Lassen National Forest, P.O. Box 767, Chester, CA 96020, (530) 258-2141

Alum Rock Park, 16240 Alum Rock Avenue, San Jose, CA 95127-1307, (408) 259-5477

Amador Ranger District, 26820 Silver Drive and Highway 88, Star Route 3, Pioneer, CA 95666, (209) 295-4251

Annadel State Park, 6201 Channel Drive, Santa Rosa, CA 95409, (707) 539-3911

Año Nuevo State Reserve, New Years Creek Road, Pescadero, CA 94060, (831) 879-2025

Ash Creek Wildlife Area, P.O. Box 37, Bieber, CA 96009, (530) 294-5824

Bidwell–Sacramento River State Park, 12105 River Road, Chico, CA 95926-4819, (530) 342-5185

Big Sur Lodge, (800) 424-4787.

Bodie State Historic Park, P.O. Box 515, Bridgeport, CA 93517, (760) 647-6142

Bothe–Napa Valley State Park, 3801 St. Helena Highway North, Calistoga, CA 94515, (707) 942-4575

Bureau of Land Management (Hollister), 20 Hamilton Court, Hollister, CA 95023-2535, (831) 630-5000

Butte Valley Wildlife Area, P.O. Box 249, Macdoel, CA 96058, (530) 398-4627

California Duck Days, (800) 425-5001

Carson Ranger District, 1536 South Carson Street, Carson City, NV 89701, (702) 882-2766

Caswell Memorial State Park, 28,000 South Austin Road, Ripon, CA 95366, (209) 599-3810

Chico Creek Nature Center, 1968 East Eighth Street, Chico CA 95928, (530) 891-4671

City of Arcata, 736 F Street, Arcata, CA 95521, (707) 822-5953

City of Oakland, Rotary Nature Center, 552 Bellevue Avenue, Oakland, CA 94610, (510) 238-2729

Clear Lake State Park, 5300 Soda Bay Road, Kelseyville, CA 95451, (707) 279-4293 or (707) 279-2267

Cosumnes River Preserve, 13501 Franklin Boulevard, Galt, CA 95632, (916) 684-2816

County of San Mateo Parks and Recreation Division, 590 Hamilton Street, Redwood City, CA 94063, (650) 363-4020

Coyote Creek Riparian Station, P.O. Box 1027, Alviso, CA 95002, (408) 262-9204

Davis Chamber of Commerce, 228 B Street, Davis, CA 95616, (530) 756-5160

Deer Creek Campground; *see* Frank Raines Regional Park.

Del Valle Regional Park, c/o East Bay Regional Park District, 2950 Peralta Oaks Court, P.O. Box 5381, Oakland, CA 94605-0381. For Del Valle information, call (510) 373-0332

Department of Fish and Game (Redding), 2440 Athens Avenue, Redding, CA 96001, (530) 225-2143

Department of Fish and Game (Yountville), P.O. Box 47, Yountville, CA 94599, (707) 944-5538

Devils Garden Ranger District, 800 West Twelfth Street, Alturas, CA 96101, (530) 233-5811

Don Edwards San Francisco Bay National Wildlife Refuge, P.O. Box 524, Newark, CA 94560, (510) 792-0222

Donner Memorial State Park, 12593 Donner Pass Road, Truckee, CA 96161, (530) 582-7892

Doran Beach Regional Park, P.O. Box 372, Bodega Bay, CA 94923, (707) 875-3540

Downieville Ranger District, 15924 Highway 49, Camptonville, CA 95922-9707, (530) 288-3231

Eagle Lake Ranger District, 477050 Eagle Lake Road, Susanville, CA 96130, (530) 257-4188

East Bay Regional Parks District, 2950 Peralta Oaks Court, P.O. Box 5381, Oakland, CA 94605-0381, (510) 562-7275

Eldorado Information Center (U.S. Forest Service), 3070 Camino Heights Drive, Camino, CA 96709, (530) 644-6048

Elkhorn Slough National Estuarine Research Reserve, 1700 Elkhorn Road, Watsonville, CA 95076, (831) 728-2822

Foresthill Ranger District, 22830 Foresthill Road, Foresthill, CA 95631, (530) 367-2224

Four Creeks Land Trust, 1002 W. Main Street, Visalia, CA 93291, (209) 738-0211

Frank Raines Regional Park, c/o Stanislaus County Parks and Recreation, 1716 Morgan Road, Modesto, CA 95358, (408) 897-3127

Golden Gate National Recreation Area, Fort Mason, San Francisco, 94123; for Presidio information, call (415) 556-0865; for Marin Headlands information, call (415) 331-1540

Golden Gate Raptor Observatory, Building 201, Fort Mason, San Francisco, CA 94123, (415) 331-0730.

Gray Lodge Wildlife Area, 3207 Rutherford Road, Gridley, CA 95948, (530) 846-5176

Grizzly Island Wildlife Complex, 2548 Grizzly Island Road, Suisun, CA 94585, (707) 425-3828

Honey Lake Wildlife Area, 728-600 Fish and Game Road, Wendel, CA 96136, (530) 254-6644

Hot Springs Ranger District, Route 4, Box 548, California Hot Springs, CA 93207, (805) 548-6503

James V. Fitzgerald Marine Reserve, P.O. Box 451, Moss Beach, CA 94038, (650) 728-3584

Jedediah Smith Redwoods State Park, 4241 Kings Valley Road, Crescent City, CA 95531, (707) 464-9533

Kern River Preserve, P.O. Box 1662, Weldon, CA 93283, (760) 378-2531

Kern Valley Bioregions Festival, Box 410, Weldon, CA 93283

Klamath Basin National Wildlife Refuges, Route 1, Box 74, Tulelake, CA 96134, (530) 667-2231

Laguna Seca Regional Park, (408) 422-6138

Lake Earl Wildlife Area, P.O. Box 1934, Crescent City, CA 95531, (707) 464-2523 or (707) 443-6771

Lake Kaweah (Corps of Engineers), P.O. Box 44270, Lemon Cove, CA 93244, (209) 597-2301

Lake Oroville State Recreation Area, 400 Glen Drive, Oroville, CA 95965, (530) 534-2409

Lake Solano County Park, 8685 Pleasants Valley Road, Winters, CA 95694, (800) 939-7275

Lake Tahoe Basin Management Unit, 870 Emerald Bay Road, Suite 1, South Lake Tahoe, CA 96150, (530) 573-2600

Las Gallinas Valley Sanitary District, 300 Smith Ranch Road, San Rafael, CA 94903, (415) 472-1734

Lassen Volcanic National Park, P.O. Box 100, Mineral, CA 96063, (530) 595-4444

Lower Trinity Ranger District, 580 Highway 96, Willow Creek, CA 95573, (530) 629-2118

McArthur–Burney Falls Memorial State Park, 24898 Highway 89, Burney, CA 96013, (530) 335-2777

McCloud Ranger District, P.O. Box 1620, McCloud, CA 96057, (530) 964-2184

Midpeninsula Regional Open Space District, 330 Distel Circle, Los Altos, CA 94022-1404, (650) 691-1200

Modoc National Wildlife Refuge, P.O. Box 1610, Alturas, CA 96101, (530) 233-3572

Mendocino Coast State Parks, P.O. Box 440, Highway 1, Mendocino, CA 95460, (707) 937-5804

Mollymawk Offshore Adventures, P.O. Box 821, Bodega Bay, CA 94923, (707) 762-5167

Mono Lake Ranger District, P.O. Box 429, Lee Vining, CA 93541, (760) 647-3000

Mount Diablo State Park, 96 Mitchell Canyon Road, Clayton, CA 94517, (925) 837-2525

Mount Tamalpais State Park, 801 Panoramic Highway, Mill Valley, CA 94941, (415) 388-2070

Muir Woods National Monument, Mill Valley, CA 94941, (415) 388-2595

Napa River Ecological Preserve, Department of Fish and Game, P.O. Box 47, Yountville, CA 94599, (707) 944-5538

National Audubon Society—*California*, 555 Audubon Place, Sacramento, CA 95825, (916) 481-5332

Natural Bridges State Beach, 2531 West Cliff Drive, Santa Cruz, CA 95060, (831) 423-4609

Pacific Ranger District, Pollock Pines, CA 95726, (530) 644-2349

Palo Alto Baylands Nature Preserve, 1305 Middlefield Road, Palo Alto, CA 94301, (650) 329-2261

Pfeiffer Big Sur State Park, #1, Big Sur, CA 93920, (831) 667-2315

Pinnacles National Monument, 5000 Highway 146, Paicines, CA 95043-9770, (831) 389-4485

Point Lobos State Reserve, Route 1, Box 62, Carmel, CA 93923, (831) 624-4909

Point Reyes National Seashore, Point Reyes, CA 94956, (415) 663-1092

Prairie Creek Redwoods State Park, Orick, CA 95555, (707) 488-2171

Richardson Bay Audubon Center and Sanctuary, 376 Greenwood Beach Road, Tiburon, CA 94920, (415) 388-2524

Rush Ranch Education Council, P.O. Box 115, Fairfield, CA 94533, (707) 428-7580

Sacramento County Regional Parks, Recreation, and Open Space, 3711 Branch Center Road, Sacramento, CA 95827, (916) 875-6672

Sacramento National Wildlife Refuge Complex, 752 County Road 99W, Willows, CA 95988, (530) 934-2801

San Francisco Recreation and Parks, 501 Stanyan Street, San Francisco, CA 94117, (415) 831-2783

San Luis National Wildlife Refuge Complex, P.O. Box 2176, Los Banos, CA 93635, (209) 826-3508

San Mateo Coast District Office, California Department of Parks and Recreation, 95 Kelly Avenue, Half Moon Bay, CA 94109, (650) 726-8819

Sequoia and Kings Canyon national parks, Three Rivers, CA 93271-9700, (209) 565-3341

Sequoia Audubon Society, 30 West Thirty-ninth Avenue, #202, San Mateo, CA 94403-4561, (650) 345-3724

Shearwater Journeys, P.O. Box 190, Hollister, CA 95024, (831) 637-8527

Shoreline at Mountain View, P.O. Box 7540, Mountain View, CA 94039, (650) 903-6392

Sierraville Ranger District, P.O. Box 95, Highway 89, Sierraville, CA 96126, (530) 994-3401

Silverado District, California State Parks, 20 East Spain Street, Sonoma, CA 95465, (707) 938-1519

Skyline Park Citizens Association, 2201 East Imola Avenue, Napa, CA 94559-0793, (707) 252-0481

Sly Park Recreation Area, P.O. Box 577, Pollock Pines, CA 95726, (530) 644-2545; for camping reservations, call (530) 644-2792.

Sonoma Coast State Beach, Bodega Bay, CA 94923, (707) 875-3483

Spenceville Wildlife Management and Recreation Area, c/o Oroville Wildlife Area, 945 Oro Dam Boulevard West, Oroville, CA 95965, (530) 538-2236

Spring Lake County Park, 2300 County Center Drive, Suite 120A, Santa Rosa, CA 95403, (707) 527-2041

Truckee Ranger District, 10342 Highway 89 North, Truckee, CA 96161, (530) 587-3558

Tule River Ranger District, 32588 Highway 190, Springville, CA 93265, (209) 539-2607

U.S. Army Corps of Engineers, Success Lake, P.O. Box 1072, Porterville, CA 93258, (209) 784-0215

Vic Fazio Yolo Wildlife Area, 45211 County Road 32B, Davis, CA 95616, (530) 757-2461

Vulture Festival, P.O. Box 410, Weldon, CA 93283

Warner Mountain Ranger District, P.O. Box 220, Cedarville, CA 96104, (530) 279-6116

Weaverville Ranger District, P.O. Box 1190, Weaverville, CA 96093, (530) 623-2121

Whiskeytown Unit, P.O. Box 188, Whiskeytown, CA 96095, (530) 241-6584

White Mountain Ranger District, 798 North Main Street, Bishop, CA 93514, (760) 873-2500

Woodland Chamber of Commerce, 520 Main Street, Woodland, CA 95695, (530) 662-7327

Yerba Buena Nursery, 19500 Skyline Boulevard, Woodside, CA 94062, (650) 851-1668

Yosemite National Park: (this is not only the name of the park, it is the name of the post office). Write to: Superintendent, Yosemite National Park, CA 95389-0577, (209) 372-0200

Appendix B: References

Allessio, L., Bish, N., Iribarne, D. (No date.) *Birds of the Lake Tahoe Basin.* Eastern Sierra Interpretive Association, South Lake Tahoe, Calif.

American Birding Association. 1994. *Birdfinding in Forty National Forests and Grasslands.* American Birding Association, Colorado Springs, Colo.

American Birding Association. 1996. *ABA Checklist: Birds of the Continental United States and Canada* (5th ed.). American Birding Association, Colorado Springs, Colo.

American Birding Association. 1998. "Directory of Pelagic Birding Trips in North America." *Winging It,* vol. 10, no. 1, p. 11. American Birding Association, Colorado Springs, Colo.

American Ornithologists' Union. 1983. *Check-list of North American Birds* (6th ed.). American Ornithologists' Union, Lawrence, Kans.

American Ornithologists' Union. 1997. "Forty-first supplement to the American Ornithologists' Union Check-list of North American Birds." *The Auk,* vol. 114, no. 3, p. 542.

American Ornithologists' Union. 1998. *Check-list of North American Birds* (7th ed.). American Ornithologists' Union, Lawrence, Kans.

Anderson, D., Fix, D., Foerster, K., Hewitt, R., Hewston, J., Leskiw, T., Lester, G.S., LeValley, R., McAllister, S., Power, J. 1995. *A Guide to Birding in and Around Arcata.* City of Arcata, Arcata, Calif.

Anderson, D. W., England, A. S. 1987. *The Biology and Natural History of California's Wild Birds.* Department of Wildlife and Fisheries Biology, University of California, Davis, Calif.

Barbour, M., Pavlik, B., Drysdale, F., Lindstrom, S. 1993. *California's Changing Landscapes.* California Native Plant Society, Sacramento, Calif.

Beedy, E. C. 1993. *Checklist of the Birds of Yolo County.* Yolo Audubon Society, Davis, Calif.

Beedy, E. C., Granholm, S. L. 1985. *Discovering Sierra Birds.* Yosemite Natural History Association, and Sequoia Natural History Association.

Bell, B., Harper, E., Johnson, D., Manolis, T., Persson, J. 1993. *Checklist of the Birds of the Sacramento Area.* Sacramento Audubon Society, Sacramento, Calif.

Bolander, G., Parmeter, B. 1978. *Birds of Sonoma County, California.* Redwood Region Ornithological Society.

Burridge, B. 1995. *Sonoma County Breeding Bird Atlas.* Madrone Audubon Society, Santa Rosa, Calif.

California Department of Fish and Game. (No date.) *Birds of the Suisun Marsh Area, California.* The Resources Agency, Department of Fish and Game, Sacramento, Calif.

California Department of Fish and Game. (No date.) *Living with California Mountain Lions.* The Resources Agency, Department of Fish and Game, Sacramento, Calif.

California Department of Fish and Game. *Outdoor California,* vol. 57, no. 3 (Special Mountain Lion Issue). The Resources Agency, Department. of Fish and Game, Sacramento, Calif.

Choate, E. A. (rev. by Paynter, R. A., Jr.). 1985. *The Dictionary of American Bird Names (Revised Edition).* The Harvard Common Press, Boston, Mass.

Cicero, Carla. 1996. *Sibling Species of Titmice in the* Parus inornatus *Complex (Aves: Paridae),* University of California Publications in Zoology, vol. 128, University of California Press, Berkeley, Calif.

Clark, J. L. 1996. *California Wildlife Viewing Guide,* rev. ed. Falcon Press, Helena, Mont.

Clark, N., Ekstrom, R., Robbins, M. 1990. *Birds of Siskiyou County.* Mt. Shasta Area Audubon Society, Weed, Calif.

Clark, W. S., Wheeler, B. K. 1987. *A Field Guide to Hawks, North America.* Houghton Mifflin, Boston, Mass.

Constantine, H. 1993. *Plant Communities of the Mono Basin.* Kutzavi Press, Mono Lake Committee, Lee Vining, Calif.

Cosumnes River Preserve. 1996. *A Field Checklist for Birds of the Cosumnes River Preserve.* Cosumnes River Preserve, Galt, Calif.

Crumpton, P. 1994. *Bird Checklist, Shasta-Trinity National Forests.* Shasta-Trinity National Forests, Redding, Calif.

DeSante, D. R. and Ruhlen, E. D. 1995. *A Census of Burrowing Owls in California, 1991–1993* (Draft). The Institute for Bird Populations, Point Reyes Station, Calif.

Dillinger, W. C. (ed.). 1981. *Birds of the Sacramento Area (Revised).* Audubon Society of Sacramento, Sacramento, Calif.

Drummond, R. 1990. *Ticks, and What You Can Do About Them.* Wilderness Press, Berkeley, Calif.

Dunn, J., Blom, E. A. T. (chief consultants). 1987. *National Geographic Society Field Guide to the Birds of North America* (2nd ed). National Geographic Society, Washington, D.C.

Dunne, P., Sibley, D., Sutton, C. 1988. *Hawks in Flight.* Houghton Mifflin, Boston, Mass.

Edwards, A. L. 1996. *Livermore Birds: Habitats, Status, Abundances, Locations.* Arthur L. Edwards, Livermore, Calif.

Edwards, A. L. 1997. *Mines Road, San Antonio Valley, Del Puerto Canyon and Corral Hollow Springtime Birding Loop.* Arthur L. Edwards, Livermore, Calif.

Farrand, J., Jr. 1983. *The Audubon Society Master Guide to Birding.* 3 vols. Alfred A. Knopf, New York, N.Y.

Fisher, C. C., Morlan, J. 1996. *Birds of San Francisco and the Bay Area.* Lone Pine Publishing, Redmond, Wash.

Gaines, D. 1988. *Birds of Yosemite and the East Slope.* Artemisia Press, Lee Vining, Calif.

Gaines, D. (rev. by Davis, L.). 1989. *Mono Lake Guidebook.* Kutsavi Books, Lee Vining, Calif.

Garrett, K., Dunn, J. 1981. *Birds of Southern California, Status and Distribution.* Los Angeles Audubon Society, Los Angeles, Calif.

Gordon, P., Hintsa, K. 1992. *Field Check-List, Birds of Mount Diablo, Contra Costa County, California.* Mt. Diablo Interpretive Association, Walnut Creek, Calif.

Green, H., Airola, D. A. 1997. *Checklist of the Birds of the Lake Almanor Area, Plumas County, California.* Helen Green, Berkeley, Calif.

Grinnell, J., Miller, A. H. 1944. *The Distribution of the Birds of California.* Cooper Ornithological Society, reprinted by Artemesia Press, Lee Vining, Calif (1986).

Gross, M. B. (ed.). 1989. *Best Birding in Napa and Solano Counties.* Napa-Solano Audubon Society, Suisun City, Calif.

Hall, C. A., Jr. (ed) 1991. *Natural History of the White-Inyo Range, Eastern California.* University of California Press, Berkeley, Calif.

Hampton, Steve. 1997. "Rare migrants in California: the determinates of their frequency," *Western Birds,* vol. 28, no. 1, pp. 30–42, Western Field Ornithologists, San Diego, Calif.

Harris, S. W. 1996. *Northwestern California Birds* (2nd ed.). Humboldt State University Press, Arcata, Calif.

Hart, J. 1996. *Storm Over Mono.* University of California Press, Berkeley, Calif.

Hatch, D. 1982. *Birds of Lassen Volcanic National Park.* Lassen Volcanic National Park, Mineral, Calif.

Heindel, M. T. 1996. "Field identification of the Solitary Vireo complex," *Birding,* vol. 28, no. 6, pp. 459–471, American Birding Association, Colorado Springs, Colo.

Hickman, J. C. (ed.). 1993. *The Jepson Manual—Higher Plants of California.* University of California Press, Berkeley, Calif.

Hunting, K. 1998. "California Mountain Plover Census," *Central Valley Bird Club Bulletin,* vol. 1, no. 2, pp. 28–29, Central Valley Bird Club, Sacramento, Calif.

Johnson, N. K. 1995. "Speciation in vireos. I. Macrogeographic patterns of allozymic variation in the *Vireo solitarius* complex in the contiguous United States," *The Condor,* vol. 97, pp. 903–919, The Cooper Ornithological Society, Lawrence, Kans.

Kaufman, K. 1990. *A Field Guide to Advanced Birding*. Houghton Mifflin, Boston, Mass.

Kaufman, K. 1997. *Kingbird Highway*. Houghton Mifflin, Boston, Mass.

Kemper, J. 1996. *Discovering Yolo County Wildlife*. Yolo Audubon Society and Yolo Basin Foundation, Davis, Calif.

Kreissman, B. 1991. *California: An Environmental Atlas & Guide*. Bear Klaw Press, Davis, Calif.

Laymon, S. A., Gallion, T., Barnes, R. A. 1996. *A Checklist of Birds of the Kern River Valley, California*. Kern River Research Center, Weldon, Calif.

Levy, C. K. 1983. *A Field Guide to Dangerous Animals of North America*. The Stephen Greene Press, Brattleboro, Vt.

Manolis, T. 1975. "The Site Guide: Honey and Eagle Lakes, California," *American Birds*, vol. 29, no. 1, pp. 19–21, National Audubon Society, New York, N.Y.

Manolis, T., Stovall, B. 1997. *Checklist of Birds of Lassen County, California*. Eagle Lake Audubon Society, Susanville, Calif.

Manolis, T., Webb, B. 1993. *Checklist of Birds of Butte County, California*. Altacal Audubon Society, Chico, Calif.

Mayer, K. E., Laudenslayer, W. F. (eds.). 1988. *A Guide to Wildlife Habitats of California*. California Department of Forestry and Fire Protection, Sacramento, Calif.

McCaskie, G., De Benedictus, P., Erickson, R., Morlan, J. 1988. *Birds of Northern California*. Golden Gate Audubon Society. Berkeley, Calif.

McCormick, M., Jensen, L., Steele, J. 1996. *Checklist of the Birds of the Sierra Valley and Yuba Pass Area*. San Francisco State University's Sierra Nevada Field Campus, Sattley, Calif.

Napa-Solano Audubon Society. 1995. *Birds (and Butterflies) of the Napa River Ecological Reserve, Napa, California*. Napa-Solano Audubon Society, Suisun City, Calif.

National Audubon Society. 1995. *Field Notes: The 95th Christmas Bird Count, 1994–95*. Vol. 49, no. 4. National Audubon Society, New York, N.Y.

National Audubon Society. 1996. *Field Notes: The 96th Christmas Bird Count, 1995–96*. Vol. 50, no. 4. National Audubon Society, New York, N.Y.

National Audubon Society. 1997. *Field Notes: The 97th Christmas Bird Count, 1996–97*. Vol. 51, no. 2. National Audubon Society, New York, N.Y.

Oliver, B., Yutzy, B., Mehden, B. V., Modeen, R., Wood, G. 1993. *Birds of Shasta County, California*. Wintu Audubon Society, Redding, Calif.

Orndurff, R. 1974. *Introduction to California Plant Life*. University of California Press, Berkeley, Calif.

Orr, R. T., Moffitt, J. 1971. *Birds of the Lake Tahoe Region*. California Academy of Sciences, San Francisco, Calif.

Peterson, R. T. 1990. *A Field Guide to Western Birds* (3rd ed.). Houghton Mifflin, Boston, Mass.

Price, J., Droege, S., Price, A. 1995. *The Summer Atlas of North American Birds*. Academic Press, London and San Diego, Calif.

Reeves, M. 1992. *Birds of Sly Park, Six-Year Study, Nov. 1986–Nov. 1992*. Sly Park Recreation Area, Pollock Pines, Calif.

Richardson Bay Audubon Center and Sanctuary. 1996. *Checklist of Birds of the Richardson Bay Audubon Center and Sanctuary*. National Audubon Society, Tiburon, Calif.

Richer, C. (ed). 1996. *San Francisco Peninsula Birdwatching*. Sequoia Audubon Society, San Mateo, Calif.

Richmond, J. 1985. *Birding Northern California*. Mt. Diablo Audubon Society, Walnut Creek, Calif.

Rising, J. D. 1996. *A Guide to the Identification and Natural History of the Sparrows of the United States and Canada*. Academic Press, San Diego, Calif.

Roberson, D. 1985. *Monterey Birds: Status and Distribution of Birds in Monterey County, California*. Monterey Peninsula Audubon Society, Carmel, Calif.

Roberson, D. 1980. *Rare Birds of the West Coast*. Woodcock Publications, Pacific Grove, Calif.

Roberson, D., Tenney, C. 1993. *Atlas of the Breeding Birds of Monterey County, California*. Monterey Peninsula Audubon Society, Carmel, Calif.

Schmidt, K. N., Hunter, J. E., LeValley, R. 1994. *Birds of the Six Rivers National Forest*. Six Rivers National Forest, Eureka, Calif.

Shearwater, D. L. 1995. "The mysteries of Cordell Bank: a gathering place for tubenoses." *Winging It,* vol. 7, no. 1, p. 1. American Birding Association, Colorado Springs, Colo.

Shuford, W. D. 1993. *The Marin County Breeding Bird Atlas*. Bushtit Books, Bolinas, Calif.

Shuford, W. D., Fitton, S. D. 1998. "Status of owls in the Glass Mountain Region, Mono County, California." *Western Birds,* vol. 29, no. 1, pp. 1–20, Western Field Ornithologists, San Diego, Calif.

Small, A. 1994. *California Birds: Their Status and Distribution*. Ibis Publishing Co., Vista, Calif.

Stallcup, R. 1992. *Field Checklist of Birds, Point Reyes National Seashore*. Point Reyes National Seashore Association, Point Reyes, Calif.

Stebbins, R. C. 1972. *Amphibians and Reptiles of California*. University of California Press, Berkeley, Calif.

Terres, J. K. 1991. *The Audubon Society Encyclopedia of North American Birds*. Wings Books, New York, N.Y.

Thelander, C. G. 1994. *Life on the Edge, A Guide to California's Endangered Natural Resources: Wildlife*. BioSystems Books, Santa Cruz, Calif.

Tuck, K. 1997. *Klamath Basin National Wildlife Refuges*. The Klamath Basin Wildlife Association, Tulelake, Calif.

Trimble, S. 1989. *The Sagebrush Ocean: A Natural History of the Great Basin*. University of Nevada Press, Reno, Nev.

U.S. Fish and Wildlife Service. 1994. *Birds of San Luis, Merced and Kesterson National Wildlife Refuges and Grasslands Wildlife Management Area*. U.S. Department of the Interior, Fish and Wildlife Service, Washington, D.C.

U.S. Fish and Wildlife Service. 1995. *Wildlife of the Klamath Basin National Wildlife Refuges*. U.S. Department of the Interior, Fish and Wildlife Service, Washington, D.C.

U.S. Fish and Wildlife Service. 1995. *Wildlife of Modoc National Wildlife Refuge, California*. U.S. Department of the Interior, Fish and Wildlife Service, Washington, D.C.

U.S. Fish and Wildlife Service. 1996. *Wildlife of the Sacramento National Wildlife Refuge Complex*. U.S. Department of the Interior, Fish and Wildlife Service, Washington, D.C.

U.S. Geological Survey. 1955. *Map of State of California (shaded relief)*. U.S. Department of the Interior, Geological Survey, Washington, D.C.

Van Wert, K. K. 1995. *Birds of the Arcata Marsh and Wildlife Sanctuary*. Friends of the Arcata Marsh, Arcata, Calif.

Westrich, L., Westrich, J. 1991. *Birder's Guide to Northern California*. Gulf Publishing Co., Houston, Tex.

Williams, Brian D. C. 1997. *Seasonal Checklist of the Birds of Nevada County*. Sierra College Natural History Museum, Rocklin, Calif.

Wintu Audubon Society. 1990. *A Checklist of the Birds of Whiskeytown—Shasta–Trinity National Recreation Area*. Southwest Parks and Monuments Assoc., Tucson, Ariz.

Wyatt, B., Stoye, A., Harris, C. 1990. *Birding at the Bottom of the Bay*. (2nd ed.). Santa Clara Valley Audubon Society, Cupertino, Calif.

Yasuda, D., Genter, C. 1995. *Birds of the Eldorado National Forest*. El Dorado National Forest, Placerville, Calif.

Yee, D. 1997. *Field Checklist of the Birds of San Joaquin County*. David Yee, Lodi, Calif.

Zeiner, D., Laudenslayer, W., Mayer, K., White, M. 1990. *California's Wildlife, Volume II: Birds*. California Department of Fish and Game, Sacramento, Calif.

Zimmer, K. J. 1985. *The Western Bird Watcher: An Introduction to Birding in the American West*. Prentice-Hall, Englewood Cliffs, N.J.

Appendix C: Reporting Rare Birds[1]

Here's what to do if you discover a bird you believe to be a rarity.

First, spread the word to other local observers. Then, call the rare bird alert telephone number (Appendix D) that is closest to your location, and give good directions to the bird. Next, document your finding by writing down a field description, providing every detail you can regarding the bird's appearance, location, and behavior. Make your notes on the spot, while you are looking at the bird, or immediately after, in case the bird disappears. Notes written later are generally less useful than notes taken immediately. Take photographs, if you can.

Send your documentation and photos, if any, to the appropriate subregional editor for *Field Notes* (formerly called *American Birds*), as listed below. Most counties in Northern California have subregional editors. If the county you saw the bird in does not have one, send your documentation to the regional editor who is in charge of the group of birds in which your rarity falls. Sightings such as yours form the bases on which the subregional editors prepare their reports regarding developments in the distributions of bird species.

Field Notes regional editors (as of 1998)

Loons to frigates, jaegers to alcids: Stephen F. Bailey, c/o Museum of Natural History, 165 Forest Avenue, Pacific Grove, CA 93950; fax: (408) 372-3256

Herons to shorebirds: Dan Singer, c/o Arroyo & Coates, 500 Washington Street, Suite 700, San Francisco, CA 94111; e-mail: dsg@isp.net

Pigeons to finches: Don Roberson, 282 Grove Acre Avenue, Pacific Grove, CA 93950; fax: (408) 373-2566; e-mail: creagrus@montereybay.com

California Bird Records Committee:

Michael M. Rogers, secretary, California Bird Records Committee, P.O. Box 340, Moffett Field, CA 94035-0340

Field Notes subregional editors (as of 1998)

Alameda County: Helen Green, 2001 Yolo Avenue, Berkeley, CA 94707; e-mail: hgreenbird@aol.com

Alpine and Calaveras counties: Penelope Bowen, 2035 Ashton Avenue, Menlo Park, CA 94025; e-mail: PbowenD@aol.com

Butte, Colusa, Glenn, Sutter, Tehama, Yuba counties: Bruce Deuel, 18730 Live Oak Road, Red Bluff, CA 96080; e-mail: 103455,2470@Compuserve.com

Contra Costa County: Steve Glover, 178 Country Brook Loop, San Ramon, CA 94523; e-mail: Sgloverccc@aol.com

Humboldt County: David Fix and Jude Clair Power, P.O. Box 4331, Arcata, CA 95518; e-mail: dfxjcp@humboldt1.com

Lake County: Jerry R. White, P.O. Box 113, Kelseyville, CA 95451

Mendocino County: Bob Keiffer, P.O. Box 354, Hopland, CA 95449; e-mail: rjkeiffer@ucdavis.edu

Modoc County: Ronnie L. Ryno, c/o Modoc NWR, P.O. Box 1610, Alturas, CA 96101; e-mail: Ryno@hdo.net

Mono County: Emilie Strauss, 1606 Hearst Street, Berkeley, CA 94703-1220; e-mail: emilie@stillwatersci.com

Monterey County: Don Roberson, 282 Grove Acre, Pacific Grove, CA 93950; fax: (408) 373-2566; e-mail: creagrus@montereybay.com

Napa and Solano counties: Robin Leong, 336 Benson Avenue, Vallejo, CA 94590-3027; e-mail: leong@community.net

---

1 Many thanks to Don Roberson for the material on reporting rare birds.

Nevada and Placer counties: Brian Williams, 204 Teton Place, Woodland, CA 95695-5928; e-mail: bwcal@sprynet.com

Sacramento and Yolo counties: Tim Manolis, 808 El Encino Way, Sacramento, CA 95864; e-mail: Ylightfoot@apci.org

San Benito County: Kent Van Vuren, 26 Vista Drive, Salinas, CA 93907

San Joaquin County: David G. Yee, 11707 North Alpine Road, Lodi, CA 95240; e-mail: dyee@cwws.net

San Mateo County: Peter J. Metropolus, 1603 Manzanita Avenue, Belmont, CA 94002

Santa Clara County: William G. Bousman, 321 Arlington Way, Menlo Park, CA 94025; e-mail: bousman@merlin.arc.nasa.gov

Santa Cruz County: David Suddjian, 801 Monterey Avenue, Capitola, CA 95010

Shasta County: Bob Yutzy, P.O. Box 990237, Redding, CA 96099; e-mail: boby@c-zone.net

Siskiyou County: Ray Ekstrom, 2209 Delphic Road, Montague, CA 96064

Sonoma County: Ruth Rudesill, P.O. Box 371, Kenwood, CA 95452

Trinity County: John F. Hunter, P.O. Box 4483, Arcata, CA 95521; e-mail: Jhunter323@aol.com

Appendix D: Rare Bird Alerts

Arcata: (707) 822-5666
Monterey: (831) 375-2577
Northern California: (415) 681-7422
Sacramento: (916) 481-0118

Appendix E: Birding Organizations

American Birding Association, P.O. Box 6599, Colorado Springs, CO 80934, (719) 578-1614

American Ornithologists' Union, c/o Division of Birds, MRC 116, National Museum of Natural History, Washington, DC 20560

Central Valley Bird Club, P.O. Box 191015, Sacramento, CA 95819

National Audubon Society—*California*, 555 Audubon Place, Sacramento, CA 95825, (916) 481-5332 (many local chapters in Northern California)

Santa Cruz Bird Club, P.O. Box 1304, Santa Cruz, CA 95061

Western Field Ornithologists, 6011 Saddletree Lane, Yorba Linda, CA 92886

Appendix F: Campground Reservations

NATIONAL PARKS

Phone (800) 365-2267 for:

Sequoia and Kings Canyon national parks

Whiskeytown National Recreation Area

Phone (800) 436-7275 for Yosemite National Park

NATIONAL FORESTS

(877) 444-6777

STATE PARKS

(800) 444-7275

OTHER CAMPGROUNDS

Del Valle Regional Park

(510) 562-2267

Laguna Seca Regional Park

(408) 422-6138

Lake Solano County Park

(800) 939-7275

Pinnacles National Monument:

Pinnacles Campground

(408) 389-4462

Spenceville Wildlife Management and Recreation Area:

Camp Far West Lake

(530) 645-0484

Nevada County Fairgrounds

(530) 273-6217

Spring Lake County Park

(707) 527-2041

Sly Park Recreation Area

(530) 644-2792

Appendix G: Recent Changes in Birds' Names

Names of birds change from time to time. The organization responsible in North America for the official list of wild birds and their names is the Committee on Classification and Nomenclature of the American Ornithologists' Union (AOU). The Committee rules on both the scientific names and the common English names.

Birders sometimes come to the conclusion that the name changes are somewhat capricious, but this is far from the case. Changes occur only after long deliberation by the Committee, usually based upon newly published research. Sometimes the changes are made to achieve standardization in the use of English names in English-speaking countries. A case in which standardization has not yet been achieved, for example, is with loons. The bird we know as the "Common Loon" is called "Great Northern Diver" in Great Britain.

Sometimes an action of the Committee results in the splitting of one species into two or three, such as when the "Northern Oriole" was split into Baltimore Oriole and Bullock's Oriole. Actually, in this particular case the split was the reversal of an earlier "lumping," that the Committee later decided, based on new research, should not have been made.

Actions of the Committee sometime result in lumping two or more species into one, as when the "Oregon" Junco, "Slate-colored" Junco, "Gray-headed" Junco, and "White-winged" Junco were all lumped into one species, the Dark-eyed Junco. In recent years there have been many more splits than lumps, and more splits are expected.

Some of the recent changes in species' names follow. Older editions of popular field guides may still contain the old names, so this list could be useful. Only those species included on the bar charts in Chapter 8 are listed.

Current name	Former name(s)
Pacific Loon	Arctic Loon (split into Arctic and Pacific)
Clark's Grebe	Western Grebe (split into Western and Clark's)
Flesh-footed Shearwater	Pale-footed Shearwater
Buller's Shearwater	New Zealand Shearwater
Short-tailed Shearwater	Slender-billed Shearwater
Great Egret	American Egret, Common Egret
Green Heron	Green-backed Heron
Brant	Black Brant (lumped with Brant)
Tundra Swan	Whistling Swan
Black Scoter	Common Scoter
White-tailed Kite	Black-shouldered Kite
Northern Harrier	Marsh Hawk
Common Moorhen	Common Gallinule
Pacific Golden-Plover	Lesser Golden-Plover (split into Pacific and American)
American Golden-Plover	Lesser Golden-Plover (split into Pacific and American)
Red-necked Phalarope	Northern Phalarope
Red-naped Sapsucker	Yellow-bellied Sapsucker (split into Yellow-bellied, Red-naped, and Red-breasted)
Red-breasted Sapsucker	Yellow-bellied Sapsucker (split into Yellow-bellied, Red-naped, and Red-breasted)
Northern Flicker	Red-shafted and Yellow-shafted Flickers were lumped
Willow Flycatcher	Traill's Flycatcher (split into Willow and Alder)
Pacific-slope Flycatcher	Western Flycatcher (split into Pacific-slope and Cordilleran)
Cordilleran Flycatcher	Western Flycatcher (split into Pacific-slope and Cordilleran)
Brown-crested Flycatcher	Wied's Crested Flycatcher

Cassin's Vireo	Solitary Vireo (split into Blue-headed, Cassin's, and Plumbeous)
Plumbeous Vireo	Solitary Vireo (split into Blue-headed, Cassin's, and Plumbeous)
Western Scrub-Jay	Scrub Jay (split into Western, Florida, and Island)
Gray Jay	Canada Jay, Oregon Jay
Oak Titmouse	Plain Titmouse (split into Oak and Juniper)
Juniper Titmouse	Plain Titmouse (split into Oak and Juniper)
American Pipit	Water Pipit
Yellow-rumped Warbler	Audubon's and Myrtle Warblers were lumped
Spotted Towhee	Rufous-sided Towhee (split into Eastern and Spotted)
California Towhee	Brown Towhee (split into California and Canyon)
Dark-eyed Junco	Oregon, Slate-colored, Gray-headed, and White-winged Juncos were lumped
Bullock's Oriole	Northern Oriole (split into Baltimore and Bullock's)
Gray-crowned Rosy-Finch	Rosy-Finch (split into Gray-crowned, Black, and Brown-capped)

The names and sequence of species in this book are consistent with the seventh edition of the *Check-list of North American Birds* (1998), published by the American Ornithologists' Union. Possessive forms of birds' names, as in Lewis's Woodpecker, are rendered in accordance with that checklist. The pronunciation of birds' names is taken from J. K. Terres, *The Audubon Society Encyclopedia of North American Birds* (1991).

Index

A listing is not given in the index for every page on which a bird species is mentioned, or the index would become unwieldy. Instead, a listing is given for a particular species if the page gives some sort of special information, or belongs to a site which is an especially good place for that species. Specialty birds are listed more frequently than non-specialties.

Some of the changes in birds' names that have occurred in recent years are shown in Appendix G (pages 394–395). In this index, when old names are listed, cross-references are given to the new names.

Abbreviations: CG=Campground; MLK=Martin Luther King; NM=National Monument; NP=National Park; NRA=National Recreation Area; NWR=National Wildlife Refuge; SB=State Beach; SF=San Francisco; SHP=State Historic Park; SP=State Park; SR=State Reserve; SRA=State Recreation Area; WA=Wildlife Area

Manzanita Lake (Lassen NP) 80
Marble Hot Springs Road (Sierra Valley) 125
Marin Headlands 207
Marina Lagoon (Foster City) 224
Martin Luther King Jr. Regional Shoreline 263
Martin, Purple 46, 197, 279, 376
McArthur Burney Falls SP 76
McArthur Swamp (Pit River) 75
McCloud River Loop 58
McGurk Meadow (Yosemite NP) 297
Meadowlark, Western 7, 62, 104, 115, 154, 162,
    194, 293, 315, 359, 380
Meiss Lake (Siskiyou County) 62
Mendocino 97
Mendocino Coast 94
Mendocino Coast Botanical Gardens 96
Mendocino Headlands SP 97
Mendoza Ranch (Point Reyes) 193
Merced NWR 294
Merganser
    Common 48, 51, 75, 84, 88, 110, 157, 169, 369
    Hooded 45, 51, 83, 157, 169, 224, 261, 336,
        368
    Red-breasted 35, 46, 138, 225, 242, 273, 369
Merlin 46, 104, 112, 138, 154, 166, 224, 369
Milepost #3 (Western Divide Hwy) 321
Milepost #74 (Kern River Valley) 325
Mill Creek Falls CG (Warner Mountains) 72
Mines Road 249
Minniear Day Use Area (Del Puerto Canyon) 253
Mitchell Canyon (Mount Diablo) 258
Miwok Trail (Sly Park) 175
Mix Canyon Road (Putah Creek) 159
Mockingbird, Northern 7, 169, 210, 220, 377
Modoc NWR 67
Modoc Plateau 13, 67, 364
Mono Lake Region 301
Monterey Peninsula 270
Monticello Dam (Putah Creek) 159
Moorhen, Common 104, 113, 154, 246, 293, 370
Moraine Trail (Lake Tahoe) 183
Moro Rock (Sequoia NP) 311
Moses Spring Trail (Pinnacles NM) 287
Mosquito Ridge 131
Moss Landing 281, 284
Mount Diablo 255
Mount Tamalpais 198
Mountain View, Shoreline at 238
Muckelroy Nature Trail (Lake Merritt) 263
Muddy Hollow (Point Reyes) 195
Muir Woods (Mount Tamalpais) 200
Municipal Wharf (Monterey) 273
Murre
    Common 34, 43, 94, 139, 191, 212, 231, 274,
        373
    Thick-billed (vagrant) 47

Murrelet
    Ancient 139, 271, 343, 373
    Craveri's 140, 271, 343, 373
    Marbled 35, 39, 231, 235, 342, 373
    Xantus's 140, 271, 342, 373

N
Napa River Ecological Reserve 145
Napa Valley 143
Natural Bridges SB 234
Neary Lagoon (Santa Cruz) 233
Nelson Avenue (Oroville) 110
New Willows (Point Reyes) 192
Night-Heron, Black-crowned 46, 48, 65, 104, 166,
    367
Nighthawk
    Common 65, 67, 81, 87, 126, 301, 374
    Lesser 254, 324, 345, 374
Nimbus Fish Hatchery (American River) 170
North Arm (Lake Almanor) 83
North Lake (Lake Merced) 216
North Park Drive (Bidwell Park) 107
North Rim (Yosemite NP) 299
North Rim Trail (Alum Rock Park) 247
Nunes Ranch (Point Reyes) 193
Nutcracker, Clark's 71, 82, 184, 304, 310, 352, 376
Nuthatch
    Pygmy 129, 180, 196, 201, 210, 215, 275, 304,
        329, 354, 376
    Red-breasted 69, 84, 178, 299, 308, 376
    White-breasted 56, 76, 99, 107, 131, 252, 296,
        376

O
Oak Hills Nature Trail (Del Valle Regional Park)
    251
Old Guadalupe Trail (San Bruno Mountain) 220
Oldsquaw 35, 47, 138, 150, 192, 261, 284, 368
Olema Marsh (Point Reyes) 196
Oriole
    Bullock's 104, 107, 120, 142, 169, 173, 195,
        202, 206, 220, 247, 312, 315, 321, 323, 359,
        380
    Hooded 210, 224, 247, 325, 359, 380
    Northern. See Oriole, Bullock's.
    Scott's 325, 360, 380
Oroville 110
Oroville WA 112
Osprey 56, 75, 83, 87, 100, 146, 157, 195, 196,
    336, 369
Otter Trail (Bobelaine) 120
Owl Rocks (Del Puerto Canyon) 254
Owl
    Barn 45, 65, 100, 105, 163, 193, 254, 373
    Barred 41, 373
    Burrowing 115, 163, 241, 242, 265, 344, 373

About the author

John Kemper has lived in California almost all his life, most of it in Northern California. He has been to every part of the state, has hiked thousands of miles on its trails, climbed its mountains, and generally inhabited its wild lands to the maximum degree possible. He has been a birder ever since he was a Boy Scout, has been to all corners of North America to see birds, and has accumulated a North American life list of 718 species. In his "other life," he worked for many years as an engineer in the scientific instruments and computer industries, became a professor at the University of California, Davis, and served for 14 years there as dean of engineering. He has a doctorate in structural mechanics from the University of Colorado. Since retiring from the university, he has served as president of his local Audubon Society, authored a book, *Discovering Yolo County Wildlife,* is active as a volunteer in California Duck Days, and leads local birding field trips.